Good Governance in Europe's Integrated Market

Edited by

CHRISTIAN JOERGES AND RENAUD DEHOUSSE

Academy of European Law
European University Institute

OXFORD
UNIVERSITY PRESS

OXFORD

UNIVERSITY PRESS

Great Clarendon Street, Oxford OX2 6DP

Oxford University Press is a department of the University of Oxford.
It furthers the University's objective of excellence in research, scholarship,
and education by publishing worldwide in

Oxford New York

Auckland Bangkok Buenos Aires Cape Town Chennai
Dar es Salaam Delhi Hong Kong Istanbul Karachi Kolkata
Kuala Lumpur Madrid Melbourne Mexico City Mumbai Nairobi
São Paulo Shanghai Singapore Taipei Tokyo Toronto

with an associated company in Berlin

Oxford is a registered trade mark of Oxford University Press
in the UK and in certain other countries

Published in the United States
by Oxford University Press Inc., New York

British Library Cataloguing in Publication Data

Data available

Library of Congress Cataloging in Publication Data

Good governance in Europe's integrated market / edited by
Christian Joerges and Renaud Dehousse.
p. cm. — (The collected courses of the Academy of European Law; v.11/1)
1. European Union. 2. European Union countries—Politics and government.
I. Joerges, Christian. II. Dehousse, Renaud. III. Series.
KJE947.G66 2001 341.242′2—dc21 2001059307
ISBN 0–19–924608–4

1 3 5 7 9 10 8 6 4 2

Typeset by Hope Services (Abingdon) Ltd
Printed in Great Britain
on acid-free paper by
Biddles Ltd., Guildford and King's Lynn

Contents

Section IV Good Governance and Democratic Theory

Notes on Contributors

Loïc Azoulay is Maître de Conférences at the Université Panthéon-Assas Paris-II. He holds a Ph.D. in Law from the European University Institute (Florence). Among his publications: 'D'une révision l'autre', in J. Rideau (ed.), *Commentaire des traités modifiés par le traité de Nice du 26 février 2001* (2001); 'La ratification du traité de Nice par la France (technique juridique et mobilisation politique)', *Annuaire Français de Relations Internationales*, vol. 2 (forthcoming); 'L'acquis et les organisations internationales', in F. Picod (ed.), *L'acquis de l'Union européenne* (forthcoming).

Renaud Dehousse is Jean Monnet Professor of EU Law at the Institut d'études politiques de Paris (Sciences Po). Professor Dehousse holds a Ph.D. in Law from the European University Institute (Florence). He has taught at the European University Institute and at the University of Pisa, Italy. His main work has been on comparative federalism and on the institutional development of the European Union. He has been adviser to various units of the European Commission on institutional issues. His recent work has focused in particular on the transformation of European governance, with specific reference to the growing importance of transnational bureaucratic structures (comitology, European agencies), as well as on the influence of the European Court of Justice on European policies. For a list of publications, see <http://www.portedeurope.org/centre_europeen/whoiswho/dehousse. htm>.

Michelle Everson is Jean Monnet Lecturer in European Law at Birkbeck College, University of London. Her primary research interests lie in the fields of European regulatory law and comparative public law, including concepts of citizenship. Recent publications include: (with C. Joerges), 'Challenging the Bureaucratic Challenge', in E. O. Eriksen and J. E. Fossum (eds.), *Democracy in the European Union* (2000), and (with G. Majone), 'Institutional Reform: Independent Agencies, Oversight, Co-ordination and Procedural Control', in O. De Schutter, N. Lebesis, and J. Patterson (eds.), *Governance in the European Union* (2001).

Christian Joerges is Professor of European Economic Law at the European University Institute (Florence). His home university is Bremen, Germany, where he held a chair in German and European Private and Economic Law and Private International Law. He was also Co-director of the Centre for European Law and Politics. His recent publications deal with the Europeanization of private law, social regulation in the internal market, transnational governance, and German legal traditions in the conceptualization of European integration. Since April 2002 he has also been a Visiting Professor at Birkbeck College, University of London.

Oliver Gerstenberg is a Dr. iur. from the J. W. Goethe-Universität, Frankfurt am Main. He is Reader in Law (on leave) at the University of Westminster, London, and is currently J. F. Kennedy Memorial Fellow (2001–2) at the Minda de Gunzburg Center for European Studies at Harvard University. His research deals with private law and constitutionalism; governance in the EU; and adjudication in the EU and WTO. His recent publications include: 'Private Law, Constitutionalism and the Limits of Judicial Role', in C. Scott (ed.), *Torture as Tort: Comparative Perspectives on the Development of Transnational Human Rights Litigation* (2001) 687; 'Denationalization and the Very Idea of Democratic Constitutionalism: The Case of the European Community', 14 *Ratio Juris* (2001) 298; 'Justification (and Justifiability) of Private Law in a Polycontextural World', 9 *Social and Legal Studies* (2000) 421.

Stefan Kadelbach has since 1997 been holder of the Chair of Public International and European Law and Co-director of the Institute of Public Law and Politics at the University of Westfalia, Münster. In 1999 he was Guest Professor at the University of Virginia. He studied at the Universities of Tübingen and Frankfurt, and obtained an LLM at the University of Virginia in 1987. In 1988 he was admitted to the Bar. He was research fellow at the University of Frankfurt from 1989 to 1996, was titled Dr. iur. in 1996 and obtained his *Habilitation* in 1996. His fields of interest are the constitutionalization of public international law, human rights and humanitarian law, and European constitutional and administrative law. His principal publications include: *Zwingendes Völkerrecht* (1992); *Allgemeines Verwaltungsrecht unter Europäischem Einfluss* (1999); *Die völkerrechtliche Haftung für die Verletzung von Fundamentalnormen (Angriffskriege und Verbrechen gegen die Menschlichkeit), Berichte der Deutschen Gesellschaft für Völkerrecht 40* (2001).

Koen Lenaerts Lic. iur., Ph.D. in Law (Leuven), LLM, MPA (Harvard), is Professor of European Law and Director of the Institute of European Law at the University of Leuven, and Judge of the Court of First Instance of the European Communities (Luxembourg). He has been Visiting Professor of Law at the Harvard Law School, at the Université Robert Schuman de Strasbourg and at the College of Europe (Bruges). His publications include *Le juge et la constitution aux États-Unis d'Amérique et dans l'ordre juridique européen* (1988), *Constitutional Law of the European Union* (with P. Van Nuffel, 1999), *Procedural Law of the European Union* (with D. Arts, 1999) as well as various articles on European Union law and comparative constitutional law in a large number of Belgian and foreign law journals. He is a Member of the *Academia Europaea*.

Peter Lindseth is Associate Professor of Law at the University of Connecticut (USA). Prior to this he was Research Scholar and Associate Director of the European Legal Studies Center at Columbia Law School, where he was also an Associate-in-Law (teaching Fellow). In addition to holding graduate Fellowships in history and the social sciences, Professor Lindseth was a Chateaubriand Fellow at the French Conseil d'Etat in 1994–5. His most recent publications include: '"Weak" Constitutionalism: Reflections on Comitology and Transnational Governance in the European Union,' 21 *Oxford Journal of Legal Studies* (2001) 145 [review article]; *Transatlantic Regulatory Cooperation: Legal Problems and Political Prospects* (2000) (co-edited with G. Bermann and M. Herdegen); and 'Democratic Legitimacy and the Administrative Character of Supranationalism: The Example of the European Community', 99 *Columbia Law Review* (1999) 628.

Charles F. Sabel, A.B., Harvard (1969); Ph.D. (1978) is Professor of Law and Social Science at the Columbia Law School. Before joining Columbia in 1995, he served as Professor of Social Science in the Department of Political Science of the Massachusetts Institute of Technology. His publications include, among many others: (with A. Fung and D. O'Rourke) 'Quale volano per gli standard internazionali di protezione sociale? Proposta per un progressivo miglioramento delle condizioni di lavoro nell'economia globalizzata', 1 *Il diritto del mercato del lavoro* (2001); (with A. Fung and D. O'Rourke) 'Ratcheting Labor Standards', World Bank Social Protection Discussion Paper No. 0011, May 2000; 'An Unlikely Democracy: The US at the Millennium', 1 *Internationale Politik und Gesellschaft* (2000); (with M. Dorf) 'A Constitution of Democratic Experimentalism', *Columbia Law Review* (1998); (with M. Priore) *The Second Industrial Divide: Possibilities for Prosperity* (1984).

Joanne Scott is a University Lecturer in EU Law, and Fellow of Clare College, University of Cambridge. She has written widely in the areas of EU law, environmental law, and the EU and the WTO. Her most recent publications include two co-edited volumes: (with G. de Búrca) *The EU and the WTO: Legal and Constitutional Issues* (2001); and (with C. Barnard) *The Legal Foundations of the Single European Market: Unpacking the Premises* (2002). She is a member of the Council for European Environmental Law.

Stijn Smismans holds a Ph.D. in Law from the European University Institute (Florence) and is currently Marie Curie Fellow at the European Centre of the Institut d'études politiques, Paris. He has published in *European Public Law* and in *European Integration online Papers*, on the role of the national parliaments in European decision-making, and on the European Economic and Social Committee. He has conducted several studies for the European Economic and Social Committee, assisting the Committee in redefining its role. His research deals with the legitimacy of European governance, and in particular with the role of social partners, interest groups and civil society in European social policy.

Amaryllis Verhoeven is currently working in the European Commission's Directorate-General for the Internal Market. She is also affiliated to the Institute of European Law of the Katholieke Universiteit Leuven as a research assistant. She has written several contributions in the field of European constitutional and economic law and legal theory, including a Ph.D. thesis on the subject of democracy and constitutionalism in the EU. She has worked as an attorney at the law offices of Cleary, Gottlieb, Steen & Hamilton. Amaryllis Verhoeven is Doctor in Law and Bachelor in Philosophy and obtained a Master of Laws degree at Harvard Law School.

Ellen Vos is Professor of European Law at the University of Maastricht. She studied law at the Universities of Utrecht and Bologna (1983–9). She was a trainee at the European Commission (winter 1989/90), the European Consumer Organization (spring/summer 1990) and the European Court of Justice (spring/summer 1993). She obtained her Ph.D. in Law at the European University Institute (Florence) (1997) and was, until November 1998, Marie Curie Fellow at the Centre of European Law and Politics (ZERP) in Bremen. She is member of the Editorial Board of the *Maastricht Journal of European and Comparative Law* and collaborator on the *Tijdschrift voor Consumentenrecht*. As of September 2001 she is the Director of Studies of the Magister Iuris Communis (LLM) Programme. Her publications and research interests concern: EU law, institutional law (comitology and agencies), free movement of goods, market integration, and risk regulation.

Table of Cases

A. European Community

European Court of Justice (alphabetical order)

Court of First Instance (alphabetical order)

E. Greece

F. Ireland

G. Italy

Corte di Cassazione (Court of Appeal)

Constitutional Court

H. Spain

I. United Kingdom

J. United States

Table of Treaties and Legislation

Abbreviations

AJCL	American Journal of Comparative Law
APA	Administrative Procedure Act
ARSP	Archiv für Rechts- und Sozialphilosophie
CFI	Court of First Instance
CMLRev.	Common Market Law Review
CRISP	Centre de recherche et d'information socio-politiques
CSTEE	Scientific Committee for Toxicology, Ecotoxicology and the Environment
EAEC	Economic and Atomic Energy Communities
ECB	European Central Bank
ECJ	European Court of Justice
ECLR	European Competition Law Review
ECSC	European Coal and Steel Community
EFA	European Food Authority
EIB	European Investment Bank
EIoP	European Integration online Papers
ELJ	European Law Journal
ELR	European Law Review
ERPL	European Review of Private Law
GATT	General Agreement on Tariffs and Trade
GMO	genetically modified organism
ILJ	Industrial Law Journal
ILM	International Legal Markets
JCMS	Journal of Common Market Studies
JEPP	Journal of European Public Policy
JHS	Journal of Historical Sociology
MLR	Modern Law Review
MLGS	multi-level governance system
NGO	non-governmental organization
OJLS	Oxford Journal of Legal Studies
RabelsZ	Rabels Zeitschrift für ausländisches und internationales Privatrecht
WHO	World Health Organization
WTO	World Trade Organization
YEL	Yearbook of European Law

SECTION I

EDITORIAL

1

The Law's Problems with the Governance of the European Market

CHRISTIAN JOERGES*

I. UN EMBARRAS DE RICHESSE?

In identifying the leitmotif for the essays which make up this volume it was at first proposed to focus on the topic 'administering Europe'.[1] As the project developed, however, the theme of 'good governance'[2] seemed more obviously to signal the search for a new conceptual framework.[3] But despite the fact that all of the authors share common research interests and even, in important respects, similar views, it would have been naïve and counterproductive to impose some pre-defined conceptual framework on them. Instead, what distinguishes this volume from a collection of articles united only by a common heading and cover is a *network effect*.

Networks co-ordinate actors without imposing a structure of hierarchical authority that is intended to serve a single given objective. Their rules of co-ordination reflect a discovery procedure that might include deliberative elements, or that might be interpreted as a product of learning and selection. This type of co-ordination does not seek to overcome divergences in the analytical premises and foci, or differences in the conceptual frameworks and normative ideas. Instead it seeks to exploit this diversity productively.

This introduction endeavours to reveal the extent to which this objective was achieved. It does so in two stages; the first is primarily descriptive, the second is more analytical.

* I owe special thanks to Alexandra George for her editing of this text—and her patience with my step-by-step approach to its production.

[1] From Everson, 'Administering Europe?', 36 *JCMS* (1998) 195.

[2] See tentatively, Joerges, ' "Bureaucratic Nightmare, Technocratic Regime and the Dream of Good Transnational Governance"; "Good Governance" Through Comitology?', in C. Joerges and E. Vos (eds), *EU Committees: Social Regulation, Law and Politics* (1999), 3 and 311.

[3] And now ties in unexpectedly well with the Commission's White Paper on 'European Governance COM (2001) 428 fimae of 25 July 2001.

The first stage (Section II) will explain the choice of the common theme of this volume, expound the overall pattern, very briefly sketch the various contents of the individual contributions, and indicate how they complement each other. Again, this presentation should not be misunderstood as an attempt to achieve some artificial harmonization by trying to camouflage differences or even tensions among the authors. Its task is to prepare the reader for the different dimensions of the common theme of the contributors, and for the divergent theoretical and methodological approaches that will come to the fore.

The second stage (Section III) seeks to provide a more analytical account. It will identify a series of overriding issues that are common to various contributions but that are approached in different ways. Such a presentation cannot be totally objective. Although an editorial should not present additional viewpoints or assessments, an unbiased, totally 'objective' selection and presentation of issues is simply impossible. What should be possible is an elucidation of ongoing debates.

II. OVERVIEW

The title of this volume does not refer to a well-defined legal discipline or to a particular policy field. Instead it designates a spectrum of activities that has evolved with the gradual integration of European markets. Market building efforts have been particularly significant since the Commission launched its famous 1985 White Paper about 'Completing the Internal Market'[4] by the magical year 1992. This project turned out to be more complex than envisaged. A look back over the last 15 years of European market building—a short time span for historians, but not for students of European integration—reveals how, and helps to explain why, the effort to modernize Europe's economies through co-ordinated efforts by Europe's political systems and many non-governmental actors had a kind of domino effect. The internal market programme and its implementation affected ever more policies and laws. National, European, governmental and non-governmental actors found themselves drawn into new arenas. Institutional innovations occurred at both the European and national levels. All these developments heralded or confirmed the erosion of territorial, nation state centred political governance and nation state constitutionalism, and a new debate about the legitimacy of European 'governance' became unavoidable.[5]

This story has been told often—and more or less comprehensively—by lawyers, political scientists and economists. 'More or less', this volume is an attempt to complement its reconstruction, and to explore and shed additional

---

[4] COM(85) 310 final of 14 June 1985.   [5] See *supra* n. 3.

light on its implications. The concepts of 'governance' and 'administration' point to continuous 'management' activities, which turned out to be indispensable even after the adoption of the internal market's new legal framework; indeed, 'management' might have been a third umbrella concept for our endeavours. 'Administration' is a term with a long and varied history; but even if reflecting the 'post-classical' developments of administrative functions, it seems to carry with it connotations of a hierarchical order or a unitary state polity. 'Governance' is a term employed primarily by political scientists to designate the phenomenon of 'governance without government' in general, and in the EU context in particular.[6]

These remarks should suffice as a first elucidation of the range of perspectives pursued in this volume, and they should provide an outline of its internal organization. They will be explored more systematically in Section III of this editorial, but that more analytical ambition should wait until a brief exposition of the individual contributions is given.

A. European Constitutionalism

When one becomes aware of the omnipresence of governance in the internal market, and then comprehends the issues dealt with by market governance, the need to understand its constitutional dimensions and its foundations in democratic theory seems self-evident. Internal democratic structures are a prerequisite for European Union membership; the EU Treaty explicitly equates 'legitimacy' with 'democratic governance', and it thus exposes the Union to that yardstick. However, any substantiation of this all-too-general premise has to face a plethora of intriguing questions. One of them asks: should we start from democratization theory when we examine the quality of the EU's legal structures? Or, does constitutional legal thought—as rooted in the democratic states—offer a firmer frame of reference? From the more mundane perspective of an editor: should we start this volume with the contribution of Koen Lenaerts and Amaryllis Verhoeven, or with that of Oliver Gerstenberg and Charles F. Sabel? We opted for the first alternative. However, this should not be interpreted as a concession to the assumed expectations of our legally trained readership. Instead it reflects the differences and commonalties of both contributions. The title chosen by the authors of 'Institutional

---

[6] The success of this term is revealing; see, e.g., Jachtenfuchs, 'The Governance Approach to European Integration', 39 *JCMS* (2001) 245; O. De Schutter, N. Lebessis and J. Paterson (eds), *Governance in the European Union* (2001) and the contributions by Schorpf and Schmitter to the symposium 'Responses to the European Commission's White Paper on Governance', edited by C. Joerges, Y. Merry and J. H H. Weiler, available at <http://www.iue.it/RSC/Governance/>.

Balance as a Guarantee for Democracy in EU Governance'[7] indicates that
they equate constitutionalism with democracy. Their exploration of this
notion must reach beyond the nation states that comprise the EU in order to
address transnational phenomena and activities. Those authors' deliberations
start with the institutional setting of the EU and its development, whereas the
authors of 'Directly-Deliberative Polyarchy: An Institutional Ideal for
Europe?' use their conceptualization of democratic processes as the starting
point for their reflections on the structures and performance of the EU in
both legal and political sciences. Readers should be aware of these differences
and choose their own starting points.

1. *Koen Lenaerts and Amaryllis Verhoeven*

These authors view the notion of 'institutional balance' as a *sui generis* construct that differentiates the EU from the constitutional state with its *trias
politica* (an institutional *specifum*) while simultaneously embodying a commitment to transnational democracy. They base this vision on a re-reading of
the historical institutional balance that flows from its judicial origins in
Meroni,[8] through an inquiry into 'the heritage of *trias politica*', and then to
two exemplary elaborations of their views. They conclude that 'the Union's
institutional balance . . . does not rest on an organic separation of powers but
on a balanced interaction between representatives of various interests'.[9] It
should be understood as the 'necessary institutional frame within which different interests can discuss with each other in order to achieve solutions that
are acceptable to all and do not unduly abridge the liberties of anyone'.[10] This
notion of institutional balance captures the regulatory functions and
acknowledges both the intergovernmental dimension and the parliamentary
model. Its normative validity is dependent upon the adequacy of both interest representation and the deliberative quality of the processes through which
the institutional actors arrive at their decisions. As Lenaerts and Verhoeven
indicate, 'institutional balance' is a necessary, but not sufficient, condition for
democratic governance.[11] Thus their exemplary discussion of the role of the
European Commission and the budgetary procedure should be read as a

---

[7] And prior as well as forthcoming publications, such as Lenaerts, 'Regulating the regulatory process: "Delegation of powers" in the European Community', 18 *ELR* (1993) 23 and
recently Lenaerts and Verhoeven, 'Towards a Legal Framework for Executive Rule-Making in
the E.U.? The Contribution of the New Comitology Decision', 37 *CMLRev.* (2000) 645; A.
Verhoeven, 'The European Union in Search of a Democratic and Constitutional Theory'
(PhD thesis on file at Leuven (2001)).

[8] Case 9/56, *Meroni & Co, Industrie Metallurgiche, SpA v High Authority of the ECSC*
[1957–58] ECR 133 and Case 10/56, *Meroni & Co, Industrie Metallurgiche, SpA v High
Authority of the ECSC* [1957–58] ECR 157.

[9] See text preceding their n. 27.   [10] See text preceding their n. 34.

[11] See esp. their n. 35.

further elaboration of their views; it is more than a mere 'application' of their institutional balance doctrine. 'Less than a government, . . . more than a secretariat': they use this rephrase[12] to frame an analysis that concludes with a plea for a 'mixture of parliamentary scrutiny and procedural guarantees ensuring, among others, the participation of interested parties (in particular of those that risk otherwise not being heard in the European forum)'.[13]

2. *Stijn Smismans and Loïc Azoulay*

Smismans and Azoulay had each originally planned to restrict themselves to a comment on the essay of Lenaerts and Verhoeven. However, they ended up delivering substantial contributions that stand alone.

The contribution of Smismans remains in the form of a comment. It follows the contribution by Lenaerts and Verhoeven in its historical reconstruction of the separation and balance of ideas about power, and then in its analyses of the EU's institutional settings. In both respects, Smismans raises intriguing queries. He states:

There is a *saut qualitative* in the way in which Lenaerts and Verhoeven [and others] . . . address the issue of interest representation compared to the traditional readings of *trias politica* and *checks and balances* [in that they] attribute to each of the Community institutions a particular interest or identify them as representative of a particular constituency.[14]

The complexity of the European multi-level system of governance is such, he adds, that it cannot adequately be reflected by the 'traditional reading' of the institutional balance principle.[15] The EU context needs—and lacks—'a normative model for functional representation'.[16]

The search for a 'new institutional balance' is also a core concern in Azoulay's contribution.[17] However, his conceptual framework is distinct. He addresses a series of tensions that need to be balanced. The potential of law to

---

[12] See, famously, Wallace, 'Less than a Federation. More than a Regime. The Community as a Political System', in H. Wallace and W. Wallace (eds), *Policy-Making in the European Community* (1983) 403.

[13] See text at p. 55.

[14] Section IIA. Smismans also discusses de Búrca's 'The Institutional Development of the EU: A Constitutional Analysis', in P. Craig and G. de Búrca (eds), *The Evolution of EU Law* (1999) 55.

[15] Section IIC.

[16] Section III; at that point, Smismans refers to 'theories of associative democracy', citing *i.a.*, J. Cohen and J. Rogers (eds), *Associations and Democracy. The Real Utopias Project* (1995); the reader will realize that he touches upon ideas presented in the contribution by Gerstenberg and Sabel.

[17] Azoulay's comment draws on his PhD Thesis defended on 'Les garanties procédurales en droit communautaire. Recherches sur la procédure et le bon gouvernement' (on file at the EUI, Florence (2000)).

resolve social problems may be jeopardized by the respect for the rule of law.[18]
The judiciary is nevertheless expected to promote 'good governance' while
simultaneously protecting individual rights and supervising public authorities. Azoulay believes that the legitimacy problems of European market governance differ significantly in the areas of economic and of social regulation.[19]
The core problem of economic regulation is the discretionary power granted
to the European Commission. In that domain adequate responses may
be achieved through procedural guarantees to the parties concerned. The
challenges in the field of social regulation in general, and of risk regulation in
particular, require more fundamental re-orientation:

The search for *legitimacy* no longer involves the *democratic* nature of the government.
It now involves local and operational forms of administrative coordination. That is
why a new form of constitutional theory seems necessary. One must be capable of
distinguishing within these complex systems between what is merely 'good management' and what might be 'good government'.[20]

With the opening of such perspectives Azoulay bridges the discourses on constitutional law, administration and democratic governance.

3. Peter Lindseth

Lindseth's contribution does not initially look 'constitutionalist'. He portrays
the EC as a supranational, administrative, non-democratic and non-national
agent.[21] The legitimacy of this institution is not directly derived from the
people but must be mediated.[22] In that sense, the legal character of the
Community is essentially 'administrative', and the juridification of Community governance seems to belong within the domain of 'administrative
law'. And, Lindseth adds, this characterization is attuned to 'technocratic
autonomy' (at least in the US).[23] Does this amount to the substitution of
national constitutional democracies by a supranational regime with an
autonomous legitimacy? Not so, Lindseth claims, if and because the
Community system depends 'on national structures of "hierarchical" govern-

---

[18] 'Les garanties procédurales en droit communautaire. Recherches sur la procédure et le
bon gouvernement', see his introductory sections and his n. 45.
[19] Ibid., see section 2 and Azoulay, 'The Judge and the Community's Administrative
Governance', 7 *ELJ* (2001) 425.
[20] Section V; text preceding n. 141.
[21] See his 'Democratic Legitimacy and the Administrative Character of Supranationalism:
The Example of the EEC', 99 *Columbia Law Review* (1999) 626 and more recently ' "Weak"
Constitutionalism? Reflections on Comitology and Transnational Governance in the
European Union', 21 *OJLS* (2001) 145.
[22] Lindseth, 'Democratic Legitimacy', *supra* n. 21, at 651, 735.
[23] Cf. Lindseth, ' "Weak" Constitutionalism', *supra* n. 21, at 152–155 where Lindseth
underlines the hierarchical dimension of American administrative law.

ment as the source . . . democratic and constitutional legitimacy',[24] the 'socio-political/socio-cultural attachment to the national constitutional bodies as the privileged expression of democratic legitimacy' persists 'as an empirical reality that cannot simply be theorized away'.[25] With these statements, Lindseth distances himself from all those who envisage the genuine legitimacy of European governance structures.[26] He lucidly defines one of the core controversies among the contributors to this volume, which the reader is invited to assess. What should be acceptable to all parties to that dispute is the inclusion of Lindseth's contribution in the section on European constitutionalism, even though he believes that European governance is largely administrative in character and remains dependent on national constitutionalism for its legitimacy.

B. Administering Europe

Europeanization is a laboratory. As the contributions to Section II of this volume prove, the distinctions between constitutional and administrative law, legislative and administrative functions—as we have inherited them in our national traditions—are being fundamentally rethought in the search for an analytically plausible and normatively attractive understanding of European governance. The same holds true for the contributions in the chapter on 'Administration'. The difference between the two chapters is gradual and one of emphasis. Lenaerts and Verhoeven review the state of the art in constitutional theory; they examine an exemplary issue of European governance but do not address the institutionalization and management of the internal market. However, their commentators and Peter Lindseth do engage in such analyses, and they deal very explicitly with the constitutional dimensions of market governance. So too do the contributions of Kadelbach, Dehousse, Everson, and Scott and Vos—albeit with differences in their emphases and orientation—which examine practices of market governance, the implementation of European policies, or the enforcement of European law. In light of these points of departure, they qualify as contributions about the 'administration' of the European market. However, they all move beyond that distinction; the 'administrative law' they advocate does reflect upon its governmental functions and legitimacy.

1. *Stefan Kadelbach*

Kadelbach's 'European Administrative Law and the Law of a Europeanized Administration' offers an elaborate account of the different layers and directions of ongoing 'juridification' processes. He distinguishes between 'three bodies' of administrative law:

---

[24] Lindseth, this vol., text preceding n. 6 and e.g. n. 29.   [25] Ibid.
[26] Ibid., n. 1 and e.g. n. 51.

(1) the internal law of European bodies ('rules and principles governing the execution of European law by institutions of the Union');
(2) the implementation of European law by national administrative bodies ('*Europeanized* national administrative law'); and
(3) the integration of European notions and principles into national systems.

These three bodies more or less faithfully mirror the experiences of national legal systems.[27] What is lacking—and unlikely to emerge in the foreseeable future—is a coherent body of law structuring the practices of 'multi-level co-operation between European, national and hybrid authorities as well as complex networks of governance'; that is, a body of law structuring exactly the type of activities that characterize so much of Europe's multi-level system of governance.

Kadelbach's account sounds pessimistic. His observations about the patchwork character of highly specific rules on the one hand and highly general principles on the other[28] seem to rephrase many German commentators' complaints about the Europeanization of private law.[29] A second glance at Kadelbach's findings allows a more optimistic reading. Europeanization *is* a highly problematic exercise if one focuses on the incremental processes of law production at the European level, and their disintegrating impact on established legal disciplines. However, if one links the rules and principles identified by Kadelbach to the realities of European governance, one detects new patterns of juridification of a new reality. These may represent—to modify Kadelbach's conceptual outlook[30]—'less than a federation, but more than a technocratic regime'.

2. Renaud Dehousse

'Misfits', and not just one, characterize Dehousse's account of the relationship between European law and the functional needs of market integration of market governance. European regulatory policies have expanded and intensified, but the legislative process proved to be much too cumbersome. The result was the increasing appropriation of decision-making by a technocratic machinery.[31] Member States sought to remain in control of that machinery through their presence and influence in the committee system, and the system developed a logic of its own.[32] Ancient doctrines are invoked against any

[27] Cf. Kadelbach, 'Verwaltungskontrollen im Mehrebenen-System der Europäischen Gemeinschaft', in E. Schmidt-Aßmann and W. Hoffmann-Riem (eds), *Verwaltungskontrolle* (2001) 205.
[28] See esp. section III, 'Elements of European Administrative Law'.
[29] See among many, Kötz, 'Gemeineuropäisches Zivilrecht', in H. Bernstein, U. Drobnig and H. Kötz (eds), *Festschrift für Konrad Zweigert zum 70. Geburtstag* (1981) 481; Hommelhoff, 'Zivilrecht unter dem Einfluß europäischer Rechtsangleichung', 192 *Archiv für die civilistische Praxis* (1992) 71 with the overview in Section IV of Kadelbach's contribution.
[30] Section V.   [31] Dehousse, this volume, Section I.   [32] Ibid., Section II.

'delegation' of discretionary ('political') powers, but new agencies are nevertheless established and embark upon an uncharted sea.[33] Dehousse does not strive for any comprehensive, theory-led cure to these failures. His analyses and suggestions are thoroughly pragmatic. Intelligent, piecemeal responses, he argues, may disappoint the theorist, but they will do in practice.

3. Michelle Everson

Everson's contribution is marked by its treatment of two complex and inter-related themes within the administration of the European market. The first is the requirement that the normative structures of European market administration (or law) take steps to ensure that the market's dominant economic rationalities are subject to constant correction and modification in the light of social and ethical values. This observation highlights the discrepancy between so many pronouncements on European market building and its exigencies. The second is the issue of how the law of market administration can maintain its integrity when adjudicating upon conflicts between economic rationalities within Europe and the various ethical and social values that seek to challenge them. Through this conceptualization of European market governance, Everson addresses the legitimacy problems of the European market policy and the potential legal contribution to their resolution.

'Socialization' of the European market—or the testing of market rationality against social and ethical concerns—is, Everson argues, a simple imperative. However, this imperative entails a vast challenge for the law that oversees European market administration. The European market polity is made up of a plurality of competing interests. In the absence of unitary political direction, the law of the European market (both national and European) must find a convincing means to imbue its decisions with the validity of adequate authority. It could thus contribute to the convincing socialization of the European market through the development of non-partisan, rational and socially sensitive forms of adjudication.

4. Joanne Scott and Ellen Vos

Scott and Vos explore two further dimensions: the role of the 'principle of precaution' in the juridification of European regulatory policies, and the 'extraterritorial' effects of that principle in international trade disputes. Internal European conflict patterns traditionally concern the imposition of 'higher' standards of protection by the Community or the defence of national regulatory concerns against European policies. The precautionary principle ranks high in the European Treaty (cf. Article 174; Articles 6 and 3; Article 95 (10)). Is it now possible—in line with firmly established law—to acknowledge the supremacy of precautionary over not-so-precautionary national law?

[33] Ibid., Section III.

Due to the highly indeterminate character of the principle, its importance in the Treaty might allow it to become a Trojan horse. Could Member States now invoke the precautionary principle in cases like *Reinheitsgebot*,[34] in which the ECJ insisted on the presentation of scientific evidence and/or consistency throughout national legislation? Are there limits on what the Community can require Member States to do in the name of precaution? Assuming that 'supremacy' would be all too odd an arbiter in controversies between national and Community expert bodies,[35] does 'precaution' imply that the EU will have to accept new trade barriers? Will it be possible to discriminate between serious health concerns and pure 'consumer panic'?

As if the complexity of its issues was not yet sufficiently sophisticated, Scott and Vos's contribution continues with an analysis of the recent career of the precautionary principle in the World Trade Organization.[36] They note that there is a tension between 'non-arbitrary, rational decision-making on the one hand, and transparency, participation and responsiveness to public opinion on the other'.[37] Scott and Vos do not content themselves with listing such dilemmas, but nor do they pretend to know how to get rid of them. However, they do offer well-elaborated recommendations about the design of legal and policy responses that would mediate between the discourses and controversies within expert communities and the concerns held by the broader public and their politically accountable decision-makers. Such deliberations seem necessary if 'precaution' is not to be permitted to replace the duty to give reasons (in Article 249) with a privilege to invoke a *Schmittian* state of emergency.

C. Democratic Theory

An editorial technique that is widely used when dealing with challenging contributions is to express high esteem and then to add that, alas, their complexity is such that they cannot adequately be presented in a brief summary. This exercise of prudence might even be wise in the case of Oliver Gerstenberg's and Charles Sabel's 'Directly-Deliberative Polyarchy: An Institutional Ideal for Europe?' This contribution is demanding and the risk of misrepresenting the authors' ideas and intentions might be substantial. However, the guiding idea of the Academy 2000's 'Specialized Courses' was to contrast legal deliberations about the governance of the internal market with theoretical reflec-

---

[34] Case 178/84, *Commission v Germany* [1987] ECR 1227.

[35] See text preceding n. 122.

[36] Most prominently with the *Communication from the Commission on the precautionary principle*, COM (2000) 1 final of 2 February 2000; cf. the critical analysis by Majone, 'The Precautionary Principle and Regulatory Impact Analysis' (International Seminar on Regulatory Impact Analysis organized by Progetto AIR, Rome, 15 June 2001).

[37] Text preceding n. 109.

tions. Rather than confirming the (foreseeable) difficulties of this exercise, my objective will therefore be to reconstruct the architecture of the Gerstenberg/Sabel contribution in a way that might be helpful for readers not familiar with its broader theoretical horizon and the work that preceded the present contribution.[38]

The introductory section offers a three-pillared summary of analyses and evaluations of the integration project: first, the erosion of the welfare state heritage; second, the tensions between the performance of European governance and quests for democratic participation; and, third, the tensions between the legitimacy that national constitutional democracies can claim and the authority exerted by European law. This is contrasted with an alternative perspective:

In a deliberative polyarchy local, or, more exactly, lower level actors (nation-states or national peak organizations of various kinds within the EU; regions, provinces or subnational associations within these, and so on down to the level of whatever kind of neighbourhood the problem in question makes relevant) are granted autonomy to experiment with solutions of their own devising within broadly defined areas of public policy. In return they furnish central or higher-level units with rich information regarding their goals as well as the progress they are making towards achieving them, and agree to respect in their actions framework rights of democratic procedure and substance as these are elaborated in the course of experimentation itself. . . .

Section I discusses a broad spectrum of conceptualization of the European polity by legal and political scientists who share—and express—interdisciplinary views about the three concerns presented in the introductory section. Proponents of economic rationality and advocates of technocratic governance and non-majoritarian institutions can be found among both lawyers and non-lawyers. The erosion of social rights, of welfare state institutions and of redistributive policies is diagnosed by constitutional lawyers and political scientists alike. Communitarian arguments are invoked from all conceivable quarters. Gerstenberg and Sabel argue that all these sceptics face a dilemma that stems from their inability to perceive and conceptualize the democratic potential of the Europeanization process.

Section II contrasts democratic experimentalism with prominent exponents of liberal democratic constitutionalism such as Ronald Dworkin, Jürgen Habermas and Frank Michelman. The title of this section ('Counterfactuals') signals Gerstenberg and Sabel's direction. They argue that all of

---

[38] See esp. Sabel, 'Learning by Monitoring: The Institutions of Economic Development', in N. Smelser and R. Swedberg (eds), *The Handbook of Economic Sociology* (1994) 137; Cohen and Sabel, 'Directly-Deliberative Polyarchy', 3 *ELJ* (1997) 313; Gerstenberg, 'Law's Polyarchy: A Comment on Cohen and Sabel', 3 *ELJ* (1997) 343; Dorf and Sabel, 'A Constitution of Democratic Experimentalism', 98 *Columbia Law Review* (1998) 270; Sabel and Cohen, 'Sovereignty and Solidarity in the EU: A Working Paper Where We Face Some Facts' (2001) (accessible at <http://www.law.columbia.edu/sabel/>).

these theoretical projects fail to conceptualize adequately the post-national and post-state developments that their designers recognize in principle.

Section III, entitled 'Countertheoreticals', draws on a host of studies that have shown how Europe's market building project was accompanied by a rebirth of regulatory policies, and how it thereby eroded 'social democratic' concerns about the demise (weakening) of the nation state. The section also examines the institutional framework generated by this unexpected course of integration events; events that seem difficult to relate systematically to either the surprising policy outcome or to a theory of democratically legitimate European governance.

It is exactly this gap that the authors seek to seal in Section IV. In this concluding part, they further substantiate the vision of democratic experimentalism by linking it, first, to legal developments (the case law on Article 28 (ex Article 30), recent developments in the jurisprudence of 'comitology',[39] and corresponding developments towards an 'experimentalist' administration in France, Italy and the UK).[40] They then connect it with political phenomena above the comitology level in the European polity and, finally, contrast it with theories of both European governance and systems theory.

III. SOME COMMON CONCERNS

The preceding chronology documented how the individual contributions complement each other through their exploration of different areas and dimensions of European market governance. It also pointed to differences in the various methodological and theoretical orientations. However, this introduction has not yet systematically explored the divergences in a way that makes the debate among the contributors more accessible. This objective will now be pursued through a description of common reference problems discussed—albeit with differing intensities and sometimes only implicitly—by the authors. The shift from a descriptive to an analytical mode will be biased by this rapporteur's own assumptions and preferences; this risk is unavoidable, and the only conceivable precautionary response is to search for transparency. It should also be mentioned that the naming of differences and controversial issues also implies a risk of misinterpretation. As Gerstenberg and Sabel point

---

[39] Case T-188/97, *Rothmans International v Commission* [1999] II-2463 ECR II-1999.

[40] Germany makes no exception; cf. e.g. Pitschas, 'Technikentwicklung und Implementierung als rechtliches Steuerungsproblem: Von der administrativen Risikoanalyse zur Innovationsfunktion des Technikrechts', in M. Kloepfer (ed.), *Technikentwicklung und Technikrechtsentwicklung—Unter besonderer Entwicklung des Kommunikationsrechts* (2000) 73 and earlier Ladeur, 'Von der Verwaltungshierarchie zum administrativen Netzwerk? Zur Erhaltung der Eigenständigkeit der Verwaltung unter Komplexitätsbedingungen', 26 *Die Verwaltung* (1993) 137.

out, the debate among the contributors is 'too frankly and invitingly exploratory to be usefully characterized through a contrast of positions that attributes to them more fixity than they pretend for themselves'.[41]

A. Regulatory Performance

The extent of the contributions' agreement in their positive evaluations of the 'quality' of European governance is remarkable. This starting point is not particularly original. The Delors Commission's legendary internal market initiatives were widely perceived to be a strategy intended to strengthen Europe's competitiveness through the abolition of technical barriers to trade and a European-wide commitment to 'deregulation'. However, it soon became apparent that European market building followed a pattern of deregulation *and* re-regulation, which led to a modernization of Europe's interventionist traditions and a true renaissance of regulatory politics.[42] Co-ordinated efforts within Member States and at the European level to 'complete' the establishment of one 'internal' European market exhibited unplanned domino effects. There were always more policies and laws to be rewritten; and national, European, governmental and non-governmental actors found themselves increasingly drawn into new arenas. Institutional innovations were required throughout the Union, and they occurred. As it gradually became apparent that all these developments signalled an erosion of territorial, nation state centred political governance and nation state constitutionalism, a new debate about the legitimacy of European governance was nurtured.

B. Institutional Choices: 'Negative' Integration and Regulatory Competition—'Positive' Integration and Agencies—'Co-regulatory' Integration by Committees

Legal commentators interpret the history of Community deregulation and re-regulation as an evolution of legal principles, legislative strategies and institutional learning. The detection of such parallels was, and continues to be, illuminating for legal and political science alike.

---

[41] Section III.

[42] For relatively early accounts see the contributions in G. Majone (ed.), *Deregulation or Re-regulation? Regulatory Reform in Europe and in the United States* (1990), and Eichener, 'Social Dumping or Innovative Regulation? Processes and Outcomes of European Decision-Making in the Sector of Health and Safety at Work Harmonization', EUI Working Paper SPS 92/28 (1992).

1. From Negative Integration to Prudent Innovation?

One particularly significant example is provided by the history of 'negative' integration. The concept of negative integration—with all its ambivalent connotations[43]—was prominent in the characterization of the Internal Market project until long after its conception.[44] As an analytical tool, the term is used to distinguish between integration oriented 'merely' around removing non-tariff barriers, and integration oriented around developing European policies ('positive integration').[45] Yet the positive/negative dichotomy tends to lead to two types of misperception. The first is to suggest that the creation of uniform market conditions merely pays tribute to pre-legal 'freedoms' and thus neglects the many innovative developments prompted by the removal of barriers to trade.

A second misperception can be traced to the legendary *Cassis de Dijon* judgment,[46] and its wishful over-interpretation by the Commission.[47] A duty was imposed on Germany to replace its liquor import restrictions. This was heralded as the establishment of the legal principle of 'mutual recognition', which implied a reliance on 'home' rather than 'guest' state control in a new period of 'regulatory competition'. But, to the disappointment of those who believed in that new option, 'mutual recognition' proved unworkable in the fine-tuning of regulatory policies that required much more comprehensive co-operation among administrative bodies.[48] And, to the surprise of its critics, mutual recognition was prudently redesigned as a means by which to grant new rights to Community citizens against overly and unreasonably paternalistic national sovereigns.[49] It exhibited fascinating innovative effects.

---

[43] Not of economists who simply distinguish between the 'removal of discrimination in economic rules and policies under joint surveillance' and a transfer of powers to common institutions (see J. Pelkmans, *European Integration. Methods and Economic Analysis* (1997), at 6.

[44] Often ascribed to J. Tinbergen, *International Economic Integration* (1954/1965) or else to Pinder, 'Positive Integration and Negative Integration: Some Problems of Economic Union in the EEC' 24 *World Today* (1968) 88.

[45] Cf. F. W. Scharpf, *Games Real Actors Play: Actor-Centered Institutionalism in Policy Research* (1997) 132.

[46] Case 120/78, *REWE-Handelsgesellschaft Nord mbH v Bundesmonopolverwaltung für Branntwein (Cassis de Dijon)* [1979] ECR 649.

[47] Communication of the Commission on the implementations of the ECJ Judgment of 20 February 1979 in Case 120/78 (*Cassis de Dijon*), OJ C 256/1980, 2–3.

[48] Cf. E. Vos, *Institutional Frameworks of Community Health and Safety Regulation. Committees, Agencies and Private Bodies* (1999), at 60.

[49] See the recent *Centros* decision which is bound to become a true landmark case: Case C-212/97, *Centros Ltd v Ervervsog Selskabsstrylsen* [1999] ECR I-1459; it is worth noting that such re-assessments can be observed among both former critics and proponents of 'regulatory competition'; see Gerken, 'Ursprungslandprinzip, Wettbewerb der Staaten und Freiheit', 50 *Ordo* (1999) 405.

2. Market Regulation Through Agencies?

The density and stringency of Europe's new regulatory machinery proved surprising, and the search for an adequate institutional model to correspond with the redesigned European regulations began with an examination of the American experience of (more or less) independent agencies.[50] The (modified) reception of that model initially seems very remarkable.

Europe established 11 agencies[51] and has recently committed itself to another.[52] Charged with market entry/exit regulation and more general, informal, information-gathering and policy-informing duties, the new European agencies apparently meet a purely technical demand for market-corrective and sector-specific regulation. Their seemingly technocratic and semi-autonomous status implicitly provides private market interests with a voice, and this gives credence to the lingering notion that internal market regulation has more to do with the 'neutral' sustenance of individual economic enterprise than with the imposition of (collective) political/social direction. Notwithstanding their placement under the Commission's institutional umbrella and the presence of national representatives within their management structures, their founding statutes (Council Directives and Regulations), permanent staff, organizational independence, varying degrees of budgetary autonomy and direct networking with national administrators, largely shield these agencies from explicitly political processes. These specifics mean that the European 'agencies' can, at best, be presented as illegitimate heirs of their American ancestors; they might be called 'independent', but they are certainly not 'regulatory'. This hybrid quality is in line with the infamous *Meroni* doctrine,[53] and this brings the agencies close to[54] the true institutional master—hero or villain—of Europe's regulatory machinery.

[50] See programmatically Majone, 'Regulating Europe: Problems and Perspectives', 3 *Jahrbuch zur Staats und Verwaltungswissenschaft* (1989) 159.

[51] For a recent overview see Chiti, 'The Emergence of a Community Administration: The Case of European Agencies', *CMLRev.* (2000) 309; Vos, 'Reforming the European Commission: What Role to Play for European Agencies', 37 *CMLRev.* (2000) 1113.

[52] See the 'Proposal for a European Parliament and Council Regulation laying down the general principles and requirements of food law, establishing a European Food Authority and laying down procedures in matters of food safety', COM(00)716 of 8 November 2000 and the comments in the contribution of Scott and Vos, Section IV, B. The proposal was adopted at Nice (according to the report at <http://www.presidence-europe.fr/pfue/static/acces5.htm>), a rarely noticed achievement of the French presidency.

[53] *Supra* n. 8.

[54] For a very careful and subtle analysis documenting the clandestine kinship of agencies to committees, see E. E. Chiti, 'Le agenzie europee' (Ph.D. Thesis on file at the EUI, Florence (2000)).

3. Comitology: Muddling Behind a 'Dark Glass'?[55]

Committees were born of a strong national desire to retain control over the setting and consequences of European regulatory norms/standards, and they thus embody the functional and structural tensions that characterize internal market regulation. First, they hover between 'technical' and 'political' considerations, or between the functional needs and the ethical/social criteria that inform European regulation. Second, they often have very fluid compositions that reflect upon the regulatory goal of balancing rationalizing technical criteria against broader political concerns, and that also forcefully highlight schisms between the political interests of those engaged in the process of internal market regulation. Committees are deeply implicated in political processes, even when they have been established with the explicit role of supporting and overseeing the implementing powers delegated to the Commission. They are the fora for the balancing of a European market-integrationist logic against a Member State's interest in the substance and costs of consumer protection and cohesive national economic development.[56] As such, they often resemble 'mini-councils'.

This does not suggest that a common institutional vision is shared by those who underline the dominant role of committees in the implementation of Europe's regulatory policies. Kenneth Armstrong[57] usefully distinguishes no less than three models used in the conceptualization: the first is a 'regulatory model' that he ascribes to Giandomenico Majone;[58] the second is the 'deliberative model' of Jürgen Neyer and the present writer;[59] and the third is Karl-Heinz Ladeur's 'heterarchical network model'.[60] He also suggests that Peter

[55] See Bradley, 'Comitology and the Law: Through a Glass, Darkly', 29 *CMLRev.* (1992) 693.

[56] The Committee literature is well documented in the individual contributions; for a particularly comprehensive reconstruction see Falke, 'Comitology and Other Committees: A Preliminary Empirical Assessment', in R. H. Pedler and G. F. Schaefer (eds), *Shaping European Law and Policy: The Role of Committees and Comitology in the Political Process* (1996) 117 and Falke, 'Comitology: From Small Councils to Complex Networks', in M. Andenas and A. Türk (eds), *Delegated Legislation and the Role of Committees in the EU* (2000) 331.

[57] K. Armstrong, *Regulation, Deregulation, Re-regulation* (2000), at 72 et seq.

[58] Armstrong refers to G. Majone, *Regulating Europe* (1996) even though Majone hardly mentions the committee system in that book; the reference does nonetheless adequately capture Majone's conceptualisation of regulation in the EU.

[59] Joerges and Neyer, 'From Intergovernmental Bargaining to Deliberative Political Processes: The Constitutionalization of Comitology', 3 *ELJ* (1997) 237; see also the references in *supra* n. 2.

[60] Esp. Ladeur, 'Towards a Legal Concept of the Network in European Standard-Setting', in Joerges and Vos, *EU Committees, supra* n. 2, at 151; Ladeur, 'Towards a Legal Theory of Supranationality: The Viability of the Network Concept', 3 *ELJ* (1997) 33; Ladeur, 'The Integration of Scientific and Technological Expertise into the Process of Standard-Setting According to German Law', in C. Joerges, K.-H. Ladeur and E. Vos (eds), *Integrating Scientific*

Lindseth's 'administrative supranationalism'[61] can be interpreted as a distinct 'principal–agent model' of comitology. Once more, we are confronted with a development in flux rather than clear-cut institutional alternatives.

In the shadow of the agency–committee divide, one can observe differences in the intensity and manner with which European institutions interact with the wider public and, more particularly, how they accommodate 'private' expertise and interests. Divergence extends far beyond a purely efficiency-seeking movement in which certain regulatory functions are left in governmental or administrative hands. Instead, difference also appears to stem from a limited but fundamental re-working of the once rigidly vertical relationship maintained between regulators and the public; some of the heavily network-oriented informational agencies habitually consult with a far wider range of national administrative and worldwide scientific technical opinion than do the more hierarchically-constructed committees and executive agencies. Agencies, committees and less formal public/private networks are clearly all *ad hoc* creatures of necessity, and they respond to an unexpected and highly differentiated demand for European market regulation in diverging ways. As such, differences in their composition and modes of operation might initially be attributed to a pragmatic impulse within the EU; that is, a mix and match attitude reminiscent of the experimental early years of national administration-building, and responsive to national, integrationist, public, private and market interests in turn.

What can lawyers do when confronted with such a mass of yet unstructured materials? They will enquire into the legal basis for all the activities they observe in the Treaty, and those operating throughout European constitutional law. They will ask whether institutions could be created to cope with the new decision-making tasks. They will wonder about the kind of law that could guide and control decision-making, and that would offer legal protection to those public actors who would like to claim or defend competencies and/or those private actors whose interests are at stake. In these queries, the host of issues mentioned in the preceding overview can easily be re-detected. What follows should be understood as a heuristic proposal offering a framework for discussion.

C. Administration?

The most basic legal operation involves the characterization of activities as falling within a legal category. As is documented by each contribution to this volume, this exercise is particularly worrisome in the case of European

Expertise into Regulatory Decision-Making: National Traditions and European Innovations (1997), at 77.

[61] Lindseth, 'Democratic Legitimacy', *supra* n. 21.

market governance. If we start from the *trias* of legislative, administrative and judicial powers as known and defined within national constitutional orders,[62] the proper characterization might initially seem quite unproblematic. The management of the internal market operates mostly within specific legislative frameworks; national and European judiciaries are entrusted with the task of protecting rights and of supervising compliance with constitutional provisions and the legality of actions taken by public authorities. It is clear that many activities required by the operation of the internal market are neither legislative nor judicial (examples include the implementation of legislative frameworks, and all the formalized acts and informal practices undertaken by the competent bodies). Does it follow that they are 'administrative' in character? The problem with such a conclusion is, of course, that it presupposes a closed set of legal categories within which 'governance' can be conceived. However, the concept of administration does not have a fixed meaning. Before claiming that European market governance should not be categorized as an administrative activity, its specific features need to be substantiated further. The following observations will focus on risk regulation. They neither suggest that this example is representative, nor that it is more problematic than, for example, economic regulatory activities.

1. Problem-solving Activities and the Normative, Ethical, Political Dimensions of Risk Regulation

The first difficulty concerns a development that is familiar within all constitutional democracies. They all assign an attendant function to the 'administrative branch', which is expressed quite emphatically (as in the German tradition) by emphasizing its subjection to the rule of law or (as in the Anglo-American tradition) the transmission-belt metaphor.[63] To point to the exhaustion of this tradition amounts to carrying coals to Newcastle. As Wolfgang Schluchter observed back in 1972,[64] the inherited (Weberian) notion of a bureaucracy governed by the rule of law rested upon an equation or compatibility of *Amtsautorität* (the power derived from the bureaucracy's sovereign) and *Sachautorität* (an authority based upon professional competences). When public administration is expected to resort to non-legal knowledge and non-legal skills, the logic of *Amtsautorität* needs to be supplemented or replaced by its problem-solving capacity. In the field of risk regulation, one feature of the required *Sachautorität* is particularly visible and worrisome.

---

[62] See Lenaerts and Verhoeven, this vol., Section I.

[63] See, famously, Stewart, 'The Reformation of American Administrative Law', 88 *Harvard Law Review* (1975) 1671, at 1674 et seq.

[64] W. Schluchter, *Aspekte bürokratischer Herrschaft: Studien zur Interpretation der fortschreitenden Industriegesellschaft* (2nd edn., 1985), at 145–176; cf. Feick, 'Wissen, Expertise und regulative Politik: Das Beispiel der Arzneimittelkointrolle', in R. Wehrle and U. Schimank (eds), *Gesellschaftliche Komplexität und kollektive Handlungsfähigkeit* (2000) 208, at 211–213.

Judgements about the social acceptability of the risks associated with, for example, the consumption of food, the licensing of pharmaceuticals or genetic engineering, not only require recourse to an infinite and uncertain body of expert knowledge; they must also balance the benefits and costs of regulatory measures. Such balancing must then pay due regard to normative, political and even ethical considerations. Two interdependent difficulties overlap. The administration is expected to use non-legal knowledge. By integrating non-legal expertise, it will strengthen its *Sachautorität*; by the same token, it will document the inadequacy of the bureaucratic *Amtsautorität*, and the case of risk regulation is a particularly dramatic illustration of this difficulty. Even within constitutional nation states, the use of the term 'administration' for the characterization of related activities is questionable. However, we can let such definitional queries rest,[65] and turn to some additional difficulties that characterize the Community context.

2. Community 'Administration'?

Whose 'will' is 'executed' in the process of implementing the law of the internal market? Which bodies can be said to function as the 'transmission belt' of what polity? These questions have an empirical and a normative dimension. The diversity of the European space renders it unlikely that one single body will be able to provide uniform responses to the normative, ethical, cultural and political dimensions of risk assessments. If such responses are to be socially acceptable within the entire internal market, they will have to be elaborated in a co-operative manner. This is not just an empirical observation. However far one stretches the notion of 'administration', its connotation of serving some higher common 'authority' cannot be upheld in a non-unitary, non-state pluralist polity. This has motivated scholars like Karl-Heinz Ladeur to ascribe the authorship of regulatory policy to 'network'.[66] Peter Lindseth,

---

[65] Udo di Fabio has, in a series of essays and his *Habilitation*, responded by creating a new legal category: '*Risikoverwaltungsrecht*' (the law of risk administration) (see, e.g., 'Entscheidungsprobleme der Risikoverwaltung. Ist der Umgang mit Risiken rechtlich operationalisierbar?', 13 *Natur und Recht* (1991) 353; *Risikoentscheidungen im Rechtsstaat. Zum Wandel der Dogmatik im öffentlichen Recht, insbesondere am Beispiel der Arzneimittelüberwachung* (1994)). The new term points to exactly those difficulties, which exclude the entrustment of traditional administrations with the problems, risk regulation has to address. In American legal literature cf. e.g. Pildes and Sunstein, 'Reinventing the Regulatory State', 62 *Chicago Law Review* (1995) 1; Manning, 'Constitutional Structure and Judicial Deference to Agency Interpretation of Agency Rules', 96 *Columbia Law Review* (1996) 612, esp. at 660 et seq.; for a very explicit link of 'non-delegation' to deliberative democracy see Sunstein, 'Nondelegation Canons', University of Chicago Law School. John M. Olin Law & Economics Working Paper No. 82 (1999). For summaries in sociology and political science on which this argument is based see Bechmann, 'Risiko und gesellschaftlicher Umgang mit Unsicherheit', *Österreichische Zeitschrift für Soziologie* (1994) 8; K. S. Shrader-Frechette, *Risk and Rationality: Philosophical Foundations* (1991); S. Jasanoff, *The Fifth Branch. Science Advisors as Policymakers* (1990).

[66] See the references in *supra* n. 60.

who defends the interpretation of the EU as a supranational administrative entity,[67] underlines the difficulty of defining a 'common good' in a Union with many masters; 'governance without government' is one concept he invokes; 'agents without principals' is another.

The notion of a networked or fused[68] administration departs from the concept of a supranational, hierarchically structured bureaucracy on the one hand, and from an intergovernmental bargaining machinery on the other. It seeks to substitute some co-operative relationship for the supranational/intergovernmental paradigm. Does this shift adequately express the tensions between the functional requirements of the internal market and the normative political dimensions of risk regulation?

In order to articulate this tension, I have resorted to a conceptual oxymoron, namely the term 'political administration'. The label does have some virtues.[69] However, as it does not capture the non-hierarchical dimension of the non-integrated, plurally-composed European polity, I have suggested the term 'good governance'. This alternative metaphor is particularly employed by international lawyers dealing with transnational governance phenomena. The term is defensible if 'good' is understood to reflect the 'legitimacy' dimension of transnational governance.[70] This dimension forms the core problem of the debate documented in this volume.

D. Expertise

Before addressing this problem more directly, one further issue (which has implicitly been dealt with earlier) needs to be raised explicitly. The practices of European market governance in general, and of risk regulation in particular, are characterized by the presence of experts of all kinds and the resort to expertise as a source of 'sound' practice. The authority of expertise threatens the realm of practical reasoning, the claim to equal participation by all con-

---

[67] See Section II A 3 above.

[68] Cf. Wessels, 'Staat und (westeuropäische) Integration. Die Fusionsthese', in M. Kreile (ed.), *Die Integration Europas* (1992) 36; 'Comitology as a Research Subject: A New Legitimacy Mix?', in Joerges and Vos, *EU Committees, supra* n. 2, at 259.

[69] It was coined by Rudolf Wiethölter in a polemic on the obstruction of an implementation of purposive salutatory provisions, through the application of 'classic' private law legislation. See Wiethölter, 'Wirtschaftsrecht', in A. Görlitz (ed.), *Handlexikon zur Rechtswissenschaft* (1972) 531, at 532.

[70] See Azoulay, this vol., and more detailed in his Ph.D. Thesis, *supra* n. 17, Titre III (paras 1090–1150); see also Joerges, '"Good Governance" in the European Internal Market: Two Competing Legal Conceptualisations of European Integration and their Synthesis', RSC Working Paper 2001 (forthcoming in A. von Bogdandy, Y. Mény and P. Mavroidi (eds), *European Integration and International Co-ordination. Studies in Transnational Economic Law—Liber amicorum Claus-Dieter Ehlermann*).

cerned in decision-making, and the accountability of elected political representatives to their constituencies. Indeed:

Specialized experts play a central role in all areas of modern life: money and banking, market and marketing developments, energy (including such diverse areas as oil and gas, nuclear, geothermal and alternative forms of energy); other natural resources such as the water we drink or the air we breathe; health and medicine; education of various types and on different levels; scientific research and new technical developments, for example in medicine and bio-technology generally; law and government. Systematic knowledge—professional, technical, and scientific—is applied to a wide range of activities and endeavours including the formulation of laws and policies, and the development of programs. This is apparent on all levels of governance, including also, of course, the level of the European Union.[71]

Laymen and experts might have comparable intelligence and virtue, but they boast different types of knowledge.[72] The expert's knowledge cannot simply be substituted or 'overruled' by the problem perceptions and preferences of the layman. It can, and should, be exposed to critical observation through a quest for counter-expertise. Such 'politicization' would not replace cognition; nor is cognition invalidated by a reference to other scientific disciplines or the

---

[71] Burns, 'The Role and Functioning of Parliament in an Era of Transition', in European Commission (Directorate General XII, Science, Research and Development, Directorate F— Human potential and mobility), *Governance and Citizenship in Europe. Some Research Directions* (2000), at 46. As Burns goes on to explain:

Increasingly, there is a 'politics of knowledge', concerning the use of new scientific and technical knowledge (Nico Stehr). Issues concern whether or not such knowledge ought to be applied and, if so, to what extent and in which ways. Although regulative issues of this sort have been around for some time (e.g. pharmaceutical products, dangerous chemicals, etc.), the scale and the contentious character of knowledge politics has increased considerably. Also, there is an ongoing scientification of politics and governance. But this is not so much in the sense of political action becoming rational action. Rather, the topics and issues that are the stuff of political debate, conflict and action—and are expressed in political discourses—are more and more generated or discovered in and through science (in this sense the scientification of political action connects with the issue of knowledge politics (and policy)). For instance, the issue of climatic change originates in climate science.

N. 7 of Burns's text; the reference is to N. Stehr, *Arbeit, Eigentum und Wissen. Zur Theorie von Wissensgesellschaften* (1994).

[72] Van den Daele, 'Objektives Wissen als politische Ressource: Experten und Gegenexperten im Diskurs', in W. van den Daele and W. Neidhardt (eds), *Kommuniktion und Entscheidung: politische Funktionen öffentlicher Meinungsbildung und diskursiver Verfahren* (1996), at 297–326; van den Daele and Neidhardt, ' "Regierung durch Diskussion"—über Versuche mit Argumenten Politik zu machen', ibid., 9. For the particularly intriguing example of pharmaceutical regulation see Feick, 'Wissen, Expertise und regulative Politik: Das Beispiel der Arzneimittelkontrolle', in R. Wehrle and U. Schimank (eds), *Gesellschaftliche Komplexität und kollektive Handlungsfähigkeit* (2000) 208; the example is so intriguing, because both the need for expertise *and* the political dimensions of regulation are hardly controversial. In Feick's account, the thoroughly professionalized EU system operates (the involvement of so many national agencies' administrators notwithstanding) in political isolation (ibid., at 230, 236).

mere fact that other experts hold other opinions. The interaction of experts and non-experts can, and should, pursue other objectives. The capture of experts by interests or unreflected patterns of thought must be revealed; the *lacunae* of knowledge must become apparent; normative and ethical issues must be recognized for what they are. However, such interactions do not readily emerge from general public communication.

This perspective suggests that a resort to expertise does not have to abolish democratic ideals; it can merely approve the inequalities by recognizing the existence of experts' deliberative privileges over the opinions of ordinary citizens.

In complex societies, the role of expertise is a key issue with important implications. To prescribe the role of experts in regulatory policy is to define the function of law in the structuring of decision-making and, ultimately, to determine which type of legitimacy is the goal in the governance of complex societies. It is beyond the scope of this introduction to present an editorial position on such matters.[73] It is instead sufficient to repeat that the expertise problem is interdependent with the issues of the following two sections. The contributions to this volume should be read and assessed accordingly.

E. Administrative Law

The law does not have ready-made solutions to all these difficulties. European market governance occurs; bureaucrats, national and Community officials continuously make decisions, develop routines and orient themselves within the legal system. The legal *lacunae* in which they operate are filled. The first task of an academic legal enquiry is to find out what kind of juridification these practices produce. Commencing with such an observational attitude postpones—rather than avoids—further examination of the theoretical challenges just outlined.

Such observation would ideally look closely at the practices of the actors and at their perceptions of the problems, and would seek to reconstruct their problem-resolving strategies. However, legal academics shy away from such *Rechtstatsachenforschung* (research into the factual background of law) and prefer to interfere only when the problems surface as legal controversies. At that stage, the controversial issues can be characterized with the help of previously existing categories. Whether these categories really 'fit' will be discussed in 'doctrinal' debates that determine how the law will 'think' and what it will 'do'.

---

[73] For a particularly lucid systematic exposition (which is close to the positions indicated here) see J. Bohman, *Public Deliberation. Pluralism, Complexity, and Democracy* (1996), esp. at 165 et seq. (on expert knowledge and democratic ideals) and 172 et seq. (on the interaction of institutions and public opinion).

Since internal market governance uses regulatory techniques borrowed from administrative lawyers, their conceptual toolkit is the first to be tested. 'Governance' and 'regulation' are not categories known to the administrative tradition, and their appearance in this volume indicates a non-fit of the inherited administrative law categories. But there is another challenge they must also accept. 'European market governance' refers to a functionally defined activity, whereas the rules and principles of 'administrative law' are understood as elements of a system with a legal logic of its own. Legal analyses of Europeanization processes tend to respect the systematic structures internal to the law, and to defend their normative coherence. Jürgen Schwarze's groundbreaking *magnus opum*[74] was an effort to detect an administrative *ius commune* for the European Union (incorporating general principles concerning the legality of administrative acts, due process requirements, notions of equal treatment and proportionality, the weight of legal certainty, protection of legitimate expectations and confidentiality, transparency, access to files, state liability, and so on), and to determine how the need for effectiveness could and should be balanced against the protection of individual rights.

However, this kind of administrative law is not very sensitive to the specifics of European governance, the interaction between national and European bodies, or the interdependence of their activities. Such issues are much more directly reflected by Stefan Kadelbach's distinctions between functionalist inspired conflict of laws approaches, federalist codification perspectives, and the defence of a plurality of national systems.[75]

Other contributions redefining the role of law in the governance of the European market are inspired by the integration theories of political theory, history and political science. An explicit search for a new analytical model and a new legal conception of the European Union leads—with compelling logic—into reflections about the 'nature' of the Union and the legitimacy of its governance structures. Methodologically-speaking, moves beyond the traditional provinces of administrative law are not original; they can be observed within every national legal system that redefines the role of its administration in response to changes in the inherited separation of powers. However, if and because the European Union is an unprecedented polity, such a move is truly 'original' at the European level.

---

[74] J. Schwarze, *Europäisches Verwaltungsrecht: Entstehung und Entwicklung im Rahmen der Europäischen Gemeinschaft* (1988) (translated as *European Administrative Law* (1992)).

[75] Cf. S. Kadelbach, *Allgemeines Verwaltungsrecht unter europäischem Einfluß* (1999) and Section V of his contribution to the present volume.

F. The Constitutionalization and Legitimacy of European Market Governance

European market governance (as this interim conclusion can be dubbed), is an activity that extends beyond the powers of the Member States and outside the institutional framework foreseen by the Treaty. The terms 'beyond' and 'outside' should not be read as assessments of its 'legality', but as analytical and normative challenges. The normative dimension of this challenge stems from the achievements of the constitutional (nation) state, which were abrogated with the project of European integration. Its analytical dimension refers to the need to redefine the meaning of constitutionalism in a non-state context. Such yardsticks might sound overly pretentious. They are nonetheless irrefutable, not only in salient cases like the BSE crisis, but also with respect to the more mundane issues with which European 'market governance' is mostly concerned.

All the contributions in all the sections of this volume address this challenge. But they operate upon different premises and pursue different perspectives. One way to understand and evaluate these positions is to reflect upon the notion of legitimate governance that they defend. Following an analytical scheme employed by Erik O. Eriksen, Johan E. Fossum and others,[76] three different conceptions of rationality—instrumental, contextual (or value-based) and communicative (or normative)—can be related to three variants of democracy and legitimate governance that in turn correspond with three ways of conceptualizing the EU:

(1) *Instrumental* rationality ties in with social choice theories, which define 'democracy' as a decision-making method or a method of preference aggregation. From such a perspective, the EU will be characterized as an institution committed to economic rationality and technocratic problem-solving.

(2) A *contextual* logic is present in republican-communitarian conceptualizations of democracy as a cultural phenomenon. Europe will therefore be understood as a community in which different national modes of allegiance and identification are to be 'harmonized'. The success of the EU depends upon the development of a shared identity and a value basis for integrating different conceptions of the good life, and a diverse range of societal interests.

(3) The *communicative* logic entails a cosmopolitan notion that is based on legal and argumentative presuppositions of a cognitive-universalist nature. Europe is designed as a rights-based, post-national union. The integration project is intended to establish a fair system of co-operation

---

[76] In the context of a project on 'Legitimate European Governance. Strategies for solving the EU's legitimacy deficits', *ARENA* (1999).

founded on basic rights and democratic procedures for deliberation and decision-making.

Although this scheme is apparently inspired by a particular epistemology[77] and my summary is quite simplistic,[78] it is helpful as a tool for placing the various positions in the controversies about European market governance. Where it seems too crude to capture the finer nuances of that debate, the scheme is still illuminating. Peter Lindseth's work can be cited as an example.[79] Lindseth portrays the EC as a supranational administrative agent, whose legitimacy cannot be directly derived from the people but must remain mediated.[80] Its administrative character seems to place the juridification of Community governance in the domain of 'administrative law'.[81] He would thus seem to be a clear candidate for the first-mentioned category.[82] However, in his review of Majone's work,[83] Lindseth rejects the severability of expertise from politics.[84] It follows that 'administrative supranationalism' cannot be exclusively legitimized through technocratic problem-solving but runs into a democratic deficit once Member States can no longer exert effective oversight. But this seems to be exactly what does occur. Lindseth notes a 'growing disconnect between structures of governance—that are being progressively denationalized and diffused throughout a complex multi-level system—and the capacity of Europeans to experience those structures as democratically and constitutionally legitimate'.[85] This analysis seems to discredit the technocratic position. It is nevertheless consistent with Lindseth's rejection as 'utopian' of the search for a genuinely transnational legitimacy that adherents to position (3) envisage. However, it follows that Lindseth would have to show how the Community's administrative supranationalism could be re-anchored in the Member States' constitutional orders. This is hardly a less utopian project.

---

[77] J. Habermas has elaborated on these concepts of rationality on many occasions, e.g. in *Theorie des kommunikativen Handelns, Band 1, Handlungsrationalität und gesellschaftliche Rationalisierung* (4th edn., 1987), at 15 et seq.; for a recent *summa* of his views on the European project see Habermas, 'Warum braucht Europa eine Verfassung?', *Die Zeit*, 29 June 2001, accessible at <http://www.iue.it/RSC/EU/Reform02.pdf>.

[78] For a fuller exposition see Eriksen, 'Deliberative Supranationalism in the EU', in E. O. Eriksen and J. E. Fossum (eds), *Democracy in the European Union. Integration through Deliberation?* (2000) 42, at 45 et seq.; Eriksen and Fossum, 'The EU and Post-national Legitimacy', *Arena Working Paper*, 26/2000.

[79] See Section II A 3 above.

[80] Lindseth, 'Democratic Legitimacy', *supra* n. 21, at 651–735.

[81] See Lindseth, ' "Weak" Constitutionalism?', *supra* n. 21, at 152–155 where Lindseth underlines the hierarchical dimension of American administrative law.

[82] In the same vein ibid., esp. at 657–662 (on 'the Community as supranational administrative agency').

[83] See references in nn. 15, 30, 38, 46.

[84] See Lindseth, 'Democratic Legitimacy', *supra* n. 21, at 686–689.

[85] Lindseth, ' "Weak" Constitutionalism?', *supra* n. 21, at 158.

In a philippic against 'infranationalism' in general, and against 'comitology' in particular, J.H.H.Weiler seems even more determined than Lindseth in his opposition to a juridification of transnational European market governance.[86] Lindseth's insistence on the 'administrative character of supranationalism' stems from his diagnosis of the flaws present in European governance. Weiler's analysis of 'infranationalism' as a 'middle-level' between (inherently political) intergovernmentalism and (truly legal) supranationalism compromises that political-legal hybrid for want of a conceptualization that would render this 'hallmark of the last decade'[87] normatively acceptable in the integration process. However, Weiler's position is more radical because he does not only list apparent deficiencies of 'infranationalist' practices[88] and flaws in academic suggestions for their cure; he goes further to reject as preposterous the very idea of 'juridifying'—let alone of 'constitutionalizing'—infranational phenomena.[89]

This principled position initially seems surprising. Not only does Weiler explicitly acknowledge the practical importance of transnational ('infranational') governance structures,[90] but he is even ready to concede that its core institution—comitology—seems to perform quite well in terms 'of both process and outcome'.[91] Why then do infranationalism and comitology not just constitute challenges for theory and practice like so many other extralegal transformations of the EU? And why resort to such stark language?

Weiler's preoccupations are probably best understood in light of his own paradigms. His diagnosis of a dual structure of the Community system portrays normative (legal) supranationalism and decisional intergovernmentalism in a functioning, albeit precarious, equilibrium.[92] 'Infranationalism' moves beyond this dual structure through its disregard of the law/politics and Member State/Community dichotomies. The Committee System is the institutionalized embodiment of these heresies; it gives a form to that subversion.

---

[86] See J. H. H. Weiler, *The Constitution of Europe. 'Do the New Clothes Have an Emperor?' and Other Essays on European Integration* (1999), at 98–99, 271–279, 283–285; Weiler, 'Epilogue: "Comitology" as Revolution—Infranationalism, Constitutionalism and Democracy', in Joerges and Vos, *EU Committees, supra* n. 2, at 339.

[87] J. H. H. Weiler, *The Constitution of Europe, supra* n. 86, at 98.

[88] His list is indeed impressive, see esp. ibid., at 283–4.

[89] Ibid., at 98–99, and Weiler, 'Epilogue', *supra* n. 86.

[90] Ibid., at 98; Weiler, 'Epilogue', *supra* n. 86, at 340; contrast Lindseth's concluding remarks in ' "Weak" Constitutionalism?', *supra* n. 21, at 163.

[91] Most outspokenly Weiler, 'Epilogue', *supra* n. 86, at 340.

[92] This theorem was first developed in J. H. H. Weiler, 'Supranational Law and Supranational System: Legal Structures and Political Process in the European Community' (Ph.D. Thesis on file at the EUI, Florence (1982)), at 117 et seq. and his 'The Community system: the dual character of supranationalism', 1 *YEL* (1981) 267. Weiler has retained this dual structure ever since, most recently in 'The Rule of Lawyers and the Ethos of Diplomats: Reflections on the Internal and the External Legitimacy of WTO Dispute Settlement', Harvard Jean Monnet Working Paper 09/00.

Such preoccupation has an empirical basis. For the purposes of this analysis, it is sufficient to point to Jürgen Neyer's report from one of his interviews with German officials. He writes: 'governments expect that their interests will be represented and defended. Their expectations are so often disappointed that they characterize their "Permanent Representatives" as "Permanent Traitors" '.[93] And yes, indeed, comitology blurs the law/politics distinction through a 'political administration'[94] that operates in the zones between normative/legal supranationalism and decisional/political intergovernmentalism.

What is so bad about all this? Political scientists tell us that:

Modern welfare states look increasingly less like hierarchical structures of legitimate authority, but more like multi-level bargaining and negotiating networks in which public actors are not obsolete, but can fulfil their functions in co-operating with private actors and groups. This is even true for the quintessential European nation-state, France.[95]

This has inevitably affected the law/politics divide even more deeply than the discovery of 'purposive' legal programmes did, and it has inspired the search for a 'proceduralization' of the category of law.[96] Such developments occur within constitutional states and are taken seriously. If this occurs within constitutional states, how could they be expected to establish legal hierarchies rather than more horizontal governance structures for transnational problem-solving? Why, then, should the substitution of legal-hierarchical constitutionalism by a 'deliberative' supranationalism be nothing but a 'semantic *faux pas*' indicative of its proponents' failure to 'grasp the real implications' of their suggestions?[97] What these proponents advocate is that the validity of democracies' legally binding restrictions be based on the exigencies of co-operation and on deliberative processes. This is an intuition that might be inspired by 'St Jürgen's noble vision of a deliberative and communicative process through which, and only through which, true democratic discourse can take

---

[93] Neyer, 'The Comitology Challenge to Analytical Integration Theory', in Joerges and Vos, *EU Committees, supra* n. 2, at 228; Neyer reports from an interview conducted with an official from the Permanent Representation of Germany in Brussels, 26 April 1996. 'Unfortunately', so he notes, 'the pun (*'ständige Vertreter'* vs. *'ständige Verräter'*) is lost in translation' (ibid., n. 34).

[94] Section II, 3 above.

[95] Börzel and Risse, 'Who is Afraid of a European Federation? How to Constitutionalize a Multi-Level Governance System', EUI Jean Monnet Working Paper 7/2000, at 6. The law has learned to live with that reality, see Somek, 'On Supranationality', 5 *EIoP* (2001); <http://eiop.or.at/eiop/texte/2001-003a.htm>, text accompanying notes 54 et seq. with references.

[96] Wiethölter, 'Proceduralisation of the Category of Law', in C. Joerges and D. M. Trubek (eds), *Critical Legal Thought: An American–German Debate* (1988) 501.

[97] Weiler, 'Epilogue', *supra* n. 86, at 347. And, one may also ask, did 'vertical' supranationalism ever have a sounder normative basis, on which one could explain how, e.g., simple directives trump national constitutional provisions?

place'.[98] And equally important: if the rise of infranationalism is really as inexorable as Weiler suggests, an erosion of the Community's dual structure seems unavoidable. The messenger who transmits this report is not to be condemned. What is at stake is a comparative evaluation of doctrinal rejections, an affirmative equation of facticity and validity, and the design of regulative ideas that guide the assessment of real-world developments.

Conceptualizing 'comitology' as an institutional core of horizontal, denationalized governance structures raises another fundamental difficulty: on whose mandate does transnational decision-making operate? In his comments on Lenaerts and Verhoeven's institutional balance approach, Smismans addresses this issue in a plea for 'functional' representation.[99] In Weiler's account, infranational actors do not 'belong' anywhere; they owe no allegiance, so they can have no mandate. Gerstenberg and Sabel's account of comitology is more ambivalent.[100] They acknowledge that:

appearances notwithstanding, comitology, . . . as an institution . . . proves capable of practical, problem-solving deliberation, and so of producing results which arguably embody the public interest in novel ways precisely by exploring the differences in current understandings of it.[101]

However, it is only a substitute for democracy. In my view, the most important flaw they identify is the insulation of comitology *telle quelle* against public discourses and opinion formation. The theoretical basis of that critique is not identical with the types of concerns raised by protagonists of 'deliberative democracy' (even though I would situate Gerstenberg and Sabel in the third of Eriksen's theory camps outlined above).[102] Gerstenberg and Sabel's account does not allow for a comparison between deliberative problem-solving and public debates. But institutionalized deliberation and public debate must interact. This must not become the Achilles heel of 'deliberative supranationalism', but it is a serious weakness of comitology as it presently operates.[103]

---

[98] Weiler, 'Epilogue', *supra* n. 86, at 347.

[99] See Section IV of his contribution to this volume. For a further thorough analysis see Section IV.II.2. of Verhoeven's Ph.D. thesis (*supra* n. 7).

[100] In the Academy version of their contribution, they were less cautious, characterizing in their section IV the assessment of comitology, cited in n. 2 above, in the outright as 'complete betrayal, betrayal and demolition of the idea of deliberative democracy'.

[101] Gerstenberg and Sabel, this volume, Introduction.

[102] Text accompanying n. 76 et seq.

[103] One should note, however, practical progress in terms of transparency and accessibility has been enormous during the last few years. The legal framework furthering such interactions is better than most critics realize (see Joerges, 'Transnationale "deliberative Demokratie" oder "deliberativer Supranationalismus"? Anmerkungen zur Konzeptualisierung legitimen Regierens jenseits des Nationalstaats bei Rainer Schmalz-Bruns', 7 *Zeitschrift für Internationale Beziehungen* (2000) 145 (' "Deliberative Supranationalism"—A Defence', 5 *EIoP* (2001);

<http://eiop.or.at/eiop/texte/2001-008a.htm>), and gets gradually strengthened (see e.g. the *Rothmans* judgment cited in n. 39 and attracting much attention and praise); and even in the worst-case scenario of the BSE crisis, one can detect considerable institutional learning (Joerges, 'Law, Science and the Management of Risks to Health at the National, European and International Level—Stories on Baby Dummies, Mad Cows and Hormones in Beef', 8 *Columbia Journal of European Law* (2001) 1, at 16–17). Equally noteworthy are the findings on the gradual formation of a European public opinion (see Eder, 'Zur Transformation national-alstaatlicher Öffentlichkeit in Europa. Von der Sprachgemeinschaft zur issuespezifischen Kommunikationsgemeinschaft', *Berliner Journal* (2000) 167; Eder and Kantner, 'Transnationale Resonanzstrukturen in Europa. Eine Kritik der Rede vom Öffentlichkeitsde-fizit', in M. Bach (ed.), *Die Europäisierung nationaler Gesellschaften (Kölner Zeitschrift für Soziologie und Sozialpsychologie* (2000) 306.

SECTION II

EUROPEAN CONSTITUTIONAL LAW

2

Institutional Balance as a Guarantee for Democracy in EU Governance

KOEN LENAERTS and AMARYLLIS VERHOEVEN*

INTRODUCTION

The notion of institutional balance is firmly wedded in the constitutional language of the European Union. Its content and function are, however, far from clear. Some authors have heralded the notion of institutional balance as a fundamental constitutional principle[1] and have drawn parallels with the principle of separation of powers.[2] Others regard it as a 'phantom' or an 'empty formula', which is interpreted by each interested party in a manner that serves its own interests.[3] As always, the truth lies probably in the middle. Although not devoid of meaning, institutional balance is, in the current state of

---

* It is stressed that the views expressed in this chapter are the authors' personal views and cannot be ascribed to the institutions to which they belong.

[1] Thus, Everling has argued that the principle of institutional balance must be respected by the Member States even when amending the Treaties upon which the Union is founded. See Everling, 'Zur Stellung der Mitgliedstaaten der Europäischen Union als "Herren der Verträge"', in *Festschrift für Rudolf Bernhardt* (1995) 1161, at 1170.

[2] Guillermin, 'Le principe de l'équilibre institutionnel dans la jurisprudence de la CJCE', 119 *Journal du droit international* (1992) 319; Jacqué, 'La légitimation active du Parlement européen ou il n'était pas nécessaire d'espérer pour entreprendre', 26 *Revue trimestrielle de droit européen* (1990) 620; Petersmann, 'Proposals for a New Constitution for the European Union: Building-blocks for a Constitutional Theory and Constitutional Law of the EU', 32 *CMLRev.* (1995) 1123.

[3] Bieber, 'The Settlement of Institutional Conflicts on the Basis of Art. 4 of the EEC Treaty', 21 *CMLRev.* (1984) 505, at 519. It is significant, for instance, that during the intergovernmental conference leading up to the Treaty of Amsterdam, the Reflection Group as well as the three institutional tenors of the European Union, the Commission, the European Parliament and the Council, all stressed the importance of maintaining the institutional balance. Each of them gave, however, a particular interpretation of that balance, in a (scarcely hidden) attempt to defend or strengthen their own position. See Craig, 'Democracy and Rule-making within the EC: An Empirical and Normative Assessment', 3 *ELJ* (1997) 105, at 107–109.

European Union law, a 'fragile principle with uncertain contents'.[4] Yet it carries, in our opinion, an important message, akin to the message inspiring the age-old doctrine of separation of powers and of 'balanced government'. A proper understanding and due application of the notion of institutional balance may, we believe, lessen the democratic deficit from which the Union is perceived to suffer.

In this contribution, we attempt to flesh out the (as yet imprecise) contours of the notion of institutional balance as it emerges from the current constitutional *acquis* and to provide it with some theoretical underpinnings. This will be done in Section I. In the ensuing sections, we will use this theoretical framework in order to tackle two unresolved questions bearing on the relationship between the institutional players within the European Union. Section II is devoted to the role of the Commission and its relationship vis-à-vis the European Parliament and Council. In particular, our focus is on how the accountability of the Commission can best be ensured. Section III then concentrates on the budgetary procedure and, in particular, on the role of the European Parliament therein.

I. INSTITUTIONAL BALANCE AND DEMOCRATIC GOVERNANCE

A. Institutional Balance: What Is It and Why Does It Matter?

The notion of institutional balance could not until recently be found in the texts of the Treaties upon which the European Communities and Union are based. The Protocol on the application of the principles of subsidiarity and proportionality, added by the Treaty of Amsterdam, now mentions institutional balance without, however, defining it.[5] The term institutional balance was used for the first time by the Court of Justice in *Meroni*. In this judgment, dating back to the early days of the European Coal and Steel Community, the Court held that:

there can be seen in the balance of powers which is characteristic of the institutional structure of the Community a fundamental guarantee granted by the Treaty to the undertakings and associations of undertakings to which it applies. To delegate a discretionary power, by entrusting it to bodies other than those which the Treaty has

---

[4] Prechal, 'Institutional Balance: A Fragile Principle with Uncertain Contents', in T. Heukels, N. Blokker and M. Brus (eds), *The European Union after Amsterdam* (1998) 273.
[5] 'The application of the principles of subsidiarity and proportionality shall respect the general provisions and the objectives of the Treaty, particularly as regards the maintaining in full of the *acquis communautaire* and the institutional balance . . .' (para. 2 of the Protocol).

established to effect and supervise the exercise of such power each within the limits of its own authority, would render that guarantee ineffective.[6]

With these words, the Court of Justice established what has come to be known as the *Meroni* doctrine, which precludes the delegation of discretionary powers to bodies other than those established by the European Treaties on the ground that this would upset a 'fundamental guarantee' contained in the balance of powers between the European institutions. It failed to establish, however, what this guarantee was and why it was important. Only in 1990, in *Chernobyl,* did the Court of Justice give further indications as to what was meant by the notion of institutional balance. It observed that the institutional balance is based on:

a system for distributing powers among the different Community institutions, assigning to each institution its own role in the institutional structure of the Community and the accomplishment of the tasks entrusted to the Community.[7]

It further held that:

Observance of the institutional balance means that each of the institutions must exercise its powers with due regard for the powers of the other institutions. It also requires that it should be possible to penalize any breach of that rule which may occur.[8]

As clarified in *Chernobyl,* institutional balance links in with the requirement set forth in Article 7 of the EC Treaty to the effect that '[e]ach institution shall act within the limits of the powers conferred upon it by this Treaty'. Thus, institutional balance concerns the balance between the institutional actors that are called, by the Treaties, to participate in European Union governance. It means that each institution should duly exercise its competencies but in doing so, respect the powers of other institutions.

Further, *Chernobyl* makes it clear that a breach of the principle of institutional balance may be judicially sanctioned. The Court of Justice considers that upholding respect of the institutional balance belongs to its fundamental task to see that the rule of law is respected. The question which arose in *Chernobyl* was whether the European Parliament had a right to bring an action for annulment against acts of the Council or the Commission. Before the Maastricht Treaty, Article 173 of the EC Treaty (now Article 230) did not recognize such a right. The Court of Justice held, however, that the absence of a *ius standi*:

may constitute a procedural gap, but it cannot prevail over the fundamental interest in the maintenance and observance of the institutional balance laid down in the Treaties establishing the European Communities. Consequently, an action for annulment

---

[6] Case 9/56, *Meroni v High Authority* [1957 and 1958] ECR 133, at 152.
[7] Case 70/88, *European Parliament v Council* [1990] ECR I-2041, at I-2072, para. 21.
[8] Ibid., para. 22.

brought by the Parliament against an act of the Council or the Commission is admissible provided that the action seeks only to safeguard its prerogatives and that it is founded only on submissions alleging their infringement.[9]

Despite the clarifications given in *Chernobyl*, institutional balance remains at present a rather elusive concept of an uncertain scope. Much of that uncertainty is due to a lack of understanding of the *ratio* of institutional balance. Why, after all, is institutional balance important, even 'fundamental', as *Chernobyl* suggests? Often, the parallel between institutional balance and the doctrine of separation of powers is drawn.[10] However, one cannot but acknowledge that institutional balance fits uneasily within the contours usually ascribed to the doctrine of *trias politica*.[11] Commonly, separation of powers is understood as an organic separation of the legislative, administrative and adjudicative function. As is well known, the European Union does not have such an organic separation although a certain functional distinction between, for instance, legislative and administrative activity can be made.[12]

Moreover, given the centrality of the legal basis requirement, there is no single institutional balance or fixed structure of institutional interaction. For each subject matter, the legal basis decides whether the Union can act, which institutions must be involved and how.[13] The three-pillar structure that was introduced by the Maastricht Treaty only adds to the existing diversity of decision-making procedures.

Finally, the notion of institutional balance is not static; it evolves over time as the Union's founding Treaties are adapted. The evolution of the institutional balance is by no means a linear process. It is influenced by various, sometimes opposing, visions of what the 'nature' of the Community and/or Union is or should be. Somewhat summarily, one can say that three different

---

[9] Case 70/88, *European Parliament v Council* [1990] ECR I-2041, at I-2072, paras 26 and 27.

[10] *Supra* n. 2.

[11] Edward, 'What Kind of Law Does Europe Need? The Role of Law, Lawyers and Judges in Contemporary European Integration', 5 *Columbia Journal of European Law* (1998) 1, at 13; Pescatore, 'L'exécutif communautaire: Justification du quadripartisme institué par les traités de Paris et de Rome', 14 *Cahiers de droit européen* (1978) 387.

[12] Lenaerts, 'Some Reflections on the Separation of Powers in the European Community', 28 *CMLRev.* (1991) 11.

[13] In the so-called *Transparency* case, the Court of Justice observed there is no general division of powers within the European Community. It concluded on that basis that the law-making powers of the Commission with respect to public undertakings (Art. 86 (3) EC) did not necessarily need to be interpreted strictly as if they were an exception to a general rule (Joined Cases 88–90/80, *French Republic and Others v Commission* [1982] ECR 2545, in particular at para. 6: 'the limits of powers conferred on the Commission by a specific provision of the Treaty are to be inferred not from a general principle, but from an interpretation of the particular wording of the provision in question').

models—the regulatory, the intergovernmental and the parliamentary model—have contributed to the particular shape of the institutional balance of today's Union.[14] Each model entails a different (constitutional) blueprint for the European integration project based on particular ideas of democratic legitimacy.[15]

If institutional balance is to be meaningful as a principle, it is important then to see why this is so. To this end, we now turn to what we believe to be the historical and intellectual roots of the concept of institutional balance, i.e., the doctrine of *trias politica*.

B. The Heritage of *Trias Politica*

The doctrine of *trias politica* or separation of powers is usually ascribed to political authors such as Locke and Montesquieu. In reality, however, the history of *trias politica* is much more complex. It has its roots in the ancient world and has been an important source of inspiration of political thinking in Renaissance Italy, seventeenth-century England and at the time the United States melted into a federal unit.[16] Further, important misgivings and confusion exist as to its content. In its pure form, the doctrine of separation of powers calls for an organic division of government in three branches: the legislature, the executive and the judiciary. To each of these branches there is a corresponding function of government: legislative, executive or judicial. Each branch of the government must be confined to the exercise of its own function and not allowed to encroach upon the function of the other branches. Furthermore, the persons who compose the three branches of government must be kept separate and distinct, no one being allowed to be at the same time a member of more than one branch. This pure doctrine has never, however, been defended in theory nor, certainly, been applied in practice. In order to provide for a stable and effective political system, it has proven necessary to combine the principle of separation of powers with other political

[14] See Caporaso, 'The European Union and Forms of State: Westphalian, Regulatory or Post-Modern?', 34 *JCMS* (1996) 29; Dehousse, 'European Institutional Architecture after Amsterdam: Parliamentary System or Regulatory Structure?', 35 *CMLRev.* (1998) 595; Majone, 'Europe's "Democratic Deficit": the Question of Standards', 4 *ELJ* (1998) 5. For a brief discussion of the models as they affect the institutional framework governing the Commission, see Section II A.2 below.

[15] The word constitutional is bracketed here since the term constitution is regarded by some authors as exclusively linked to the state (among others, Grimm, 'Does Europe Need a Constitution?', 1 *ELJ* (1995) 282). Hence, speaking of a constitution for Europe would imply, in their opinion, promoting a statal vision for Europe.

[16] On the history and various strands in the *trias politica* doctrine, see, in particular, M. Vile, *Constitutionalism and the Separation of Powers* (1969).

ideas, such as the idea of balance and, in particular, the concept of checks and balances.[17]

Yet why is *trias politica* important and what is its link to democracy? In order to answer this question, we will turn to what Montesquieu says about it in his famous Eleventh Book of *De l'esprit de lois*. Montesquieu's basic concern is with building a constitutional system capable of safeguarding the political liberty of its citizens.[18] As Montesquieu warns, democracies (i.e., systems based on a 'rule by the people') do not of themselves vouchsafe the liberty of their citizens. At the most, they give them an illusion of liberty which comes with taking part in the 'general will' that dictates what should be done and what not.[19] Liberty can only be found in systems of limited government:

[P]olitical liberty is to be found only in moderate governments; and even in these it is not always found. It is there only where there is no abuse of power. But constant experience shows us that every man invested with power is apt to abuse it, and carry his authority as far as it will go.[20]

Therefore, he concludes:

To prevent this abuse, it is necessary from the very nature of things that power should be a check to power.[21]

This is, precisely, what constitutions are about. Constitutions are designed to place the necessary limits on governmental power, by dividing it and subjecting it to mutual forms of control, in order that the liberty of the citizens be preserved. A similar message can be found in Article 16 of the French Declaration of human rights of 1785:

Toute société dans laquelle la garantie des droits n'est pas assurée, ni la séparation des pouvoirs déterminée, n'a point de constitution.[22]

---

[17] M. Vile, Constitutionalism and the Separation of Powers (1969), at 2; Alen, 'Scheiding of samenwerking der machten?', 1 *Academiae Analecta (Mededelingen van de Koninklijke Academie voor Wetenschappen, Letteren en Kunsten van België)* (1990).

[18] The title of the Eleventh Book is significant in this respect: '*Des lois qui forment la liberté politique dans son rapport avec la constitution*'.

[19] Cf. Rousseau's famous precept to subject the will of the individual to the '*volonté générale*' and the virulent criticism against this interpretation of liberty by, for instance, Isaiah Berlin (Berlin, 'Two concepts of liberty', in *Four Essays on Liberty* (1969) 118).

[20] Montesquieu, *supra* n. 18, Eleventh Book, Chapter IV. ('*La liberté politique ne se trouve que dans les gouvernements modérés. Mais elle n'est pas toujours dans les États modérés; elle n'y est que lorsqu'on n'abuse pas du pouvoir. Mais c'est une expérience éternelle que tout homme qui a du pouvoir est porté à en abuser; il va jusqu'à ce qu'il trouve des limites*'.)

[21] Ibid. ('*Pour qu'on ne puisse abuser du pouvoir, il faut que, par la disposition des choses, le pouvoir arrête le pouvoir*'.)

[22] ('A society in which rights are not guaranteed and a separation of powers is not organised, has no constitution.') The existence or absence of a system of separation of powers marked the difference, according to eighteenth-century political writers, between a democracy (that knows no such separation) and a republic. Whereas we would call, today, a republic a

In Chapter IV, *De la Constitution de l'Angleterre*, Montesquieu recalls, then, that there are three essential governmental functions, the legislative, the executive and the judicial, each of which must be assigned to a specific governmental body in order to arrive at a limited and therefore moderate government. Yet the separation he calls for is nowhere absolute. With reference to the English constitution, he allows for and even recommends a certain degree of institutional interaction between the bodies in charge of the governmental functions—in fact the ideal he portrays comes close to that of the 'checks and balances' that the authors of *The Federalist Papers* would advocate.[23]

Yet there is a deeper strand behind Montesquieu's call for a division of governmental power. The dispersion of power over various institutions that sometimes act separately and at other times are called upon to co-operate is by no means arbitrary. Each institution represents a particular interest and particular views. The balance of powers is supposed to reflect the ideal balance between the different interests within a society.[24] The ideal of separation of powers as defended by Montesquieu links in with the republican ideal that sees the democratic process as an institutionalized—and thus civilized—dialogue between different interests, which is capable of uncovering the 'common good' for all.[25] The American revolutionary idea of balanced

'constitutional democracy', a democracy, understood in this way, is a form of popular despotism. See, among others, I. Kant, *Zum Ewigen Frieden (Eternal Peace)* (first edition 1795); also *The Federalist Papers* No. 10 (Madison).

[23] In particular *The Federalist Papers* Nos 10, 62 and 63 (Madison) and 78 (Hamilton). The central idea of *checks and balances* is that each branch of authority can fulfil its tasks in an efficient way only when at least one other branch co-operates to that effect, thus controlling the use the first makes of its powers.

[24] Thus Montesquieu concludes as regards the legislative function for instance: *'ainsi, la puissance législative sera confiée, et au corps des nobles, et au corps qui sera choisi pour représenter le peuple, qui auront chacun leurs assemblées et leurs délibérations à part, et des vues et des intérêts séparés'.* ('Therefore, legislative powers shall be entrusted to an aristocratic body representing the people, each of which will have separate meetings and discussions and different views and interests'.)

[25] Cf. the interpretation of Montesquieu's thinking by Charles Eisenmann: *'Le gouvernement modéré, c'était pour lui [Montesquieu] un gouvernement où l'élaboration de l'ordre social et, plus généralement, la direction de la collectivité, le gouvernement de la société n'appartiendrait pas, en dernier ressort, à un organe simple, – corps ou individu, – mais à un organe composé, formé de différents facteurs sociaux auxquels il voulait donner le moyen de faire valoir leurs conceptions et leurs intérêts, ou de leurs représentations, et dont les décisions exprimeraient, par conséquence, la volonté commune et concordante, seraient le fruit de l'accord de ces différents éléments, qui pourraient ainsi se faire mutuellement opposition, se limiter, c'est-à-dire se contraindre les uns et les autres sur une ligne moyenne également acceptable pour tous les citoyens, également respectueuse de leurs intérêts'.* ('Moderate government was for him [Montesquieu] a system of governance in which the establishment of the social order and the exercise of public power did not, in final order, belong to the realm of a single body or individual, but rather of a complex body, composed of various social factions capable of promoting their views and interests, or of the

government within the framework of a constitution was led by a similar concern to gear deliberations towards the attainment of the public good.[26]

The _trias politica_ defended by Montesquieu (again, not a pure theory of separation of powers) is highly relevant for the European Union of today. The Union's institutional balance does not rest on an organic separation of powers but on a balanced interaction between representatives of various interests.[27] Thus, the European Parliament represents 'the peoples of the States brought together in the Community';[28] the Council represents the Member States' governments;[29] the Committee of the Regions gathers 'regional and local bodies'[30] and the Economic and Social Committee represents 'the various categories of economic and social activity'.[31] The Commission represents no constituency, yet its members are called upon to act 'in the general interest of the Community'.[32] One could complement this list by referring to the many instances wherein European law provides for the participation of functional interests in European governance (apart from the Economic and Social Committee already mentioned above). The participation of organized labour and management in the making of European social policy is but one example.[33]

Interpreted against the background of tradition, institutional balance within the European Union can be seen as the necessary institutional frame within which different interests can discuss with each other in order to achieve

representatives thereof. Therefore, the decisions of such a body would express the general interest; they would be the result of an agreement between different views, that would oppose and limit each other and force all to find a middle ground equally acceptable to all citizens and equally respective of their interests.') Eisenmann, 'L'esprit des lois et la séparation des pouvoirs', in _Mélanges R. Carré de Malberg_ (1993) 165, at 188–189.

[26] See, in this respect, for instance, Madison's ardent defence of representative government: 'the effect of the . . . difference [between a direct democracy and a representative republic] is . . . to refine and enlarge the public views, by passing them through the medium of a chosen body of citizens, whose wisdom might best discern the true interests of their country, and whose patriotism and love of justice, will be least likely to sacrifice it to temporary or partial considerations'. _The Federalist Papers_; _supra_ n. 23, No. 10.

[27] For an outstanding analysis, see Jacqué, 'Cours général de droit communautaire', 1 _Collected Courses of the Academy of European Law_ (1990, 1) 237, at 289.

[28] Article 189 of the EC Treaty. See also nn. 86 to 91 below and accompanying text.

[29] See Article 203 of the EC Treaty: 'The Council shall consist of a representative of each Member State at ministerial level, authorized to commit the government of that Member State'.

[30] Article 263 of the EC Treaty.   [31] Article 257 of the EC Treaty.

[32] Article 213 of the EC Treaty. On the role of the European Commission, see Section II below.

[33] Articles 138 and 139 of the EC Treaty. On the possibilities of participation of non-governmental organizations and other non-voluntary organizations in the European decision-making process, see Verhoeven, 'Europe beyond Westphalia: Can Postnational Thinking Cure Europe's Democracy Deficit?', 5 _Maastricht Journal of European and Comparative Law_ (1998) 369, at 382 et seq. See also below.

solutions that are acceptable to all and do not unduly abridge the liberties of anyone.[34] Institutional balance is the prime device that brings together the various interests within the Union in a balanced manner and ties their discussions into an institutional frame in which, it is hoped, the narrow pursuit of self-interest can be overcome and replaced by a more emphatic, constructive debate on the 'public good' within the European Union. It is, thus, hoped to enhance the deliberative nature of institutional decision-making at the European Union level.[35]

Institutional balance is one of the main tenets underscoring the federal nature and ambitions of the Union. Federalism is a means to structure the relationship between interlocked authorities in such a way that a balance can be achieved between the need for common action in order to pursue efficiently a set of common values, and the need to see the identity of the different actors taking part in the common action being preserved.[36] Federalism prescribes that power be dispersed, both vertically, between the central authority (the locus of the common action) and the component entities, as well as horizontally within the central authority, in order to ensure that that authority duly reflects all different interests present in the federal whole.

Institutional balance concerns the horizontal dimension of the division of powers called for in federal systems. The horizontal dimension—balanced interaction among different actors and institutions within the Union—necessarily entails a vertical dimension, however.[37] In this sense, institutional

[34] In a similar sense, see Craig, *supra* n. 3, in particular at 113–119.

[35] On the virtues of deliberative democracy, see among others J. Habermas, *Between Facts and Norms* (1997); S. Benhabib (ed.), *Democracy and Difference* (1996). Various scholars have used the model of deliberative democracy in an attempt to lessen the EU's legitimacy crisis (among others, Curtin, 'Civil Society and the European Union: Opening Spaces for Deliberative Democracy', 7 *Collected Courses of the Academy of European Law* (1999, 1) 185; Joerges and Meyer, 'From Intergovernmental Bargaining to Deliberative Political Processes: The Constitutionalization of Comitology', 3 *ELJ* (1997) 273; Joerges, 'Good Governance through Comitology?', in C. Joerges and E. Vos (eds), *EU Committees: Social Regulation, Law and Politics* (1999) 311, with critical comments by Weiler, 'Epilogue: "Comitology" as revolution—Infranationalism, constitutionalism and democracy', ibid., at 339). Our argument here is that a proper understanding of institutional balance can contribute to more democracy since it focuses on issues of interest representation and fair procedure (see below). Institutional balance does not, however, address other issues that are also of importance in the deliberative-democratic model, such as, for instance, the quality of informal processes of will-formation (that must inform institutional levels of decision-making).

[36] Thus, emphatically, the federal ideal does not presuppose the structure of the nation state. It only requires an institutional set-up designed to pursue common values and objectives. See, in this respect, Lenaerts, 'Federalism: Essential Concepts in Evolution—the Case of the European Union', 21 *Fordham International Law Journal* (1998) 746. See also D. Elazar, *Exploring Federalism* (1987), who expresses at 12 that 'using the federal principle does not necessarily mean establishing a federal system in the sense of a modern federal state'.

[37] See in detail, K. Lenaerts, *Le juge et la constitution aux Etats-Unis d'Amérique et dans l'ordre juridique européen* (1988), in particular at 340–566.

balance affects 'the conditions under which the Member States, that is to say, the States that are parties to the Treaties establishing the Communities and the Accession Treaties, participate in the functioning of the Community institutions'.[38]

C. Institutional Balance as a Legal and Political Principle of EU Governance

1. The Role of Institutional Balance as a Legal Principle

The function of institutional balance as a legal principle, i.e., a principle that may be used in courts, is limited yet not unimportant. As mentioned before, institutional balance links in with Article 7 of the EC Treaty, which requires each institution to act within the limits of the powers conferred on it by the Treaties. The underlying *ratio* is, as discussed, a desire to see all relevant interests duly represented and interacting at the European level in accordance with the provisions of the European constitution. The principle of institutional balance requires the European institutions, positively, to assume fully the political responsibilities conferred on them by the Treaties and, negatively, to refrain from 'abusing' their powers, i.e. using them in a way that usurps the powers granted to other institutions. From the institutional balance case-law of the Court of Justice, one can distil the following three principles:[39]

(1) Each institution should enjoy a sufficient independence in order to exercise its powers.[40]

(2) Institutions should not unconditionally assign their powers to other institutions.[41]

---

[38] Case C-95/97, *Région wallonne v Commission* [1997] ECR I-1787, at I-1791, para. 6. In that case, the Court of Justice (in our opinion rather unfortunately) reasoned that the institutional balance (which, among others, seeks to safeguard the position of the Member States in the European Union) risked being upset if regional authorities were accorded a right of access to the Court. Compare Case T-288/97, *Friuli Venezia v Commission* [1999] ECR II-1871, where a region was permitted to challenge a State aid decision addressed to the Member State of which it was part but concerning an aid granted by the region concerned.

[39] See Lenaerts and Van Nuffel in R. Bray (ed.), *Constitutional Law of the European Union* (1999) 414.

[40] Accordingly, each institution is entitled to regulate its own organization and manner of operation (including internal decision-making procedures) within the limits of the rules set forth in the Treaties (see, e.g., Case 5/85, *AKZO Chemie v Commission* [1986] ECR 2585, at 2615–2616, paras. 37–40). In addition, Art. 10 of the EC Treaty requires Member States to refrain from taking any measure that might interfere with the internal functioning of the Community institutions (see, e.g., Case C-345/95, *France v European Parliament* [1997] ECR I-5215, at I-5242, para. 32).

[41] See the *Meroni* case, *supra* n. 6. See also Case 98/80, *Romano* [1981] ECR 1241, at 1256, para. 20.

(3) Institutions may not, in the exercise of their powers, encroach on the powers and prerogatives of other institutions.[42] This is particularly true of the European Parliament's power to take part in the Community legislative process. In an elucidating judgment, the Court of Justice held that the European Parliament's participation constitutes 'an essential factor in the institutional balance intended by the Treaty'. The reason is that '[a]lthough limited, it reflects at the Community level the fundamental democratic principle that the peoples should take part in the exercise of power through the intermediary of a representative assembly'.[43] The *ratio* of the institutional balance principle—preserving a balanced interplay between various interests in EU governance—comes clearly to the fore here.

As *Chernobyl* highlights,[44] institutional balance is a fundamental rule which may, as the case may be, move the Court of Justice to take a corrective action—even acting *contra legem*—when this is needed to see that rule respected. Thus, the Court of Justice in *Chernobyl* accorded *ius standi* rights to the European Parliament in order to enable that institution to defend its prerogatives in court. The question is, however, how far the Court can go in this respect. The Court itself is bound by the principle of institutional balance: it should stay within the limits of the tasks and powers assigned to it, among others, in order not to upset the political balance between institutions and other actors within the European Union intended by the *Herren der Verträge* ('Masters of the Treaties').

To be sure, the European Treaties do not require the Court of Justice to act as a passive *'bouche de la loi'*. Article 220 of the EC Treaty provides that 'the Court of Justice shall ensure that in the interpretation and the application of this Treaty the law is observed'. The Court of Justice has read in Article 220 a recognition of 'the law' as a source of law that enables it to have recourse to general principles of law (such as human rights and rule of law considerations) when interpreting and applying Community law.[45] Accordingly, it held in *Brasserie du Pêcheur* that the principle of institutional balance did not prevent it from recognizing in European law a general right to compensation of

---

[42] Case 149/85, *Wybot v Faure* [1986] ECR 2391, at 2409, para. 23; Case 25/70, *Einfuhr- und Vorratsstelle Getreide v Köster* [1970] ECR 1161, at 1170, paras. 8 and 9 (as regards the *Köster* case, see also below).

[43] Case 138/79, *Roquette Frères v Council* [1980] ECR 3333, at 3360, para. 33 and Case 139/79, *Maïzena v Council* [1980] ECR 3393, at 3424, para. 34.

[44] Case 70/88, n. 7 above.

[45] The other institutions have approved such an interpretation. See Joint Declaration of the European Parliament, the Council and the Commission of 5 April 1977, OJ 1977 C 103/1: 'Whereas, as the Court of Justice has recognized, that law comprises, over and above the rules embodied in the Treaties and in secondary Community legislation, the general principles of law and in particular the fundamental rights . . .'.

individuals in case of breaches of that law.[46] Yet Article 220 of the EC Treaty does not entitle the Court to substitute itself for the political decision-makers.[47] Neither can it depart from EU law as it stands any time the application of that law would, in its opinion, lead to 'unbalanced' solutions. In his Opinion in *Chernobyl*, Advocate-General Van Gerven argued that, while it is the province of the Court to uphold the institutional balance as it is set out in the Treaties (and grant the necessary procedural rights thereto, even *contra legem*), the Court cannot change the institutional balance in favour of one or other institution or political actor. The task of rendering the institutional balance more 'balanced' is one that belongs to the constituent power of the Union, i.e. to the Member States themselves as *Herren der Verträge*. Thus, he argued that the Court should make a distinction:

> between the interpretation of the Treaty with a view to ensuring that there is an adequate and coherent system of legal protection and its interpretation in a manner which might interfere with the delicate political balance between the institutions . . . Whereas the first is the inalienable task of the courts, the second falls to the (primary) legislature.[48]

Making that distinction—drawing the line between an acceptable interpretation and an unacceptable interference with the institutional balance—might not always be easy, however. For instance, one knows that pursuant to Article 230 of the EC Treaty, individuals can bring an action for annulment against acts of the Community institutions not addressed to them only if they are directly and individually concerned by such acts. This precludes, in principle, individual actions against acts of a general normative nature. In *Codorniu*, the Court of Justice held, nevertheless, that an action for annulment brought by Codorniu against a Council regulation reserving the right to use the term 'crémant' solely for French and Luxembourg producers of sparkling wines was admissible.[49] The effect of that provision was to prevent Codorniu from using its graphic trademark 'Gran Cremant de Codorniu', which it had registered in Spain in 1924 and used traditionally both before and since its registration. In view of these circumstances, the Court of Justice held that Codorniu had established the existence of a situation which, from the point of view of the contested act, differentiated it from all other traders. In a later case, the Court of Justice stated that Codorniu's application had been found admissible exceptionally because, although the regulation was a legislative act, it had

---

[46] Joined Cases C-46/93 and C-48/93, *Brasserie du Pêcheur and Factortame* [1996] ECR I-1029, at I-1143–1144, paras. 24 to 30.

[47] See, e.g., Case 109/75 R, *National Carbonising Company v Commission* [1975] ECR 1193, at 1202, para. 8; Case 415/85, *Commission v Ireland* [1988] ECR 3098, at 3118, paras 8 and 9; Case C-249/96, *Lisa Grant* [1998] ECR 623, at 648, paras 35 and 36, and at 651, paras 47 and 48.

[48] Joined Cases C-46/93 and C-48/93, n. 46 above, I-1136, para. 6.

[49] Case C-309/89, *Codorniu v Council* [1994] ECR I-1853.

adversely affected 'specific rights' of the applicant,[50] namely its proprietory right in a trademark. Expanding on *Codorniu*, it could be argued that an action for annulment of a legislative act brought by an individual must be held admissible if and when such an action is necessary for the effective legal protection of the fundamental rights of that individual. Whether the Court of Justice would be prepared to accept such an argument, as well as whether it could validly do so given the institutional balance chosen by the constituent Member States (*in casu*, the position of private parties in the judicial process), remain open questions, however.[51] One cannot but admit that at Member State level also, the right to seek the annulment of a legislative act that breaches fundamental rights is not always guaranteed.[52]

2. The Role of Institutional Balance as a Political Principle

As a political principle, the scope and potential of institutional balance is much broader. Institutional balance requires the makers of the European constitution to shape institutions and the interactions between them in such a manner that each interest and constituency present in the Union is duly represented and co-operates with others in the frame of an institutionalized debate geared towards the formulation of the common good. At the same time, the formulation of the common good should never lead to an unequal and unnecessary sacrifice of individual liberty.

As a political principle, institutional balance must guide and complement the shaping of the legal basis requirement which prescribes the objective and nature of the measure that can be adopted, as well as the procedural requirements for its adoption and the institutions competent to adopt it. In (re-) shaping the European constitution—today an almost permanent activity given the pace at which intergovernmental conferences succeed each other— one should duly reflect upon two essential questions: which institutions should be competent to deal with a particular matter and how should they proceed.

This requires, first, a reflection on the particular role the institution in question is called upon to play in the EU decision-making process. Which—if any—interest does the institution represent? Does it do so in an adequate manner, i.e., does the legal frame governing that institution allow it to be truly representative? Are there other interests that, as yet, have insufficient institutional

---

[50] Case C-10/95 P, *Asocarne v Council* [1995] ECR I-4149, at I-4163, para. 43.

[51] Joined Cases T-172/98, T-175/98 to T-177/98, *Salamander and Others v European Parliament and Council*, judgment of 27 June 2000, not yet published; see further, Lenaerts, 'The Legal Protection of Private Parties under the EC Treaty: a Complete and Coherent System of Judicial Review?', in *Scritti in Onore di Giuseppe Federico Mancini* (1998) II, 591–623.

[52] Case T-173/98, *Unión de Pequeños Agricultores v Council*, order of 23 November 1999, not yet published.

means to participate in decision-making at the European level? Many problems arise here. The absence of a uniform electoral procedure for the European Parliament and the shaky conditions in which the 'civil dialogue' at the EU level takes place are but some examples.

Further, it requires a reflection on the ways in which the European Treaties call on the institutions to interact in the decision-making process. Do the procedures set up by the Treaties allow for a duly 'institutionalized' debate likely to bring about results that approximate to the common good, given the subject matter to be decided upon? Or do they, by contrast, facilitate a concentration of power in the hands of one institution, at the risk of crushing the interests represented by others? In this respect, a *laudatio* must go to the oft-criticized Treaty of Amsterdam, which did away with (almost) all imbalances between the European Parliament and the Council in the co-decision procedure. Yet again, much remains to be done.

In this context, it should be kept in mind that the current European Treaties only concern part of the 'institutional balance' as it exists in practice. It has been observed that a gap exists between the formal constitution and the way the European Union really functions.[53] Substantial elements of constitutional reality operate in the margins of or wholly outside the formal constitutional framework. The whole area of executive rule-making within the European Union is characterized by intricate institutional elements such as comitology committees and agencies and operates in a constitutional twilight zone, regulated only by a few and ambiguous Treaty provisions, some case-law of the European courts, incomplete pieces of secondary legislation and a number of declarations and interinstitutional arrangements. The new comitology decision, adopted on 28 June 1999, improves that situation, but only to a limited extent.[54] Similarly, an adequate frame for recently introduced decision-making procedures, such as social policy legislation resulting from agreements between social partners, is still lacking.[55]

---

[53] De Búrca, 'The Institutional Development of the EU: A Constitutional Analysis', in P. Craig and G. de Búrca (eds), *The Evolution of EU Law* (1999) 55, at 61.

[54] Council Decision 99/468/EC laying down the procedures for the exercise of implementing powers conferred on the Commission, OJ 1999 L 184/23. Three declarations made in respect of this decision were included in the Council's minutes and set out in OJ 1999 C 203/1. See for an analysis, Lenaerts and Verhoeven, 'Towards a Legal Framework for Executive Rule-Making in the E.U.? The Contribution of the New Comitology Decision', 37 *CMLRev.* (2000) 1, and also below.

[55] See in particular Art. 139 of the EC Treaty. In the absence of an adequate legal framework, the Court of First Instance has stepped in and has required the Commission and Council, when deciding on whether or not to ratify social policy agreements, to ensure the representativity of the social partners involved in the agreement. It held, in this context, that the participation of the social partners in the legislative process constituted a form of participatory democracy (compensating for a lack of involvement by the European Parliament; Case T-135/96, *UEAPME v Council* [1998] ECR II-2335).

In the remainder of our contribution, we will use institutional balance as a political principle in order to reflect on two current problems of European institutional law that strike us as particularly poignant: the role of the European Commission and the question of its accountability, and the budgetary procedure.

II. THE EUROPEAN COMMISSION: PARLIAMENTARY SUPERVISION VERSUS INDEPENDENCE?

A. The Legitimacy of Commission Action: A Continuing Quest for Standards

1. The 'Most Original and Unprecedented' Institution

In accordance with current (Western) thought, all governmental power must be legitimate, that is, it must be capable of justifying itself *vis-à-vis* those over which it is exercised. Further, legitimacy equals, for us, democratic legitimacy. We accept to be governed to the extent we are able to consider ourselves as the (ultimate) source of that governance. Concomitantly, we accept rules to the extent we are, in one way or another, 'makers' of those rules. Democracy as self-rule by the people is not, however, an absolute value: we are willing, for instance, to give up on democratic participation if such is necessary in order to achieve efficiency, but only up to a certain extent. On important issues of political life, we want to rule ourselves, moreover, we want at all times to be able to watch over those who govern us, even when our direct participation is low.

European governance is no different in this respect. However, the fact that Union governance does not follow the traditional patterns developed in the framework of the nation state makes issues of democratic legitimacy particularly problematic in the Union. For two centuries, the nation state was the sole framework of reference in which politics was conducted and in which the democratic ideal was implemented. The transition from the statal model to the constitutional set-up of Union governance forces us to reconsider traditional thoughts on how democratic governance is to be ensured. Moreover, there is no agreement as to the organizational and political nature of the Union. The Union is perpetually evolving; its current institutional set-up is but a 'new stage in the process of creating an ever closer Union'.[56] Therefore, the challenge of how to solve the Union's democratic deficit is very much a 'question of standards';[57] it depends on what one understands the Union to be and how one wishes it to evolve.

---

[56] See Article 1 of the EU Treaty.   [57] Majone, *supra* n. 14.

The ever-continuing 'battle' over the nature of the Community and/or Union[58] has left a particular mark on the Commission. The role of the European Commission has always been controversial.[59] Heralded by some as the very motor of European integration, it has been debunked by others as a group of pretentious technicians (De Gaulle) or faceless bureaucrats (Douglas Hurd). Its future in the institutional structure of the European Union remains contested, today perhaps more than ever. The Treaty of Amsterdam failed to take a position on the reform of the institutions—among others the Commission—required in the light of enlargement. Instances of fraud, mismanagement and corruption on behalf of some of its members forced the Santer Commission to collectively resign on 16 March 1999[60] and fuelled a debate and a series of measures and proposals on the reform of the Commission.[61]

---

[58] Typically, models of integration focus primarily on the Community. The non-Community aspects of integration—second and third pillar—are usually left outside the conceptual analysis; they are often considered to constitute (but) a form of international co-operation taking place in the margins of the true locus of integration, the Community.

[59] Studies concentrating on the role of the Commission include G. Edwards and D. Spence, *The European Commission* (1994) 311; Dewost, 'La Commission ou comment s'en débarraser?', in *L'Europe et le droit. Mélanges en hommage à Jean Boulouis* (1991) 181; Gosalbo Bono, 'The Commission after Amsterdam: its Future in an enlarged Union', in T. Heukels, N. Blokker and M. Brus (eds), *The European Union after Amsterdam* (1998) 69; Laursen, 'The Role of the Commission', in S. Andersen and K. Eliassen (eds), *The European Union: How Democratic is it?* (1996) 119; Lequesne, 'La Commission européenne entre autonomie et dépendance', 46 *Revue française de sciences politiques* (1996) 389; J.-V. Louis and M. Waelbroeck, *La Commission au coeur du système institutionnel des Communautés européennes* (1989); Timmermans, 'Effectiveness and Simplification of Decision-making', in J.A. Winter, D. Curtin, A. Kellermann and B. de Witte (eds), *Reforming the Treaty on European Union. The Legal Debate* (1996) 133.

[60] One will recall the stream of events that led to the resignation of the Santer Commission. Over the course of 1998, various instances of mismanagement, fraud and nepotism leaked to the press and to the European Parliament (which was briefed, among others, by civil servants of the Commission itself). Alarmed by the allegations, on 17 December 1998 the European Parliament refused to grant a discharge to the Commission for the 1996 financial year. The Commission did not react. On 14 January 1999, the Parliament failed by a narrow margin to obtain the necessary majority to pass a motion of censure. It proposed, however, that a committee of independent experts be set up under the auspices of the European Parliament and the Commission to examine the way in which the Commission detected and dealt with fraud, mismanagement and nepotism (Resolution of the European Parliament of 14 January 1999, B4–0065, 0109 and 0110/99, see <http://www.europarl.eu.int/dg3/experts/en/reso14en. htm>). The Committee submitted a devastating report on 15 March 1999. The day after, all members of the Commission collectively resigned.

[61] Of particular interest in this respect are the first and second reports of the Committee of independent experts, see <http://www.europarl.eu.int/experts/en/default.htm>, as well as the White Paper on the European Commission's internal reforms, see *Europe Documents*, No. 2178–2179 of 9 March 2000, 1–20.

One reason for this controversy is the fact that the Commission fits uneasily in classical institutional theory. As of today, the Commission remains the 'most original and unprecedented of the institutions', as Walter Hallstein, its first president, wrote.[62] It is less than a government—and altogether different—but surely more than a secretariat of an international organization. The place of the Commission in the overall institutional balance of the Union is highly uncertain. Contrary to, for instance, the Council and the European Parliament, it is not a representative body, yet its members are called to act in the 'general interest of the Community'.[63] Nor is it subject to classical mechanisms of political control as national governments are. It retains, as of today, a rather large institutional autonomy vis-à-vis both the Council and the European Parliament. Concomitantly, it is not clear whence the Commission derives the necessary democratic legitimacy and how its day-to-day accountability vis-à-vis the European public can be ensured.

2. Which Constitutional Blueprint for the Commission?

In line with the overall models for the Community/Union (the regulatory, the federal/statal and the intergovernmental) mentioned before, three models have over time been advanced for the Commission.[64] Each model has contributed, to a greater or lesser extent, to the current institutional shape of the Commission and retains its advocates today. As will be explained, each model rests on particular ideas on institutional balance and democratic legitimacy.

(a) The regulatory model: the Commission as an independent expert body

The regulatory model views the Community[65] as a special purpose organization ('*Zweckverband*') or an agency, whose purpose is to address a number of issues over which it can achieve a greater efficiency than the Member States acting individually.[66] In that view, the goal of European integration is primarily economic not political. The task of the European institutions is not to edict norms regarding broad, political matters but to develop regulatory solutions for a series of socio-economic problems. Typically, this model places

---

[62] W. Hallstein, *Europe in the Making* (1972) 45.   [63] Article 213 of the EC Treaty.
[64] See also Rometsch and Wessels, 'The Commission and the Council of Ministers', in Edwards and Spence, *supra* n. 59, at 202.
[65] Non-Community forms of integration usually fall outside the regulatory model's analytical focus.
[66] See, among others, Everson, 'Administering Europe?', 36 *JCMS* (1998) 195; Lindseth, 'Democratic Legitimacy and the Administrative Character of Supranationalism: the Example of the European Community', 99 *Columbia Law Review* (1999) 628; Majone, 'The Agency Model: the Growth of Regulation and Regulatory Institutions in the European Union', 3 *EIPA Scope* (1997) 9; Majone, 'The Rise of the Regulatory State in Europe', 17 *West-European Politics* (1994) 77; Majone, *supra* n. 14. See also various contributions in G. Majone (ed.), *Regulating Europe* (1996) and in Joerges and Vos, *supra* n. 35; McGowan and Wallace, 'Towards a European Regulatory State?', 3 *Journal of European Public Policy* (1996) 560.

an emphasis on the centrality of a strong, independent 'expert' European
Commission in the European integration process.

The regulatory model harks back to the historic origins of the Commission
and its predecessor, the High Authority. Jean Monnet created the High
Authority as a dynamic and enlightened technocracy, capable of defining and
furthering the European interest.[67] Article 9 of the original ECSC Treaty
stressed the independent and supranational character of the High Authority:

The Members of the High Authority shall be completely independent in the performance of their functions, in the general interest of the Community. In the discharge
of their duties they shall neither seek nor take instructions from any Government or
from any other body. They shall refrain from any action incompatible with the supranational character of their functions.

Each Member State undertakes to respect this supranational character and not to
seek to influence the members of the High Authority in the performance of their
tasks.[68]

The High Authority was empowered to take binding decisions, acting mostly
alone and sometimes together with the Council of Ministers. Other institutions included a Common Assembly with only supervisory powers (the term
parliament was deliberately avoided) and, interestingly, a Consultative
Committee representing interest groups (the predecessor of the current
ECOSOC).

The accountability of the High Authority vis-à-vis any representative
organ—the Assembly or other—was low. Legitimacy of High Authority
action was to be secured by essentially 'non-majoritarian' means. A first legitimacy ground was to be sought in the expertise of the institution. Thanks to
its expertise, the High Authority was expected to bring about material benefits (peace, prosperity) that, in turn, would produce a 'shift of loyalty' from
the national to the European level in the minds and hearts of the European
people.[69]

Further, the independent status of the High Authority was defended by
reference to the specific functions with which the institution was entrusted.
Hallstein summarized this by saying that the Commission (the High
Authority's successor) was 'at once a motor, a watchdog and a kind of honest

---

[67] The High Authority of the ECSC was modelled on the High Authority of the Ruhr
which formerly supervised the German coal and steel industries on behalf of the Allied Powers
after the Second World War.

[68] Quoted from Laursen, *supra* n. 59, at 122. Significantly, the reference to the term supranational could not be found in the EEC Treaty (adopted in 1957), and was dropped in the
ECSC Treaty as a result of the Merger Treaty (adopted in 1965).

[69] This went hand in hand with a belief in the 'spill-over', i.e. the belief that a sufficiently
strong integration in limited fields would automatically lead to integration in ever widening
fields. In this belief, economic integration was to be the driving force for political integration.

broker'.[70] As a broker of interests, it was to bring together both national interests (the interests of the different Member States) and sectoral interests (the Consultative Committee, called upon to give its opinion on the High Authority's actions, fitted into that design). As a guardian of the Treaties, it was to see to it that no Member State (or enterprise) failed to live up to its obligations under the Treaty.

Formal legitimacy, i.e. legality, was sought in the administrative character of the High Authority's powers. The ECSC Treaty entrusted the High Authority with specific, well-circumscribed powers for ensuring that 'the objectives set out in this Treaty are attained in accordance with the provisions thereof'.[71] The delegation by the Member States (and their parliaments, which ratified the Treaty) of technical, administrative powers to a supranational High Authority was considered not to be different in essence from the delegation of powers to national executives. In the logic of delegation, accountability could be ensured through legal and political controls designed to prevent *ultra vires* activity (to this end, the Assembly gathered members of national parliaments entrusted with the task to control whether the High Authority stayed within the limits of its delegated powers). No direct democratic accountability was considered necessary.

The Economic and Atomic Energy Communities were patterned on the same model. However, contrary to the ECSC, their founding Treaties contained much less detail, leaving broader, political decision-making powers to the Community institutions themselves.[72] Accordingly, the balance of powers between the Commission (the EEC and EAEC version of the High Authority) and the Council was tilted in favour of the latter: whereas the Commission retained an exclusive power to propose, the latter was to decide. With the advent of the EEC/EAEC, and as a result of the steady broadening of Community competencies, the original justifications for Community activity—and in particular for the (still rather) independent role of the Commission—lost force. It was indeed no longer evident to consider the Commission an 'expert body'.[73] Similarly, the delegation logic—according to

---

[70] Hallstein, *supra* n. 62, at 22, and further Laursen, *supran* n. 59.

[71] Article 8 of the ECSC Treaty.

[72] This difference between the ECSC and the EEC/EAEC Treaties is usually captured by the terms *'traité-loi'* and *'traité-cadre'*, respectively.

[73] The argument regarding expertise has been developed in particular by Majone (see references at *supra* n. 66). Majone has observed that European integration has shown little progress in politically sensitive areas (such as social policy, labour policy and foreign security) whereas it has substantially advanced in others (single market, technical standards, environment), i.e., in areas where 'technical' concerns of efficiency, risk reduction or wealth distribution significantly outweigh issues of redistribution. Given these findings, his precept is to concentrate at the EU level on matters where expertise is the most important asset in the decision-making process, and to leave more sensitive 'redistributional' matters to be decided at the national level.

which the Community institutions only exert delegated powers which they must exercise within set limits so as to leave policy choices as much as possible in the hands of the Member States—became less convincing.[74] Much in line with the delegation logic, Advocate-General Lagrange would in *Costa v ENEL*, in order to defend the democratic legitimacy of Community rule-making (and hence its primacy over national law), still argue that

Community regulations, even the most important ones, are not legislative measures nor even, as is sometimes said, 'quasi-legislative measures' but rather measures emanating from an executive power (Council or Commission) which can only act within the framework of the powers delegated to it by the Treaty and within the jurisdictional control of the Court of Justice. It is certainly true to say that the Treaty of Rome has, in a sense, the character of a genuine constitution, the constitution of the Community . . .; but for the greater part the Treaty has, above all, the character of an 'outline law'[75] and this is a perfectly legitimate method where a situation of an evolutionary nature such as the establishment of a common market is concerned, in respect of which the object to be attained and the conditions to be realized (rather than the detailed rules for its realization) are defined in such a way that the generality of the provisions need not exclude precision: we are still far from the 'carte blanche' given to the executive by certain national parliaments.[76]

The argument that Community powers were only administrative in kind was rather unconvincing, however, given the often far-reaching political consequences of Community acts. Significantly, Lagrange admitted already in *Confédération nationale de producteurs de fruits et légumes,* rendered two years before *Costa,* that measures adopted by the E(E)C institutions could not easily be considered as purely administrative and therefore that 'limited powers' were not sufficient to ensure an adequate control on decision-making within the EEC:

One might ask, and you know that some people do ask themselves today, whether on such a matter, impinging as it does on the field of legislation, the proper counter-weight to the action of governments represented in the Council ought not to be sought in a more effective participation by the parliamentary organ of the Community.[77]

As will be discussed later, the Commission's role as broker of interests and guardian of the Treaties remains an important one.

---

[74] Nonetheless, it is still used today in an attempt to vest the legitimacy of the Community legal order. See Lindseth, *supra* n. 66.

[75] *'Une loi-cadre'* in the original French text.

[76] Opinion of Advocate-General Lagrange in Case 6/64, *Costa v ENEL* [1964] ECR 604–605.

[77] Opinion of Advocate-General Lagrange in Joined Cases 16 and 17/62, *Confédération nationale de producteurs de fruits et légumes v Council* [1962] ECR 486.

(b) The parliamentary model: the Commission as a federal government

Defendants of the parliamentary model (associated historically with Altiero Spinelli and his group of federalists) usually foster a federal-statal model for Europe. The central institution in this model is the European Parliament, which should be transformed into a first chamber of *Bundestag*-type body, whereby the Council and the Commission should assume, respectively, the roles of a second chamber/*Bundesrat* and of a federal government. In its pure form, this view argues that the Commission should draw a democratic mandate from the European Parliament and develop into a fully-fledged government. If taken to its logical end, this model would do away with most of the features that characterize the current 'independent' Commission, such as, among others, its right of initiative.[78] No one today advocates this model in its pure form, not even the European Parliament,[79] yet it remains very influential in more attenuated versions. As suggested, this model seeks in parliamentary scrutiny (exercised, it is argued today, jointly by the European Parliament and the Council acting in a bicameral logic) the most important, even unique, source of democratic legitimacy for the European Commission.

(c) The intergovernmental model: the Commission as an administrative secretariat to the Council

The intergovernmental model stresses the fact that the European Union is an international organization, albeit a rather integrated one, in which the Member States are and remain the main actors. In this view, the democratic legitimacy lies essentially with the Member States. The emphasis lies therefore on the role of the Council (and, as the case may be, the European Council), which must closely watch over Commission action. In this reading, comitology is interpreted as a means to ensure a sufficient control by the Member States over executive rule-making within the Commission (see below).

None of the three views (dynamic and enlightened technocracy, federal government, secretariat to the Council) adequately corresponds to the role of the Commission,[80] nor do they provide on their own an adequate framework for safeguarding the accountability of Commission action. We will argue instead that accountability is to be ensured through a mixture of parliamentary scrutiny and procedural guarantees ensuring, among others, the participation of interested parties (in particular of those that otherwise risk not being heard in the European forum).

[78] See among others the critique by Dewost, *supra* n. 59.

[79] At the last intergovernmental conference, the European Parliament no longer asked, for instance, to obtain a right of initiative, although such a right would be essential if a federal-statal model were followed.

[80] In the same sense, see Rometsch and Wessels, *supra* n. 64, who argue instead that the role of the Commission is essentially one of a 'promotional broker'.

B. Balancing between Independence and Parliamentary Supervision: An Overview of Ends and Means

1. Why Parliamentary Scrutiny?

In the White Paper on internal reforms it presented in March 2000, the Commission stated that it needed to be 'independent, accountable, efficient and transparent, and guided by the highest standards of responsibility'.[81] Finding a right mix between these requirements is by no means easy, however, as a desire for independence and efficiency might conflict with the need to ensure accountability. Traditionally, more weight has been given to the independence of the Commission than to its accountability; in fact, mechanisms of political control have traditionally been weak.

In our opinion, the Commission needs a certain degree of independence in order to be able to advance the interests of the European Union in an efficient manner and in particular to perform properly its rather unique tasks as a broker of interests and guardian of the Treaties. Yet independence should be clearly understood. What the Commission needs is an absence of the exertion of undue influence by partisan interests, whether national, sectoral or of any other kind (e.g., interests of business leaders). Independence should not mean, however, the absence of institutionalized forms of democratic control. While advocates of the regulatory model have argued that an independent Commission can be controlled by nobody and yet be 'under control',[82] we very much doubt that an anonymous control coming from a set of legal constraints geared towards an enhanced transparency, rationality and an equitable participation of interested parties in the decision-making process is sufficient.[83] In our opinion, these elements of democratic legitimacy, although important, should be complemented by mechanisms of parliamentary scrutiny. National parliaments are not well-placed to control the Commission (they must, in the first place, ensure the accountability of the Council).[84] By

---

[81] *Supra* n. 61. Many of these ideas have now matured in the White Paper on European governance, which the Commission adopted on 25 July 2001. This contribution was finalized, however, well before the White Paper on governance saw the light.

[82] See Majone, 'Europe's democracy deficit: a question of standards', 4 *ELJ* (1998) 26, borrowing from American theory on independent agencies.

[83] See, e.g., Majone, *supra* n. 66.

[84] The Amsterdam Treaty includes a Protocol No. 13 'on the role of national parliaments in the European Union', which seeks to enhance the 'scrutiny by individual national parliaments of their own government in relation to the activities of the Union'. To this end, the Protocol stipulates that the national parliaments should receive all Commission consultation documents and proposals for legislation, and that a period of six weeks shall elapse between the communication by the Commission of a proposal to the Council and the European Parliament, and the date at which discussions in the Council may start. Hitherto, the influence of the national parliaments on the Council has been rather low (see e.g. Dehousse, 'La CIG 2000: vers une réforme incomplète des institutions européennes', 1674 *CRISP* (2000) 10).

contrast, the European Parliament has a crucial role to play in ensuring the accountability and responsibility of the Commission.

Parliamentary scrutiny of Commission activity must not necessarily take the forms it assumes at national level. A revival and transposition to the European context of traditional thinking inspired by Rousseau is not desirable. The European Parliament does not represent a European people nor, certainly, a European general will (in fact, institutional balance is precisely designed to ensure that a plurality of interests duly participates in the formulation of a European common good). The Commission does not at present function as an agent and emanation of the Parliament nor should it in the future. While the European Parliament lacks the necessary status to operate convincingly as a principal, the Commission should retain more independence of action than agents traditionally enjoy. Yet parliamentary scrutiny of Commission action is important, in our opinion, for the following reasons.

First, as the European Human Rights Court stressed in *Matthews*, the European Parliament 'represents the principal form of democratic, political accountability in the Community system'.[85] On the basis of direct elections by universal suffrage, it represents the 'peoples of the States brought together in the Community'[86] in their capacity, we submit, of European *citizens* rather than nationals of their own Member States. In fact, if the bicameral logic that underscores the co-decision procedure is to make sense, the European Parliament should represent the European citizens (like, say, the German *Bundestag*) whereas the Council should be called to represent the same individuals in another capacity, that is, as nationals of their own state (like the *Bundesrat*). Recent evolutions confirm the European Parliament's vocation to represent the European citizens: examples are the extension of voting rights to EU residents who are not nationals in elections for the European Parliament,[87] the EC Treaty's call for the constitution of political parties at the European level,[88] as well as the fact that all MEPs may participate in debates

[85] ECHR, *Matthews v United Kingdom*, No. 24833/94, Judgment of 18 February 1999, at para. 52. On the basis of an analysis of the current composition and powers of the European Parliament, the ECHR concluded that the European Parliament can be considered a 'legislature' for the purposes of Art. 3 of Protocol No. 1 to the European Human Rights Convention, which aims at safeguarding the right to vote in elections for the legislature. Hence, it condemned the denial of voting rights in European Parliament elections to inhabitants of Gibraltar.

[86] Art. 189 of the EC Treaty.

[87] Art. 19 (2) of the EC Treaty introduced by the Maastricht Treaty. See also Council Directive 93/109 laying down detailed arrangements for the exercise of the right to vote and stand as a candidate in elections to the European Parliament for citizens of the Union residing in a Member State of which they are not nationals, OJ 1993 L 329/34.

[88] Art. 191 of the EC Treaty, introduced by the Maastricht Treaty, stipulates that 'political parties at the European level are important as a factor for integration within the Union. They contribute to forming a European awareness and to expressing the political will of the citizens

and decision-making in policy spheres in which not all Member States participate.[89] One cannot but recognize, however, that as of today, the national links still play an important role—too important in our opinion—in the Parliament's composition (thus, each Member State has a fixed number of EP representatives[90] and elections for the European Parliament are still organized at the national level in accordance with national procedures).[91]

Second, control by the European Parliament can enhance the transparency of Commission action vis-à-vis the general public. The European Parliament retains a unique position in this respect, as it provides a forum where the Commission can explain itself vis-à-vis representatives of the European citizens. This can help to shield off the Commission against sometimes ill-directed and partisan critiques of (mostly national) media and accordingly, nationally-oriented public opinion.[92] It is well-known that 'Brussels' often functions as a scapegoat for various evils for which national governments or even third parties—business leaders for example—are (at least co-) responsible.

Third, and more in particular as regards executive rule-making, the exercise of control by the European Parliament is necessary to safeguard that the Commission stays within the limits of the powers delegated to it by the Community legislator (of which the European Parliament is a part) and within the policy orientations established by the latter.[93]

Fourth, parliamentary scrutiny also constitutes an effective means to control whether the Commission respects the 'rules of the game' when operating

of the Union'. Hitherto, no such parties exist. In the European Parliament, members form political groups on the basis of their political affinities, but such groups are relevant only for action within the Parliament (political groups receive funds for a secretarial staff and participate in the Conference of the Presidents of political groups, which sets the agenda for the European Parliament); its members do not politically act as a front outside. Significantly, a political group must always comprise members of more than one Member State and the minimum number of MEPs required to form a political group reduces in function of the number of nationalities present in the group (minimum 23 members if they come from 2 Member States, 18 members if they come from 3, and 14 if they come from 4 Member States). Thus, national diversity enhances a group's chance to be recognized as a political group (see EP Rules of Procedure, Art. 29, para. 2). This underscores the truly European vocation of the MEPs.

[89] Resolution of the European Parliament of 19 January 1994, OJ 1994 C 44/88.

[90] Article 190 (2) of the EC Treaty.

[91] Article 190 (4) of the EC Treaty calls for the establishment of a uniform electoral procedure or, at least, of principles common to all Member States when organizing elections for the Parliament. See, in this respect, the Resolution of the European Parliament on a draft electoral procedure incorporating common principles for the election of Members of the European Parliament, dated 15 July 1998 (A4-0212/1998).

[92] In the same sense, it is stated in the Second Report on Reform of the Commission of the Committee of Independent Experts, Chapter 7, at para. 7.14.3, that: 'Giving full account to Parliament . . . is . . . a form of self-defence for ministers and commissioners against the unhappy predicament of being submitted to the unfocused and uninformed criticism by press and public opinion'. On transparency and the role of the European Parliament, see also below.

[93] See below.

as a broker of interests and guardian of the Treaties. Efficient mechanisms of political control constitute an attractive alternative to a detailed regulation of Commission action, which would unduly clip the Commission's wings, encourage an attitude of legalism and could lead to a little desirable culture of litigation, wherein, ultimately, administrative discretion is replaced by judicial discretion.[94]

Finally, the European Parliament is in a position effectively to sanction the Commission (although, as will be discussed, the current sanctioning mechanisms are not entirely adequate).

In our view, the Commission should be accountable to the European Parliament (i.e., it should account for its actions towards that institution) and the Parliament should be able to hold the Commission politically responsible for its actions (i.e., to attach effective political consequences to the conduct of Commissioners).[95] Mechanisms to ensure accountability and political responsibility are set forth in the founding Treaties, in the Rules of Procedure of the European Parliament, as well as, importantly, in interinstitutional agreements. Thus, on 5 July 2000 the European Parliament and the Commission concluded a new 'Framework Agreement' designed, among others, to 'strengthen the responsibility and legitimacy of the Commission, to extend constructive dialogue and political cooperation' and 'to improve the flow of information' between the two institutions.[96]

2. Mechanisms to Ensure Accountability

The European Treaties ensure in several ways that the Commission gives account of its actions before the European Parliament. The European Parliament has a right to put oral or written questions to the Commission.[97] Oral questions are placed on the agenda for a parliamentary sitting and must be referred to the Commission at least a week beforehand. One of the members of the Commission must answer them. Written questions must be answered within six weeks (three weeks for so-called 'priority questions') and the answers are published together with the questions in the C series of the

[94] On the dangers of over-regulation, see, among others, Dehousse, 'Towards a Regulation of Transnational Governance', in Joerges and Vos, *supra* n. 35, at 123; Harlow, 'Codification of EC Administrative Procedures? Fitting the Foot to the Shoe or the Shoe to the Foot?', 2 *ELJ* (1996) 3.

[95] On the difference between accountability and political responsibility, see the Second Report on Reform of the Commission of the Committee of Independent Experts, Chapter 7 ('Integrity, Responsibility and Accountability in European Political and Administrative Life').

[96] Available on the website of the European Parliament (Doc. C5–0349/2000). The EU institutions often use interinstitutional agreements in order to render the procedures set forth in the Treaties more effective, without, however, being entitled to amend these procedures or alter the institutional balance. Interinstitutional agreements may be binding (see further Lenaerts and Van Nuffel, *supra* n. 39, at 590).

[97] Art. 197 of the EC Treaty.

Official Journal.[98] Members of the Commission may also freely attend the meetings of the European Parliament and, at their request, be heard on behalf of the Commission.[99] Further, the Commission must draw up an annual report on the activities of the European Union[100] and other reports on specific sectors of Community policy.

More specific rules regarding accountability can be found in the provisions dealing with the Commission's implementing powers, and, in particular, its powers to implement the budget and to adopt measures implementing basic (legislative) acts. In connection with the Parliament's supervision of the implementation of the budget, the Commission must submit a number of reports to the European Parliament and give hearings.[101] The rights of information of the Parliament in connection with the executive rule-making procedure will be discussed below.

The new Framework Agreement sets out the conditions under which confidential information from the Commission must be forwarded to and handled by the European Parliament. The aim is to give a greater access to information to the European Parliament than the general public enjoys, so that the Parliament can duly exercise its powers of scrutiny. In principle, no information should be refused to the European Parliament on the grounds of its confidential nature.[102] Access to confidential information within the European Parliament is subject, however, to strict procedural conditions and security requirements.

In addition, the European Parliament has rather large powers of investigation. It can, among others, set up an internal temporary committee of inquiry in order to investigate alleged contraventions or maladministration in the implementation of Community law (as it did for example in the BSE crisis).[103]

---

[98] See the European Parliament's Rules of Procedure, Rules 42–44.

[99] Article 197 of the EC Treaty.

[100] Articles 200 and 212 of the EC Treaty. For other reports, see Lenaerts and Van Nuffel, *supra* n. 39, at 321.

[101] Articles 275 and 276 of the EC Treaty. The Framework Agreement adds that reports on the implementation of the budget must be submitted 'at regular intervals'.

[102] As an exception, information relating to infringement proceedings and competition proceedings that are not yet covered by a final Commission decision, will not be transmitted to the European Parliament. In addition, confidential information from a State or an institution or an international organization can be forwarded only with the agreement of the body in question. Under pressure of the Council, the European Parliament and the Commission deleted the requirement, taken up in a prior draft of the Framework Agreement, for States, institutions or international organizations, to duly justify an eventual refusal to grant access to information to the European Parliament on the grounds of secrecy reasons resulting from national or Community legislation (see also Declaration No. 35 attached to the Amsterdam Treaty).

[103] Except where the alleged facts are being examined before a court and while the case is still subject to legal proceedings. See Article 193 of the EC Treaty and Decision 95/167 of the European Parliament, the Council and the Commission of 19 April 1995, OJ 1995 L 113/2 and Article 136 of the European Parliament's Rules of Procedure.

The political weight of such committees might not, however, be significant. Thus, the European Parliament resorted to the solution of a committee of independent experts (and not to the temporary committee of enquiry solution) after it had failed to remove the Santer Commission from office by a motion of censure. Although the move for an independent committee—operating under the auspices of both the Parliament and the Commission—was criticized as a 'surrender' by the Parliament of its supervisory powers, it has led, in practice, to results that a parliamentary committee might not have achieved.[104]

3. Mechanisms to Ensure Political Responsibility

Since the resignation of the Santer Commission, the issue of the political responsibility of the Commission vis-à-vis the European Parliament has been high on the political agenda.[105] Much and fruitful thought has been devoted to the question for what the Commission and/or its members should be held responsible and how the European Parliament can act. The Second Report of the Committee of independent experts contains ground-breaking material where it establishes the criteria against which the political responsibility of the members of the Commission must be assessed.[106] It draws a distinction between individual and collective responsibility. Individual responsibility of Commissioners must cover the whole range of competencies and activities for which they are responsible and must relate to 'their own personal, managerial and operational shortcomings in the functioning of their departments, even when the blame for these cannot be laid on them personally'.[107] The collective responsibility of the Commission as a body may be engaged when decisions have been taken by the Commission as a body, but also where the Commission as a whole fails to react to the mismanagement on the part of one colleague of which it is aware or should have been aware.[108]

The European Parliament has, in the current state of the law, only limited means to sanction the Commission or its members.[109] The European

---

[104] The saga of the resignation of the Santer Commission can usefully be compared to that of the mad cow crisis. For an analysis of the latter, see Chambers, 'The BSE Crisis and the European Parliament', in Joerges and Vos, *supra* n. 94, at 95–107.

[105] For academic comments, see among others Rodrigues, 'Quelques réflexions juridiques à propos de la démission de la Commission européenne. De la responsabilité des institutions communautaires comme "manifestation ultime de la démocratie"?', 430 *Revue du Marché Commun et de l'Union européenne* (1999) 472; Tomkins, 'Responsibility and Resignation in the European Commission', 62 *MLR* (1999) 744; van Gerven, 'Ethical and Political Responsibility of EU Commissioners', 37 *CMLRev.* (2000) 1.

[106] *Supra* n. 61.   [107] Ibid., para. 7.14.9.   [108] Ibid., para. 7.10.1.

[109] The Parliament can of course use its veto right in the investiture procedure to prevent a second term of office in the (unlikely) event the Member States would nominate an outgoing President or outgoing members that have come under severe criticism from the European Parliament (for the investiture procedure, see below).

Parliament can adopt a motion of censure, in which case the Commission (as a body) must resign.[110] The conditions are very strict, however: while the motion may be submitted by one-tenth of the MEPs, the vote on the motion cannot be held until at least three days after it has been submitted. In order for the motion to be carried, it must obtain a two-thirds majority of the votes cast, representing a majority of MEPs.[111] It comes as no surprise then that, although the Parliament has hitherto held seven votes on motions of censure, no motion has been carried.[112]

In addition, the European Parliament has an exclusive right to grant an annual discharge to the Commission in respect of the implementation of the budget.[113] In this connection, the European Parliament may ask to hear the Commission give evidence with regard to the execution of expenditure or the operation of financial control systems. The Commission must also submit any necessary information to the European Parliament at the latter's request.[114] Refusal to grant discharge represents a strong political reprimand for the Commission. It is a public statement by the European Parliament that either the Commission's management of European funds has been irregular or uneconomic or that the Commission has failed to respect the political objectives set when the budget was adopted. Yet European law does not provide sanctions in case discharge is refused.[115] In practice, the European Parliament has sought to pressurize the Commission by adding 'observations' in the decision giving discharge on which the Commission must act or by delaying the

[110] Article 201 of the EC Treaty.

[111] On 14 January 1999, a motion of censure against the Santer Commission was rejected.

[112] Lenaerts and Van Nuffel, n. 39 above, at 296. In the framework of the current IGC, some delegations have proposed to introduce a 'motion of confidence', the precise contours of which, however, remain rather vague.

[113] Article 276 of the EC Treaty. The European Parliament acts here on a recommendation from the Council, acting by a qualified majority.

[114] Article 276 (2) of the EC Treaty. The Framework Agreement adds that if new aspects come to light concerning previous years for which discharge has already been given, the Commission must forward to the Parliament all necessary information with a view to arriving at an acceptable solution.

[115] In 1977, Commissioner Thugendhat, then responsible for the budget, reportedly stated that 'refusal to grant discharge is a political sanction which would be extremely serious: the Commission thus censured would, I think, have to be replaced' (quoted in R. Corbett, F. Jacobs and M. Shackleton, *The European Parliament* (3rd edn., 1995) 224, at 241). On the two occasions on which the Parliament refused to grant it discharge, the Commission did not do so, however. In November 1984, the Parliament refused discharge for the 1982 fiscal year, but as the Commission was at the very end of its term, no further consequences were given. The refusal, on 17 December 1998, to grant a discharge to the Santer Commission for the 1996 budget was followed by a motion for censure, which however was not carried. See also Baziadoly, 'Le refus de la décharge par le Parlement européen', 354 *Revue du Marché Commun et de l'Union européenne* (1992) 58.

grant of discharge in order to obtain further information.[116] Hence, discharge becomes an instrument to ensure a proper flow of information to the European Parliament rather than a real sanctioning mechanism.

It should be noted also that the Treaties do not provide for a mechanism that would allow the European Parliament to act against an individual Commissioner. The mandate of a member of the Commission only ends when he or she resigns or is compulsorily retired by the Court of Justice on application by the Council or the Commission (not the European Parliament).[117] In the wake of the Santer Commission débâcle, MEPs called for the possibility to censure individual Commissioners.[118] In practice, such an action appears politically difficult to achieve, as it risks being interpreted as an action against a particular nationality or political colour or might raise difficult issues of collegiality within the Commission. As the Second Report suggests, it is better to leave that matter to the Commission President, who could act, as the case may be, on objections made by the European Parliament.[119] In the Framework Agreement, the European Parliament and the Commission have agreed that if the Parliament expresses, with due political support, a lack

---

[116] Also the Council may, in its recommendation to the Parliament, adopt 'comments' which the Commission must respect. Since the Maastricht Treaty, Art. 276 (3) of the EC Treaty indeed reads that '[t]he Commission shall take all appropriate steps to act on the observations in the decisions giving discharge and on other observations by the European Parliament relating to the execution of expenditure, as well as any comments accompanying the recommendations on discharge adopted by the Council. At the request of the European Parliament or the Council, the Commission shall report on the measures taken in the light of these observations and comments and in particular on the instructions given to the departments which are responsible for the implementation of the budget. The reports shall also be forwarded to the Court of Auditors'.

[117] See Articles 215 and 216 of the EC Treaty. In accordance with Art. 216 of the EC Treaty, compulsory retirement may take place if a commissioner 'no longer fulfils the conditions required for the performance of his duties or if he has been guilty of serious misconduct'. Of course, a (former) member of the Commission may be brought before the Court of Justice for failure to respect his or her Treaty obligations. Thus, the Council started legal proceedings against former Commissioner Bangemann on the grounds that his acceptance of a seat on the Board of Directors of Telefónica conflicted with his duties of discretion with regard to post-mandate employment enshrined in Article 213 (2) of the EC Treaty. The matter has been settled in the meantime (see Council Decision 200/44 EC, ECSC and Euratom, OJ 2000 L 16/73).

[118] See the Resolution of the European Parliament of 23 March 1999 on the resignation of the Commission and the appointment of a new Commission, OJ 1999 C 177/19.

[119] Para. 7.14.26. Tomkins suggests an alternative solution. He advocates the creation of an ad hoc, independent body to monitor and supervise good administrative behaviour (Tomkins, *supra* n. 105, at 762). In our opinion, the creation of such a body would inevitably raise the *'quis custodet custodies'* question. As a result, the findings of such an independent body would need to be advisory only, whereby the Parliament (or as the case may be the President of the Commission) would retain the final say. Yet the question would then be whether the same functions could not be carried out by temporary committees of enquiry set up within the European Parliament in accordance with Art. 193 of the EC Treaty.

of confidence in a member of the Commission, the President of the Commission will examine seriously whether he should request that member to resign. Individual responsibility vis-à-vis the Commission President can only work, however, if two conditions are met. The President should have the power to change the assignments of the members of the Commission and, as the case may be, dismiss them. Currently, the President has the former power (although there is no firm constitutional basis for it),[120] but not the latter, at least not as a matter of law.[121] Second, the European Parliament should be able to hold the President responsible in case he fails to keep his team in line with standards of good governance. The only legal possibility here is the motion of censure, yet, as mentioned, the conditions for a successful motion are onerous. If and when the Treaty of Nice comes into force, the President's powers will significantly increase in this respect.[122]

Again, as the result of the saga of the resignation of the Santer Commission, there might now well be a climate change—say, a greater willingness on behalf of Commission members to live up to (as yet still murky) standards of good governance and to draw political conclusions if they are found seriously to breach these standards. Much will depend, ultimately, on the integrity of the members of the Commission as well as of the MEPs themselves, lest parliamentary scrutiny loses credibility.[123] Yet a further formalization of the rules on responsibility seems long overdue.

4. Towards a Reform of the Commission Investiture Procedure?

The members of the Commission are appointed by the Member States by common accord. The Commission 'must include at least one national of each of the Member States but may not include more than two Members having

---

[120] See declaration No. 32 attached to the Amsterdam Treaty and Art. 3 of the Rules of Procedure of the Commission adopted on 16 September 1999. Under the Framework Agreement, a Commissioner must appear before the relevant parliamentary committee at its request in case his or her responsibilities are changed in a substantial way.

[121] Upon taking office, the members of the Prodi Commission undertook to resign if the President would ask them to do so. In its opinion for the current intergovernmental conference adopted on 26 January 2000 (COM (2000) 34 final), the Commission pressed for a formal incorporation of this undertaking in the Treaties.

[122] Thus, Article 217 EC will provide that the President of the Commission can allocate, and reshuffle the allocation of responsibilities and duties, which the individual members must carry out under the President's authority. Further, a member of the Commission will need to resign at the President's request, with the approval of the College.

[123] The European Parliament's own record is not the greatest. At the end of March 2000, the European Parliament's own auditors issued, for instance, a report in which they vehemently criticized the way the institution spends taxpayers' money (abuses alleged included overcharging by outside contractors, fraudulent allowance claims by officials, breaches of public procurement rules and widespread pilfering of the Parliament's property): see *European Voice*, 30 March–5 April 2000.

the nationality of the same state'.[124] This has meant, in practice, that each Member State appointed its Commissioner(s) without interference from the others.[125] Despite their strong national political links (Commission members are appointed by Member States and, crucially, depend on them for the renewal of their term of office), the EC Treaty aims at ensuring the Commissioners' independence in various ways. Commission members must be 'chosen on the grounds of their general competence' and their 'independence must be beyond doubt'.[126] Also, '[i]n the performance of their duties, they shall neither seek nor take instructions from any government or from any other body'. The Member States, in turn, have undertaken 'not to seek to influence the Members of the Commission in the performance of their task'.[127] Moreover, the members of the Commission are appointed for a fixed term[128] and cannot be dismissed by the Member States.

Since the early days of the Community, the European Parliament has pressed for a say in the appointment of the Commission, which it considered a crucial means to influence policy.[129] The Parliament argued that granting it government-building powers would greatly enhance its own respectability vis-à-vis the European citizen.[130] As of the Maastricht Treaty, the Commission's term of office has been made to coincide with that of the European Parliament. The aim was to make the Commission's composition reflect the outcome of the elections for the European Parliament. Since the Treaty of Amsterdam, the Member States nominate, first, the person they intend to appoint as President of the Commission. The nomination then has to be approved by the European Parliament. Next, the national governments nominate, by common accord with the nominee for President, the other persons whom they intend to appoint as members of the Commission. The nominees for President and members of the Commission must be approved by the European Parliament as a team, upon which they can be appointed by the Member States.[131]

---

[124] Article 213 (1) of the EC Treaty.

[125] Donnelly and Ritchie, 'The College of Commissioners and their Cabinets', in Edwards and Spence, *supra* n. 59, at 34.

[126] Ibid.   [127] Article 213 (2) of the EC Treaty.

[128] Initially four years, since the Maastricht Treaty extended to five years, in order to have the term of office of Commissioners coincide with the term of the elected European Parliament (Art. 214 of the EC Treaty).

[129] See the Resolution of the European Parliament of 27 June 1963, OJ 1963 1916/63.

[130] Corbett *et al.*, *supra* n. 115, at 249.

[131] Article 214 of the EC Treaty. The Treaty of Nice will replace the nomination by the Member States, acting together in common accord, with nomination by the Council, in its special composition of Heads of State or Government, on the basis of a qualified majority. The main reason for this amendment is to prevent one Member State from blocking the designation of the future President of the Commission, as the UK did with respect to the nomination of the Commission's President in 1994.

The new investiture procedure introduced by the Treaty of Amsterdam has been heralded as 'a forceful impetus with a view to politicizing and Europeanizing the selection of the European executive'.[132] We tend to disagree, acknowledging, however, that only the future will tell on this point (much depends, indeed, on how the new investiture procedure is applied in practice). As of today, one cannot say that the European citizens are really able—via their representatives in the European Parliament—to choose the members of the Commission (and thus to weigh on the European agenda-setting). First, the powers of the European Parliament are much too weak in this respect. True, the European Parliament has acquired a veto right as regards the choice of both the President and the Commission as a body—not, significantly, over the choice of an individual member—but it cannot suggest candidates itself. Faced with an all-or-nothing situation, the European Parliament is not likely to withhold its approval, although it might voice certain concerns and try to solicit undertakings from candidate-Commissioners.[133] A much better option (at least if one is serious about the Parliament's involvement) would be to let the European Parliament choose the candidate for President first and to submit this choice afterwards to the Council for approval.[134] In this respect, the European Parliament's position might have been stronger under the Maastricht Treaty, where it had a right to be consulted *before* the President was nominated (and thus to suggest candidates) and thereafter to approve the investiture of the college as a whole.[135]

---

[132] Nentwich and Falkner, 'The Treaty of Amsterdam: Towards a New Institutional Balance', 15 *EIoP* (1997) <http://www.eiop.or.at/eiop/texte/1997-015a.htm>.

[133] The designation of the Prodi Commission, which took place under the Amsterdam rules, testifies to the relative weakness of the European Parliament. Mr. Prodi was nominated by the Berlin European Council on 24 March 1999, several months before the elections for the European Parliament, which were to be held in June 1999 (see *Europe Documents*, No. 2131/2132 of 27 March 1999, 16). The circumstances were of course rather exceptional: all its members having resigned on 16 March 1999, the Santer Commission felt no longer able to take new political initiatives (cf. Guidelines drawn up by the outgoing European Commission for its activities during the interim period, *Europe Documents*, No. 2133 of 9 April 1999). The nomination of Mr. Prodi was approved by the Parliament shortly thereafter for the remainder of the term (Resolution of the European Parliament of 5 May 1999, No. B4–0453/99). A new candidate-team of Commissioners was prepared soon thereafter by Mr. Prodi and the Member States. It was nominated on 19 July 1999, approved by the new European Parliament on 15 September 1999 and finally appointed by the representatives of the governments of the Member States on the same day (OJ 1999 L 248/30).

[134] Hix, 'Executive Selection in the European Union: Does the Commission President Investiture Procedure Reduce the Democratic Deficit?', 21 *EIoP* (1997) <http://www.eiop.or.at/eiop/texte/1997-021.htm>.

[135] The appointment in 1994 of the Santer Commission did not follow this procedure, however, but rather the one codified now in the Amsterdam Treaty. See Lenaerts and De Smijter, 'Le Traité d'Amsterdam', 46 *Journal des Tribunaux—Droit européen* (1998) 25, at 33, footnote 131. Already in 1983, the European Council decided that, before appointing the

Further, the European Parliament's own representativity remains rather weak. Less than half of the European Union's electorate voted in last year's parliamentary elections.[136] National campaigns still tend to concentrate on national issues. If, for instance, the Christian Democrats replaced the Socialists as the European Parliament's strongest group as a result of the 1999 elections, that 'victory' has to be analysed in light of a declining popularity of the left in the Member States and not in light of a purportedly more attractive political programme for European Union governance presented by the Christian Democrats (in fact, such programme could not even exist given the absence of transnational political parties). Admittedly, there is a (viciously) circular relation between powers and representativity (part of the low voter turn-out can be explained precisely by the fact that the European Parliament cannot appoint the Commission). One cannot but remark, however, that the steady increase of the powers of the European Parliament has not resulted in a more positive image of that institution in the eyes of the general public.[137]

In our opinion, a full-blown parliamentary investiture procedure is not necessarily beneficial. As mentioned, the Commission is not an agent of the European Parliament nor should it be. It assumes its *own* responsibility—to further the Community interest—which the Treaties have directly entrusted to it. Further, if the Commission becomes an emanation of a parliamentary majority, the European Parliament risks losing its 'critical distance', which enables it to exercise its supervisory role effectively. However, the existing imbalance between the Member States and the European Parliament as regards the nomination of the European Parliament remains an unhappy anomaly, certainly in light of the fact that it is incumbent on the European Parliament to ensure the accountability of the Commission's political action vis-à-vis the general public. For that reason, we suggest that the European Parliament be put on an equal footing with the Member States, at least as regards the choice of the Commission President. The position of the latter vis-à-vis the other members of the Commission has been steadily increased, among others as a result of the Amsterdam Treaty. As mentioned, the nominee for President must now agree with (and hence can oppose) the individual Member States' choices as regards candidate-members of the Commission. Further, the Commission has to 'work under the political guidance of its

President of the Commission, the Member States would seek the opinion of the enlarged bureau of the European Parliament and that, after the members of the Commission had been appointed, the European Parliament would vote on the Commission's proposed programme (see the Solemn Declaration of Stuttgart of 19 June 1983, *Bull EC* (6–1983) point 1.6.1.).

[136] Arguably, if voting had not been compulsory in Belgium, Italy and Luxembourg, the turnout would have been even more depressing.

[137] On the lack of representativity of the European Parliament, see generally J. Blondel, R. Simmott and P. Svensson, *People and Parliament in the European Union. Participation, Democracy and Legitimacy* (1999) 287.

President'.[138] Giving the European Parliament a greater say in the choice of the President (and at the same time, further strengthening the latter's role) could ease the current tension between the need for a more representative Commission, on the one hand, and the continuing struggle of Member States to continue each to have 'their' Commissioner, appointed by them at their liking.[139] One could think, in this respect, of a procedure whereby the President is elected by common accord of the European Parliament (acting with a simple majority) and the Council (acting, preferably, with a qualified majority) on the basis of a dual list, drawn up by the Council and by the European Parliament.

Alternatively (and in our opinion even better) one could envisage introducing a presidential system, whereby the President of the European Commission would be directly elected by the European public (in several rounds, as in the French system, or after 'primary' elections, as in the United States). This, in turn, would require—and stimulate—the formation of genuine European political parties and, concomitantly, political will-formation in the Union.

C. Parliamentary Supervision in Action: The Commission's Role in the Legislative and Executive Process

1. The Role of the Commission in the Legislative Process

Whereas the Commission has independent regulatory[140] powers under the ECSC Treaty, the Commission under the EC Treaty in principle only proposes and the Council, mostly together with the European Parliament, disposes.[141] The right of initiative endows the Commission, however, with a

---

[138] Article 219 (1) of the EC Treaty. In Declaration No. 32 (on the organization and functioning of the Commission) the intergovernmental conference added that 'it considers that the President of the Commission must enjoy broad discretion in the allocation of tasks within the College, as well as in any reshuffling of those tasks during a Commission's term of office'. Art. 3 of the new Rules of Procedure of the Commission (OJ 1999 L 252/41) now firmly establishes the right of the President to assign to members of the Commission specific fields of activity and to change these assignments. It also establishes the principle that Commission decisions are taken by a majority of its members, irrespective of the nature and tenor of the decision (Art. 8).

[139] The desire of all Member States to have (one or two) 'own' Commissioner(s) renders difficult the debate on the size and composition of the Commission, one of the major issues to be decided upon by the current intergovernmental conference.

[140] We deliberately avoid the term 'legislative' here, since the ECSC Treaty sets forth detailed rules containing policy choices that leave little other than administrative and supervisory tasks to the Commission, even when it is entitled to act alone (without the Council).

[141] Only in exceptional cases does the Commission have original legislative powers under the EC Treaty (notably in Article 86 (3) of the EC Treaty, which concerns the application of the competition rules to public undertakings).

crucial role in the European policy-making process. First, the Commission's right of initiative is exclusive or nearly so. In principle, no European institution can legislate in the absence of a proposal from the Commission.[142] Only in very limited circumstances can the Council adopt an act on its own initiative.[143] As an exception, measures provided for in the new Title IV of the EC Treaty (visa, asylum and other policies relating to the free movement of persons) can be adopted 'on a proposal of the Commission or on the initiative of a Member State'.[144] Yet the Member States' right of initiative is temporary only and expires five years after the entry into force of the Amsterdam Treaty (i.e., on 30 April 2004). The Commission's monopoly of initiative under the EC Treaty stands in a stark contrast with the fact that, for matters covered by the second and third pillar of the Union, it shares the right of initiative with the Member States.

Further, the Commission exercises its right of initiative independently and with an absolute discretion, except for the few instances in which the Treaty imposes an obligation on the institutions to legislate. This means that it falls on the Commission to decide whether the Community should act and if so, on what legal basis (this, in turn, determines the type of decision-making procedure to be followed).[145] It also decides what content and, as the case may be, what provisions as regards further implementation the proposal should contain. The Commission cannot be compelled to submit a proposal. Although both the Council and the European Parliament have a right to request the Commission to do so,[146] the Commission keeps a wide margin of discretion as to the manner in which it follows up on such a request. The Commission has given an undertaking to the European Parliament, however, that it will take account of requests to submit a legislative proposal and that it will provide a prompt and sufficiently detailed response.[147] Arguably, a

---

[142] Case C-301/90, *Commission v Council* [1992] ECR I-221.

[143] Such own initiative measures are usually limited to certain specific organizational matters only, such as the determination of the languages of the institutions (Art. 290). In very exceptional cases, however, they may concern important political decisions, such as the introduction of the third stage of Economic and Monetary Union (Article 121 (3) of the EC Treaty) or the decision to allow State aid in exceptional circumstances (Article 88 (2) of the EC Treaty).

[144] Article 67 of the EC Treaty. See, e.g., Council Regulation (EC) No. 1346/2000 of 29 May 2000 on insolvency proceedings, OJ 2000 L 160/1, which was adopted pursuant to an initiative from Germany and Finland.

[145] Of course, the choice of legal basis should be based on objective grounds.

[146] Art. 208 of the EC Treaty empowers the Council, acting by a simple majority vote, to 'request the Commission to undertake any studies the Council considers desirable for the attainment of the common objectives, and to submit to it any appropriate proposals'. Art. 192 of the EC Treaty confers on the European Parliament, acting by a majority of its Members, the right to 'request the Commission to submit any appropriate proposal on matters on which it considers that a Community act is required for the purpose of implementing this Treaty'.

[147] See Article 4 of the Framework Agreement on relations between the European Parliament and the Commission, *supra* n. 96.

similar duty exists as regards requests brought by the Council, since it would seem to flow from the general duty of interinstitutional loyalty.[148]

The Commission's right of initiative ensures it a significant influence during the entire decision-making process. If the Council wants to amend the Commission's proposal, it must act unanimously.[149] As long as no decision has been reached, the Commission may at all times amend its proposal or even withdraw it. The Commission might do so, for instance, if it dislikes proposed amendments in the Council that may obtain the unanimous consent of the Member States.[150] Thus, for instance, in November 1986 it withdrew its proposal with regard to the Erasmus scheme for student exchanges. According to Mr. Marin, then responsible for the matter, this was done in order to prevent the Council from depriving the scheme of all significant content.[151]

Given the importance of the Commission's monopoly of initiative and its originality (no government in statal systems enjoys a similar monopoly) it is worth looking at the reasons why it was introduced. Its *ratio* appears to be essentially one of making the decision-making process more deliberative and more geared towards the attainment of the interests of all in the Community—including the interest of the Community itself (that is, the interest to achieve common solutions over and above national factionism). As Emile Noël, the Commission's long-time secretary-general explained in 1973, the Commission's monopoly of initiative created a dialogue between the Commission (representing the Community interest) and the Council (representing the national interests) in the decision-making process. Duties linked to the Commission's power of initiative are those of reflection, preparation, thinking ahead, co-ordination and conciliation. Thanks to the initiative of the Commission, decision-making would be less arbitrary and 'identify more with co-ordination, conciliation, conviction and encouragement'.[152]

---

[148] Compare Case C-65/93, *Parliament v Council* [1995] ECR I-643. Further, the EC Treaty expressly refers to an obligation to give reasons in Art. 11 (2) of the EC Treaty, which deals with the procedure for authorizing a closer co-operation. The Commission is bound to 'submit its conclusions to the Council without delay' in the event that the Council or a Member State requests it to make a recommendation or a proposal pursuant to Art. 115 of the EC Treaty in order to enable the Council to legislate on EMU matters. Having regard to the cautious wordings of that provision, it does not require the Commission, however, to submit a proposal formally.

[149] The Council must, moreover, stay within the limits of what constitutes an 'amendment', that is, it has to stay within the subject-matter and the objectives of the original proposal (e.g., Case C-408/95, *Eurotunnel* [1997] ECR I-6315, at I-6354–6355, paras. 37–39). Of course, the unanimity requirement only applies when the Council must act on a formal proposal of the Commission, not in the few cases where a simple 'recommendation' suffices.

[150] One should note, however, that the Commission loses the right to withdraw its proposal once, in the co-decision procedure, the matter is referred to the Conciliation Committee.

[151] Usher, 'The Commission and the Law', in Edwards and Spence, n. 59 above, at 147.

[152] Noël, 'The Commission's Power of Initiative', 10 *CMLRev.* (1973) 123, at 124.

There are other advantages as well. The Commission's exclusive right of initiative has enabled it to drive for the (relatively) high level of integration in the many policy fields that we know today. As the experience with the second and third pillar testifies, the Member States are in a much weaker position to propose such initiatives. Initiatives undertaken by the Member States risk giving rise to mistrust on the part of other Member States. In fact, the Treaty of Amsterdam gave the Commission a right of initiative in the second and third pillar together with the Member States (who had until then enjoyed an exclusive right of initiative) in order to overcome the inertia and paucity of results that had characterized these domains.

Further, the Commission's monopoly of initiative can contribute to the consistency and, thus, the overall quality of European legislation. In an ever-enlarging European Union, this is no small advantage.[153]

The monopoly of initiative allows the Commission to act as a 'broker' between interests that might otherwise not, or only insufficiently, be heard at the European level. Before a proposal is adopted, the Commission carries out preliminary soundings and discussions with representatives of governments, industry, the trade unions, special interests groups and, where necessary, technical experts.[154] In various instances, it draws up so-called Green Papers and White Papers on which it invites comments. The Commission, thus, becomes a marketplace for ideas and interests.[155] Brokerage continues when the Commission's proposal is under discussion at the legislative level. In fact, the rule that the Council can only amend the Commission's proposal with unanimity constituted an important—and for a long time sole—means to ensure that comments and amendments made by the European Parliament were effectively taken into account. If the Commission backs the position of the Parliament, it amends its proposal to that effect, thereby forcing the Council to accept the Parliament's position (unless the Council unanimously rejects it). As mentioned, the Commission has also promised, in principle, to withdraw proposals that the European Parliament rejects, thus precluding the adoption of such legislation.

With the introduction and increasing generalization of the co-decision procedure, the Commission's role as promoter of the European Parliament's interest has become much less important.[156] Co-decision allows the European Parliament directly to negotiate with the Council. As it disposes of

---

[153] Gosalbo Bono, *supra* n. 59, at 97.

[154] Thus the Commission, describing itself on <http://europa.eu.int/comm/role_en.htm>.

[155] Mazey and Richardson, 'La Commission européenne: une bourse pour les idées et les intérêts', 46 *Revue française de sciences politiques* (1996) 409.

[156] Boyron, 'The Co-decision Procedure: Rethinking the Constitutional Fundamentals', in P. Craig and C. Harlow (eds), *Lawmaking in the European Union* (1998) 147; Kreppel, 'What affects the European Parliament's Legislative Influence? An Analysis of the Success of EP Amendments', 37 *JCMS* (1999) 521; see also Lenaerts and Van Nuffel, *supra* n. 39, at 451.

a veto right, it no longer depends on the Commission to see its position effectively taken into account. One will recall that the co-decision procedure consists of various stages.[157] The procedure begins with a stage in which the European Parliament delivers an opinion on a proposal from the Commission, which may include amendments. If the Council approves all amendments contained in the opinion of the European Parliament (or in case no opinion is issued), it may adopt the proposed act as amended by a qualified majority. Thus, at this stage, a qualified majority in the Council and a simple majority in Parliament suffice to override a Commission proposal. In theory, the Commission could prevent this by withdrawing its proposal or modifying it. That would be counterproductive, however, as it might lead to interinstitutional conflict. By way of an interinstitutional agreement, the Commission has, therefore, committed itself to 'exercise its right of initiative in a constructive manner with a view to making it easier to reconcile the positions of the European Parliament and the Council'.[158] It has declared, in that respect, that it would organize meetings so that the principal participants can consider compromise texts before the first reading by the European Parliament (one of its principal aims being to ensure that the Council does not reach a political agreement before the first reading of the Parliament, in which case the procedure risks becoming a lengthy or even fruitless one).[159]

If the Council does not agree with the European Parliament's opinion, it adopts a common position (and renders its reasons for doing so public). In a second reading, the European Parliament may approve the common position, adopt amendments or reject it (if it does not act within set time limits, the act is deemed to be adopted). The Commission must, in turn, deliver an opinion on the European Parliament's amendments. The Commission has, in theory, an important political leverage here. If it delivers a negative opinion, the Council can only adopt the said amendments with unanimity. Yet the Commission's 'victory' in case no such unanimity is found (that is, in case at least one Member State agrees with its view) is limited, since it disqualifies itself from a later stage of the legislative process. In fact, if the Council and the European Parliament find no agreement in the second reading, the Conciliation Committee must be convened, in which case the Commission loses influence. The Commission can, of course, also withdraw its proposal in the second reading but if it does so, it openly puts the European Parliament out of play. As this might lead to interinstitutional conflict, the Commission

---

[157] Article 251 of the EC Treaty. See, for an extensive discussion, also Lenaerts and Van Nuffel, *supra* n. 39, at 447.

[158] Point 3 of the Joint Declaration of the European Parliament, the Council and the Commission of 4 May 1999 on practical arrangements for the new co-decision procedure, OJ 1999 C 148/1.

[159] *Europe Documents*, No. 7504 of 9 July 1999, at 10.

would probably rarely be tempted to do so (one might ask even whether withdrawing a proposal in the second reading can be reconciled with the requirement of loyal co-operation set forth in Article 10 EC).

The Conciliation Committee is composed of the members of the Council or their representatives and an equal number of representatives of the European Parliament. It is the last chance for a legislative measure to be adopted: unless an agreement is found there and agreed upon by the Council (by a qualified majority) and the Parliament (by a simple majority), no legislation can be passed.[160] The Commission takes part in the Conciliation Committee's deliberations and must 'take all the necessary initiatives with a view to reconciling the positions of the European Parliament and the Council'.[161] This has been interpreted to mean that the Commission can no longer withdraw a proposal once it reached the conciliation stage, nor force the Council to decide by unanimity if it issues a negative opinion.

Thus, the Commission's influence in the co-decision procedure is limited, even more so in fact than in law. Its only means to influence policy consists of ensuring that its initial proposal is likely to meet the concerns of the Council and the European Parliament. Given its mandate, it should also ensure that the concerns of the Community in general are addressed. Prior consultations with all interested parties are key in this respect. The Commission cannot—and should not—(as a rule) use its powers to promote its policy views in the legislative process once that process is en route by way of 'aggressive' means such as withdrawing the proposal or forcing the Council towards unanimity. Having said this, the Commission's role remains an important one. While its role as an independent policy-maker decreases, the Commission should increasingly focus on its tasks of mediation, brokerage of interests and safeguarding that the *acquis communautaire* and overall consistency of Community law, as well as Union policy, are respected.[162]

The aforementioned advantages of the Commission's right of initiative—making the process more participatory and deliberative—only work if the Commission takes the responsibilities that come with that right seriously. At present, the Commission often consults with many interests before it launches a proposal but in a rather pragmatic, case-by-case, and unsystematic manner. The Commission has, however, issued a set of interesting communications (on its dialogue with special interests groups[163] and on how to

---

[160] Before the Treaty of Amsterdam, there was still a possibility of a so-called 'third reading', i.e. the Council had the option to confirm its common position with a qualified majority in case the Conciliation Committee could not reach an agreement. The act would then stand as adopted, unless the European Parliament rejected it with a majority of its members.

[161] Article 251 (4) of the EC Treaty.   [162] Cf. Article 3 of the EU Treaty.

[163] 'An open and structured dialogue between the Commission and special interest groups' (93/C63/02).

increase the transparency of its work,[164] for instance) that may be binding on it under the *patere legem quem ipse fecisti* principle. Further, it has opened a special internet website setting out working tools that enable officials to promote the participation of socio-economic circles and representatives of civil society in the legislative process.[165]

The Framework Agreement submits the use, by the Commission, of its monopoly of initiative to various constraints that are designed to improve the dialogue with the European Parliament in the legislative process. Thus, the Commission has agreed not to make public any legislative initiative or significant initiative or decision before notifying and, for politically important matters, informing the European Parliament. Further, it undertakes to take the utmost account of amendments adopted by the European Parliament in the second stage of the co-decision procedure. A decision not to adopt such amendments must be based 'on important grounds' and must be explained to the Parliament. Of even more significance is the undertaking in principle to withdraw a legislative proposal that the European Parliament has rejected (outside the co-decision procedure). The Commission can only maintain such proposals on important grounds that, again, must be explained to the European Parliament.

The Council has criticized this undertaking, arguing that it unduly abridges the autonomy of the Commission and thus upsets the institutional balance between the Commission, Parliament and Council.[166] In our view, the Commission's undertakings are well in line with the *ratio* underlying the monopoly of initiative (making the legislative process more deliberative) and the overall duty of sincere co-operation among the institutions. It should be noted, moreover, that the Commission has already made similar undertakings in favour of the Council. Thus, as part of the Luxembourg Compromise of January 1966, the Commission had undertaken duly to consult the Member States before launching a legislative initiative, and not to submit a proposal to the Parliament or render it public before it had formally submitted it to the Council. On that occasion, the Council argued that these undertakings did not abridge the Commission's monopoly of initiative, they only obliged the Commission to use that monopoly well.[167]

Finally, the time has come, we think, to accord also to the European Parliament some right of initiative in the legislative process. One could think of granting it a right to 'co-initiate' a proposal. Before a proposal is launched

---

[164] 'Increased transparency in the work of the Commission' (93/C63/03).

[165] <http://europa.eu.int/comm/secretariat_general/sgc/lobbies>. On the Commission's role as a broker of interests, see further Mazey and Richardson, *supra* n. 154.

[166] See *Agence Europe*, No. 7757 of 13 July 2000, at 12.

[167] *Bull EC* (3-1966) 5, at 6: ('Cette consultation ne porte pas atteinte au pouvoir d'initiative et de préparation que la Commission tient du Traité, elle oblige seulement cette institution à en user à bon escient.')

by the European Parliament, the Commission would still need to give its assent (in order to enable the Commission to engage the social and/or civil dialogue, to control the consistency of European law and the preservation of the *acquis communautaire*), yet such an assent could not be unreasonably withheld.[168]

2. The Commission's Implementing Powers and the Comitology Issue

The Commission has been entrusted with a wide range of executive functions. According to Article 211, fourth indent, of the EC Treaty, the Commission 'exercise(s) the powers conferred on it by the Council for the implementation of the rules laid down by the latter'. The Commission enjoys, in practice, broad powers to issue decisions and regulations in order to implement legislative acts, now mostly adopted by the Council and the Parliament. Since such executive rule-making endows the Commission often with wide policy-making powers, the Council has, since the sixties, sought to limit the discretion of the Commission through the so-called comitology system. Under this system, the Commission must, before it takes an implementing act, seek the advice of a committee of national representatives in accordance with procedures that, in certain cases, enable the Council to take over the work of implementation. Comitology finds a legal basis in Article 202, third indent, of the EC Treaty and is further regulated by the so-called Comitology Decision of 28 June 1999.[169]

In short, there are three types of comitology procedures. In the advisory procedure,[170] the advice of the committee of national representatives is not binding.[171] In the management procedure,[172] the Commission must communicate the implementing measures to the Council forthwith if they are not in accordance with the opinion of the committee (awaiting the Council's response, the Commission can defer their application). The Council can then amend the executive measures within a short period of time. The regulatory procedure[173]—a procedure that is to be used for measures of a normative scope that closely approximate to legislation[174]—is the most complex. In that case, if the Commission fails to have the support of a qualified majority of the members of a regulatory committee, it must submit the proposed measures to

---

[168] Arguably, the Commission is currently already under a duty (flowing from Art. 10 of the EC Treaty) duly to consider launching an initiative where the European Parliament consistently (and with reason) requests it to do so. See above.

[169] *Supra* n. 54. For a discussion and critique, see Lenaerts and Verhoeven, ibid.

[170] Article 3 of the Comitology Decision.

[171] The Commission must take, however, the 'utmost account of it'. Further, the opinion of the committee, as well as the Commission's position as regards that opinion (and, at their request, the position of individual Member States), must be recorded in the minutes.

[172] Article 4 of the Comitology Decision.   [173] Article 5 of the Comitology Decision.

[174] Article 2 of the Comitology Decision.

the Council (contrary to the management procedure, it cannot adopt the measures itself). It must also inform the European Parliament, which may inform the Council if it considers that the proposed executive measures are *ultra vires* (i.e., exceed the powers granted to the Commission in the basic instrument). The Council can then oppose the adoption of the measures, in which case the Commission can either submit an amended proposal (to the Council), submit a legislative proposal (to the Council and, often, the European Parliament) or start a new executive process altogether. The Council must act with a qualified majority, however, and relatively quickly (within three months); if it fails to act, the Commission will adopt the implementing measures.

The fact that, as a result of the current ascendancy of the co-decision procedure, the comitology system empowers one 'branch' of the Community legislature (the Council) to the detriment of the other (the European Parliament) has long been justified by the argument that the Member States have original executive powers, which they can freely delegate to the Commission. Hence, *qui peut le plus peut le moins*: if the Member States (through the Council) can delegate powers to the Commission, they can also subject these powers to conditions designed to keep control over the executive process.[175] As we have argued elsewhere,[176] we do not think that this view correctly states the institutional balance as it exists today in the Union. In our opinion, the Commission has original executive powers.[177] The preponderance of the Council in the comitology system can be justified as an instance of executive federalism. It corresponds to the need to involve in the decision-making process those that are most directly affected by it, i.e., those who must implement the decisions at the national level. The European Parliament should, however, be ensured a due supervision over the executive rule-making process within the framework of comitology, in order to ensure

---

[175] Kortenberg, 'Comitologie: le retour', 3 *Revue trimestrielle de droit européen* (1998) 317. The *Köster* case, *supra* n. 42, seemed to sustain that argument; it certainly has been interpreted in that way.

[176] Lenaerts and Verhoeven, *supra* n. 54.

[177] This follows from Art. 202, third indent, of the EC Treaty, according to which the Council can only 'in specific cases' exercise implementing powers itself. Much depends, of course, on how the notion of 'implementation' is defined. Neither the Treaties nor the new Comitology Decision define implementation. Implementation is normally understood as everything that is not legislation itself. In a contribution to the IGC 2000, Jean-Claude Piris suggests, however, reserving the co-decision procedure to general legislative acts that cover only general principles, essential rules and objectives. 'Subordinated' acts that are intended to develop and clarify such legislative acts could then be adopted by the Council, acting by a qualified majority and after consultation of the European Parliament. This proposal risks narrowing the scope for 'implementing acts', and thus to narrow the sphere of competences of the Commission (see Discussion Paper for the Working Party of Representatives of the Governments of the Member States, SN 3068/00 of 30 May 2000, available on the website of the Council).

that the Commission (and Council) do not act ultra vires and respect essential procedural safeguards.

The new Comitology Decision meets this requirement to some extent. It accords the European Parliament substantial rights of information (Article 7) and a (limited) right of intervention when the Commission plans to act ultra vires (Article 8). An agreement between the European Parliament and the Commission has further elaborated these rights.[178] The European Parliament's right of information includes a right to receive agendas for meetings of comitology committees, the summary records of the meetings (including the results of votings) as well as lists of authorities and organizations to which the committee members belong. Pursuant to its right of intervention, the European Parliament should be in a position to defend its legislative prerogatives in a timely and efficient manner against the implementing authority. If the European Parliament adopts a resolution to this effect, it forces the Commission to re-examine the draft implementing measures. The Commission is not obliged to follow the European Parliament's view, but must state the reasons why it refuses to do so. Taken together, the right of information and of intervention ensure that the European Parliament can effectively exercise political and legal controls on the executive process involved in the framework of comitology, in particular in order to safeguard that the rule of law (and the principle of institutional balance, which is part thereof) is respected.

Apart from delegated rule-making, the Commission's executive powers also include powers directly to administer certain Treaty policies vis-à-vis national governments and individuals, such as competition and State aid policy; powers to supervise the way national bodies implement and enforce Community law in their own internal orders;[179] the powers to administer various safeguard clauses provided for by the Treaties or by secondary legislation;[180] and, importantly, the power to implement the budget of the European Communities.[181] The latter includes the power to administer major European funds and programmes. Given the potential for fraud and abuse (as recent events have testified) sufficient parliamentary supervision is needed here as well.

---

[178] OJ 2000 L 256/19.

[179] This follows from its role as a guardian of the Treaties (see above).

[180] Safeguard clauses allow for waivers of Community obligations, granted for a limited period of time, in certain policy fields. Given their often politically sensitive nature, the Commission has to act in collaboration with the Member States when applying (certain) safeguard measures (this is now regulated in the new Comitology Decision, *supra* n. 54.

[181] Article 274 of the EC Treaty provides that 'the Commission shall implement the budget, in accordance with the provisions of the regulations made pursuant to Article 279, on its own responsibility and within the limits of the appropriations, having regard to the principles of sound financial management'.

III. THE BUDGETARY PROCEDURE: 'CHEQUES AND IMBALANCES'[182]

A. Overview of the Budgetary Procedure

1. Introduction

The budget of the European Union and the procedure for its adoption[183] are prime examples of the *sui generis* nature of the Union, striking an uneasy middle ground between an international organization and a more vertically-integrated structure akin to that of federal states.[184] The discord and confusion on the respective roles of the Council, the European Parliament and the Commission in budgetary matters have always been paramount.[185] As of today, this remains the case. The budgetary procedure has largely escaped the recent wave of constitutional amendments. It has been subject only to some tinkering, largely in the frame of interinstitutional agreements.

Initially, the budget of the three Communities was not very different from that of international organizations. International organizations are financed by national contributions calculated, typically, on the basis of the relative wealth of the participating states. Similarly, the EEC and the EAEC had initially only financial contributions from the Member States (each contributing to a fixed percentage), although the Treaties put the Commission under a

---

[182] Quote borrowed from *The Economist*, 20 November 1999, at 40.

[183] On the budget of the European Union and the budgetary procedure in general, see The Philip Morris Institute for Public Policy Research, *Do We Need a New Budget Deal?* (1995); Corbett, *supra* n. 115, at 224–244; Dutheil de La Rochère, 'Au-delà de Maastricht: le financement de la future Europe', 1 *Revue des affaires européennes* (1995) 101; Griese, 'Die Finanzierung der Europäischen Union', 33 *Europarecht* (1998) 462; B. Kerremans and H. Matthijs, *De Europese Begroting* (1997); Kolte, 'The Community Budget: New Principles for Finance, Expenditure and Budget Discipline', 25 *CMLRev.* (1988) 487; H. Smit and P. Herzog, *The Law of the European Community. A Commentary to the EC Treaty*, No. 5–671; Schmidhuber, 'Die Notwendigkeit einer neuen Finanzverfassung der EG', 26 *Europarecht* (1991) 329; Strasser, 'Les finances publiques communautaires face aux échéances et aux nécessités', 1 *Revue des affaires européennes* (1992) 60; S. Walder, *The Budgetary Powers of the European Economic Community* (1992).

[184] Also as regards its content, the budget of the European Union can be situated somewhere in the middle. International organizations devote by far the largest part of their revenue to administrative costs (salaries, real estate, etc.). The Union uses its revenue to implement a wide range of policies decided upon at the European level, whilst running costs constitute only a relatively modest element. On the other hand, the budget of the Union is still small compared to that of States, given the Union's focus on regulatory rather than redistributive policies (see on the latter point, Majone, *supra* n. 66, at 77 et seq.).

[185] One will recall, for instance, that the notorious empty chair crisis of July 1965 was occasioned by ambitious proposals of the Commission to convert proceeds of the common external tariff and levies on agricultural imports into 'own resources'.

duty to investigate the institution of a system of own resources.[186] In 1970, such a system of independent, Community-owned resources was introduced.[187] The creation of the own resources system came with an amendment of the budgetary procedure. As long as the Community was financed by Member State contributions, each Member State retained an obvious control over Community institutions and programmes and a rather large fiscal autonomy (each State was free to determine how the revenue necessary to finance its share of the Community budget was raised). The loss of national parliamentary control on budgetary affairs as a result of the own resources system was 'compensated' by a substantial increase of the budgetary powers of the European Parliament.[188] As a result, the budgetary authority of the European Community (and now Union) now consists of two arms: the Council and the European Parliament.[189] As will be discussed, the role of the European Parliament with respect to the budget remains, however, a rather imbalanced one.

2. The Collection of Revenue

The role of the budgetary authority as a whole and of the European Parliament in particular as regards the revenue side of the budget is limited. The sources of revenue and the maximum amount of revenue that can annually be called upon are set forth in so-called 'own resources decisions'. These decisions are taken by a unanimous Council on a proposal from the Commission and after consulting the European Parliament, and are thereafter adopted by the Member States in accordance with their respective constitutional requirements.[190] The revenue system is further specified in decisions taken by the Council, acting unanimously.[191]

Currently, the revenue system is still governed by the Fourth Decision on Own Resources of October 1994,[192] but a new decision, adopted in

---

[186] By contrast, the ECSC has operated from the outset with its own resources, consisting of levies on the production of coal and steel and direct borrowings on the capital market (Articles 49 and 50 of the ECSC Treaty).

[187] Council Decision 70/243/ECSC/EEC/Euratom of 21 April 1970 on the replacement of financial contributions from Member States by the Communities' own resources, OJ 1970 L 94/19.

[188] Treaty of 22 April 1970 amending certain budgetary provisions of the Treaties establishing the European Communities and of the Treaty establishing a single Council and a single Commission of the European Communities. For an assessment of the budgetary reform of the early seventies, see Bustin, 'Financing the European Economic Community: Autonomy and the Problem of Parliamentary Control', 13 *Harvard International Law Journal* (1972) 481.

[189] See Part V, Title II of the EC Treaty, Articles 268 to 280.

[190] Article 269 of the EC Treaty.   [191] Article 279, indent (b), of the EC Treaty.

[192] Decision 94/728/EC, OJ 1994 L 293/9.

September 2000, is soon to take effect.[193] The Communities' own resources consist of four sources of revenue:[194] (1) custom duties; (2) agricultural levies; (3) VAT-based contributions; and (4) a variable percentage of each Member State's gross national product (GNP), determined each year in the course of the budgetary procedure. The first two sources constitute the so-called 'traditional own resources'. The fourth source of income was introduced in 1988 as a response to a chronic lack of means to cover the Community's growing expenses. It borrows from the classical mechanism of intergovernmental transfers—the Member States themselves decide how to collect the money necessary in order to finance their GNP-based contributions—but is nevertheless an 'own' resource, in that the percentage of GNP that is to be paid (and thus the total amount of the GNP-based revenue) is established on a yearly basis by the budgetary authority of the European Union, i.e., the Council and the European Parliament. That independence has a limit, however: the total amount of own resources (comprising all four sources) may not exceed 1.27 of EU GNP.[195]

Within the framework of the applicable own resources decision, the budgetary authority establishes each year the total amount of revenue and the distribution thereof over the various sources. Given the fact that revenue and expenses must be in balance,[196] the decision on expenditure directly influences the amount of revenue to be collected each year. Since the European Parliament has the final word as regards non-compulsory expenses (see above), the question has been raised whether it has the power to amend the revenue side of the draft budget as well. The Council has consistently sought to deny the existence of such a right. In defence of its position, it has referred to the general spirit of the European budget as a 'budget of expenditure', i.e., a budget based solely on the need to finance projected Community expenditure, akin to budgets of international organizations. The Court of Justice has not yet ruled on the matter.[197] It appears fair to accord the European

---

[193] Council Decision 2000/597/EC, Euratom of 29 September 2000 on the system of the European Communities' Own Resources. This decision will take effect as of 1 January 2002. It only contains technical corrections, but imposes an obligation on the Commission to undertake, before 1 January 2006, a general review of the Own Resources system, among others, in the light of the effects of enlargement. In this context, the Commission should study the possibility of modifying the structure of the Own Resources, among others, by creating new autonomous resources.

[194] In addition, there is miscellaneous revenue, such as the proceeds of the Community tax on officials' salaries, fines imposed for infringement of competition rules and a proportion of the levies on the production of coal and steel.

[195] Article 3 of the Fourth Own Resources Decision. This percentage is maintained in the new Decision, subject to technical adjustments (in order to take account of a new statistical method for calculating GDP) to be adopted by the Commission.

[196] Article 268 of the EC Treaty.

[197] The issue came before it most recently in Case C-284/90, *Council v European Parliament* [1992] ECR I-2277. In that case, the Council sought the annulment of the final

Parliament a right to make amendments to the revenue side of the budget where the amendments necessarily ensue from amendments made in respect of non-compulsory expenditure, or where the European Parliament and the Council disagree about the correct application of the own resources decision or other relevant provisions. The European Parliament cannot use its powers, however, in order to frustrate the powers of the Council or the Member States.[198]

3. The Allocation of Expenditure

Article 272 of the EC Treaty governs the rather unwieldy procedure for adopting the budget. As a general matter, the budget is adopted in stages. On the basis of a preliminary draft drawn up by the Commission, the Council adopts a draft budget by a qualified majority. It then presents that draft to the European Parliament. After the first reading by the Parliament (in which it can suggest modifications), the Council has the final word on compulsory expenditure, i.e. expenditure necessarily resulting from the Treaties or from acts adopted in accordance therewith.[199] The Parliament takes the final decision on non-compulsory expenditure at the second reading. At the completion of the procedure, the President of the European Parliament declares that the budget is adopted.[200]

The European Parliament has four major powers. It has, first, a right to increase or to reduce expenditure, within certain defined limits. Second, it can redistribute spending from one sector of the budget to another (without an increase or decrease). Third, even without amending the expenditure, it can amend the remarks that specify the use that is to be made of the appropriations. It considers these remarks as binding.[201] Finally, it can reject the whole annual budget or any supplementary budget by a majority of its members and

adoption of the budget by the European Parliament, among others, on the grounds that the Parliament had amended the revenue side thereof. The Court of Justice did not expressly address the matter. It did, however, pronounce on whether the amendments made to the revenue side were lawful in the particular circumstances, which would appear to constitute implied recognition of the Parliament's right of amendment. See also the comments by de Witte, in 41 *Sociaal-Economische Wetgeving* (1993) 757 and Van den Bossche, in 31 *CMLRev.* (1994) 653.

[198] This is the view defended by Advocate-General Jacobs in Case C-284/90, *supra* n. 195. Article 272 of the EC Treaty, which governs the procedure for the adoption of the budget, seems to buttress this position, by stating in its para. 10 that '[e]ach institution shall exercise the powers conferred upon it . . . with due regard for the provisions of the Treaty and for acts adopted in accordance therewith, in particular those relating to the Communities' own resources and to the balance between revenue and expenditure'.

[199] Article 272 (4) second sentence of the EC Treaty.

[200] Article 272 (7) of the EC Treaty.

[201] Thus, for instance, it modified certain aid provisions in the 1990 budget procedure in order to exclude the possibility of payments to China following the dramatic events of Tienanmen Square in the summer of 1989. See Corbett *et al.*, *supra* n. 115, at 235.

two-thirds of the votes cast 'for important reasons'. In case no budget is voted at the start of the financial year, the Commission is only allowed to spend each month one-twelfth of the expenditure included in the previous year's budget or in the draft budget under preparation (or before it was rejected), whichever is the lower. This allows the Union to function but does not allow new activity. To date, the European Parliament has used this power on three occasions.[202]

With respect to the European Parliament's right to amend the draft budget, a distinction must be drawn between compulsory and non-compulsory expenditure. As regards compulsory expenditure, the European Parliament can make modifications to the draft budget with a majority of the votes cast. If the effect of a modification is to increase the total expenditure of an institution, it will be accepted only if the Council expressly does so with a qualified majority. If a proposed modification does not have that effect (because, for instance, it is compensated for by a proposed reduction in another expenditure), the proposed modification stands as accepted unless the Council rejects it with a qualified majority within the prescribed time-limit. Therefore, the Council has the last word as regards compulsory expenditure, although the European Parliament can, of course, express its dissatisfaction by rejecting the budget as a whole.

As regards non-compulsory expenditure, the European Parliament can propose amendments by a majority of its members.[203] The Council, in turn, can modify these amendments. On a second reading, however, the European Parliament can overturn the Council's position provided that it does so with a majority of its members and three-fifths of the votes cast, and provided it stays within certain limits. In particular, non-compulsory expenditure can increase from one year to another by no more than what is called the 'maximum rate of increase', a percentage determined by the Commission in light of certain macro-economic factors.[204] Nevertheless, the maximum percentage may be exceeded in two ways. The European Parliament can always enter amounts totalling at least half the maximum rate. Thus, if the Council enters increases in the draft budget that account for all or most of the maximum rate, the Parliament still retains the right to further increase the budget by an amount equal to half the rate. In practice, this has meant that the Council

---

[202] The first rejection took place, not surprisingly, in the budgetary procedure that immediately followed the first direct elections to the European Parliament (see the Resolution of 13 December 1979, OJ 1980 C 4/37) and further the Resolutions of 16 December 1982 (OJ 1983 C 13/67) and of 13 December 1984 (OJ 1985 C 12/90).

[203] The quorum necessary to effect amendments to non-compulsory expenditure is therefore more difficult to reach than that required for modifications to compulsory expenditure, where a majority of votes cast suffices.

[204] In particular, the economic growth, the average variation in the budgets of the Member States and the rates of inflation in the Member States (see Article 272 (9) of the EC Treaty).

enters an amount of half of the maximum rate, leaving it to the Parliament to decide on the other half. Further, the Treaty allows the budgetary authority (Parliament and Council) to increase the maximum rate set by the Commission if it considers that the activity of the Union so requires it.[205] Of course, any increases in expenditure must stay within the maximum limit of available revenue, established in the relevant own resources decision.

Since 1988, the debates about increases of the expenditure take place within the framework of a so-called financial perspective, established by way of an interinstitutional agreement between the European Parliament, the Council and the Commission.[206] The financial perspective sets out in advance the ceilings for the budget of the coming years, not just in overall terms but also by category of (major) expenditure. The financial perspective has radically altered the debates between the European Parliament, the Council and the Commission, among others, as regards increases beyond the maximum rate.[207] On the one hand, it has helped to keep Union expenditure under control (by the Member States), in particular by constraining the European Parliament's power unilaterally to increase the budget. On the other hand, it has allowed for yearly increases in spending well beyond the maximum rate of spending, without there being (too much) obstruction from the Member States.[208]

In addition, the establishment of the financial perspective is typically coupled with arrangements that improve the budgetary procedure and in particular buttress the position of the European Parliament (without, of course, amending the Treaty framework as such). Thus, the 1999 interinstitutional agreement seeks to strengthen institutional collaboration by planning regular triangular meetings (between the President of the Council, the chairman of the European Parliament's committee on budgets and the Commissioner responsible for the budget) at decisive moments in the budgetary procedure, if necessary followed by a conciliation procedure involving the Council and a

[205] To this end, the Council must act with a qualified majority and the European Parliament with a majority of its members and three-fifths of the votes cast.

[206] The first interinstitutional agreement came as a response to a decision by the European Council to impose a strict budgetary discipline (see interinstitutional agreement of 29 June 1988 on budgetary discipline and improvement of the budgetary procedure, OJ 1988 L 185/33). The current financial perspective, covering the period 2000–2006, has been adopted by way of an interinstitutional agreement of 6 May 1999, OJ 1999 C 172/1. See for a discussion, Bache, 'Agenda 2000: Les enjeux et résultats de la négociation sur le cadre financier pour la période 2000–2006', 429 *Revue du Marché Commun et de l'Union européenne* (1999) 372.

[207] For an early assessment of the changes affecting interinstitutional co-operation, see Timman, 'La procédure budgétaire pour l'exercice 1989 et la première application de l'accord interinstitutionnel', 326 *Revue du Marché Commun et de l'Union européenne* (1989) 235.

[208] In the 1999 interinstitutional agreement, it is established that, while the financial perspective for the period 2000–2006 may be adjusted, revisions of the compulsory expenditure may not lead to a reduction of the amount available for non-compulsory expenditure.

delegation from the Parliament with the Commission as a participant.[209] In order to overcome disagreement as to the classification of expenditure, it also establishes a definition of compulsory expenditure[210] and, more importantly, a list classifying each heading or sub-heading of the financial perspective as compulsory or non-compulsory.[211] In case agreement on the classification of expenditure can still not be reached, the said conciliation procedure applies. These interinstitutional arrangements have led to less disruptive and more equilibrated budget-adoption procedures.[212]

B. Problems of Democratic Accountability

Having the people decide on the budget is one of the cornerstones of the democracy. Historically, parliamentary democracy has grown out of the demand of taxpayers to decide on how their money should be collected and spent ('no taxation without representation'). As regards the budget of the European Union, the line of accountability towards the people of Europe runs, however, in a rather indirect and opaque manner. Over time, the European Parliament has gained more powers in the budgetary procedure yet its powers appear affected by a striking lack of balance. In particular, there is lack of balance between the European Parliament's budgetary and legislative powers and worse, between its powers as regards, respectively, the revenue and expenditure sides of the budget.

As discussed, the European Parliament has rather large powers as regards expenditure (it has the final say over non-compulsory expenditure, which now accounts for the major part of the budget). It uses these powers to exert pressure during the policy-making process, in particular in areas where its decision-making powers are limited (such as, for instance, in the second and third pillar). In itself, that is not problematic. Thanks to the leverage it has in budgetary matters, the European Parliament has been able to ensure that the powers it has in the decision-making process—however limited they are—are duly respected. As regards common foreign and security policy, i.e., second pillar matters, the European Parliament only has a right to be consulted on

[209] Cf. Annex III of the 1999 interinstitutional agreement.

[210] See para. 30 of the interinstitutional agreement: 'The institutions consider compulsory expenditure to be such expenditure as the budgetary authority is obliged to enter in the budget by virtue of a legal undertaking entered into under the Treaties or acts adopted by virtue of the said Treaties'.

[211] The interinstitutional agreement provides also that only multi-annual programmes adopted under the co-decision procedure can contain financial provisions that are binding on the institutions during the budgetary procedure. If financial provisions are incorporated in other kinds of acts, they serve only as an illustration.

[212] For an example, see Discors, 'La procédure budgétaire pour 1998: une idylle interinstitutionnelle', 423 *Revue du Marché Commun et de l'Union européenne* (1998) 681.

the 'main aspects and the basic choices' and to be 'regularly informed'.[213] It has, however, a substantial leverage in the budgetary field. Whilst administrative expenses related to CFSP are always charged to the general budget, operational expenses are also charged to the budget, unless the Council decides otherwise (acting unanimously).[214] In practice, the Council will not do so as the alternative—raising separate government contributions—offers less guarantees for a secure funding. When operational expenses are charged to the budget, the European Parliament is in a position, however, to refuse funding for operations it is opposed to or otherwise to impose its views. In order to avoid blockage, the Commission, Council and European Parliament agreed that when the Council adopts a decision in the field of CFSP entailing expenditure, it must immediately send the European Parliament an estimate of the cost envisaged (i.e., the so-called *fiche financière*). The Commission also informs the budgetary authority of the implementation of CFSP actions.[215] In this way, the European Parliament can be sure that its limited powers in CFSP decision-making are not just a dead letter, but serve as an instrument of control and influence.

At the same time, the legal basis requirement prevents the European Parliament and the Commission from upsetting, by way of the budgetary procedure, the institutional balance for decision-making purposes intended by the *Herren der Verträge*. For some time, the European Parliament argued that if money was entered in the budget, then it had to be implemented by the Commission in accordance with the wishes of the budgetary authority. This view was strongly resisted by the Council which argued that a budgetary entry was not a sufficient legal basis. The Court of Justice corroborated the Council's view, deciding that implementation by the Commission of Community expenditure relating to any significant Community action requires not only the entry of the relevant appropriation in the budget but also the prior adoption of a basic act of secondary legislation.[216] The 1999 interinstitutional agreement further specifies the legal basis requirement. In particular, it lists certain exemptions where the Commission can use expenditure without a prior basic act.[217]

---

[213] Article 21 of the EU Treaty.

[214] Article 28 (3) of the EU Treaty. Expenditure for operations having military or defence implications must remain outside the budget, however.

[215] These agreements were set out in an interinstitutional agreement of 16 July 1997, incorporated thereafter in the 1999 interinstitutional agreement.

[216] Case 16/88, *Commission v Council* [1989] ECR 3457, at 3486, paras. 16–19, and in particular, Case C-106/96, *United Kingdom v Commission* [1998] ECR I-2729, at I-2755, para. 26.

[217] Essentially these include appropriations for pilot schemes of an experimental nature or for preparatory acts (up to certain limits), as well as appropriations for actions carried out by the Commission pursuant to its own specific powers or intended for the internal operation of the institutions.

The European Parliament's large powers as regards expenditure are problematic, however, in the light of the fact that it cannot (or almost not) decide on revenue. As a result, the European Parliament is in a position to allocate and, as is often the case, increase expenditure in the draft budget adopted by the Council without being responsible for determining the type of revenue needed to cover that expenditure.[218] This situation is sometimes referred to as the 'luxury of revenue irresponsibility'. It negatively affects the status of the European Parliament *vis-à-vis* the European citizen,[219] particularly when considered in the light of recurrent reports on irresponsible financial behaviour by the institution and some of its members. In fact, it is difficult to see how the European Parliament can be truly representative of the European peoples in the absence of powers to raise revenue—the (inverted) dictum 'no representation without taxation' might well hold true here.[220]

The ensuing lack of accountability cannot be effectively redressed at the national level. Under the current system, Member States must set aside provisions on a yearly basis in their own budgets in order to comply with their obligations vis-à-vis the Union (and in particular, to finance their part of the GNP-based resource). Consequently, debates on the revenue part of the budget of the European Union take place in the national parliaments, whilst these parliaments do not decide on the expenditure side nor on how the budget is implemented and controlled. This has, again, several negative effects. First, it leads to rather one-sided attitudes of calculating how much one, as a State, 'spends' on the Union and how much one 'gains' from it. That attitude has led, in the Fourth Own Resources Decision, to complicated and not necessarily fair corrections for so-called budgetary imbalances, measured by the differences between contributions to and receipts from the budget, in favour of the United Kingdom.[221]

Second, the revenue each Member State has to pay is adjusted automatically to the overall level of expenditure under the allocation rules that establish a current ceiling for VAT and GNP-based contributions. That means that if expenditure goes up, the Member States will have to pay more. Since their impact on the amount of yearly expenditure is relatively low, this opens the door to facile critiques as to the financial irresponsibility of the European Union and the spendthrift nature of its institutions. Given the lack of balance

[218] The budgetary interventions of the European Parliament usually imply an increase in expenditure, see Kerremans and Matthijs, *supra* n. 182, at 152.

[219] See *supra* n. 135 and accompanying text.

[220] A. Peijpers, *De mythe van het democratisch tekort* (1999).

[221] These corrections were a concession made by the Member States at the 1984 Fontainebleau summit, in reply to then British Prime Minister Margaret Thatcher's notorious statement 'I want my money back'. The Fifth Own Resources Decision of 2000 maintains the UK correction, subject to some technical adjustments, but the contribution of some Members will be reduced in order to 'finance' this correction.

between its powers of expenditure and of revenue, the European Parliament thus becomes an easy scapegoat in national budgetary debates.

A solution could consist in granting the European Parliament powers to decide, with the Member States, on the amount and type of revenue to be raised. This would force the European Parliament, when deciding on spending, to be flexible on the question of how to raise the necessary money as well. Making it responsible for the revenue side, along with its expenditure powers, would greatly enhance the European Parliament's accountability vis-à-vis the European citizen. It would also reduce the risk of 'nationalist' reflections fuelled by national parliamentary debates on the European budget.

Granting the European Parliament revenue powers would mean a fundamental overhaul of the current own resources system, not only in terms of procedure (who decides on revenue and how) but also in terms of the type of revenue to be collected. It could pave the way, for instance, for the introduction of a system of European taxes. In our opinion, such reforms are long overdue. In a 1998 report, the Commission pointed out that the current own resources system failed to live up to the requirements of financial autonomy, transparency, simplicity and cost-effectiveness.[222] In particular, it noted with concern that the proportion of the GNP-based resources in the overall revenue has steadily increased, thus weakening the financial autonomy of the Union.[223] Further, the collection of the traditional own resources (custom and agricultural levies) appears to be cumbersome and has given rise to many instances of fraud. Transparency and simplicity are also affected by the complicated correction mechanisms in favour of the United Kingdom. Others have criticized the own resources system for being unjust, as it would impose a heavier burden on small incomes than on large ones.[224] As mentioned, the new decision on own resources that will take effect as of 1 January 2002 leaves the basic structure of the current own resources system intact.

As a remedy, the suggestion has been made to replace the current resources system by a series of European taxes.[225] In our opinion, the introduction of a system of European taxes would entail various advantages in terms of democracy. Apart from the obvious advantages suggested above (reduction of instances of fraud, a more equitable division of the fiscal burden), it could heighten citizens' awareness of European Union matters.[226] The current

---

[222] Report of the Commission on the operation of the own resources system, COM (1998) 560 final; see also *Agenda 2000—Financing the European Union, Bull EC* (1998) Suppl. 2.

[223] In 1998, the Commission forecast that the proportion of GNP-based revenue would come close to 50 per cent in 1999!

[224] This critique was voiced, among others, by Dieter Biehl, professor in economics, and noted down in Dutheil de La Rochère, *supra* n. 182, at 103.

[225] In its report on the operation of the own resources system (n. 220 above), the Commission suggests the introduction of a withholding tax on interest, a CO_2/energy tax, a communications tax or even taxes on personal and corporate income.

[226] Which is one of the fundamental aims of the Union, cf. Article 1 of the EU Treaty.

revenue system offers little transparency and is too much dominated by the Member States themselves. EU taxpayers simply do not know how (part of) their money is transferred to 'Brussels'. Although it is their money the Member States collect, it is the money of the Member State that is transferred to the Union (one speaks of the German contribution, the UK contribution, etc.). Arguably (and perhaps somewhat ironically), a system of European taxes, making citizens feel when and how much they pay for the operation of the European Union, could draw the Union closer to its citizens; at least it would make them more concerned about what happens there.[227] As many studies indicate, a lack of proper involvement, the absence of a feeling that what happens at the European Union level really matters in their daily lives, accounts for many of the problems commonly associated with the democratic deficit.[228]

One might object that amending the own resources system in this manner would require an unacceptable surrender of national sovereignty.[229] If the political will for an overall reform is lacking, an intermediary solution could consist of a harmonization of national fiscal systems and instruments so that, for each European taxpayer, a uniform 'contribution for Europe' could be established over and above its national (personal or company) income, it being understood of course that the overall fiscal burden would not increase. The current discussions on a possible introduction of qualified majority voting for fiscal matters might be a first step in this direction.

In conclusion, the current budgetary system appears no longer tenable. In the absence of a system guaranteeing transparency and a proper involvement of the European peoples, money issues will continue to undercut the already fragile basis of legitimacy upon which the Union rests.

` [227] In the same sense, Scrivener, 'A Strategy for the EU Budget in the 21st Century', in *Do We Need a New Budget Deal?*, Paper of the Philip Morris Institute for Public Policy Research (June 1995), at 60–71. See on the connection between a potential European tax and citizenship, Weiler, 'European Citizenship and Human Rights', in Winter *et al.*, *supra* n. 59, at 57.

[228] See among others, Blondel *et al.*, *supra* n. 136; Hedetoft, 'National Identities and European Integration: Integration "From Below": Bringing People Back In', 18 *Revue d'intégration européenne* (1994) 1; and the results of recurrent Eurobarometers, published regularly in the *Bulletin of the European Union*.

[229] That, surely, is the dominant feeling today. Following up on its 1998 report, on 8 July 1999 the Commission submitted to the Council a proposal for a new own resources system. The proposal contains a few rather technical adjustments only. As the proposal admits, its 'objective is to improve the operation of the Union's financing system while retaining the principal elements. The European Council [meeting in Berlin in March 1999] considered the time was not yet ripe to embark on a radical restructuring of the own resources system'.

3

Institutional Balance as Interest Representation. Some Reflections on Lenaerts and Verhoeven

STIJN SMISMANS*

INTRODUCTION

Lenaerts and Verhoeven argue that a proper understanding and application of the notion of institutional balance may lessen the democratic deficit from which the Union is perceived to suffer. Therefore, they distinguish between institutional balance as a legal principle and as a political principle of EU governance. The former mainly corresponds with the 'traditional' court-led reading of the concept of institutional balance, whereas the latter provides a broader normative tool to shape European governance. The latter interpretation is used by the authors to analyse the role of the European Commission and the question of its accountability, and the budgetary procedure. The aim of my contribution is not to analyse the merits of these two 'case studies', though they contain very interesting proposals, such as the introduction of a presidential system and a system of European taxes. My focus will be on the definition of institutional balance formulated by the authors.

I will first describe the 'traditional' interpretation of the institutional balance (section I) to better distinguish the particular features of the definition provided by Lenaerts and Verhoeven, which could be called an 'institutional balance of interest representation'. This 'new reading' of the institutional balance—which has equally been developed by Craig[1] and de Búrca[2] and has

* Marie Curie Research Fellow at the European Centre, Institut d'Etudes Politiques, Paris. I am grateful to Gráinne de Búrca, Renaud Dehousse and Christian Joerges for comments on an earlier draft and to Zaria Greenhill for stylistic and linguistic help.

[1] Craig, 'The Nature of the Community: Integration, Democracy, and Legitimacy', in P. Craig and G. de Búrca (eds), *The Evolution of EU Law* (1999) 1, at 36–41.

[2] De Búrca, 'The Institutional Development of the EU: A Constitutional Analysis', in ibid., at 57–60 and 73–75.

been suggested by Curtin,[3] and Joerges and Neyer[4]—offers a potential normative tool to structure European governance, but it needs further clarification (section II). In particular, I will argue that its potential can only be realized to the full if well-known narratives on territorial representation are complemented by narratives on functional representation (section III).

I. THE 'TRADITIONAL' INSTITUTIONAL BALANCE

The 'traditional' institutional balance has mainly been developed as a legal principle. It was the case law of the Court of Justice (see *Meroni*[5] and *Chernobyl*[6]) which defined the institutional balance as 'a fundamental guarantee granted by the Treaty', which consists of a system for distributing powers among the different Community institutions, assigning a precise role to each institution in the institutional structure of the Community and in the accomplishment of the tasks entrusted to the Community. The Court ensures respect of the rule of law by monitoring the observance of the institutional balance, i.e., each of the institutions must exercise its powers with due regard for the powers of the other institutions.

However, rules cannot justify themselves simply by being rules, without reference to considerations beyond themselves.[7] Put differently, respect of the institutional balance as such does not suffice to ensure legitimate EU governance. Therefore, the institutional balance as a legal principle has been linked to elements of 'democratic procedure' and more particularly to territorial representation. A distinction could be made between the intergovernmentalist interpretation of the institutional balance and the parliamentary one. In the intergovernmentalist interpretation the institutional balance is above all a device to retain the supranational bureaucracy of the Commission under control of the European Parliament and especially of the Council, and the legitimacy of this institutional balance finds its legitimization in the constituent power of the Member States as *Masters of the Treaty*. This power is assumed to be rooted in the democratic procedures within the Member States. In the parliamentary interpretation of the institutional balance the focus is on the 'legitimating role' of the European Parliament which 'although limited, reflects at the Community level the fundamental democratic principle that the peoples

---

[3] Curtin, 'Civil Society and the European Union: Opening Spaces for Deliberative Democracy', 7 *Collected Courses of the Academy of European Law* (1999, 1) 185.

[4] Joerges and Neyer, 'From Intergovernmental Bargaining to Deliberative Political Processes: the Constitutionalization of Comitology', 3 *ELJ* (1997) 273.

[5] Case 9/56, *Meroni v High Authority* [1957 and 1958] ECR 133, at 152.

[6] Case 70/88, *European Parliament v Council* [1990] ECR I-2041, at I-2072, paras. 21 and 22.

[7] Obradovic, 'Policy Legitimacy and the European Union', 34 *JCMS* (1996) 191, at 197.

should take part in the exercise of power through the intermediary of a representative assembly'.[8] It is not incidental that the principle of institutional balance has been formulated most extensively by the Court in a case (*Chernobyl*) concerning the prerogatives of the European Parliament. As described by Lenaerts and Verhoeven, in *Chernobyl* the Court even took a corrective action *contra legem* in order to ensure the prerogatives of the Parliament within the institutional balance. The combination of institutional balance and democratic input via the European Parliament has largely dominated legal debate on the European democracy deficit[9] and it concurs with the dominance of the parliamentary model in the broader academic and political debate on the issue.[10]

The 'traditional' interpretation of the institutional balance built on the case law of the Court is characterized by three elements:

(1) It is above all a legal principle, namely it is a Treaty-based guarantee: the balance of power among the institutions as enshrined in the Treaty (though *Chernobyl* shows that the Court can interpret this Treaty-based balance by making recourse to general principles of law).

(2) It concerns the five Community Institutions—the EP, the Council, the Commission, the Court of Justice and the Court of Auditors—and especially the balance of powers among the first three institutions as controlled by the Court of Justice.

(3) As a normative argument for legitimate EU governance the traditional interpretation of institutional balance links the rule of law with an assumed democratic input via territorial representation either expressed via the *Masters of the Treaty* and the Council—as particularly stressed in the intergovernmentalist interpretation—or via the European Parliament—as stressed in the prevailing parliamentary view.

This traditional reading of the institutional balance has a slightly fictional ring when compared to the current institutional reality of European governance. As mentioned by Lenaerts and Verhoeven and more extensively developed by de Búrca,[11] substantial elements of European governance operate in the margins of or wholly outside the formal constitutional frame as defined by the institutional balance. The traditional reading of the institutional balance does

---

[8] Case 138/79, *Roquette Frères v Council* [1980] ECR 3333, at 3360, para. 33 and Case 139/79, *Maïzena v Council* [1980] ECR 3393, at 3424, para. 34.

[9] See, for instance, Mancini and Keeling, 'Democracy and the European Court of Justice', 57 *MLR* (1994) 191; Michael O' Neill, 'Democracy and the EU: Legal Perspectives on the Political Debate', 1 *Irish Journal of European Law* (1995) 48; Ress, 'Democratic Decision-Making in the European Union and the Role of the European Parliament', in D. Curtin and T. Heukels (eds), *Institutional Dynamics of European Integration* (1994) 153.

[10] Dehousse, 'European Institutional Architecture after the Amsterdam Treaty: Parliamentary System or Regulatory Structure?', 35 *CMLRev.* (1998) 595, at 601.

[11] de Búrca, *supra* n. 2.

not correspond with the complex reality of European governance with its three pillar structure and with its gradual proliferation of formal and informal bodies beyond the five Institutions. It is striking that the institutional balance does not take account at all of forms of functional participation and representation that are part of the institutional reality.

The problem is not simply one of 'institutional imbalance' which could (after the intervention of the Court of Justice) be adjusted by bringing the institutional practice into conformity with the Treaty-based norm of institutional balance. The gap between institutional reality and formal constitution as expressed by the institutional balance is so big that one can question whether the latter can (still) be assumed to ensure the rule of law and the legitimacy of European governance. As stated by de Búrca, 'if the institutional development and expansion of the Union materially outgrows the basic constitutional structure established in the Treaties, and that structure is neither adequately supplemented nor modified by secondary norms nor by judicial adaptation, the notions of institutional balance and constitutional legitimacy presupposed by that structure become increasingly empty'.[12] The real challenge is thus to provide a constitutional framework for the complex reality of European governance. A 're-interpreted' institutional balance may serve as a tool to shape that framework.

II. THE 'NEW' INSTITUTIONAL BALANCE: POLITICAL PRINCIPLE AND BALANCE OF INTEREST REPRESENTATION

According to Lenaerts and Verhoeven, 'a proper understanding of institutional balance can contribute to more democracy since it focuses on issues of *interest representation* and fair procedure' (emphasis added).

The institutional balance requires the makers of the European constitution to shape institutions and the interactions between them in such a manner that each interest and constituency present in the Union is duly represented and co-operates with others in the frame of an institutionalized debate geared towards the formulation of the common good. At the same time, the formulation of the common good should never lead to an unequal and unnecessary sacrifice of individual liberty.

The definition of institutional balance in terms of fair interest representation has equally been developed by Craig[13] and de Búrca[14] and has been suggested by Curtin,[15] and Joerges and Neyer.[16] The common argument is that each institution represents a different interest or constituency, and that their interaction ensures deliberation geared to the attainment of the common good.

---

[12] de Búrca, *supra* n. 2, at 56.   [13] Craig, *supra* n. 1.   [14] de Búrca, *supra* n. 2.
[15] Curtin, *supra* n. 3.   [16] Joerges and Neyer, *supra* n. 4.

This 'new reading' of the institutional balance differs considerably from the traditional interpretation:

(1) Institutional balance is above all used as a political principle, i.e., as a normative tool to shape the institutional framework of the Treaty. It thus refers to a norm beyond the Treaty which is sought in political and democratic theory. This in turn will influence the institutional balance as a legal principle which ensures the respect of the institutional framework laid down in the Treaty.[17]

(2) It is not by definition limited to the relation EP–Council–Commission nor to the five Community Institutions.

(3) Normative considerations are not limited to territorial representation but refer to various forms of interest representation.

This new reading also raises many questions; can such an institutional balance be retraced to the idea of *trias politica* as Lenaerts and Verhoeven argue? (A); can the European institutions be considered to represent a particular interest or constituency? (B); and which institutions and organs can be considered part of the institutional balance? (C).

A. *Trias Politica* and Interest Representation

Lenaerts and Verhoeven indicate the doctrine of *trias politica* as the historical and intellectual roots of their broadened concept of institutional balance. One could reconstruct the evolution of *trias politica* to this interpretation of the institutional balance in the following three steps.

The first interpretation of *trias politica* is the strict separation of powers commonly attributed to Montesquieu. In this interpretation each institution ensures a particular function—legislative, executive and judicial. In the EC/EU such an organic understanding of the principle of separation of powers is not possible[18] (though a functional definition of the separation of powers can be provided).[19]

---

[17] Moreover, as the traditional reading and the attitude of the Court of Justice has also shown, even as a legal principle institutional balance cannot be separated entirely from normative considerations beyond the rule of law.

[18] An organic interpretation of the European institutional balance has been given by Pescatore, 'L'exécutif communautaire: justification du quadripartisme institué par les traités de Paris et de Rome', 14 *Cahiers de droit européen* (1978) 387. Pescatore identified an organic 'quadripartite institutional balance' within the European Communities rather than a *trias politica*. However, such an organic interpretation—even if 'quadripartite'—is ever more problematic, not least since the Council's increasing involvement in implementation (via comitology) makes Pescatore's identification of the Commission as the one and only real executive body more difficult.

[19] Lenaerts, 'Some Reflections on the Separation of Powers in the European Community', 28 *CMLRev.* (1991) 11.

In a second step the focus is more on a balance of powers than on a strict separation of powers. As Lenaerts and Verhoeven suggests even Montesquieu's *trias politica* can be read in that sense.[20] It is, however, the thinking of the US Founding Fathers which best developed the idea of a system of *checks and balances* as a way of protecting the liberties of individuals against a concentration of powers in one single authority and as a tool to prevent factions acting adversely to the rights of other citizens or to the aggregate interests of the community.[21] This system of *checks and balances* rather than a *trias politica* seems apt for the EC/EU. It stresses the idea of dividing up power by creating different institutions which control each other via necessary cooperation, rather than the idea that the legislative, executive and judiciary powers need by definition to be divided among three institutions and that each institution should be identified with one function. Although the institutional balance in the Treaty seems to derive more from power interests—and more precisely from the Member States' desire to retain control—than from a liberal or pluralist political ideology,[22] there is much to say for the European institutional balance as a democratic guarantee against the concentration of power. However, this general interpretation of a system of *checks and balances* gives few indications as to which institutions should be created and how they should relate to each other. As soon as these questions are formulated, the issue of interest representation comes to the fore, which brings us to the third step in the argument.

There is a *saut qualitatif* in the way in which Lenaerts and Verhoeven (and equally Craig and de Búrca) address the issue of interest representation compared to the traditional readings of *trias politica* and *checks and balances*. Lenaerts, Verhoeven, Craig and de Búrca attribute to each of the Community institutions a particular interest or identify them as representative of a particular constituency.[23] Instead of a negative formulation of *checks and balances* as a guarantee against concentration of power, a positive formulation of 'mixed government' can be made according to which any decision should have the support of institutions representing different interests.

---

[20] See also W. J. Witteveen, *Evenwicht van Machten* (1991), at 34, as cited by E. Vos, *Institutional Frameworks of Community Health and Safety Regulation—Committees, Agencies and Private Bodies* (1999), at 86.

[21] See P. P. Craig, *Public Law and Democracy in the United Kingdom and the United States of America* (1990), at 58.

[22] Dehousse, 'Comparing National Law and EC Law: The Problem of the Level of Analysis', 42 *AJCL* (1994) 761, at 771.

[23] In the words of Lenaerts and Verhoeven: 'each institution represents a particular interest and particular views'. In the words of de Búrca: 'Since each of the institutions . . . represents a different constituency, the notion of institutional balance can be presented as a way of ensuring the adequate participation and representation of different constituencies within the European Community process'. de Búrca, *supra* n. 2, at 60.

For Montesquieu, however, the issue of interest representation was entirely addressed by the legislative body which had to represent the aristocracy in one chamber and the people in another chamber. For Madison 'national representatives operating above the fray would be able to disentangle themselves from local pressures and deliberate on and bring about something like an objective public good'.[24] The emphasis was placed on the need to establish a large republic so that factional interests would be so heterogeneous that they could not dominate the institutions.[25] *Checks and balances* were a sort of safeguard in case national representatives did not have the virtue to disentangle themselves from factional interests rather than a clearly balanced system of interest representation in which various institutions representing different constituencies interact and ensure deliberation on the common good.

Gargarella, however, gives a reading of Madison in which *checks and balances* and interest representation concur. He argues that Madison did indeed recognize the variety of factions in society but was also convinced that a division between two groups was omnipresent in society, namely the division between those who hold property (the minority) and those who are without property (the majority). The main idea of the system of *checks and balances* was to give equal power to both 'the few' and 'the many', as two separate and opposite groups. The House of Representatives (based on direct elections) would express the interests of the majority, while the interests of the minority would be expressed and protected by the executive power, the Senate, and the judiciary (based on indirect elections).[26] Yet even such a reading of Madison's *checks and balances* in terms of interest representation[27] cannot provide a practical tool-box for the interpretation of institutional balance in the EC/EU. If ever a system of interest representation based on a division 'property holders–non-property holders' has been justified, it is surely not the case for systems of governance in the twenty-first century. Due to industrialization, informatization and globalization people identify with various groups and

---

[24] Sunstein, 'Interest groups in American Public Law', 38 *Stanford Law Review* (1985–1986) 29, at 42.

[25] Craig, *supra* n. 21, at 332–333; and H. F. Pitkin, *The Concept of Representation* (1972), at 191–196.

[26] See Gargarella, 'Full Representation, Deliberation, and Impartiality', in J. Elster (ed.), *Deliberative Democracy* (1998) 260, at 264–269.

[27] Gargarella's reading of Madison is surely not the most common one. Pluralist theorists, for instance, tend to read Madison as the forefather of the idea of interest group competition, and thus focus on Madison's theory of the 'problem of factions'; e.g., R. A. Dahl, *A Preface to Democratic Theory* (1956), chap. 1. Republican theorists argue that the pluralist idea that the result of interest group competition *is* the public good is absent from Madisonian and Federalist thought. They stress that Madisonian thought includes the idea of a common good, and that checks and balances served as a restraint against factional tyranny in the event that national representatives failed to fulfil their responsibilities. See Sunstein, *supra* n. 24, at 44; and Craig, *supra* n. 21, at 333.

territorial levels. The challenge is to provide a system of interest representation in which people feel represented on an equal basis in their various identities.

The reconstruction of the argumentation to retrace institutional balance to the theories of *trias politica* and *checks and balances* suggests that one has to be cautious in using old theories to legitimize new ones. Neither *trias politica* nor *checks and balances* were primarily thought of in terms of interest representation, and even where they introduced elements of interest representation their argumentation cannot simply be transposed to a system of multi-level governance in the twenty-first century. This does not invalidate the normative value of the concept of institutional balance as a system in which balanced interaction between institutions representing different interests ensures deliberation on the common good. Yet to use it as a political principle to structure European governance one should clarify what is meant by such concepts as 'representation' and 'interest'.

B. European Institutions and Interest Representation

Can the European institutions be considered to represent a particular interest or constituency? The concept of representation has multiple meanings.[28] Often it refers to a principal–agent relation which invokes both elements of authorization and of accountability. But representation can also mean 'showing similarity', e.g., a parliament is often assumed to be a microcosmic representation of society. Things or persons can also symbolically represent something or somebody, e.g. both a flag and a president can symbolically represent a country. This example also shows that representation need not necessarily be of a person or persons; abstractions, too, can be represented. In fact representation always involves a certain level of abstraction. Even where an agent has to represent one single individual he/she cannot entirely know all the wishes of that person. This is where the concept of interest comes to the fore.[29] One can represent the (abstract) interest of a single person but also of a group of persons (e.g., the interest of the labour movement). While an interest can still be retraced to some wishes and desires as long as a person or a group of persons are represented, this is no longer the case when representation means 'standing for' pure abstract ideas such as 'the interest of world peace' or 'the national interest'.

In political theory, representation has most commonly been identified with parliament as a representative body regularly accountable to the people via

---

[28] See Pitkin, *supra* n. 25; and A. H. Birch, *The Concepts and Theories of Modern Democracy* (1993), at 69–79.

[29] Pitkin, ibid., at 156.

territorially-based elections (in which case the debate has largely focused on whether a parliamentarian should be representative of the nation as a whole or of the constituency in which he/she is elected).[30] Yet some would also argue that a government is 'representative' when it enjoys popularity among its subjects, i.e., people consider the government representative because it addresses their preferences and desires adequately.[31]

Within the European institutional balance the European Parliament is said to 'represent the peoples of the States brought together in the Community' and the Council is argued to represent 'the Member States' governments'. In these cases 'representation' does not only mean standing for such abstractions as 'the interest of the European peoples' or 'the interests of the Member States/national interests' but it refers also to the direct or indirect 'electoral mandate' of the Parliament and the Council. For the Commission, representation cannot be thought of in terms of electoral authorization and accountability. Thus Lenaerts and Verhoeven state that the Commission, 'contrary to the Council and the European Parliament, . . . is not a representative body'. However, in the first part of their chapter they mention the Commission as an institution which is part of the institutional balance which ensures a 'balanced interaction between representatives of various interests'. Does the Commission represent a particular interest or particular views? The representative nature of the Commission can only be thought of in terms of 'standing for an abstract idea', in this case 'the general interest of the Community'. Such 'standing for' can be deduced from the Commission's institutional prerogatives. If 'the general interest of the Community' is understood as the pursuit of the objectives of the Treaty, the Commission as institution can be assumed to best represent this interest given its institutional role as 'guardian of the Treaty'. Its composition—at least one national of each of the Member States, who are 'chosen on the grounds of their general competence and whose independence is beyond doubt' and who shall in the performance of their duties 'neither seek nor take instructions from any government or from any other body'[32]—and *modus operandi*—principle of collegiality—sustain the credibility of this assumption.

With some goodwill one could also argue that the Court of Justice represents the abstract interest of justice or rule of law, and the Court of Auditors the interest of financial accountability.

However, defining the five European Institutions in terms of interest representation raises several issues:

(1) One should distinguish between the supposed representative nature of an institution and the role of the persons acting within that institution. This

---

[30] Birch, *supra* n. 28, at 71; and J. R. Pennock, *Democratic Political Theory* (1979), at 332–334.

[31] Pitkin, *supra* n. 25, at 229.　　　[32] Article 213 of the EC Treaty.

raises, for instance, the traditional debate on the role of the European Parliament as representative of the peoples and the representative position of the parliamentarian therein. It means also that one cannot simply assume that the Commission represents 'the general interest of the Community' for the only reason that the members of the Commission are called to act in that interest. The members of the Economic and Social Committee, for instance, are equally required to act in all independence 'in the general interest of the Community'.[33]

(2) The position of the Commission also illustrates how difficult it is to identify which interest an institution represents. When 'the general interest of the Community' is understood as the pursuit of the objectives of the Treaty, the Commission could be assumed to represent this interest. Yet could 'the general interest of the Community' not equally be understood as the general interest of all European citizens? And would then, for instance, the European Parliament not be best placed to represent this interest? Moreover, it is precisely the institutional balance which is hoped to overcome the pursuit of self-interest and to arrive at constructive debate on the public good. Could the final outcome of this process not be defined as 'the general interest of the Community'?

(3) The answer to which interest an institution represents will differ according to which normative approach will be used, be it a parliamentary, intergovernmental or regulatory model. Lenaerts and Verhoeven show how the role of the Commission within the institutional balance will differ according to the normative model that is applied. They also argue that none of the three models correspond to the current complex reality of European governance. Yet the question is then on which normative framework can suggestions for reform of the institutional relations be based.

By identifying the 'representative nature' of the five Community Institutions one can better address the question whether all of them should be part of the institutional balance. In particular, one can question whether institutions which merely 'stand for an abstract interest' without reference to a constituency should be considered part of the institutional balance? Where Lenaerts and Verhoeven define institutional balance as balanced interaction between representatives of various interests, the Court of Justice and the Court of Auditors are not included in the list of institutions which they identify as representing a particular interest. Nevertheless, they further state that the Court itself is bound by the principle of institutional balance. One could argue that in the latter case the authors refer to the institutional balance as a legal principle which includes the five Institutions as enshrined in the Treaty, whereas in the former case they refer to the institutional balance as a political

---

[33] Article 258, of the EC Treaty.

principle which does not include institutions merely representing an abstract interest. Nonetheless, this would not resolve the position of the Commission, which also does not represent a constituency.

Consequently, a normative framework is needed which can identify the representative nature of the various institutions and which can justify their 'representative role' within the institutional balance. Moreover, one should also ask whether institutions other than the current five (can) play a representative role within the institutional balance.

C. How encompassing is the Institutional Balance?

As argued above, the traditional interpretation of the institutional balance is concerned with the five Community Institutions and especially with the EP–Council–Commission relation. In the first part of their chapter, Lenaerts and Verhoeven define institutional balance in broader terms including also other organs enshrined in the Treaty, such as the Economic and Social Committee and the Committee of the Regions. Moreover, they add that 'one could complement this list by referring to the many instances wherein *European law* accommodates for the participation of functional interests in European governance' (emphasis added). This formulation suggests that the institutional balance could also include the many bodies and representative structures for functional participation established by secondary European law.[34]

It is not clear whether these considerations concern the institutional balance as legal principle or as political principle, or whether it only refers to what they call ' "the institutional balance" as it exists in practice'. The latter expression is confusing when one is used to the concept of institutional balance as a 'normative standard', either to adapt institutional practice to the norm of the Treaty (legal principle) or to adapt institutional practice to a more fundamental norm based on democratic theory (political principle). If one does not use the concept of institutional balance to describe the actual institutional practice but only as a legal or political principle, the question remains: which institutions should be considered part of that balance?

Even as a legal principle the concept of institutional balance need not, by definition, be limited to the five Community Institutions as in the 'traditional reading' of that balance. One could consider the institutional balance to be composed of all the institutions whose role is defined in the Treaty.[35] The

---

[34] It should be noted, though, that Lenaerts and Verhoeven give as the only example the participation of organized labour and management in the making of European social policy; i.e., precisely an institutional structure for the participation of functional interests which *is* (partially) enshrined in the Treaty.

[35] In a similar sense, Vos, *supra* n. 20, at 88.

Court of Justice would ensure this institutional balance as a legal principle, i.e., it will ensure that the prerogatives of all these organs are respected. The underlying idea is that the relationship between all these institutions, as defined by the Treaty, would ensure debate on the public good which will lead to 'solutions that are acceptable to all and do not unduly abridge the liberties of anyone'. Thus, in certain policy domains—as expressed in the legal basis— a 'representative debate on the common good' is only assumed to have taken place when also the ESC and/or the COR are consulted, representing respectively the 'various categories of economic and social activity' and the 'regional and local bodies'. If the 'democratic input' of these institutions is taken seriously as part of the institutional balance[36] the Court should protect the prerogatives of these bodies in the same way as it has done for the five Community Institutions. Case law on the prerogatives of the European Parliament, especially when it had still merely consultative power, may be a source of inspiration. In *Roquette Frères*, for instance, the Court protected the prerogatives of the EP—in that case its consultative power—arguing that it reflects at Community level 'the fundamental democratic principles that the peoples should take part in the exercise of power through the intermediary of a representative assembly'; it therefore ruled that the Council should not act before the EP's opinion is received, and the Council must use all the available means to receive timely advice from the EP.[37] Acknowledging the 'democratic input' of the ESC and the COR within the institutional balance, comparable requirements could be formulated in cases where the Treaty provides compulsory consultation of these institutions.[38]

Also the participation of management and labour in European social policy, as enshrined in Articles 138 and 139 of the EC Treaty, can be considered

[36] One could note that when the Court built up the supranational features of the Community in *Van Gend en Loos*, stressing the direct links between citizens and the European level, it stated that 'the nationals of the states brought together in the Community are called upon to cooperate in the functioning of this Community through the intermediary of the European Parliament and the Economic and Social Committee'. Case 26/62, *Van Gend en Loos* [1963] ECR 8.

[37] Case 138/79, *SA Roquette Frères v Council* [1980] ECR 3333, at 3360, paras 33–36.

[38] One could also ask whether the ESC and the COR as part of the institutional balance should not have standing to call the Court of Justice to ensure that their functions are respected. Under Article 230 EC Treaty this is currently not possible. It is unlikely that the Court would accord to the ESC and the COR *ius standi* without Article 230 EC being changed. In the case of the EP, which lacked equally such right under Article 230 (then 173 EEC) Treaty, the Court has only accorded *ius standi* after the EP had acquired cooperation power (Case 70/88, *Chernobyl* [1990] ECR I-2041) and even then with reluctance (Case 302/87, *Parliament v Council (Comitology)* [1988] ECR 5615). The most practical way to ensure that the ESC and the COR—in accordance with their representative role in the institutional balance—would have *ius standi* to defend their prerogatives (even if merely advisory) is to provide such right in Article 230 EC Treaty; which implies a Treaty revision and brings us thus to the level of 'institutional balance as a political principle'.

to be part of the 'legal' institutional balance. Though not an 'organ' with legal personality and own administration, we have to do here with a procedure— or 'institution' in the broad sense of the word—endorsed by the Treaty which guarantees the representation of certain interests. The Court of First Instance has recognized in *UEAPME* that this procedure is an expression of the principle of democracy, namely that the participation of the parties representative of management and labour could compensate for the lack of parliamentary involvement in these cases.[39] Yet, the Court has refrained from using the concept of institutional balance in this context.

Is the list of institutions to be considered part of the institutional balance as legal principle thus complete? Or should organs such as the European Central Bank (ECB) or the European Investment Bank (EIB), which are equally enshrined in the Treaty, also be part of the list?[40] If institutional balance is defined as a legal principle stressing respect of the prerogatives of all institutions/organs that are enshrined in the Treaty, those organs could also be included. However, by including automatically all organs enshrined in the Treaty in the institutional balance, the concept would be reduced to a simple application of the rule of law and would be emptied of its 'legitimating potential', be it either its link with territorial representation as in the traditional reading, or its role of balanced interest representation geared towards the formulation of the common good as in the new reading. Consequently, institutional balance as a legal principle cannot be isolated from normative considerations.

If institutional balance is used as a 'political principle' one cannot take a positivist approach and simply refer to the Treaty. The broad definition of institutional balance as a political principle raises questions not only on which institutions and organs currently provided by the Treaty should be part of the institutional balance but equally on whether other institutions not currently provided by the Treaty should be included in that balance. This institutional balance may also include 'the many instances wherein European law accommodates the participation of functional interests in European governance'. It does not follow that the institutional balance can be guaranteed by secondary European law. As a political principle the institutional balance is a normative tool to shape the European constitutional framework, i.e., it addresses the question of which interaction of institutions should be enshrined in the Treaty (and then ensured as a legal principle) to realize legitimate governance.

---

[39] '. . . the principle of democracy on which the Union is founded requires—in the absence of the participation of the European Parliament in the legislative process—that the participation of the people be otherwise assured, in this instance through the parties representative of management and labour who concluded the agreement which is endowed by the Council . . .' Case T-135/96, *UEAPME v Council* [1998] ECR II-2335, at 2371.

[40] See in this sense Vos, *supra* n. 20, at 88.

As argued above, the traditional reading of the institutional balance does not reflect the complexity of European governance. To ensure the rule of law and legitimate governance, the constitutional framework should be adjusted. Such 'adjustment' does not mean that the Treaty should be a detailed descriptive account of the entire institutional practice. Nevertheless, the Treaty should provide an institutional balance which identifies the role of the main institutions (beyond the current five), their relationships and the way in which they ensure adequate representation and legitimate governance. Moreover, the constitutional framework should provide constitutional norms—such as principles of accountability, transparency, good administration and political and judicial control—to structure the complex 'infranational reality' of European governance and more precisely to define the relation of these infranational structures to the main identified (representative) institutions. Such a framework can only be shaped taking account of normative considerations about the nature of EU governance, the form of democratic process and types of representation. In particular, narratives of territorial representation should be complemented by normative considerations about functional representation.

III. WHO IS AFRAID OF FUNCTIONAL REPRESENTATION?

The traditional reading of the institutional balance has defined the legitimacy of EU governance in terms of rule of law and territorial representation. Yet, as already mentioned, the European institutional practice also includes many forms of functional participation, i.e., the participation in European policy-making of private interest groups, public interest groups, social partners, NGOs, voluntary organizations and/or civil society organizations.[41] They participate via informal lobbying and via formalized representative structures. Such functional representation includes fora like the ESC and advisory committees as well as procedures for consultation of the social partners and civil society. The 'new' reading of the institutional balance opens the door for these forms of functional representation as possible elements of the institutional balance which gears deliberations towards the attainment of the public good.

However, to date the broadened definition of institutional balance has not yet led to a profound analysis of how functional participation should be insti-

---

[41] These concepts are partially overlapping, and the given definitions depend strongly on the context. The concept of 'interest groups' could cover many of these groups. Yet 'interest groups' has often been identified with 'private interests' so that other concepts have been sought to name groups as voluntary associations or trade unions. The concept of functional participation enables the distinction of the participation of all these intermediary groups from participation via territorial representation or from direct citizen participation.

tutionalized and constitutionalized. Also Lenaerts and Verhoeven focus with their two 'case studies' especially on the traditional EP–Council–Commission relationship—though in an innovative manner. In that context functional participation is used as an argument to state that the Commission represents 'the general interest of the Community' pointing to the Commission's practice of consulting various interests. One might be tempted to see the institutional balance as a balance between the EP, the Council and the Commission, in which on the one hand the EP and the Council represent the democratic input via territorial representation and on the other hand the Commission 'absorbs' the role of functional representation. However, such interpretation cannot be taken for granted, neither descriptively nor normatively.

Descriptively one should note that even within the EP–Council–Commission trio the Commission is not the sole focus of functional participation. The European Parliament, for instance, organizes hearings to involve civil society organizations. Moreover, as equally acknowledged by Lenaerts and Verhoeven, the Rome Treaty established the Economic and Social Committee precisely to represent 'the various social and economic categories' and the EC Treaty provisions on the social dialogue provide opportunities for functional participation which go beyond the mere consultation of the social partners by the Commission. Beyond the Treaty, European secondary law provides several organs, independent of the Commission, which facilitate functional participation. European agencies, for instance, enhance functional participation via the establishment of networks.

Normatively one should ask how functional representation should be addressed at the constitutional level. Can functional representation be ensured within an institutional balance limited to the EP–Council–Commission trio? Which legal (and/or Treaty) provisions should then be taken to ensure that the Commission or EP represent the variety of interest groups? Consequently, the problem of defining the interest or the constituency represented by the institutions composing the institutional balance should be linked to the question of how to proceduralize the participation of interest groups in the main institutions. Several authors have explored the idea of codifying and developing a detailed regulation of the participation of interested parties in European decision-making by virtue of an (American-type) Administrative Procedure Act (APA) which would impose stringent requirements on the administration in terms of procedural law of rule-making, transparency, public participation and judicial review.[42] Would such

---

[42] Curtin, *supra* n. 3, at 266; Shapiro, 'Codification of Administrative Law: The US and the Union', 2 *ELJ* (1996) 26; Harlow, 'Codification of EC Administrative Procedures? Fitting the Foot to the Shoe or the Shoe to the Foot', 2 *ELJ* (1996) 3; Vos, 'EU Committees: the Evolution of Unforeseen Institutional Actors in European Product Regulation', in C. Joerges and E. Vos (eds), *EU Committees: Social Regulation, Law and Politics* (1999) 19; and Dehousse,

an APA enable the Commission to absorb the role of functional representation? Or should still other institutions (equally subject to the APA) ensure functional representation? Should this or these institutions then be part of the institutional balance? As already mentioned, the Economic and Social Committee is enshrined in the Treaty to represent the 'economic and social categories' and it could be considered part of an institutional balance that ensures deliberation on the common good via a balanced interaction between institutions representing different interests or constituencies. It has even been argued that the Economic and Social Committee could be developed into an associative parliament, becoming the central forum for civil society organizations within the European institutional set-up.[43] In recent years the Committee has indeed developed several initiatives to become a broader 'representative forum of organized civil society' rather than a mere committee representing occupational interests,[44] and the Nice Treaty has made a small change in the definition of the Committee's composition to confirm this development.[45] However, even if the Economic and Social Committee's composition and competence changed more profoundly[46] it would never be able to monopolize the role of functional representation within the multi-level polity which is the EU. Yet it does not follow that the (reformed) Economic and Social Committee cannot play a particular representative role within the institutional balance. Moreover, there is no reason to state *a priori* that the recognition of an institution (or institutions) ensuring functional representation within the institutional balance cannot be combined with the introduction of an APA. Both techniques are not, by definition, alternatives but can be complementary.

In order to be able to answer whether (new) bodies for functional participation should be part of the institutional balance and whether an APA would be able to structure functional participation within the traditional or within a broadened institutional balance there is need for more developed narratives on functional participation. However, despite the extended character of func-

'Towards a Regulation of Transitional Governance? Citizens' Rights and the Reform of Comitology Procedures', in ibid., at 109.

[43] Van der Voort, *In Search of a Role. The Economic and Social Committee in European Decision Making* (1997), at 325–338.

[44] See Smismans, 'The European Economic and Social Committee: towards deliberative democracy via a functional assembly', 4 *EIoP* (2000) 12, at <http://eiop.or.at/eiop/texte/2000-012a.htm>.

[45] According to the new Article 257 EC, the Committee will be composed of 'representatives of the various economic and social components of organised civil society' and no longer of 'representatives of the various social and economic categories'.

[46] The Nice Treaty will not change substantially the current role of the Economic and Social Committee; its competence and the appointment procedure of its members remain unchanged and even the new definition of its composition retains the former list of 'socio-economic categories' which should 'in particular' be represented in the Committee.

tional participation, it is surprising to note that this issue has hardly been addressed in normative debate on EU governance. On the one hand, there is a broad descriptive literature on EU lobbying[47] and on the social dialogue.[48] On the other hand, the democratic deficit debate has centred on territorial representation and the parliamentary model and, since Maastricht, on issues such as citizenship, subsidiarity and transparency.[49] The latter has sometimes been linked to the participation of interest groups but a broader normative account on the role of functional participation and representation in the EU has not developed—despite the increasing popularity of normative accounts on the nature of EU governance.[50]

This lack of a normative account of functional participation can be explained by the dominance of territorial representation within political theory and by the general identification of democracy with territorial representation within the practice of the (European) nation states. Functional participation has theoretically most commonly been addressed with reference to the concepts of (neo-)pluralism and (neo-)corporatism. Both have above all been used as descriptive models of interest intermediation;[51] the first mainly identified with the US, the second with the Western European nation states. However, pluralism soon took *Sein* for *Sollen*;[52] the process of interest group competition was assumed to be the best guarantee to define the common good. Neo-pluralists, on the contrary, acknowledged that such an assumption could not be taken for granted, given the imbalances of resources among the

---

[47] E.g., Claeys *et al.* (eds), *Lobbying, Pluralism and European Integration* (1998); J. Greenwood, *Representing Interests in the European Union* (1997); J. Greenwood, J. R. Grote and R. Karsten (eds), *Organized Interests and the European Community* (1992); S. Mazey and J. Richardson (eds), *Lobbying in the European Community* (1993); H. Wallace and A. Young (eds), *Participation and Policy-making in the European Union* (1997).

[48] E.g., Bercusson and Van Dijk, 'The Implementation of the Protocol and Agreement on Social Policy of the Treaty on European Union', *International Journal of Comparative Labour Law and Industrial Relations* (1995) 3; G. Falkner, *EU Social Policy in the 1990s. Towards a Corporatist Policy Community* (1998); Falkner, 'The Maastricht Protocol on Social Policy: Theory and Practice', 6 *Journal of European Social Policy* (1996) 1; Gadbin, 'L'association des partenaires économiques et sociaux aux procédures de décision en droit communautaire', 36 *Revue trimestrielle de droit européen* (2000) 1; Marginson and Sisson, 'European Collective Bargaining: A Virtual Prospect?', 36 *JCMS* (1998) 505.

[49] de Búrca, 'The Quest for Legitimacy in the European Union', 59 *MLR* (1996) 349.

[50] E.g., R. Bellamy, V. Bufacchi and D. Castiglione (eds), *Democracy and Constitutional Culture in the Union of Europe* (1995); D. Beetham and C. Lord, *Legitimacy and the EU* (1998); Cohen and Sabel, 'Directly-Deliberative Polyarchy', 3 *ELJ* (1997) 515; Joerges and Neyer, *supra* n. 4; MacCormick, 'Democracy, Subsidiarity, and Citizenship in the "European Commonwealth"', 16 *Law and Philosophy* (1997) 331; A. Weale and M. Nentwich (eds), *Political Theory and the European Union* (1998).

[51] The early pluralists called themselves 'empirical democratic theorists' since they would analyse how politics really worked. D. Held, *Models of Democracy* (2nd edn., 1996), at 199.

[52] Birch, *supra* n. 28, at 164.

interest groups. Legal provisions were required to ensure 'equal access' for interest groups. Neo-pluralism thus developed as a normative model which greatly inspired the shaping of interest intermediation in US administrative law.[53] On the European continent, though, neo-corporatism was developed to describe systems of interest intermediation which were clearly distinct from the American pluralist description. But authors as Schmitter and Lehmbruch stressed that they did not use 'neo-corporatism' as a normative model.[54] They also used the prefix 'neo' to clearly distinguish 'liberal corporatism' in the democratic European states from the 'authoritarian corporatism'[55] developed in the authoritarian regimes of fascist Italy and Germany and the Spanish and Portuguese dictatorships, and from the normative models of corporatism that had degenerated in these regimes. In the first part of the twentieth century several theories on functional participation and representation were developed on the European continent, going from the British pluralists, guild socialism and anarcho-syndicalism to corporatist theories based on the idea of 'organic solidarity and morality' within a corporation (bringing management and labour together in each sector or profession).[56] The latter was recuperated by extreme right-wing ideology. Though the theories of 'functional representation' were more divers than corporatist theories, and though even the latter differed seriously from what the authoritarian regimes made out of it,[57] the issue of functional representation seems to have become a taboo in democratic theory.[58] Democratic theory has entirely returned to issues of territorial representation whereas theories on interest intermediation have limited themselves to giving a descriptive account of how interest group participation is structured. Parallel to this lack of normative theories, constitutional and administrative law on the European continent pay little attention to func-

---

[53] See M. Shapiro, *Who Guards the Guardians?* (1988), at 36–54; Stewart, 'The Reformation of American Administrative Law', 88 *Harvard Law Review* (1975) 1667; Sunstein, *supra* n. 24.

[54] 'Defining corporatism in terms of its praxis, the concept is liberated from its employment in any particular ideology or system of ideas', Schmitter, 'Still the Century of Corporatism?' in P. C. Schmitter and G. Lehmbruch (eds), *Trends Toward Corporatist Intermediation* (1979) 7, at 8.

[55] These concepts are used by Lehmbruch, 'Consociational Democracy, Class Conflict, and the New Corporatism', in ibid., 53, at 53; Schmitter uses the concepts of 'societal corporatism' and 'state corporatism', see Schmitter, 'Modes of Interest Intermediation and Models of Societal Change in Western Europe', in ibid., 63, at 67.

[56] P. Q. Hirst (ed.), *The Pluralist Theory of the State: Selected Writings of G. D. H. Cole, J. N. Figgis, and H. J. Laski* (1989); Hyman, 'Pluralism, Procedural Consensus and Collective Bargaining', *British Journal of Industrial Relations* (1978) 16; G. A. M. Vogelaar, *Democratie en Corporatisme* (1945).

[57] As the corporatist theorist Bowen had already put it in 1947, 'the actual political and economic organization of the Third Reich did not even roughly correspond to the specifications laid down by any of the main schools of corporatist theory', cited in A. Black, *Guilds & Civil Society* (1984), at 233.

[58] Ibid., at 234.

tional participation. So issues such as collective agreements among the social partners—sometimes with the value of a law—are exiled to the sector of (collective) labour law, safely separated from constitutional design and democratic theory. Lacking a normative model, and contrary to what is sometimes assumed, the 'neo-corporatist' interest intermediation in the European countries is less subject to legal provisions than interest group participation in the US, inspired by the neo-pluralist model.[59]

The lack of a normative model for functional representation[60] and the lack of a legal translation thereof may no longer be tenable. Even at national level, forms of functional participation and representation have multiplied and the idea that legitimate governance can be resumed in territorial representation combined with 'neutral bureaucratic implementation' is ever more a fiction. Moreover, citizens show increasing dissatisfaction with the limits of territorial representation.

At the European level there are extra reasons to provide a normative and legal framework for functional participation. The debate on the lack of a European demos[61] and of a European public sphere[62] has illustrated the particular difficulties of building the legitimacy of European governance on territorial representation. Participation via the intermediary of groups might be an additional source of legitimacy for European governance.

I am not pleading to establish at European level whatever proposed model of functional representation, be it of British or American, pluralist or corporatist design. I argue, though, that functional participation should be taken seriously as an issue of constitutional design, given the extensive nature of the phenomenon and the limits of territorial representation. The idea of European governance legitimized by an institutional balance between the EP, the Council and the Commission, retraced entirely to democratic input via territorial representation, does not correspond to reality. The 'new' reading of the institutional balance recognizes that various types of representation can constitute an institutional equilibrium ensuring legitimate governance. Functional representation can thus complement territorial representation.

---

[59] According to Salisbury, 'no democratic nation even remotely approximates the seriousness of the American effort to regulate the details of group-government interactions'. Salisbury, 'Why No Corporatism in America?', in P. C. Schmitter and G. Lehmbruch (eds), *Trends Toward Corporatist Intermediation* (1979) 213, at 221.

[60] More recently theories of associative democracy have been developed. However, they have not (yet) been translated in institutional and legal practice and discours. E.g., P. Hirst, *Associative Democracy* (1994); and J. Cohen and J. Rogers (eds), *Associations and Democracy. The Real Utopias Project* (1995).

[61] Weiler, Haltern and Mayer, 'European Democracy and Its Critique', 18 *West European Politics* (1995) 4.

[62] Meyer, 'European Public Sphere and Societal Politics', in M. Telo (ed.), *Démocratie et construction européenne* (1995) 123.

However, to realize to the full the potential of the 'new' reading one needs a narrative which can guide and theoretically defend the organization of functional representation, in the same way as we are accustomed to narratives of territorial representation.

4

The Judge and the Community's Administrative Governance

LOÏC AZOULAY

INTRODUCTION

The field of relationships between the Community judge and its administration is dominated by the chronology and complexity of the process of European integration. Between these two agents of the integration process the link is neither immediate nor universal. But as it is taking shape and developing today, it is becoming a nodal point of the Community's institutional balance.

We must first understand how the link can be forged and what its present meaning is (see Section I). It is in the Community's economic administration that the judge's role is most important. In this area, the judge seeks to resolve the major difficulty attaching to his function: to *supervise* the administration without *constraining* it in its action. This judicial strategy leads to a new understanding of the Rule of Law founded on procedure (see Section II). This is, however, limited within the Community administration to individual proceedings. In the general context of the regulatory system the question is no longer how to ensure *protection* of individuals involved without endangering the *efficiency* of administrative action, but becomes how to organize *coordination* of all persons interested without endangering the *flexibility* that is the basis for the administrative system. How are we to move from 'good administration' to 'administrative democracy'? (see Section III). This question raises the old problem of the legitimacy of public action (see Section IV). The very notion of administration needs today to be rethought. The classic sense of a technical instrument in the service of the legislator has to be augmented by the idea of administration as a central form of governance, remote from the classical models of political representation and judicial review. This is the meaning of a new institutional balance (see Section V).

I. THE ORIGIN OF THE ADMINISTRATIVE JUDGE

The Community's institutional balance rests on an 'essentially legislative conception' of integration, leaving little room for the administration.[1] In the initial plan of the Community structure, it has to be borne in mind that:

national administrations are called on to play an important part, given that the Community administration is only exceptionally a territorial one. While normative execution is, according to the case, ensured by the Community authorities alone, or the national authorities jointly, or by national authorities alone, administrative enforcement rests essentially on the national administrations, which are thus concerned by the founding treaties, and more generally by Community law, which come to form part of the set of texts of which they are to ensure implementation.[2]

The Community administration has accordingly to be regarded chiefly as one for conception rather than enforcement. Within the Community, this distinction has come to be seen almost as an axiom.[3] That the Commission possesses a certain power of direct enforcement has to be accepted, but this is limited and in every case subsidiary.[4] This is the original conception the Community has of 'executive federalism'.[5]

   This last feature has been notably highlighted. It still marks whole major areas of the integration process.[6] The principle of it is continually reaffirmed.[7] Yet it can no longer claim to be absolutely true. The Community's administrative dimension, with its source from the outset in Article 211 EC, became manifest as from the nineties.[8] The prospect of a single market opened up in 1986 by the Single European Act was to promote development of anticompetitive practices and slippage of economic construction towards social

---

[1] G. Majone, *La Communauté europeenne: un Etat régulateur* (1996) 37.
[2] Rideau, 'Traités constitutifs et Administrations dans l'Union et les Communautés européennes', 16 *Annuaire européen d'administration publique* (1993) 239, at 240.
[3] See, e.g., Pescatore, 'L'exécutif communautaire: justification du quadripartisme institué par les traités de Paris et de Rome', 14 *Cahiers de droit européen* (1978) 387.
[4] Cf. Case C-476/93 P, *Nutral v Commission* [1995] ECR I-4125.
[5] Cf. Lenaerts, 'Regulating the Regulatory Process: "Delegation of powers" in the European Community', *ELR* (1993) 23, at 28.
[6] See esp. R. Barents, *The Agricultural Law of the EC. An Inquiry into the Administrative Law of the European Community in the Field of Agriculture* (1994).
[7] The Declaration relating to the protocol on application of the principles of subsidiarity and proportionality annexed to the Amsterdam Treaty reaffirms that 'the implementation in administrative terms of Community law is in principle incumbent on Member States, in accordance with their constitutional systems'. It adds, however, that 'the supervision, monitoring and implementing powers conferred on the Community institutions pursuant to Articles 202 and 211 of the Treaty establishing the European Community shall not be affected'.
[8] See J. Schwarze, *European Administrative Law* (1992); M. P. Chiti, *Diritto amministrativo europeo* (1999).

regulatory policies. It is no coincidence that the extension of the Commission's powers to all areas of competition policy[9] and the enhancement of its competence in environment, health and consumer safety matters[10] date from just this period. This move from market integration to 'regulation' has been amply studied.[11] But one of its least noted effects is the growth of the Community administration. As a result of this evolution, the administration has in fact taken on a primary role, not just to 'ensure the functioning and development of the common market', but still more to drive the process of market building.[12]

In this rise of the Community administration the judge has had a special part to play. He no longer appears as the constitutional judge enabling the emergence of the 'legal and economic constitution' of Community Europe.[13] The great period of judicial activism coincides with the first twenty-five years of European integration. What we are now seeing is a twofold contrary movement of 'rise in jurisdictional power' and 'decline in jurisprudential power'.[14] This movement corresponds exactly to the birth of the Court of First Instance of the European Communities as the Community's 'true administrative judge'.[15] While its creation marks the end of the judicial teleology of integration, it would be wrong to think that all the issues have disappeared. At the centre of the previous period was the 'empty chair crisis' and consequent development of a genuine 'law of market integration'.[16] At the heart of the new period is the 'mad cow crisis' and the need to invent a new 'law of economic and social regulation'.[17] Lawyers' attention has shifted accordingly. It is no longer centred on the efficacy of judicial cooperation mechanisms[18] but

---

[9] See Gerber, 'The Transformation of European Community Competition Law', 35 *Harvard International Law Journal* (1994) 97.

[10] Cf. R. Dehousse et al., *Europe After 1992. New Regulatory Strategies*, EUI Working Paper Law, 92/3, Florence (1992).

[11] One reference that has become indispensable is G. Majone, *La Communauté européenne: un Etat régulateur* (1996); see also Dehousse, 'Integration *v* Regulation? On the Dynamics of Regulation in the European Community', 30 *JCMS* (1992) 383.

[12] See Streeck, 'From Market-Making to State-Building? Reflections on the Political Economy of European Social Policy', in S. Leibfried and P. Pierson (eds), *European Social Policy. Between Fragmentation and Integration* (1995) 389.

[13] See K. Lenaerts, *Le Juge et la Constitution aux Etats-Unis d'Amérique et dans l'ordre juridique européen* (1988).

[14] See, in French law, Linotte, 'Déclin du pouvoir jurisprudentiel et ascension du pouvoir juridictionnel en droit administratif', 36 *Actualité juridique–Droit administratif* (1980) 632.

[15] R. Dehousse, *La Cour de justice des Communautés européennes* (1994), at 32.

[16] See P. Pescatore, *Le droit de l'intégration. Emergence d'un phénomène nouveau dans les relations internationales selon l'expérience des Communautés européennes* (1972).

[17] See in general Frison-Roche, 'Le droit de la régulation', 7 *Dalloz* (2001).

[18] Weiler, 'The Community System. The Dual Character of Supranationalism', 1 *YEL* (1981) 257.

on the possibility of creating the conditions for legitimate governance in Europe.[19]

This is the new challenge for the law in Europe: creating 'good government'. Is the judge capable of bringing in some features of legitimacy?

II. THE JUDGE'S ROLE IN DEVELOPING A 'GOOD ADMINISTRATION'

In the areas of economic regulation the Community has developed a system of administration reflecting the tensions and contradictions of a period of integration. This system undoubtedly began with Council Regulation 17/62 creating a system of centralized control in anti-trust matters.[20] It was subsequently extended to all branches of economic regulation.[21] It is based essentially on the use of deterrent powers and the adoption of individual measures. Guarantees of individual protection have been in the texts since 1962. But it is the judge who strove within the various systems to pick out the general, enhanced instruments for protecting those involved (see A below). This development today lets us speak of a true 'jurisdictionalized' administration (see B); but this development is not without limits (see C).

A. The Jurisdictional Limits to Administrative Discretionality

Discretionary power is the principle of all the Commission's administrative interventions. In this sector it enjoys an 'executive competence' close to a reserved area.[22] Taking its model from the ECSC High Authority and its function directly from the treaty, it has general, autonomous decision-making powers.[23]

The Community judge has justified this discretion on the ground that these decisions ultimately rest on 'complex assessments'.[24] It follows that the

---

[19] Joerges, ' "Good Governance" Through Comitology?', in C. Joerges and E. Vos (eds), *EU Committees: Social Regulation, Law and Politics* (1999).

[20] See Ellis, 'Les règles de concurrence du Traité de Rome applicables aux entreprises', 15 *Revue internationale de droit comparé* (1963) 299.

[21] Thus, in relation to merger control (Council Regulation 4064/89, OJ 1989 L 395/1, rectified version OJ 1990 L 257/13, amended in 1997, OJ 1997, L 180/1), control of State aids (Council Regulation 659/1999, OJ 1999 L 83/1), anti-dumping control (Council Regulation 384/96, OJ 1996 L 56/1).

[22] D. Triantafyllou, *Des compétences d'attribution au domaine de la loi. Etude sur les fondements juridiques de l'activité administrative communautaire* (1997), at 280–282.

[23] Case 41/69, *ACF Chemiefarma v Commission* [1970] ECR 661.

[24] See Ritleng, 'Le juge communautaire de la légalité et le pouvoir discrétionnaire des institutions communautaires', 55 *Actualité juridique–Droit administratif* (1999) 645.

judge refuses to 'substitute his own evaluation for the Commission's'.[25] Accordingly, judicial control is in principle limited control.[26] That does not mean it is zero. On the contrary, the enhancement of control in recent years in the CFI case law is noteworthy. It relates first to the facts.[27] But in this sense, it is first and foremost procedural.

From an analysis of the CFI case law it clearly emerges that

in cases where the Commission has a power of evaluation in order to carry out its tasks, the respect for procedural guarantees conferred by the Community legal system in administrative proceedings is of all the more fundamental importance.[28]

This passage is a remarkable pointer to the latest stage of Community case law on review of economic administration. The review has not so much been reduced as transferred. The logic it reveals is the one gradually emerging in Community administrative law: the granting of major discretionary power to the administration henceforth corresponds to respect for extended procedural guarantees. This can be schematically reconstructed as follows: discretionary power is legitimate and must be respected, so that review is limited; but limited review does not mean that there should not be strict control, this will accordingly relate essentially to respect for procedural rights enshrined by the judge over and above the texts.

This review is based on the principle that guides every action by the judge in his mission to ensure 'respect for the law' (Article 220 EC):

in all Member State legal systems intervention by the authorities in the sphere of private activity of any person, whether physical or legal, must have a legal basis and be justified by grounds provided for by law, and . . .these systems consequently, though in different ways, provide protection against intervention that might be arbitrary or disproportionate. The need for such protection must be recognized as a general principle of Community law.[29]

The principle of *legal protection* applies on the one hand to 'protection through the existence of an appropriate legal basis which at the same time furnishes the points of reference for the review bodies'[30] and on the other to

---

[25] Case T-3/93, *Air France v Commission* [1994] ECR II-121.

[26] For a comparison of control in the various areas of complex economic intervention, see the conclusions of Advocate-General Cosmas presented on 28 March 1996 in *Re Germany et al v Commission* [1996] ECR I-5161.

[27] See Lenaerts, 'Le Tribunal de première instance des Communautés européennes: regard sur une décennie d'activités et sur l'apport du double degré d'instance au droit communautaire', 56 *Cahiers de droit européen* (2000) 323.

[28] Case T-7/92, *Asia Motor France et al v Commission* [1993] ECR II-694. This formula first appeared in *Technische Universität München* and has since several times been repeated by the Court and CFI (Case C-269/90, *Technische Universität München* [1991] ECR I-5499).

[29] Joined Cases 46/87 and 227/88, *Hoechst v Commission* [1989] ECR 2924.

[30] Cf. D. Triantafyllou, *Des compétences d'attribution au domaine de la loi. Etude sur les fondements juridiques de l'activité administrative communautaire* (1997), at 206.

Judicial protection.[31] This is the principle that today enables protection to be extended to the stage of administrative procedure. Thus, the introduction of procedural guarantees attests a remarkable extension of the Rule of Law in the Community'.[32] In Community law there exists, alongside the famous 'right to the judge', a real 'right to the procedure'.[33] This right is assuredly contributing to the construction of a new mode of 'administrative governance'.

B. A 'Jurisdictionalized' Administration

The form of this governance is the outcome of an interaction between Community case law and the Commission's administrative practices. For his part the judge identifies a common, unwritten principle: 'the general principle of the rights of the defence'. Following a procedure of extension by analogy he ensures its application in all individual procedures well beyond the areas where the texts had enshrined them. Accordingly, 'respect for the rights of the defence in all proceedings against a person liable to lead to an adverse act constitutes a fundamental principle of Community law that must be ensured even in the absence of any regulation concerning the procedure'.[34] This formula means that the content of the guarantees is amplified, their field of application extended and their effects reinforced.[35]

---

[31] In this form it is Advocate-General W. van Gerven who supplies the most rigorous definition: 'In this context we mean by *legal protection* the possibility belonging to any holder of a right, a power or a prerogative to approach the judiciary power on their own initiative, i.e. their own judgment, in order to assert that right, power or prerogative' (Conclusions presented in Case C-70/88, *Parliament v Council* [1990] ECR I-2058).

[32] In the strict sense this notion concerns the fact that 'neither the Member States nor the institutions can escape the checking of their acts against the fundamental constitutional charter, the Treaty' (Case 294/83, *The Greens v European Parliament* [1986] ECR 1339). Jacqué points out that 'a Community of law is not a Community of norms, but a Community in which jurisdictional control of respect by the authorities for the rule of law is assured' (Jacqué, 'La Constitution de la Communauté européenne', 6 *Revue universelle des droits de l'homme* (1995), at 406–407). But he does not yet mention this extension to pre-litigation procedure.

[33] For this expression see G. Isaac, *La procédure administrative non contentieuse* (1968), at 219.

[34] Case C-32/95 P, *Commission v Lisrestal et al.* [1996] ECR I-5396. This formula replaces one ensuring 'respect for the rights of the defence in any proceedings likely to lead to *sanctions*, notably fines or penalty payments' (Case 85/76, *Hoffmann-La Roche v Commission* [1979] ECR 511; our emphasis). In the *Lisrestal* case, Advocate-General La Pergola clearly affirmed: 'we find equally devoid of foundation the observations made by the Commission to the effect that the decision attacked does not have the nature of a sanction, and on the absence of procedural rules concerning the protection in question of the enterprises involved'. For 'it is the nature of an *adverse act*, but not necessarily of a *sanction*, that constitutes the necessary and sufficient condition for the addressee of the act to be guaranteed such a right' ([1996] ECR I-5381).

[35] On all these points, L. Azoulay, *Les garanties procédurales en droit communautaire. Recherches sur la procédure et le bon gouvernement* (thesis on file at the EUI, Florence 2000).

Far from slowing this development, the Commission has in some respects anticipated it. Efforts have been made in order, apart from any new obligation, to strengthen the independence of the institution charged with taking decisions relating to competition. These have seen the creation of the position of *hearing counsellor*, whose role is to ensure 'respect for the rights of the defence, while taking account of the need for effective application of the competition rules'.[36] This difficult conciliation role, sometimes regarded as impossible,[37] seems by now to have become well-integrated[38] and established.[39] In the same sense, the CFI has recognized that by 'establishing a procedure of access to the file in competition cases the Commission has imposed on itself rules going beyond the requirements formulated by the Court'; accordingly, 'it should be noted that the Commission cannot depart from the rules it has thus imposed on itself'.[40] At present, it is a Commission communication that lays down the *internal* rules of procedure for processing requests for access to the file.[41] The Commission thus opens itself up to interpretation of recent developments in the case law and its own practice. This type of act enables it to set its own 'case law' in an already highly normalized context. Such acts fit perfectly into what has been called 'reflexive legality' and an 'organizational conscience'.[42] They should end up by being integrated into the regulation framework.[43] But their existence corresponds to a spontaneous concern to 'securitize' individuals and 'moralize' the administration. The

---

[36] Art. 2 of the Commission Decision of 12 December 1994, OJ 1994 L 330/67.

[37] See Louis, 'Droits de la défense et efficacité des procédures: l'inconciliable peut-il être concilié?', in Association Européenne des Avocats (AEA) (ed.), *Un rôle pour la defense dans les procédures communautaires de concurrence* (1997) 39.

[38] See the opinion of a DG IV hearing counsellor, Gilchrist, 'Rights of Defence and Access to File', in ibid., at 29.

[39] Advocate-General Vesterdorf states that since the Commission has chosen to bring in rules going beyond the administrative procedural guarantees respect for which the case law requires, or which result from written regulation bases, 'it may at least be affirmed that it must necessarily respect them, even though it was not legally bound to give itself those rules' (Advocate-General Vesterdorf's conclusions, Case T-1/89, *Rhône-Poulenc v Commission* [1991] ECR II-889).

[40] Case T-7/89, *Hercules Chemicals v Commission* [1991] ECR II-1739.

[41] OJ 1997 C 23/3.

[42] In relation to economic organizations see G. Teubner, *Le droit, un système autopoiétique*, translated from German by N. Boucquey and G. Maier (1993), at 101 et seq.; G. Teubner, *Droit et réflexivité. L'autoréférence en droit et dans l'organisation*, translated from German by N. Boucquey and G. Maier (1994), at 46–47.

[43] By inserting them in a Regulation: 'it is appropriate to ensure compatibility between the current administrative practices of the Commission and the case law of the Court of Justice and Court of First Instance of the European Communities' (Commission Regulation 2842/98, OJ 1998 L 354/18, recital no. 10 (anti-competitive practices); Commission Regulation 447/98, OJ 1998, L 61/1, recital no. 3 (mergers); recital no. 10 (anti-competitive practices); Council Regulation 659/199, OJ 1999 L 83/1, recital no. 3 (State aids).

Commission thus intends to approach the standards of a 'good administration'.[44] The principle of such administration is now enshrined in Article 41 of the Charter of Fundamental Rights of the European Union, proclaimed at Nice.

The Commission remains, however, under review by the judge. On the one hand, the judge assures the parties directly concerned of judicial protection against the risks of attenuation of the guarantees in practice. In this sense the judge affirms that 'respect for the rights of the defence cannot be obstructed by technical and legal difficulties that an efficient administration can and must overcome'.[45] Likewise, any temptation to 'paternalism', which would amount to sacrificing individual rights in the name of the good faith and goodwill of the authorities,[46] is rejected by the judge.[47] On the other hand, he has accentuated formal protection of third parties interested in the outcome of the procedures. In relation to them protection is reduced in order not to endanger the need for efficiency of administrative review. The judge recognizes this requirement by practically divorcing the 'rights of the defence' from the 'procedural rights', which are poorer, as acknowledged by third parties.[48] But he compensates for this attenuation by recognizing an obligation to give extended reasons and the granting of Judicial guarantees.[49] This largely explains the extension of the right of appeal to interested third parties in all areas of competition policy.[50]

---

[44] Cf. C. D. Ehlermann, 'The European Administration and the Public Administration of Member States with regard to Competition Law', 16 *ECLR* (1995) 454.

[45] Case T-30/91, *Solvay SA v Commission* [1995] ECR II-1819.

[46] Making the whole fairness of the procedure rest entirely on the good faith of the administrative services is a recurrent tendency visible in the Commission's argumentation (see e.g. Case 155/79, *AM & S v Commission* [1982] ECR 1584; and most recently Cases T-305 to 307/94, T-313 to 316/94, T-318/94, T-325/94, T-328 to 329/94 and T-335/94, *Limburgse Vinyl Maatschappij NV et al. v Commission* [1999] ECR II-1029).

[47] In this sense, the Community judge 'takes rights seriously' (Weiler and Lockhart, ' "Taking Rights Seriously" Seriously: The European Court of Justice and Its Fundamental Rights Jurisprudence', 32 *CMLRev.* (1995) 51 and 579).

[48] See originally, in relation to anti-competitive practices, Cases 142 and 156/84, *BAT and Reynolds* [1987] ECR 4573.

[49] See, in exemplary fashion, Cases T-371/94 and T-394/94, *British Airways et al. and British Midland Airways v Commission* [1998] pt 64 ECR II-2436.

[50] This extension has come about on the basis of participation by third parties in the administrative procedure: thus, in relation to anti-competitive practices, Case 26/76, *Metro v Commission* [1977] ECR 1975; Case 75/84, *Metro v Commission* [1986] ECR 3021; in relation to State aids, Case 169/84, *Cofaz v Commission* [1986] ECR 414; Case C-198/91, *Cook v Commission* [1993] ECR I-2487; in relation to merger control, Case T-3/93, *Air France v Commission* [1994] ECR II-121; Case T-96/92, *CCE de la Société des grandes sources v Commission* [1995] ECR II-1231; in relation to anti-dumping, Case 191/82, *Fediol v Commission* [1983] ECR 2913; Case 264/82, *Timex v Council and Commission* [1985] ECR 849; Case 358/89, *Extramet Industrie v Council* [1991] ECR I-2532.

What this displays is the progressive 'jurisdictionalization' of the Community administration. The economic administration is a system of enquiry and of adjustment of the various interests involved. Assignment of this 'quasi-jurisdictional function' justifies the introduction of procedural guarantees.[51] These guarantees do not of course compare with those in judicial proceedings: they do not upset the organization of the administrative system to the point of converting it into an 'impartial independent tribunal'. On this point, the Community case law has remained firm: the Commission is an administrative body and 'cannot be termed a "court" within the meaning of Article 6 of the European Convention of Human Rights'.[52] The practical result is that application of the principle of the rights of the defence must be subordinated to the 'general reservation that it must be compatible with the requirements of effective administration'.[53]

The jurisdictionalization can be seen as a sure way to preserve both the *efficiency* of administrative decisions and the legal *security* of the persons involved. In an economically complex environment, public action is uncertain. The granting of procedural guarantees gives the addressees of decisions and interested third parties the security of being heard either by the administration or, as a last recourse, by the judge. Security is ensured within the Community system through procedure. This development of 'Community administrative procedural law' owes much to the case law.[54] One might today hope, alongside the fragmentation of the substantive legal systems, for a codification of the procedural rules.[55]

---

[51] English-speaking writers are in the best position to grasp this. T. C. Hartley has called these procedures 'quasi-judicial', adding that even if the case law does not use this notion 'it has become increasingly clear that it is not possible to make sense of the cases unless one adopts some such notion' (T. C. Hartley, *The Foundations of European Community Law. An Introduction to the Constitutional and Administrative Law of the European Community* (1994), at 369, 378). In English law, a body engages in judicial or quasi-judicial activity when it can take decisions liable to affect the rights of individuals adversely: this was the solution arrived at in 1963 by the House of Lords in the famous case *Ridge v Baldwin* [1964] AC 40. See also Wymeersch, 'La fonction quasi-juridictionnelle', *Revue de droit international et de droit comparé* (1982) 214.

[52] See, e.g., Cases 209 to 215 and 218/78, *Van Landewyck v Commission* [1980] ECR 3248.

[53] Advocate-General Warner's conclusions in case 133/77, re *NTN v Council* [1979] ECR 1262.

[54] See Weber, 'Il diritto amministrativo procedimentale nell'ordinamento della comunità europea', 2 *Rivista italiana di diritto pubblico comunitario* (1992) 393.

[55] In this connection see Harlow, 'Codification of EC Administrative Procedures? Fitting the Foot to the Shoe or the Shoe to the Foot', 2 *ELJ* (1996) 3; Shapiro, 'Codification of Administrative Law: The US and the Union', 2 *ELJ* (1996) 26.

C. The Limits to Jurisdictionalization

However, this development has its limits. First, it defines a balance, hard to maintain, between the requirements of protection and the imperatives of efficiency. In general terms the judge has displayed remarkable capacity to reconcile these two requirements. But in some cases the balance of the case law becomes fragile. The *Sytraval* case supplies a remarkable example.[56] In this state-subsidy case, several companies and associations under French law lodged a complaint with the Commission regarding the existence of aid supplied illegally by the French government to a competitor company in the postal sector. In 1992, the Commission took a decision to reject the complaint. In the complainants' appeals, the CFI considered the classical question of the soundness of the Commission's consideration of the complaint in terms of the requirement to give *reasons*. But it took advantage in order to impose a new procedural logic. In its judgment giving reasons is associated with impartiality and elevated to the level of a fundamental principle governing the whole procedure. Impartiality thus becomes the matrix from which there follows a whole consistent set of guarantees granted to third parties, in particular the right to be heard at the stage of prior considerations. This means the CFI is breaking not just with the organization of control of public aid but with the general idea that governed the adoption of the principle of the rights of the defence in all competition proceedings: i.e. a procedure split in two in which the right to be heard comes only at a second stage and remains limited to the decision's addressees alone. Now, on the basis of this case-law, there are two contrary convictions, that in relation to procedural guarantees the procedure is a unit, and that all those involved are entitled themselves to constitute the object of the proceedings. This judgment involves a questioning of the Commission's control over the procedures. Its logic implies a re-allotment of the parties' roles in the decisional procedure.

However, this logic was to be rejected by the Court of Justice. The judgment was quashed in the appeal on points of law.[57] According to Advocate-General Lenz, followed by the Court, 'the Court clearly went beyond the normal framework of these principles and ended by considering not the existence of adequate reasons but the substantive exactness of these reasons'.[58] The Court accordingly moved to reducing the rights of third parties to a mere obligation to consider the complaint with care and diligence. There is, however, an ensuing risk of extending its own review to the suitability of the

---

[56] Case T-95/94, *Sytraval and Brink's France v Commission* [1995] ECR II-2651.

[57] Case C-367/95 P, *Commission v Sytraval and Brink's France* [1998] ECR I-1719.

[58] Advocate-General Lenz's conclusions in Case C-367/95 P, *Commission v Sytraval and Brink's France,* § 59, I-1740.

Commission's action.[59] In fact the Community judge does not in these matters stop fluctuating between a position of *withdrawal* in relation to the Commission's discretionary power and one of *intrusion* into administrative action. This dilemma has to do with the very nature of the jurisdictionalization of the system. It sets up a system of permanent monitoring and enquiry that subordinates individual participation to the imperatives of the enquiry and leads to a certain concentration of powers in favour of the controlling authorities (the Commission and the Court).

Second, this development is of limited scope. It comes up against a major obstacle: rejection by the judge of any transposition of procedural guarantees into normative procedures.[60] This exclusion arises from an initial confusion of the legislative and the executive function in the Community institutional system. It is justified by the desire to preserve the discretionary nature of economic policy choices made by the Community institutions.[61] It is reflected in general terms in the litigation system, both through strict conditions on admissibility of appeals against acts of general scope, and through limited review by the judge. It does not follow that all controls are impossible. The judge has allowed some liberalization of the admissibility conditions and enhanced recourse to the principles of equality, proportionality and legitimate trust in relation to this type of act. But Ritleng has clearly shown that 'the enhancement in instruments of control brought by recourse to the general principles of law is tempered by the fact that the Court, from the reticence it has displayed in reviewing respect for them, has simultaneously imposed self-limitation of their scope'.[62] In a judgment of 19 November 1998, the Court confirmed that the intensity of judicial review must be less the more 'the act concerned is of general scope'.[63]

III. FROM 'GOOD ADMINISTRATION' TO 'ADMINISTRATIVE DEMOCRACY'?

The Community regulatory system has developed on a variety of bases. 'The pluralist inspiration of the decision-making process' and the 'permeability of

---

[59] In this sense see the analyses by H. P. Nehl, *Principles of Administrative Procedure in EC Law* (1999).

[60] In this sense Case T-521/93, *Atlanta et al v Commission* [1996] ECR II-1707; Case T-122/96, *Federolio v Commission* [1997] ECR II-1559; Case T-199/96, *Bergadem and Goupil v Commission* [1998] ECR II-2805.

[61] Cases 116 and 124/77, *Amylum v Council and Commission* [1979] ECR 3527.

[62] D. Ritleng, *Le contrôle de la légalité des actes communautaires par la Cour de justice et le Tribunal de première instance des Communautés européennes* (1998), thesis on file at the University of Strasbourg, at 504.

[63] Case C-150/94, *United Kingdom v Council* [1998] ECR I-7235.

the Commission to economic, social and intergovernmental interests and concerns' can no longer be doubted today.[64] They testify to a recent, profound and general transformation of administrative goals, procedures and institutions in the Community (see A below). The opening is apparent particularly at three levels: scientific, social and political (see B). Most important for an understanding of the evolution of the Community system is to see how these various levels can interact and overlap in a general, consistent system of monitoring, control and information (see C).

A. Transformation of the Regulatory System

Till the late eighties, the Commission was fairly hostile to any openings. It was long confined to developing favoured relations with certain national industrial groups.[65] This restriction can be explained by a strong desire on the Commission's part to assert a 'European political style' reflecting an integration process seen as autonomous.[66] Mazey and Richardson have studied this behaviour as the action of a 'powerful but youthful bureaucracy' taking a 'pragmatic, unplanned' approach.[67] Wessels rightly pointed in this connection to the formation of a 'mega-bureaucracy' of a 'corporatist' type.[68]

The Single European Act proved decisive in this connection.[69] It affirmed the concern that was progressively to become central in the European decisional process: how to formalize pluralist, open dialogue with a maximum of interests? This concern became even more pressing at the time of the debate on democracy and subsidiarity that followed the Maastricht Treaty.[70] Since

---

[64] Mangas Martín, 'Pluralisme politico-social et processus décisionnel au sein des institutions communautaires', in *Melanges en hommage à Michel Waelbroeck* (1999) 483.

[65] McLaughlin and Greenwood, 'The Management of Interest Representation in the European Union', 33 *JCMS* (1995) 143.

[66] Mazey and Richardson, 'La Commission européenne, une bourse pour les idées et les intérêts', 46 *Revue française de science politique* (1996) 409.

[67] Mazey and Richardson, 'De la liberté des mœurs politiques à un style européen de politique publique?', in Y. Mény, P. Muller and J.-L. Quermonne (eds), *Politiques publiques en Europe* (1995), at 100.

[68] Wessels, 'The Growth and Differentiation of Multi-Level Networks: A Corporatist Mega-Bureaucracy or an Open City?', in H. Wallace and A. R. Young (eds), *Participation and Policy-Making in the European Union* (1997), at 36. It will be noted that in this area concepts vary, sometimes going so far as to contradict each other: thus, for instance, what Wessels calls a 'corporatist' policy is termed 'pluralist' by Ayberk and Schenker (Ayberk and Schenker, 'Des lobbies européens entre pluralisme et clientélisme', 48 *Revue française de science politique* (1998) 725). It is therefore important to precisely define the terms used. What is meant here is a policy where 'interest groups are branded as social actors exercising direct or indirect pressure on power without participating in its exercise', and in their relations, 'the groups are in almost perfect competition'.

[69] In this sense see Mazey and Richardson, *supra* n. 65.

then the movement has only accelerated. And thus 'Brussels, the open city' was born.[71]

This policy of openness enables the Commission, which has limited resources and means, to gather the reliable information it lacks.[72] By associating addressees with the preparation of decisions it further ensures legitimacy and a certain effectiveness to the policies laid down by the Commission.[73] In the *European public policy space*,[74] where resistance is high and means of control fairly weak, this collaboration is proving essential. In parallel with the expansion of expertise, the growth in consultation and the acceptance of the policy committee procedures precisely coincide with implementation of the *subsidiarity principle*.[75]

The openness principle is enshrined in Article 1 of the Treaty on European Union:

This Treaty marks a new stage in the process of creating an ever closer union among the peoples of Europe, in which decisions are taken as openly as possible and as closely as possible to the citizen.

From this wording the Commission today derives the need to set up a 'new governance' as an element in the introduction of 'participatory democracy' to the Union.[76] This principle is manifested in both the Commission's internal organization and its external procedures.[77] This is true particularly of social regulation in the areas of the environment, consumer health and safety at work.[78]

---

[70] See van Gerven, 'The Legal Dimension: The Constitutional Incentives and Constraints on Bargained Administration', in F. Snyder (eds.), *Constitutional Dimensions of European Economic Integration* (1996) 75.

[71] Wessels, 'The Growth and Differentiation of Multi-Level Networks: A Corporatist Mega-Bureaucracy or an Open City?', in H. Wallace and A. R. Young (eds), *Participation and Policy-Making in the European Union* (1997) 17.

[72] Wallace, 'Introduction', in ibid., at 9.

[73] In general D.J. Galligan, *Due Process and Fair Procedures. A Study of Administrative Procedures* (1996), at 282.

[74] On this concept see Muller, 'La mutation des politiques publiques', *Pouvoirs* (April 1994) 63.

[75] In this sense see McLaughlin and Greenwood, *supra* n. 65, at 143. This point is confirmed in the Protocol annexed to the Amsterdam Treaty on application of the principles of subsidiarity and proportionality, which provides that the Commission shall endeavour to make 'broad consultations' (pt 9).

[76] Commission discussion document, *The Commission and NGOs: strengthening the partnership*, COM (2000) 11 final, 6.

[77] See European Commission, *White Paper on Commission Reform*, 1 March 2000.

[78] G. Majone, *La Communauté européenne: un Etat régulateur* (1996); Joerges, 'The Market without the State? The "Economic Constitution" of the European Community in the Rebirth of the Regulatory Politics', 19 *EIoP* (1997).

B. Openness in the Decision-Making Process

To understand present developments, one must distinguish among the ancillary procedures associated with the decision-making process: expertise, participation and the committee procedures. In fact, these various procedures manifestly interweave into a complete tapestry, very complex to analyse.

1. Expertise

Expertise is increasing in importance in all sectors of new social regulation and at all levels of administrative activity. A mere glance at health or environment regulations should convince one of this. It is supposed to be at the centre of a system aimed at reconciling social protection with innovation and technical progress.[79] This system favours extension of the area of risks calling for scientific assessment.[80] Far from being limited, as in economic regulation, to a management technique, expertise in social regulation becomes a genuine 'structure of government'.

The Committee's scientific consultation system has been thoroughly reorganized following the BSE crisis. The aim is to restore credibility and public trust in the scientific assessment process.[81] Rules of internal organization have been laid down around three general principles: '*excellence, independence and transparency*'.[82] Additionally, the cooperation and scientific coordination procedures have been institutionalized. Today, creation of a Food Agency is being considered as a desirable substitute for the existing scientific network:[83] the Authority proposed by the Commission has the ambition of becoming the 'scientific reference for the whole of the Union', the 'centre' of a 'network of scientific contacts in Europe and further afield'.[84] The European Environ-

---

[79] See Van den Daele, 'Scientific Evidence and the Regulation of Technical Risks: Twenty Years of Demythologizing the Experts', in N. Stehr and V. Ericson (eds), *The Culture of Power Knowledge. Inquiries into Contemporary Society* (1992) 323.

[80] Vos, 'Market Building, Social Regulation and Scientific Expertise: An introduction', in C. Joerges, K.-H. Ladeur and E. Vos (eds), *Integrating Scientific Expertise into Regulatory Decision-Making. National Traditions and European Innovations* (1997) 127.

[81] EC Commission, Green Paper, *General Principles of Food Legislation*, COM (97) 176 final, 36.

[82] Commission communication, *Consumer Health and Food Safety*, COM (97) 183 final, 10.

[83] Cf. Valverde, Piqueras García and Cabezas López, 'La "nouvelle approche' en matière de santé des consommateurs et de sécurité alimentaire: la nécessité d'une agence européenne de sécurité des aliments', 4 *Revue du marché unique européen* (1997) 31.

[84] EC Commission *White Paper on Food Safety*, COM (1999), 719 final, 5 and § 37. On the reasons for setting up an 'Authority', a model based more on interinstitutionality and less autonomous than an 'Agency', see P. James, F. Kemper and G. Pascal *The future of scientific advice in the EU* (Report commissioned by the European Commission), December 1999, website of the Directorate-General for Health and Consumer Protection.

ment Agency is to succeed the experimental programme to collect and systematize environmental information in the Community.[85] In general, the institution of independent agencies 'contributes to creating an epistemic Community'.[86]

The Community seeks consensus. It has set up a general research method: '*risk analysis*'.[87] Recently introduced in the area of public health, because of the urgency of the problems arising there, it has three stages. First, *risk evaluation*, which is the basis for the scientific opinions. This phase favours cooperation and coordination of the various competent authorities. Second, *risk management*, denoting adoption of a norm based on the outcome of scientific assessment and reaching the 'desired level of protection'. Finally, *risk communication*, consisting in assuring 'broadest possible' access by all interested parties to the scientific opinions and the policy decisions. This is the 'interface between the academic world, the policy world and the other components of civil society'.[88] Risk analysis consists in instituting 'participatory expertise'.[89] The object is to have various 'learning systems' coexist within the expertise procedure, characterized by 'operations for selecting actors and data, through validating tests, hierarchical relations and decisions'.[90]

2. Participation

Risk administration in the areas of economic and social regulation cannot be content with being supported on scientific expertise. In a context of uncertainty it requires participation and discussion by all interested parties so as to secure information and anticipate responses.[91]

As from 1974, the Economic and Social Committee noted 'a tendency to the multiplication of specific consultation bodies it fears might lessen the privileged nature of its consultative mission leading to dilution of the

[85] Council decision of 27 June 1985 adopting a Commission work programme concerning an experimental project to collect, coordinate and collate information on the state of the environment and natural resources in the Community, EC OJ 1985, L 176/14.

[86] On the agency's network-type organization see L. Metcalfe, 'Etablissement de liens entre les différents niveaux de gouvernance: intégration européenne et mondialisation', 66 *Revue internationale des sciences administratives*, (2000) 153.

[87] Commission communication, *Consumer Health and Food Safety*, COM (97) 183 final, 20–21; EC Commission *White Paper on Food Safety*, COM (1999) 719 final, para 12; Commission communication on recourse to the precautionary principle, COM (2000) 1 final.

[88] Commission communication, *Consumer Health and Food Safety*, COM (97) 183 final, 21.

[89] E. Naim-Gesbert, *Les dimensions scientifiques du droit de l'environnement. Contribution à l'étude des rapports de la science et du droit* (1999), at 665.

[90] Lascoumes, 'L'expertise peut-elle être démocratique?', 8 *Le monde des débats* (1999).

[91] Godard clearly shows the need for 'deliberative procedures' founded on 'expert information' in 'Le principe de précaution: une nouvelle logique de l'action entre science et démocratie', 11 *Philosophie politique* (2000) 17.

consultative function in the Communities'.[92] However, well aware of the Commission's need to take consultation with 'very specialized committees' it claimed for itself 'broader attention to problems of a general nature, so as to pursue its own true mission'. General opinion on major economic and social policy lines remains its own specific area. But from then on the fear of seeing consultative committees set up by the Commission multiply was confirmed. There are today a great number of committees made up of representatives of economic and social interests.[93] Alongside consumer committees on health, consultative forums on the environment are growing.[94] Nor should one over-look the constant presence of informal consultation procedures on an *ad hoc* basis.[95]

Recently, the Commission has sought to give these forms of association a coherent image. In its communication on 'promoting the role of associations and foundations in Europe' the Commission takes as its 'new policy objective' 'the construction, ultimately, of true **civil dialogue** at European level to sup-plement the political dialogue with national authorities and the social dia-logue with the social partners'.[96] The partners and modalities of this dialogue are to be understood broadly: it includes both social and economic groups, formal and informal consultation procedures. Alongside political democracy, supplementing rather than substituting for it,[97] civil dialogue should lead to the creation of a true 'participatory democracy' founded on European civil society. That was the ideal affirmed by Commission President Romano Prodi in January 2000.[98]

---

[92] Economic and Social Committee, *Opinion on the place and role of the Economic and Social Committee in the Community institutional system, and prospects for its development*, EC OJ 1974, C 111/37, III.1.

[93] Ciavarini-Azzi counts 57 committees of this type that met in 1995 ('Comitology and the European Commission', in Joerges and Vos, *supra* n. 19, at 51.

[94] Commission Decision 93/701/CE of 7 December 1993 creating a General Consultative Forum on the environment EC OJ 1993, L 328/53; Commission Decision 97/150/EC of 24 February 1997 creating a European Consultative Forum on sustainable development, EC OJ 1997, L 58/48. In general, see Gadbin, 'L'association des partenaires économiques et sociaux organisés aux procédures de décision en droit communautaire', 36 *Revue trimestrielle de droit européen* (2000) 1.

[95] Commission Secretariat-General, *The Commission and Interest Groups*, <europa.eu.int/comm/secretariat_g...obbies/droits_obligations/droits_fr.htm>.

[96] Commission communication, *Promoting the Role of Associations in Europe* COM (97) 241 final, 9 (our emphasis).

[97] The Commission takes care to specify that 'the decision-making process in the European Union is legitimized first and foremost by the elected representatives of European citizens', and 'in this context, dialogue between the European Commission and the NGOs *usefully supple-ments* the institutional process at political level' (Commission discussion document, *The Commission and the NGOs: Strengthening the Partnership* COM (2000) 11 final, 1.3.1., 2.; our emphasis).

[98] Discussion document published on 18 January 2000, COM (2000) 11 final.

3. The Committees

In a third stage following on the previous ones the political element of great importance in the decision process comes in: the committee procedures. Their creation goes back to the development of the Common Agricultural Policy; but social regulatory policies brought out their importance.[99] These procedures, with their basis in Article 202 EC, involve having the Commission assisted by a committee of national representatives.[100] The committee system expresses the desire to ensure Member State presence in the adoption stage of measures for implementing basic texts.[101] The 'comitology' has today taken on such importance that the Community is often presented as a 'government of committees'.[102]

The comitology has aroused lively institutional controversy. This controversy seems to have found a provisional end or rest in the Decision of 28 June 1999 laying down the detailed rules for exercising the enforcement powers conferred on the Commission.[103] The efficiency of the committee system is no longer doubted today. Everyone recognizes that far from being an obstacle to integration the system is instead an effective support to the development of cooperation among the Union's administrations. It facilitates the implementation of Community law.

Empirical studies have shown that comitology is not 'the Member States' Trojan horse inside the Commission citadel'.[104] They bring out a complex functional and deliberative administration. According to Wessels, the comitology can be defined as the locus of '*fusion*' among the various national

[99] See Joerges, 'Bureaucratic Nightmare, Technocratic Regime and the Dream of Good Transnational Governance', in Joerges and Vos, *supra* n. 19, at 3.

[100] For a full bibliography see R. H. Pedler and G. F. Schaefer (eds), *Shaping European Law and Policy. The Role of Committees and Comitology in the Political Process* (1996) 195.

[101] Wessels counts some 410 of them in 1997, a figure confirmed by the Commission Services in 'Comitology: fusion in action. Politico-administrative trends in the EU system', *JEPP* (1998) 219. The number of opinions handed down by these committees doubled between 1971 and 1994, going from 1,400 to 2,800. For a full statistical analysis of the committee system sector by sector see Falke, 'Comitology and Other Committees: A Preliminary Empirical Assessment', in Pedler and Schaefer, *supra* n. 100, at 117.

[102] See Sidjanski, 'Communauté européenne 1992: gouvernement de comités?', 48 *Pouvoirs* (1989) 71. The term is of more than purely descriptive value: it also displays the ambition to seek a new constitutional system for organizing the powers. This was at least the intention of K. C. Wheare, who elaborates on the term in analysing the British governmental process, in *Government and Committee: An Essay on the British Constitution* (1955).

[103] See the detailed analysis in Lenaerts and Verhoeven, 'Towards a Legal Framework for Executive Rule-Making in the E.U.? The Contribution of the New Comitology Decision', 37 *CMLRev.* (2000) 645.

[104] Cf. Weiler, 'Epilogue: "Comitology" as Revolution—Infranationalism, Constitutionalism and Democracy', in Joerges and Vos, *supra* n. 19, at 341.

administrative and political systems. This system suggests the possibility of a 'shared use of powers'.[105] This merger is not the outcome of a definite policy project; it is more the product of the demand by competent, specialized national actors for access to the Community process. This pressure is supposed to create a 'partnership' bringing the various levels of State powers together: the bringing together of the various levels and of all participants' own interests in order to reach a result will lead to high productivity and a high degree of acceptance by all those involved.[106] Still in search of rare, costly information that can justify their presence, the various participants find themselves in a 'mutual learning' position.[107] This conception reduces the influence of considerations of a policy nature. In this system all *formalism* must be discarded: the formal rules are clearly subordinated to this search for a solution to problems on a consensus basis.[108] Undoubtedly, and in the eyes of the participants themselves, the committees' power of influence depends more on expertise and the consensus they are able to produce than on their statutes and legal powers.[109] In these conditions the *formalities* (controlling the calendar, running the secretariat and the chair) become decisive. It is through these apparently minor mechanisms that the Commission ensures its control of these procedures.

C. Networked Administration

The interaction of these various levels gives rise to a complex, specialized, autonomous administrative system. It is best described in terms of a 'network'. One would have to go further into the meaning of this term, today used in the most varied contexts. Suffice it here to note the multiple introduction of cooperation and coordination mechanisms involving several partners in solving one and the same problem. This definition is enough to give an account of three essential features of the new Community administrative organization.

(1) The network has no sharp distinction between internal organization and outside action. At outside level partnership relations should develop, since the action calls for support from outside expertise, concertation

[105] Wessels, 'Comitology: Fusion in Action. Politico-administrative Trends in the EU System', 5 *JEPP* (1998) 217.

[106] Ibid.

[107] Joerges and Neyer, 'Multi-Level Governance, Deliberative Politics, and the Role of Law', EUI, Conference RSC, Florence, 9–10 December 1996, 45–48.

[108] Wessels, *supra* n. 105, at 225.

[109] See Van Schendelen, 'EC Committees: Influence Counts More Than Legal Powers', in Pedler and Schaefer, *supra* n. 100, at 34.

with the interest groups that actually form the network[110] and the delegation of some tasks to organs themselves organized in networks.[111] It is within the Commission that connections should be established among these various outside contact points. Internally, the Commission's various divisions constitute 'the central core of a vast "network of reflection" which includes, in addition to experts from the national administrations, independent consultants who may also be from outside the European Union, academics, and representatives of economic and professional organizations and regional bodies'.[112] This is the general approach the 'new Commission' seems to wish to take. It regards development of an 'externalization policy' and of more effective coordination as desirable.[113] This need is relatively new.[114] In a complex environment, information is scarce. To define and adapt regulatory policies in such an environment, information has to circulate. It thus requires the introduction of specific institutional mechanisms for coordinating the competent authorities involved, be they public or private, academic or political, and for participation by all relevant persons. Thus, complex forms of *co-implementation* grow up.[115] With the affirmation through the nineties of the legitimacy

[110] In this sense see Ayberk and Schenker, 'Des lobbies européens entre pluralisme et clientélisme', *Revue française de science politique* (1998) 725.

[111] The organization of European standardization supplies the most visible example of this. In this area, 'the Commission did not see fit to try to create a bureaucratic pyramid. Instead, since transparency and consistency in testing and certification work are very important, the Commission has since 1986 advocated the need for a European organization capable of acting as a pole of attraction, a forum where all interested parties could meet, exchange information and experience and especially find all the technical instruments for setting up mutual recognition agreements, or downright European certification systems' (McMillan, 'La "certification", la reconnaissance mutuelle et le marché unique', *Revue du marché unique européen* (1991) 201). Dehousse also adapts the formula to European agencies in 'Regulation by networks in the European Community: the role of European agencies', *JEPP* (1997) 246.

[112] Majone, *supra* n. 1, at 92.

[113] This need is clearly formulated by the Committee of Independent Experts set up in early 1999 by the European Parliament to throw light on the Commission's dysfunctions (on this point see Rodrigues, 'La nouvelle Commission Prodi face à ses engagements. Est-ce la fin de la crise?', *Revue du marché commun* (1999) 678). It is reflected in the Commission's new rules of procedure, especially in Articles 18 and 19, which stipulate: 'To meet special needs, the Commission may set up specific structures charged with specific missions, the powers and working methods of which it shall determine'; 'to ensure the efficacy of the Commission's actions, its services shall work in close cooperation and in coordination in order to develop and implement decisions' (EC OJ 1999, L 252/41).

[114] See the comparative study by Cini, 'La Commission européenne: lieu d'émergence de cultures administratives. L'exemple de la DG IV et de la DG XI', 46 *Revue française de science politique* (1996) 457.

[115] See Chiti, 'The Emergence of a Community Administration: The Case of European Agencies', 37 *CMLRev.* (2000) 309.

of these new forms, a *'network'*, *'heterarchical'* institutional structure replaced an organization founded on autarchy and hierarchy.[116] The consequence is certainly greater autonomy and flexibility, but undoubtedly also a greater risk of confusion among public and private interests.

(2) The network ignores the opposition between interventionist administration and abstentionist administration. The new administrative system tries to give a modest place to direct control, to the benefit of procedural, decentralized techniques. Basing himself on the example of regulation in the area of biotechnology, Landfried suggests that 'the result of the European policy is more than a technocratic regime and more than promotion of negative integration'.[117] The network constitutes 'a specific form, between hierarchy and the market'.[118] The research of the American institutionalist school and the new institutionalist economics have emphasized the importance of this form in economic organization. Now there is a striking isomorphism between the organization of the new economy and certain aspects of the administrative organization being set up. Lehmbruch has sought to theorize these systems of interaction between government bureaucracies and private-interest associations. Going beyond pluralist and corporatist models, he sees in these *procedures of 'intermediation'* of public and private interests the 'emergence of networks that will end by becoming institutionalized'.[119] These analyses are valuable to an understanding of current developments in the Community.

(3) Finally, the network rejects the alternative between supranational integration and intergovernmental integration. The hypothesis of the intergovernmentalist school that the Community institutions should remain totally subject to national governments does not apply to the Community administration, the role and means of which largely escape political negotiation. However, no administrative action can be developed without national administrative authorities being associated with it: the setting up of committees, agencies and standardization agencies show the presence of national experts. The point is not just for States to regain

---

[116] See Ladeur, 'Towards a Legal Concept of the Network in European Standard-Setting', in Joerges and Vos, *supra* n. 19, at 151.

[117] Landfried, 'Beyond Technocratic Governance: The Case of Biotechnology', 3 *ELJ* (1997) 256.

[118] L. Boltanski and E. Chiapello, *Le nouvel esprit du capitalisme* (1999) 131.

[119] Lehmbruch, 'The Organization of Society, Administrative Strategies and Policy Networks', in R. Czada, A. Héritier and H. Keman (eds), *Institutions and Political Choices. On the Limits of Rationality* (1998) 61. This work should be compared with that of Philippe Schmitter and Wolfgang Streeck, who developed a notion of 'private interest government' in 'Community, market, state—and associations? The prospective contribution of interest governance to social order', in W. Streeck and P. C. Schmitter (eds), *Private Interest Government. Beyond Market and State* (1985).

lost influence. Their presence facilitates cooperation and the placing in common of scarce resources, chiefly information. To highlight this development, political scientists have developed a 'multi-level system' model.[120] This new model does not deny the role of States in the conduct of 'high politics' nor in controlling the integration process through the treaties:[121] the point is mainly to show the intensity and originality of the new levels of integration, of an administrative nature.

IV. THE LEGITIMACY OF ADMINISTRATIVE ACTION

This development does not cease to raise questions. Following this brief analysis, a Community decision can be seen as:

(1) a factual judgement established by experts who attest its truth;
(2) crowned by a fact and value judgement made by the Commission, which assures its legitimacy; and
(3) possibly monitored by forums of enlightened citizens that ensure credibility.

This system leads to some concentration of powers in the Commission's hands and to openness limited to the closest, best armed and best informed interests. It can be seen that it involves risks of *exclusion* for those without the resources needed to participate, and risks of *dilution of responsibilities* by multiplying contacts and actors in the decision. This raises the question whether legal guarantees exist that are capable of providing a framework for this pluralism and flexibility, without reducing their expression. The need today is to know whether we are not being duped by the 'spirit of openness'. The old question of the legitimacy of public action arises again.[122] But what is needed are new answers. The system being set up displays a renewed questioning of the two pillars of our classical conceptions of democracy: the principle of judicial protection and that of political representation.

---

[120] See esp. Scharpf, 'Community and autonomy: multi-level policy-making in the European Union', 1 *JEPP* (1994) 219.

[121] The distinction between 'high' and 'low' politics was established by S. Hoffmann in the international relations context in 'Obstinate or Obsolete: The Fate of the Nation State and the Case of Western Europe', 95 *Daedalus* (1966) 862.

[122] Cf. N. Lebessis and J. Paterson, *Accroître l'efficacité et la légitimité de la gouvernance européenne. Un agenda de réformes pour la Commission,* Cellule de prospective de la Commission des C.E., CdP (99) 750, Bruxelles, 1999.

A. The Rejection of 'Juridification'

A network cannot be run the way isolated behaviour on a market is supervised. In such a regulatory system, by nature flexible and procedural, the legal constraint is not absent. But it is recognized that the law has a cost, lying in an 'artificial rigidity' and a simplicity incapable of 'offering solutions to profound problems arising in modern society'.[123] In the area of the environment the Commission has accepted that 'the exclusively legal approach has often proved inefficient or impracticable'.[124] The elimination of all binding rules does not follow. But one can see individual protections being replaced by monitoring instruments and collective participation to promote consensus. In general terms this new form of regulation favours participation. But it rejects all excessive formalism. There are no longer any parties directly *protected*. There are only interested actors that at this or that stage deserve to be *associated* with running the decision process. It follows that the legal pathway tends to be discarded. It is perceived as an ossification in a complex system favouring consensus. It 'hinders a response to this increasingly essential need appearing with the growth of complexity: to mobilize citizens' imaginations and talents' to make action less costly and more effective.[125]

That does not mean that development of these procedures could remain without consequences in the case law. On several occasions the Court of Justice has reacted. Basing itself either on new interpretations of classical principles drawn from its case law, like the 'democratic principle' or the 'principle of institutional balance', or on new principles like the 'precautionary principle', it has laid down new legal guarantees.[126] Thus, recourse to expertise can now be seen as one of the guarantees for complex decisions.[127] The democratic principle has been extended to economic and social participation.[128] Finally, transparency and the 'proper performance of procedures' become means for controlling committee procedures.[129] The fact remains that these

---

[123] In this sense see Willke, 'Le coût du principe de légalité', in C.-A. Morand (ed.), *Figures de la légalité* (1992) 127.

[124] Commission Report on progress in implementing the Community policy and action programme for the environment and sustainable development, COM (95) 624 final, 4. In general see Macrory, 'Environmental Law: Shifting Discretions and the New Formalism', in O. Lomas (ed.), *Frontiers of Environmental Law* (1991) 8.

[125] M. Crozier, *Etat moderne, Etat modeste. Stratégie pour un autre changement* (1987), at 248.

[126] See Scott and Vos, 'Administering Europe in an Age of Uncertainty: The Precautionary Principle in Community Law', this volume.

[127] See Case C-212/91, *Angelopharm* [1994] ECR I-171; Case 151/98 P, *Pharos v Commission* [1999] ECR I-8157; Case C-157/96, *National Farmers' Union et al.* [1998] ECR I-2211.

[128] Case T-135/96, *UEAPME v Council* [1998] ECR II-2335.

[129] Case T-188/97, *Rothmans International v Commission* [1999], II-2463; Case C-244/95, *Moskof* [1997] ECR I-6441; Case C-263/95, *Germany v Commission* [1998] ECR I-441. We would note that the Commission's recent proposal on public access to documents takes note

advances are limited and isolated. They impose fairly weak constraints on the general deployment of the procedures.[130] And that will be so as long as the Court remains attached to the classical instruments of institutional balance.

B. The Limits to Political Representation

To the question of new legitimacy, 'the most obvious answer is that the Union already has a far better way of checking technocratic policy-making than a system of supplementary law-making subject to judicial review. . . . The Council does not delegate its law-making powers but exercises all its legislative powers itself'.[131] It would thus suffice to transpose into Community law the American doctrine of 'non-delegation' that today seeks to restore the preponderance of the independent impartial law-maker over subordinate administrative authorities.[132] But the Council is far from displaying the requisite qualities of a legitimately elected law-maker, since its legitimacy basis is 'international (representativity), not directly popular'.[133] To be sure, 'Council members come from democratically selected governments and enjoy the confidence of national parliaments', and 'their actions on the Council can be controlled by national parliaments, as happens in certain cases'.[134] But the decision process does not escape the general deterioration of the opinion-forming process into a technocratic arrangement and a negotiated compromise that is affecting all constitutional democracies.[135] Moreover, the Council seems 'technically' short of resources to take this sort of decision. That is why it has had to multiply delegations and the introduction of technical committee procedures under Commission responsibility.

We may then invoke the rise of co-decision and control by Parliament. But however desirable a highly placed parliament in the European Union might be, it could not be counted among sure ways of ensuring the legitimacy of

of this case law, since it is provided that it should apply to the committees (COM (2000) 30 final).

[130] See the exemplary Case C-321/95 P, *Greenpeace Council et al. v Commission* [1998] ECR I-1651.

[131] Shapiro, 'Codification of Administrative Law: The US and the Union', 2 *ELJ* (1996) 45.

[132] J.-H. Ely, *Democracy and Distrust. A Theory of Judicial Review* (1980), at 131.

[133] Pescatore, 'L'exécutif communautaire: justification du quadripartisme institué par les traités de Paris et de Rome', 34 *Cahiers de droit européen* (1978), 393.

[134] Jacqué, 'Cours général de droit communautaire', 1 *Collected Courses of the Academy of European Law* (1990, 1) 237, at 284. The author continues: 'it is none the less the case that *de facto* democratic control at national level remains theoretical . . .'.

[135] On this point see Héritier, 'The Accommodation of Diversity in European Policy-making and its Outcomes: Regulatory Policy as a Patchwork', EUI, Working Paper SPS, 96/2, Florence (1996).

Community action. Not only does it not have the necessary technical resources to guide the administration, but it has no direct control over the administration from the very fact of the network system set up by the Council and Commission and the pressures for which it is itself the forum.[136] Undoubtedly, Parliament's powers, enhanced by the Amsterdam Treaty, to exercise indirect control over the Community bureaucracy are legitimate and should be strengthened.[137] The course of the BSE crisis shows that.[138] But it seems hard to shift the whole responsibility for regulating risk on to parliamentary control alone.[139]

V. THE SEARCH FOR A NEW INSTITUTIONAL BALANCE

At the same time as making 'government by judges' undesirable, Community integration has made the idea of a 'system of representative government addressing a *demos* of citizens'[140] obsolete. The search for *legitimacy* no longer involves the *democratic* nature of the government. It now involves local and operational forms of administrative coordination. That is why a new form of constitutional theory seems necessary. One must be capable of distinguishing within these complex systems between what is merely 'good management' and what might be 'good government'.[141] 'Good management' amounts just to the concern to pursue serious enquiries and obtain scientific consensus. 'Good government' is further capable of conceiving 'the redistribution of forms of expertise' and the opening of the procedure to all persons concerned[142] (see part A below). To move from the first to the second, a new institutional balance seems necessary (see part B).

[136] Harlow, 'A Community of Interests? Making the Most of European Law', 55 *MLR* (1992) 331; Rideau, 'Les groupes d'intérêt dans le système institutionnel communautaire', 3 *Revue des affaires européennes* (1993) 49.

[137] In this connection one might cite participation by Parliament in appointing members of the Commission, the possibility of creating temporary committees (as happened in 1996 for the 'mad cow crisis'), appointment of the Ombudsman with the role of monitoring cases of 'maladministration', the right to consider petitions, and last but not least, budget control.

[138] Wright, 'Can the European Parliament Punish European Commission Officials? Who Takes the Blame for the BSE Mess?', *European Food Law Review* (1998) 39; Chambers, 'The BSE Crisis and the European Parliament', in Joerges and Vos, *supra* n. 19, at 95.

[139] Compare Fisher, 'Drowning by Numbers: Standard Setting in Risk Regulation and the Pursuit of Accountable Public Administration', 20 *OJLS* (2000) 109.

[140] Leca, 'Sur la gouvernance démocratique: entre théorie et méthode de recherche empirique', 1 *Politique européenne* (2000) 125; equally Delwit, de Waele and de Munck, 'Europe: la représentation démantelée', 17 *L'événement européen* (1992) 143.

[141] On this distinction see Leca, 'Le gouvernement en Europe, un gouvernement européen?', 15 *Politiques et management public* (1997) 21.

[142] J. de Munck, *L'institution sociale de l'esprit. Nouvelles approches de la raison* (1999), at 191.

A. Prospects for 'Good Government'

Failing a State structure, the principle of government has to be sought in social integration.[143] The question is no longer to allot subjective rights to individuals or seek an unfindable 'European people', but to stimulate on each problem the integration of the various representative interest systems within a single procedure. How can government be conceived apart from representation, whether legislative or judicial? What alternative can one offer to the sovereignty of the general will and subjective right? How can, within complex systems, individual autonomy and a common project once again become associated?

In recent years these questions have stimulated much research. That research has in common the fact of being based on the design of existing networks. The idea is to offer institutional solutions enabling unjust practices and illegitimate social usages to be denounced in the very name of the principles on which the regulated sectors are based. These new measures have the ultimate objective of constituting a 'common legal language' for all today's complex social problems that cannot be coped with by the classical means of political representation.[144]

Thus, to the classical constitutional model based on *representative government*, Charles Sabel opposes an institutional model based on *administrative government*.[145] The idea of representation is not thrown out. It remains a central point in social organization, since it allows general objectives to be assigned and common values affirmed. But new forms for administering social matters must be found. The Constitution no longer constitutes *either its origin or its objective*. Its creative capacity, lying in an exceptional original moment,[146] has to be transferred to plural, local organizations. Sabel calls for the formation of multiple, decentralized constitutional orders.[147] The reference model is close to that of the firm, since 'the firm represents the archetype of organization in a situation of complex collective learning'.[148]

---

[143] This was already John Dewey's position in *The Public and its Problems. An Essay in Political Inquiry* (1946), in *John Dewey. The Later Works* (1984), at 278, 259–260; cf. Lefort, 'Droits de l'homme et politique', in *L'invention démocratique. Les limites de la domination totalitaire* (1991), at 45.

[144] Teubner, ' "Altera pars audiatur": le droit dans la collision des discours', 35 *Droit et société* (1997) 99.

[145] Cohen and Sabel, 'Directly-Deliberative Polyarchy', 3 *ELJ* (1997) 313; Dorf and Sabel, 'A Constitution of Democratic Experimentalism', 98 *Columbia Law Review* (1998) 270.

[146] Which Bruce Ackerman calls '*constitutional moments*' in *We the People. Foundations* (1991).

[147] Sabel, 'Constitutional Ordering in Historical Context', in F. Scharpf (ed.), *Games in Hierarchies and Networks. Analytical and Empirical Approaches to the Study of Governance Institutions* (1993) 65.

[148] Favereau, 'Règles, organisation et apprentissage collectif: un paradigme non standard pour trois théories hétérodoxes', in A. Orléan (ed.), *Analyse économique des conventions* (1994) 128.

Administrative government is a 'collective arrangement' bringing together a heterogeneous set of actors operating thanks to a *learning* mechanism. Within constitutional orders, it stimulates processes of discussion on specific problems based on a general coordinated learning mechanism (*learning by monitoring*).[149] This mode of government undoubtedly presupposes a central unit. But this would no longer act as a hierarchical, centralizing, state-type structure. The role of a central authority is essentially to seek the persons concerned, define responsibilities, act as arbiter in discussion and ensure coordination and the follow-up to solutions adopted. This is the 'strong procedural power' that can be called 'administration'.[150]

B. A New Distribution of Responsibilities

What can we draw from this brief analysis for research into the Community system? The theory of 'deliberative polyarchy' is at present extending its proposals to the European order.[151] In our view there follows both a new sharing of tasks and a new institutional balance.

First, the procedure must remain open to all sorts of competences, be they economic, social, political or ethical. This conception applies to action, the carrying out of which is guided no longer only by calculation or association of interests, but by a process of *socialization*. This last conception can refer to Karl Polanyi.[152] The procedure is capable of 'socializing the economy' by enabling social groups directly concerned to engage in the reviewing and definition of policies.

It would also be necessary for interest groups to be able to take part in work of the 'expert committees' and 'policy committees'. The policy committees should no longer be regarded as 'closed shops'.[153] The groups should no longer be shut up in consultative committees with no real power. Thus, for instance, according to the Economic and Social Committee 'one has to ask how far the exchange of information needed in this connection among Member States' representatives, producers, industry, commerce, workers and consumers should be institutionalized. One should contemplate participa-

---

[149] See Sabel, 'Learning by Monitoring: The Institutions of Economic Development', in N. Smelser and R. Swedberg (eds), *The Handbook of Economic Sociology* (1994) 137.

[150] See B. Latour, *Politiques de la nature. Comment faire entrer les sciences en démocratie* (1999), at 269.

[151] Gerstenberg and Sabel, 'Directly-Deliberative Polyarchy: An Institutional Ideal for Europe?', this volume.

[152] Cf. K. Polanyi, *La Grande Transformation. Aux origines politiques et économiques de notre temps* (translated from English by C. Malamoud) (1983).

[153] Falke and Winter, 'Management and Regulatory Committees in Executive Law-making', in G. Winter (ed.), *Sources and Categories of European Union Law. A Comparative and Reform Perspective* (1996) 571.

tion by the various groups involved in the standing committee on human food'.[154]

The autonomy of the various competences has to be respected, but organized in such a way as to make collaboration and confrontation possible. This complementarity of autonomy and cooperation is fully in line with the *principle of institutional balance* enshrined by the Court of Justice in interinstitutional relations: it has now to be transposed into the administrative sphere. Adversary procedures should be organized.[155] The creation has been proposed of 'hybrid forums' composed of a variable group made up, according to the problem dealt with, of heterogeneous interest groups.[156] These forums should in any case be preferred to the present autarchical arrangements of the comitology. In this way a 'public space of expertise' might be created.[157]

Secondly, on this basis there should also be clarification of the separation and coordination of 'legislative functions, official control and others'.[158] All the difficulties raised in this study turn around a new definition of the Commission's role. Leaving a great part of coping with problems up to persons concerned and the defining of essential requirements to the legislator, it has to take on above all 'procedural responsibilities'. Responsibility is considered not just from the viewpoint of organizational science as 'the function of simulation and forecasting in a complex process',[159] 'the understanding and establishment of relations between the organization and its network of partners'.[160] It is here considered from the legal viewpoint as guaranteeing the correct unfolding of the procedure, and respect for essential procedural rules.[161] The administration is the guarantor of the autonomy of the persons involved and of the structuring of responsibilities at the various levels

---

[154] Economic and Social Committee Opinion on the 'Commission Green Paper "General principles of food legislation in the European Union" ', EC OJ 1998 C 19/61, I. 3.5.1.

[155] 'What is abnormal is when the conflict is resolved within, rather than between, centres of power', Chambers, 'The BSE Crisis and the European Parliament', in Joerges and Vos, *supra* n. 19, at 102.

[156] Cf. Callon and Rip, 'Humains, non-humains: morale d'une coexistence', in J. Theys and B. Kalaora (eds), *La terre octroyée. Les experts sont formels!* (1992) 140.

[157] See P. Roqueplo, *Entre savoir et décision, l'expertise scientifique* (1997), at 55.

[158] See the question as approached (but not settled) by the Commission communication on *Consumer Health and Food Safety* COM (97) 183 final, 17–18.

[159] Bourcier and Koubi, 'Responsabilisation des décideurs et systèmes d'information', 55 *Actualité juridique—Droit administratif* (1999) 7.

[160] Metcalfe, 'Etablissement de liens entre les différents niveaux de gouvernance: intégration européenne et mondialisation', 66 *Revue internationale des sciences administratives* (2000) 164.

[161] We would note that the 'principle of procedural responsibility' was provided for by the Italian Law of 7 August 1990 laying down the principles of administrative procedure (Cassese, 'Les droits des administrés en Italie à la suite de la loi du 7 août 1990', 43 *Etudes et Documents—Conseil d'Etat* (1991) 251).

involved. This leads to a rule of *inputability* in the event of breach of those rules at whatever level that may occur.[162]

In this sense the legislator is charged with determining the 'essential requirements' on the basis of which the normative resolution procedure is to be engaged. The distinction should accordingly be dropped between 'policy questions' and 'technical questions', a source of so much confusion and conflict. Taking standardization law as the model,[163] the legislator, and first and foremost Parliament, defines the essential requirements, the 'value system' and the objects to aim at.[164] Accordingly, Parliament exercises 'procedural' control over the Commission, and the Community administration in general. The point is not to give it a 'right of evocation'. It is in fact the Parliament's task to keep itself informed of progress with procedures and where necessary intervene to recall the principles that have to be respected in implementing European policies. Accordingly, it ought to have a very broad information right.[165] It does not replace the executive; it has to concentrate on defining and monitoring respect for the essential requirements. The Court remains the guardian of this balance.[166]

The judge's role in this new balance consists first of *allocating the responsibilities* to the various actors in the network. On the other, it consists in

[162] Advocate-General La Pergola's conclusions in *re Commission v Lisrestal* (C-32/95 P) put this point very well: 'separation of the various institutional levels involved in a procedure and establishment of the resultant financial relations is one thing, and protecting firms another. The functioning system does not compromise protection for the firm, since ultimately it is destined to create, for economic operators too, advantages representing interests guaranteed by Community law. . . . We fail to see how it could be denied that this right to act in turn includes the essential interests of the firm benefiting from the correct course of the administrative procedure in the decision, relating to the outcome or the amount of the aid granted it' ([1996] I-5380). In a note he adds: 'One factor having to do with organization might also be taken into account. The Member State undoubtedly has the role of intermediary between the Commission and the firms, and is, as the Court has affirmed, the Commission's sole interlocutor. This manifestly meets a *concern for efficiency* and for the principles of sound management that must necessarily inspire administrative activity. *But it is none the less the case that, from the viewpoint of organization science, the national administration has to be analysed as playing the part of "agent" of the Community administration. We feel it is legitimate to infer regarding this organization that any omissions committed by the State in its capacity as intermediary have to be **chargeable** to the Commission*' (I-5380, note 20).

[163] Cf. the Commission's Report to the Council and the European Parliament on *Efficacy and legitimacy in European standardization in the context of the New Approach*, SEC (98) 291, Bruxelles, 1998.

[164] This distinction between essential and accessory goes back to the *Köster* case law (Case 25/70, *Köster* [1970] ECR 1161).

[165] In this connection it has been proposed that Parliament should have full access to the committee documents, without protection of privacy being able to be brought against it, as against private persons (Lenaerts and Verhoeven, n. 103 above). On the need to integrate the European Parliament into the work of the scientific committees, see P. James, F. Kemper and G. Pascal (Report commissioned by the European Commission), *supra* n. 84, at 16.

[166] Case C-303/94, *Parliament v Council* [1996] I-2943.

protecting the autonomy of the various actors, be they institutional, public or private. It thus refrains from organizing powers, distributing competences and judging the appropriateness of decisions taken. He enters in at the point where network connections are broken, enabling re-incorporation into the procedure of those 'excluded' from the network, concerned but isolated and disorganized.

VI. CONCLUSION

These analyses would merit further consideration and refinement. But one thing seems certain: it is time to broaden our conception of the principle of institutional balance to bring in the complex phenomenon of Community administration.[167] Over and above that, the evolution of the Community system is setting out what has perhaps become the major political theme of the institutional orders that are arising in complex societies. Classically, it is the 'form of government' that conditions the production of law by the 'good legislator' and its application by the 'good judge'.[168] On the contrary, in the new economic and social orders, the political dimension lies in local, direct formalizations of the 'collective', where the legal means has to be discovered anew. One can no longer be content with a general, abstract political form. Today, the terms of the classical formula have to be inverted. It is the 'form of law', that will supply the tools for building 'good government'.

[167] Cf. Lenaerts and Verhoeven, 'Institutional Balance as a Guarantee for Democracy in EU Governance', this volume.

[168] See e.g., Ost and Lenoble, 'Rationalité juridique et mythes fondateurs', *ARSP* (1980) 519; Ost and Van de Kerchove, 'Rationalité et souveraineté du législateur, "paradigmes" de la dogmatique juridique?', 62 *Rivista internazionale di filosofia del diritto* (1985) 227.

5

Delegation is Dead, Long Live Delegation: Managing the Democratic Disconnect in the European Market-Polity

PETER LINDSETH

I. INTRODUCTION: DELEGATION AND COMMUNITY GOVERNANCE

Is it any longer useful to think of the regulatory system in the European Community in terms of authority 'delegated' from the national level? The direction of the Community's development in the decade and a half since the adoption of qualified-majority voting for internal market measures, as well as the concomitant expansion of the comitology system, would seem to support a negative response. Over the last fifteen years, it has become increasingly obvious that the production of regulatory norms in the Community involves a complex array of actors operating at multiple political levels—supranational, national, regional and local. Among the major players in this multi-level system are administrative officials, quasi-public standard-making bodies, business interests, trade unions, public advocacy groups, 'epistemic communities' of scientific and technological experts, as well as elected officials both legislative and executive (not to mention lawyers and judges). The diffuse and fragmented nature of normative power in the Community system is reflective of the character of the European integration project as a whole, which aims to create a *sui generis* market-polity transcending national borders. Although the semblance of traditional hierarchical 'government' may persist on the national level (a debatable assertion in itself), the Community reality is arguably one of polyarchical 'governance', a term used precisely because it seems to avoid the implication that there exists any privileged source of normative power (or democratic legitimacy) at the summit of the system.

From this perspective, although national constitutional traditions may mandate that we view regulatory norm-production merely in terms of a delegation from the national parliament (and hence properly subject to the parliament's control and supervision), the complexities of the European regulatory system make it difficult to sustain the same view at the supranational level. In the Community system, the modes of governance and distribution of powers simply do not divide neatly into traditional constitutional categories—legislative, executive and judicial. Thus, it would no longer seem useful to think about the Community system in terms of the classic *trias politica* upon which national constitutional orders have been built, with the people's legislative power personified or embodied in a parliament at the centre of the system. One might fairly say that, in trying to understand the Community, the notion of a delegation from the national level should be avoided precisely because it suggests a principal–agent relationship between national parliaments and the producers of regulatory norms that does not exist. Even if the norm-producing 'agents' in the Community (never easy to identify) could be said to derive their authority from their purported constitutional 'principals' at the national level, the process of regulatory norm-production in the Community operates with so much effective autonomy that it would seem impossible for anyone realistically to assert that the agents work under the control or supervision of a national constitutional principal in any meaningful hierarchical sense. Rather, in this polyarchical regulatory environment, national parliaments (the locus of democratic legitimacy in classical constitutional theory), as well as national government ministers (who derive their own legitimacy from the parliament), are merely one set of actors among many, with certain powers at their disposal but hardly a decisive influence over the regulatory process. Indeed, one might well say that national legislatures and executives are themselves simply 'agents' in a diffuse regulatory system comprised of 'agents without principals'.

In such a system, it might seem difficult to claim—as an interpretation rooted in traditional state-based conceptions of administrative and constitutional law might lead one to do—that the foundation of the normative authority in the European market-polity is a delegation of legislative power from constitutional principals at the national level—the Member State parliaments. For many thoughtful commentators, several of whom are represented in this volume,[1] the fact that delegation has little empirical-analytical utility in this way may also suggest that it should be abandoned as a normative-legal principle as well. From such a perspective, it is time to reconceptualize the legal and democratic underpinnings of the Community system—to remove them finally and definitively from the confines of national administrative and constitutional thinking—and to explore alternative means of legitimizing the Community's regulatory output in decentralized, non-hierarchical ways that are more congruent with the polyarchical character of the integration project.

[1] E.g., Oliver Gerstenberg and Charles Sabel, Koen Lenaerts and Amaryllis Verhoeven, Michelle Everson, and Christian Joerges.

The favoured mechanism in this regard is a dramatically expanded range of transparency and participation rights for the social interests affected by Community regulation, as well as a heightened obligation on the part of Community regulators to disclose the scientific bases of their proposed rules and standards. Making Community norm-production more accessible to outside groups and their autonomous expertise is undoubtedly a normatively attractive undertaking. In its most sophisticated form, this alternative theory of legitimation in the Community seeks to build a new kind of deliberative democracy based on new forms of political participation, transparency and information exchange, free from the constraints of hierarchical, plebiscitarian, 'demos'-based constitutionalism at the national level.[2] If properly designed, we are told, such a system could not only legitimize the Community governance in non-hierarchical terms but it could also foster the kind of policy experimentalism and attention to best practices that are more likely to yield innovative regulatory solutions to the complex problems facing Europe and elsewhere.

My purpose here is not to criticize proposals for greater participation, transparency and experimentalism in the Community system; these should be favoured in their own right wholly apart from whether they constitute an entirely new form of democratic legitimation.[3] My purpose, rather, is to question precisely this latter claim to a novel kind of 'non-hierarchical' or 'directly deliberative' democratic legitimacy—not on the theoretical plane, but rather as a realistically achievable socio-political/socio-cultural programme, at least in the near term. It is certainly possible, in principle, to *conceive* of democracy in directly-deliberative and non-hierarchical ways, and extremely sophisticated models have been advanced to do so. Legitimacy, unfortunately, is not solely a question of what is conceptually possible. If that were so, then scholarly solutions to the myriad of constitutional challenges in the EU could be unproblematically translated into institutional and legal reality, without being filtered through a complex process of political, social and cultural contestation at the national level.

The principal weakness in these reconceptualizations of democratic and constitutional legitimacy in the Community, it seems to me, is that they fail to account for one socio-political/socio-cultural fact. For better or worse, prevailing understandings of what makes a system 'democratic' are still wedded in important respects to the hierarchical governmental institutions of the nation state, which remain the primary focal point of political identity in Europe.[4]

---

[2] See in particular the contribution of Gerstenberg and Sabel in this volume.

[3] See n. 46–49 below and accompanying text.

[4] Cf. Wood, 'Building "Europe": Culture, History and Politics', 11 *Journal of Historical Sociology* (1998) 397; Deflem and Pampel, 'The Myth of Postnational Identity: Popular Support for European Unification', 75 *Social Forces* (1996) 119; Shore, 'Transcending the Nation-State? The European Commission and the (Re-)discovery of Europe', 9 *Journal of Historical Sociology* (1996) 473.

Prevalent conceptions of democracy in Europe are still intimately bound up with the idea that there must exist certain publicly 'constituted' bodies (most importantly, but not exclusively, a parliament) that are broadly understood to embody or express the capacity of a historically cohesive political community—again, the 'demos'—to rule itself. This historically-grounded condition of democracy may carry with it all sorts of negative implications and consequences; nevertheless, as a cultural presupposition, it retains a capacity to order thinking and to give meaning to social and political action affecting whether and how a regulatory regime is *experienced* as democratic.[5]

It is for this reason that a programme constructed primarily (or even exclusively) on conceptions of non-hierarchical or directly-deliberative legitimation in the Community strikes me as problematic. The persistent socio-political/socio-cultural attachment to national constitutional bodies as the privileged expressions of democratic legitimacy is an empirical reality that cannot simply be theorized away. This attachment is a background constraint so fundamental as to be sometimes overlooked in non-hierarchical theories of Community governance. The legitimacy of national constitutional government flows from a long and complex history—social, political and legal—out of which national political communities and their corresponding governing structures emerged over several hundred years. Stable constitutional structures on the national level have derived their legitimacy—even if imperfectly and not without significant moments of overt and covert contestation by divergent interests—from a symbolic quality. This quality is grounded in the popular perception that governmental hierarchies on the national level (be they legislative, executive, or judicial) have come to embody or express, *in a historical sense*, the capacity of the national political community to rule itself.

In light of the historical-rootedness of national constitutional orders, it is questionable whether any supranational regulatory system constructed primarily or exclusively on non-hierarchical mechanisms of legitimation can be experienced as democratic in any broadly acceptable sense, unless popular understandings of the nature of democratic self-rule are themselves radically transformed. This absence of democratic legitimacy at the supranational level

---

[5] On the relationship of 'experience' and meaningful political action, see Thompson, 'History and Anthropology, Lecture Given at the Indian History Congress (30 December 1976)', in E. P. Thompson, *Making History: Writings on History and Culture* (1994) 222, who argued in an analogous context: 'historical change eventuates . . . because changes in productive relationships are *experienced* in social and cultural life, refracted in men's ideas and their values, and argued through their actions, their choices and their beliefs'. Rather than focusing on productive relationships, as Thompson did, I am focusing on how changing *structures of public governance* are 'experienced' in relation to historically-rooted ideas and values of democracy. Those ideas and values obviously evolve historically in relation to the changing structures of governance, but my basic premise is that prevailing ideas and values of democracy have still remained attached to national institutions even as normative power increasingly becomes denationalized.

may well be surmounted over time, but in a half century of economic and to a lesser extent political integration, Europe has proven unable to overcome it fully—at least so far. For the time being, therefore, this suggests that the Community system will continue to depend on national structures of hierarchical 'government' as the source of this kind of traditional, historically-grounded democratic and constitutional legitimacy.

Should the Community's continuing dependence on national legitimation be regarded as troubling? It should *only if* one begins with the premise that the Community, given its seemingly autonomous normative powers, must also possess its own fully autonomous legitimacy, apart from delegations from the national level. This premise, I believe, is historically mistaken. National constitutional orders in the twentieth century were built on the realization that national parliaments could not—indeed, should not—be the exclusive locus of legislative power in the administrative state. The resultant diffusion and fragmentation of normative power conferred a significant degree of rule-making authority on executive and administrative bodies—as well as on quasi-public and even traditionally private entities—but, importantly, never also conferred on them a fully autonomous constitutional legitimacy. The foundation of administrative legitimacy at the national level is generally not constitutional but rather simply legislative, rooted not in direct democratic control but in other forms of political and legal supervision.

The foundation of Community legitimacy is not radically different. The Community system draws its authority not from a direct constitutional enactment of some definable European 'demos' but rather from lawful transfers of normative power from national parliaments as representatives of their respective national communities.[6] Like administrative governance on the national level, the key sources of legitimacy in the Community are found in political and legal, and not directly democratic, control mechanisms. From this perspective, Community institutions operate as a multi-function agency—a category Americans know well—with executive, legislative and adjudicative

[6] It is of course true that Community institutions have also benefited from several transfers of normative power directly from the 'peoples' of certain Member States, via popular referenda revising their respective constitutions. Even if such referenda took place in all Member States—and they have not—they should not be analogized to a constitutional transfer of sovereignty that might occur on the national level, from the 'people' to national parliaments, executives, or courts. Constitutional amendment (whether by referendum or not) was necessary *as a matter of domestic law*, not because the several European 'peoples' intended to create a separate entity with independent constitutional status, but because the revised EC Treaty permitted the exercise of an autonomous rule-making power *outside the confines of the nation state*, thus infringing upon national sovereignty. See, e.g., the decision of the French Conseil constitutionnel, no. 97-394 DC, 31 Dec. 1997, Cons. const., *Rec.* 344 (holding that France needed to amend its constitution prior to the entry into effect of certain provisions of the Treaty of Amsterdam of 1997, following the same logic that the Conseil applied to the Maastricht Treaty in Decision no. 92-308, 9 Apr. 1992, Cons. const., *Rec.* 55).

jurisdiction stretching across vast areas of economic and social regulation, unique in that it takes its mandate from multiple political principals, i.e., the Member State parliaments and their electorates.

The transfer of regulatory authority to the Community system in the second half of the last century, I would suggest, is simply the *denationalized manifestation of a diffusion and fragmentation of normative power away from national parliaments* which began to accelerate at the national level in the 1920s and 1930s and then reached its full fruition in the post-war decades. Indeed, it was only in the post-war decades that the decline of parliaments in national constitutional orders was reconciled in any stable way with historical conceptions of democratic and constitutional legitimacy inherited from the eighteenth and nineteenth centuries. European integration built directly on this reconciliation of administrative governance and parliamentary democracy, and thus it is no coincidence that supranationalism emerged as a viable political project in western Europe at precisely the moment in history when the basic constitutional foundations of administrative governance at the national level were also secured.[7]

II. THE RECONCILIATION OF ADMINISTRATIVE GOVERNANCE AND PARLIAMENTARY DEMOCRACY: MEDIATED LEGITIMACY

Writing in the mid-1930s in support of his claim of an irreversible 'crisis of parliamentary democracy', Carl Schmitt noted how constitutional developments in every major industrialized country since the First World War fell into a common pattern, characterized by the suppression of the constitutional distinction between legislative and executive power.[8] The apparent degradation of parliaments in the national constitutional orders of western Europe (Schmitt focused on Germany, France and Britain, along with the United States) was the result, he asserted, of an effort to 'simplify' the legislative process, in order to keep legislation 'in harmony with the constant changes in

---

[7] See W. Mattli, *The Logic of Regional Integration* (1999), at 99–100 (asserting a catalysing effect of 'commitment institutions'—Commission and ECJ—as a condition of successful regional integration). This effect would not have been possible, I assert, if the legitimacy of administrative governance had not been settled by the end of the 1950s. See also Opinion of Advocate-General Lagrange in Case 6/64, *Costa v ENEL* [1964] ECR 604–605, discussed in the contribution of Koen Lenaerts and Amaryllis Verhoeven in this volume.

[8] Schmitt, 'Une étude de droit constitutionnel comparé: L'évolution récente du problème des délégations législatives', *Introduction à l'étude du droit comparé: Recueil en l'honneur d'Edouard Lambert*, 3rd and 4th parts (1938). The article appeared originally in German as 'Vergleichender Überblick über die neueste Entwicklung des Problems der gesetzgeberischen Ermächtigungen (Legislative Delegationen)', *Zeitschrift für ausländisches öffentliches Recht und Völkerrecht* (1936) 252.

the political, economic and financial situation'.[9] For Schmitt, this effort responded to what he claimed was 'an insurmountable opposition between the concept of legislation in a parliamentary regime and the evolution of public life over the course of the last decades', which had obliged the concentration of legislative power in the executive.[10]

To Schmitt, however, it was wrong to characterize this constitutional evolution 'by the pejorative word dictatorship',[11] because in his mind it represented instead the 'triumph' of an older constitutional legality, one rooted in the thinking of Aristotle and St. Thomas Aquinas, 'over the concepts of legislation and of constitution peculiar to separation of powers regimes'.[12] Schmitt's evident purpose was to justify the Nazi regime as both a more genuine expression of purportedly traditional European precepts of governance, as well as a harbinger of things to come throughout the industrialized world. It was only in Germany, however, that this phenomenon had reached its logical conclusion, Schmitt argued, in that it was the Germans who in 1933 had fully dispensed with conventional notions of 'separation of powers' by instituting a system of what he called 'governmental legislation'.[13]

Did the demands of modern governance and 'the concepts of legislation and of constitution peculiar to separation of powers regimes' prove as contradictory as Schmitt predicted? To the contrary, among the major constitutional achievements in western Europe after the Second World War (apart from the development of effective mechanisms for the protection of individual rights), was in the development of mechanisms of governance to surmount what Schmitt had claimed was 'insurmountable'. Although legal and institutional approaches would differ in particulars, the process of reconciling delegation and parliamentary democracy would follow the same basic pattern in most western European states. The vast majority of rules of general application (i.e., legislative rules) would no longer be in the form of traditional legislation passed by the national parliament but would now take the form of regulations or other subordinate legislation produced in the executive and an increasingly complex and diffuse administrative sphere. The democratic legitimation of these rules would no longer be directly through a vote of individual legislators as such, but rather through the hierarchical control or supervision of the administrative sphere by government ministers (who were in turn responsible before parliament), supplemented by forms of direct legislative oversight and legal controls enforced by courts or other specialized administrative tribunals.

In countries like France and the Federal Republic of Germany, however, efforts were made in another direction as well, toward the protection of the

---

[9] Ibid., at 200.   [10] Ibid., at 204.   [11] Ibid., at 201.   [12] Ibid., at 210.
[13] Ibid., at 205. Of course, after 1940, France joined Germany in this camp. See D. Rusu, *Les décrets-lois dans le régime constitutionnel de 1875* (PhD Thesis on file at the Université de Bordeaux, 1942), at 178 (citing Schmitt with approval).

'core' democratic functions of the legislature through the development of substantive constitutional constraints on the nature and scope of delegation. Article 80(1) of the West German Basic Law, for example, authorized the federal parliament to delegate either to the federal government, a federal minister or a Land government the power to issue *Rechtsverordnungen*—regulatory ordinances with the force of law. That authorization, however, was subject to one very important proviso: the 'content, purpose and scope' (*Inhalt, Zweck, und Ausmaß*) of the delegation had to be specified in the enabling legislation itself, thus prohibiting indeterminate delegations of the Weimar type. The French constitution of 1946 seemed to take an even more restrictive line— providing in Article 13 that '[t]he National Assembly alone shall vote *la loi*. It cannot delegate this right'—although this provision was never subsequently interpreted as prohibiting shifts in normative authority to the executive even as its precise limitations remained the subject of some controversy. The aim of Article 13 was to avoid a return to the open-ended *décrets-lois* which became common in the final years of the Third Republic.

Defining the substantive consequences of these delegation constraints would occupy both German and French judges over the course of the 1950s. In its very first decision applying Article 80(1) to a proposed delegation, the Bundesverfassungsgericht stated in 1951:

The Basic Law in this as in other respects reflects a decision in favour of stricter separation of powers. The Parliament may not escape its lawmaking responsibilities by transferring part of its legislative authority to the Government without considering and precisely determining the limits of the delegated authority.[14]

What emerged in the post-war jurisprudence of the Constitutional Court was not an inflexible, absolutist non-delegation doctrine—by its terms, Article 80(1) in fact *authorized* delegation—but rather a more subtle approach. The Court relied on a series of analytical formulas to constrain the executive's normative autonomy while nevertheless allowing the delegation to proceed.[15]

---

[14] BVerfGE 1, 14, 60. My reading of the Article 80(1) case law of the Constitutional Court is greatly indebted to Currie, 'Separation of Powers in the Federal Republic of Germany', 41 *AJCL* (1993), at 218–219, and to W. Mößle, *Inhalt, Zweck und Ausmaß: Zur Verfassungsgeschichte der Verordnungsermächtigung* (1990).

[15] These included: the *Vorhersehbarkeitsformel*, which focused on whether the content of any future regulation was foreseeable from the statute itself; the *Selbstentscheidungsformel*, which focused on whether the legislature had itself decided the limits of the regulated area as well as the goals of the regulation; and the *Programmformel*, which focused on whether the statute had defined with sufficient clarity the regulatory programme. The Court also relied on the presence in regulatory statutes of Bundestag veto powers over measures adopted by the executive—in effect, a kind of direct legislative oversight— viewing this veto power as compensation for the increased concentration of authority in the executive brought about by the delegation itself. See, e.g., BVerfGE 8, 274, 319–322 (1958); for a discussion, see Currie, *supra* n. 14, at 233. Where Länder interests are implicated, the Bundesrat also possesses a right of veto that derives directly from the Basic Law itself. See Article 80(2).

Even though the Bundesverfassungsgericht sought to avoid applying Article 80(1) in an excessively strict sense, it also recognized the need to protect what it understood to be, in light of historical experience, the 'essential' functions of the people's elected legislative representatives. This *Wesentlichkeitstheorie*, or 'theory of essentialness', directly intersected with the Court's constitutional obligation to protect individual rights: where a regulatory programme implicated such rights or some other fundamental aspect of public policy, there was a heightened constitutional obligation on the part of the legislature to make the policy decisions itself on the face of the statute, rather than delegating that power to the executive. This heightened obligation derived less from the terms of Article 80(1) than from the overall structure and ethos of the Basic Law as establishing a system of separation of powers under the rule of law, in which only the Parliament was understood as possessing the necessary 'democratic legitimation' to decide questions of fundamental public policy.[16] As the Court would later make clear, the *Wesentlichkeitstheorie* was rooted directly in the constitutional guarantee of democracy:

The democratic legislature may not abdicate [its] responsibility at its pleasure. In a governmental system in which the people exercise their sovereign power most directly through their elected Parliament, it is rather the responsibility of this Parliament above all to resolve the open issues of community life in the process of determining the public will by weighing the various and sometimes conflicting interests.[17]

In France, a similar understanding of the democratic function of delegation constraints would also emerge in the post-war decades. In its famous advisory opinion of 6 February 1953, the Conseil d'Etat stated that, although Article 13 of the 1946 constitution prohibited recourse to open-ended decree-laws of the type common in the late Third Republic, it did not prevent the legislature from 'determining *souverainement* the competence of the regulatory power'.[18] The Conseil found that there was no absolute prohibition contained in Article 13 but rather two broad limitations, one as to subject-matter, the other as to indeterminacy. Consistent with established administrative

[16] Mößle, *supra* n. 14, at 35.

[17] BVerfGE 33, 125, 159 (1972). This translation is drawn from Currie *supra* n. 14, at 224. It should be stressed that the principles of non-delegation developed in West Germany in the post-war decades did not apply merely to the transfer of rule-making power from the legislature to the executive and administrative sphere. Rather, it applied more generally to the broad diffusion and fragmentation of normative power that has characterized modern governance, whether to public corporations, professional associations, or local government. See BVerfGE 12, 319 (1961) and BVerfGE 19, 253 (1965) (applying constitutional restrictions to delegations to public corporations); BVerfGE 32, 346 (1972) (local government); BVerfGE 33, 125 (1972) (occupational associations); and BVerfGE 77, 1 (1987) (legislative committees).

[18] Advisory Opinion of 6 February 1953, reprinted in Y. Gaudemet, B. Stirn, T. Del Farra and F. Rolin (eds), *Les grands avis du Conseil d'Etat* (1997), at 63–64.

jurisprudence,[19] the Conseil d'Etat found that 'certain matters are reserved to legislation', notably anything affecting the individual rights and liberties now incorporated by reference into the preamble of the 1946 constitution. In these sensitive domains, the legislature must formulate 'the essential rules' itself, although it may also grant authority to the government to 'complete' them. The constitution also prohibited a delegation that, 'by its generality and its imprecision', constituted an abandonment by the National Assembly to the government of 'the exercise of national sovereignty'. In this sense, the Conseil viewed the need for constitutional constraint on delegation as a direct consequence of the democratic character of the constitution itself.

The constitutional environment in France obviously changed dramatically in 1958 both in terms of substance and institutional structure. Nevertheless, these changes, at least insofar as concepts of delegation are concerned, were less dramatic than originally supposed, despite the contrary implication of the new constitutional text (notably Articles 34 and 37) which now suggested that the executive possessed its own autonomous 'regulatory' powers. The prevailing jurisprudence of both the Conseil d'Etat and the newly-established Conseil constitutionnel strived to maintain (perhaps quixotically) the constitutional centrality of the legislature in the production of regulatory norms. Both bodies have extensively interpreted the realm of legislation so that it is now understood to reach effectively all subject-matters, thus undermining the purportedly autonomous character of the government's normative authority.[20] The Conseil constitutionnel and the Conseil d'Etat have interpreted the government's powers as generally being limited to *mise en oeuvre*—or merely legislative implementation.[21] Moreover, the subsidiary nature of the government's regulatory powers manifested itself in another manner as well, in the subjection of these powers to general principles of law as enforced by the *juge administratif*.[22]

---

[19] C.E., 4 May 1906, *Babin, Rec.* 362, concl. Romieu.

[20] For an overview, see Favoreu, 'Les règlements autonomes n'existent pas', 3 *Revue française de droit administratif* (1987) 871.

[21] Thus, 'in the quasi-totality of the cases' the determination of whether a matter falls within the legislative or regulatory domain turns on 'the secondary or subsidiary nature of the question involved (and not [on] the nature of the matter concerned)'. Ibid., at 878.

[22] The purportedly 'autonomous' character of the government's regulatory power in the constitution of 1958 led some observers to question whether these general principles of law could any longer be used in the legal control of decrees adopted pursuant to Article 37. The Conseil d'Etat disposed of this concern fairly quickly, holding in 1959 that the general principles of law were themselves of a constitutional character, rooted in the rights and liberties incorporated by reference in the preamble to both the 1946 and 1958 constitutions. They were thus superior to regulatory norms produced under Article 37 and applicable to the control of all governmental action in a *recours pour excès de pouvoir*. C.E. Sect., 26 June 1959, *Syndicat général des ingénieurs-conseils, Rec.* 394.

If we shift our attention to post-war Britain (the third European country on which Schmitt focused in the mid-1930s),[23] we find of course that it never abandoned parliamentary supremacy as a fundamental constitutional doctrine. Thus, explicit recourse in that country to judicially-enforced constraints on delegation was out of the question. The focus of British efforts to constrain delegation would therefore be, at least initially, parliamentary and procedural, notably through the rationalization of parliamentary oversight mechanisms ('laying' procedures) under the Statutory Instruments Act of 1946, as well as through a parallel effort a decade later to rationalize administrative adjudication and judicial review under the Tribunals and Inquiries Act of 1958. For much of the immediate post-war decade, however, the British courts deferred to the political imperatives of Parliament and the government in the exercise of normative power outside the parliamentary realm.[24] Over the decade following the passage of the Tribunals and Inquiries Act, however, the courts would reverse this trend.[25] In other words, after a decade of quiescence, the British courts began to assert their place in the post-war constitutional settlement of administrative governance in the United Kingdom by becoming more active defenders of individual rights in the face of executive and administrative action, albeit within the confines imposed by British constitutional tradition.

In some sense, British judges simply confronted through administrative case-law the same constitutional reality that their French and German counterparts also confronted through their written constitutional texts and jurisprudence. The diffusion and fragmentation of normative power both to, and within, the executive and administrative spheres directly challenged historically-grounded notions of 'separation of powers'—in which the legislature would make the norms of general application, the executive would implement those norms as an agent of the legislature, and judges would adjudicate

---

[23] See, *supra* n. 9 and accompanying text.

[24] This led to a series of disturbing precedents regarding the limited application of principles of natural justice (*Nakuda Ali v Jayaratne* [1951] AC 66, and *R v Metropolitan Police Commissioner ex parte Parker* [1953] 1 WLR 1150); deference to the discretionary powers of the administration (see, e.g., *Robinson v Minister of Town and Country Planning* [1947] KB 702); and a broad reading of statutory provisions precluding judicial review (see, e.g., *Woollett v Ministry of Agriculture and Fisheries* [1955] 1 QB 103).

[25] A now-famous series of major cases would reinvigorate the application of principles of natural justice (*Ridge v Baldwin* [1964] AC 40); impose much stricter judicial limits on ministerial discretion (*Commissioners of Customs and Excise v Cure & Deeley Ltd* [1962] 1 QB 340); give a much more narrow reading to preclusive clauses (*Anismic Ltd v Foreign Compensation Commission* [1969] 2 AC 147); and more generally use the doctrine of *ultra vires* to review a broad range of administrative illegalities. For a summary, see B. Schwartz and H. W. R. Wade, *Legal Control of Government: Administrative Law in Britain and the United States* (1972), at 299. For a detailed historical consideration of increasing judicial activism in the early 1960s, see J. Griffith, *Judicial Politics Since 1920: A Chronicle* (1993), ch. 4.

disputes as to the meaning and implementation of those norms. In the subsequent decades, few could deny that western European public law was now confronted by a much more complex reality. National legislatures, rather than specifying regulatory norms directly in the statute itself, now more often than not simply conferred power on executive bodies to make the rules via some form of subordinate legislation, subject to certain general statutory guidelines (*lois-cadres* in the French parlance). National executives thus came to enjoy not merely extensive legislative powers but also, concomitantly, broad adjudicative powers as well (at least in the first instance) over the vast array of disputes which arose in the implementation of the administrative programmes under their charge. And as a consequence, national judicial power increasingly became concerned with the particulars of public (i.e., administrative and constitutional) law, taking on an important role in the supervision of the normative functions of the executive and the administration.[26]

What these judicial controls suggest, however, is that even as power shifted out of the parliamentary realm, the executive and administrative spheres never gained the ability to legitimize their normative activities in an autonomous manner. Rather, oversight by other branches—both judicial and legislative—continued to play important roles. Thus, even if the concentration of authority in the executive branch seemed to signify a 'fusion' rather than a 'separation' of powers in the traditional sense (as Schmitt claimed), historically-grounded notions of democratic and constitutional government were, after a period of significant historical struggle, maintained through a separation of the *mechanisms of legitimation*—legislative, executive and judicial—something Schmitt could never appreciate.[27] In this way, administrative governance never attained—and has not attained—a kind of autonomous constitutional legitimacy, but rather its legitimacy has remained *mediated* through the traditional branches of government that are themselves historically endowed with constitutional authority.

III. ADMINISTRATIVE GOVERNANCE IN THE COMMUNITY SYSTEM: MANAGING THE DEMOCRATIC DISCONNECT

The fact of widespread normative autonomy in the Community system does not mean that it should be freed from similar forms of traditionally legitimate (and legitimizing) oversight and control. The Community system at best enjoys a kind of 'technocratic' legitimacy rooted in its capacity to generate sound policy outcomes, supplemented by a (judicially-enforced) 'legal' legit-

---

[26] For an eyewitness account of the resulting *complexification* of public law during this period, see Braibant, 'Du simple au complexe: quarante ans de droit administratif (1953–1993)', 45 *Etudes et Documents du Conseil d'Etat* (1993) 409.

[27] See, e.g., C. Schmitt, *Der Hüter der Verfassung* (1931).

imacy derived from its operation within the lawful bounds of its delegated power. As for 'democratic' legitimacy, however, the Community acts essentially as a supranational administrative agent with an attenuated relationship to the perceived ultimate source of its normative powers: national parliaments *severally* as representatives of their national political communities.[28]

What is conventionally understood, then, to be a 'democratic deficit' in Community institutions is really better understood as a 'democratic disconnect', in recognition of the increasingly attenuated nature of direct national control and oversight over Community norm-production. The notion of a democratic deficit focuses our attention exclusively on the Community level and implies that democratization of supranational norm-production can take place through changes made largely if not entirely within the confines of supranational institutions (e.g., an augmented role of the European Parliament) or within supranational regulatory processes (e.g., greater transparency and participation in the comitology system). The notion of a democratic disconnect, by contrast, focuses our attention on the relationship between supranational institutions and national oversight and control. It does not deny the need for greater transparency and participation in the Community regulatory system, but it suggests that any democratization strategy must, at least in part, include a rethinking of the linkages between supranational norm-production and democratic legitimation derived from the national level.

At its inception, European integration built directly on elements of the post-war constitutional settlement which supported administrative governance at the national level as well. First, and most importantly, it built on the constitutional predominance of the national executive, not merely as a 'legislator' in its own right but also as the first line of democratic legitimation over policy-making in subordinate administrative bodies, whether national or supranational. It also built on a kind of enabling legislation in a new guise— the various *traités-cadres* of the three European communities—which, like *lois-cadres* on the national level, did not specify most regulatory norms directly but rather delegated this normative power to executive and technocratic institutions, albeit ones which now extended beyond the nation state (the Council and the Commission). Finally, the process of European integration entailed an important judicial component, not merely to review the legality of Community regulation but also, somewhat more unexpectedly, to scrutinize the conformity of Member State law with the goals of market integration as set forth in the treaties, something akin to supranational 'constitutional' review.

---

[28] Cf. Dahl, 'Can International Organizations be Democratic? A Skeptic's View', in I. Shapiro and C. Hacker-Gordón (eds), *Democracy's Edges* (1999) 19. I explore the legal implications of this perspective in detail in Lindseth, 'Democratic Legitimacy and the Administrative Character of Supranationalism: The Example of the European Community', 99 *Columbia Law Review* (1999) 628.

It is, I would suggest, precisely *because* the Community's constitutional underpinnings have built directly on the foundations of administrative governance on the national level that the Community has been able to survive for so long without obvious democratic legitimacy of its own. Rather than demonstrating a breach between the Community's low normative legitimacy as a democratic body and its high social acceptance,[29] the Community's durability owes to a popular appreciation that its legitimacy is not constitutionally autonomous but rather flows from its essentially administrative character and from the oversight by political institutions that themselves possess democratic and constitutional legitimacy (primarily national executives). From the Community's inception, committed European federalists (and technocrats) like Jean Monnet saw the essence of supranationalism as normative autonomy from even national executive control. However, what developed institutionally over the subsequent decades was in fact fairly consistent with the constitutional underpinnings of administrative governance on the national level in the post-war decades. Much of the institutional politics of European integration in its first thirty years would centre around the largely *successful* effort by national executives to assert their hierarchical legal authority (either severally or collectively) over Community rule-making.[30]

Of course, running contrary to the effort of national executives to maintain hierarchical control has been the jurisprudence of the European Court of Justice, through the development of such fundamental doctrines as direct effect, supremacy and implied powers. Here too, however, one can still maintain that a form of mediated legitimacy—albeit not through the national executive—has played an important role. The ECJ's jurisdiction to rule on

---

[29] This is the position taken in Weiler, 'Bread and Circus: The State of European Union', 4 *The Columbia Journal of European Law* (1998) 233, at 235.

[30] The first step was the creation of a 'Special Council of Ministers' in the Treaty of Paris despite the absence of such an institution in the original Monnet draft treaty for the ECSC. See generally the contributions in K. Schwabe (ed.), *Die Anfänge des Schuman-Plans 1950/51* (1988). The second and perhaps more important step was the dramatic augmentation of the Council's role under the Treaty of Rome, which deviated significantly from the more limited role of the Council under the ECSC. See generally the contributions in Enrico Serra (ed.), *Il Rilancio dell'Europa e i Trattati di Roma* (1989). The process continued in the 1960s and 1970s with the establishment of the COREPER as a parallel bureaucracy rivalling the Commission in Brussels; the Luxembourg Compromise of 1966, effectively perpetuating unanimous voting despite treaty provisions to the contrary; and ultimately the establishment of the European Council in 1974, as an organ of executive oversight outside the treaty framework. In its actual decisional practice (at least until 1986), European integration thus seemed to involve less 'a surrender of limited areas of national sovereignty to the supranation', as Milward phrases it (A. S. Milward, *The European Rescue of the Nation-State* (1993), at 4), and more a surrender of sovereignty by the *national legislature* to the *national executive*, working in conjunction with its fellow national executives in the Council of Ministers or European Council, aided both by national administrators at home and in the COREPER, as well as by a new supranational technocracy in the European Commission.

the conformity of Member State law with Community law has depended critically on the willingness of national courts to make preliminary references under the old Article 177 (now Article 234). Moreover, although the resulting constitutionalizing jurisprudence of the ECJ was sometimes profoundly intrusive into national constitutional orders, the adjudicative activism of the Court remained a largely incremental phenomenon. As such, the decisions of the Court did little to alter the basic public perception of the Community as an essentially technocratic institution; that is, as an extension of national forms of administrative governance to the supranational level. Indeed, one might well assert that, even as it deployed the conceptual vocabulary of constitutionalism to justify its actions, the real function of the Court was to acclimatize Europeans to the existence of the new supranational administrative regime.[31]

At successive stages since the mid-1980s (more specifically 1986, 1992, and 1997), the Community system gained an increasing degree of relative legislative autonomy from direct national control through the expansion of qualified-majority voting in the Council. There are two ways to interpret the post-1986 changes. First, one may argue that, taken together, they constituted a major 'constitutionalizing' step, in that they established a relatively autonomous legislative process at the supranational level that in some ways can claim to be representative of a new political community that cannot be understood in exclusively national terms. At first glance, there seems a kernel of truth in this, particularly when viewed in conjunction with the expansion of the powers of the European Parliament in the legislative process, which has given the Community the appearance of moving (slowly) toward the establishment of a genuine parliamentary system at the supranational level. In many respects, the advent of qualified-majority voting in the Council and

---

[31] The comparison with the history of American federal regulatory institutions on this point is intriguing. American lawyers will recall that when the Supreme Court finally abandoned its narrow reading of federal power to regulate interstate commerce in *NLRB v Jones & Laughlin Steel Corp* 301 US 1 (1937), it was in connection with an agency that is as 'judicial' as they come. The National Labor Relations Board, until relatively recently, almost never made rules. Rather, it used a common-law method of precedent more reminiscent of nineteenth-century practice, which perhaps made the transition to a federal regulatory state less threatening (I am grateful to Peter Strauss for this insight). Indeed, it was not until nearly three decades after *Jones & Laughlin Steel* that there was the explosion in rule-making we associate with the modern American regulatory state. See Strauss, 'From Expertise to Politics: The Transformation of American Rulemaking', 31 *Wake Forest Law Review* (1996) 755–756, nn. 33–34 and accompanying text (referring to the 'tremendous expansion . . . in the prominence, use and development of rulemaking' in the United States in the 1960s). Ironically, a similar thirty-year interval elapsed in Europe before the explosion in legislative-type rule-making at the supranational level, from the adoption of the Treaty of Rome in 1957 to the adoption of the Single European Act in 1986. In the interim, it was the Court of Justice, in its adjudicative capacity, that exercised primary responsibility for the enforcement of the common market norms set forth in the treaties.

co-decision in the Parliament marked the beginning of true supranationalism in the Community; its exercise of core legislative powers were freed from the requirement of formal approbation by the democratically-accountable executives in each Member State, as supranational adjudicative power had long been.

Nevertheless, the better way of interpreting these changes, I believe, avoids the language of supranational constitutionalism and instead views them as reflective of changes in the nature of administrative governance both nationally and supranationally over the same period. Like the earlier development of European institutions, the move toward increased supranational normative autonomy in the Community in the middle 1980s and throughout the 1990s merely extended upon developments also taking place in national administrative states. In France and Britain, for example, there was the increasing recourse to, or experimentation with, decentralized administrative control as the principal means of market regulation, through *autorités administratives indépendantes* and quasi-autonomous regulatory offices. In Germany, the complexity of modern administration began to overwhelm the old notion of a 'Chancellor democracy', leading some commentators to speak instead merely of a 'coordination democracy', in which the Chancellor served only as a policy manager at the centre of a highly pluralist institutional network.[32] All of these national developments reflected the broader recognition that the administrative state's old dependence on the executive's direct hierarchical political control over regulatory action was ill-adapted to the needs of contemporary regulation, which necessitated both greater decentralization as well as more regulatory and institutional experimentation.

How did European public law respond to these developments? Not by the abandonment of delegation constraints, to be sure, which merely took on a new and indirect form. In some sense, paradoxically, the first line of constraint was through qualified-majority voting itself. The Member State executives were arguably willing to risk the relative degree of regulatory autonomy that qualified-majority voting entailed precisely because they sought to restore some semblance of intergovernmental control over the harmonization of technical non-tariff barriers to trade, which to date had effectively been controlled by the ECJ in its free movement of goods jurisprudence. The post-1986 approach of minimal harmonization, when combined with qualified-majority voting,

was better than the alternative of letting the judicial process continue to make the necessary policy choices incrementally. . . . In other words, Member States were led to prefer political legislation, even at the risk of being pushed into the minority on a vote

---

[32] See generally Padgett, 'Introduction: Chancellors and the Chancellorship', in S. Padgett (ed.), *Adenauer to Kohl: The Development of the German Chancellorship* (1994), in particular at 18–19 and the sources cited at n. 19.

concluding Council deliberations among the Member States, to a kind of 'creeping legislation' through the judicial process, to which they were completely external.[33]

Supplementing this attempt to reassert political control via qualified-majority voting was also the introduction of several other legal mechanisms or principles designed functionally—if not formally—to preserve indirect national hierarchical control over the otherwise autonomous rule-making in the Community system. These include not merely comitology—the often obscure yet critically important system of nationally-dominated committees charged with making the detailed norms needed to implement regulatory policy in the Community—but also the subsidiarity principle, the pillar structure, and a growing range of opt-outs, derogation rights and 'closer cooperation' provisions that contribute to the increasing 'flexibility' of Community governance. Indeed, one might fairly view the expansion of the powers of the European Parliament, normally taken as evidence of constitutionalization, as in fact an indirect national control mechanism, in that it serves as one more constraint on the Commission's autonomous proposal powers, thus favouring the national regulatory status quo by making it more difficult to adopt harmonized legislation at the Community level.[34]

All of these changes, I would suggest, attempt to strike a similar balance. On the one hand, consistent with the notion of delegation, they attempt to maintain some measure of national control, even if indirectly, over the process of otherwise autonomous norm-production in the Community system. On the other hand, they reflect the realization, born of experience under the old unanimity regime, that the construction of the single market requires a relatively autonomous regulatory process operating outside the confines of the nation state, in order to overcome the inevitable collective-action problems that the Member States otherwise face. The insertion of these discretion-constraining features into European public law—the most tangible manifestation of the effort to 'manage the democratic disconnect'—suggests that the Member States still very much see themselves as the constitutional principals in the Community's political and legal system, which is understood as deriving its legitimacy from a delegation from the national level. From this perspective, in normative-legal terms at least, the Community's regulatory system, diffuse and fragmented though it may be, must still be regarded as an agency of the Member States. The Community system admittedly enjoys broad discretion in the regulatory domains delegated to it (like an independent, administrative 'fourth branch of government'[35]) but without any

[33] Lenaerts, 'Some Thoughts about the Interaction Between Judges and Politicians', *University of Chicago Legal Forum* (1992), at 110–111.

[34] See Moravcsik and Nicolaïdis, 'Keynote Article: Federalist Ideals and Constitutional Realities in the Treaty of Amsterdam', 36 *JCMS* (1998) 21.

[35] Majone, 'The European Community. An "Independent Fourth Branch of Government"?', in G. Brüggemeier (ed.), *Verfassungen für ein Ziviles Europa* (1994) 23.

autonomous constitutional legitimacy of its own, which continues to be derived from the national level.[36]

It should perhaps be unsurprising that, in its infamous and much criticized *Maastricht Decision*, the German Federal Constitutional Court would stress similar themes in its analysis of the constitutional foundations of the Community's normative power. One commentator has focused on the purportedly Schmittian premises underlying the decision,[37] but this interpretation is ironic (to say the least), as the earlier discussion of Schmitt's views on delegation and separation of powers should indicate. The emphasis which the *Maastricht Decision* placed on the differing functions of national constitutional bodies (parliament, government and courts) as representatives and protectors of the democratic rights of the national demos—and hence the Court's recourse to notions of delegation to *uphold* the Maastricht Treaty (a sometimes overlooked fact[38])—could hardly be further from Schmitt's own views on the subject.

For Schmitt, writing in the mid-1930s, the traditional precepts of separation of powers inherited from the eighteenth and nineteenth centuries (at the core of which was the parliament) simply could not be reconciled with the exigencies of modern governance. Constraints on delegation in the interest of separation of powers were an illusion, designed to surmount what Schmitt insisted was insurmountable. For the German Constitutional Court in the *Maastricht Decision*, by contrast, the shift in legislative power outside the parliamentary realm (including to the supranational level in the post-war decades) could indeed be reconciled with democracy as long as the mechanisms of mediated legitimacy—whether executive, legislative or judicial— were preserved. This was, in important respects, simply a restatement of the post-war constitutional settlement of administrative governance in the supranational context. The Court's ultimate reservation of *Kompetenz-Kompetenz* was a recognition that, vis-à-vis constitutional government at the national level, supranational organs are of an essentially administrative character and therefore should not be the ultimate judge of the scope of their own delegated authority.

One would think, given the fundamental nature of the claims made by the Bundesverfassungsgericht in the *Maastricht Decision*, that perhaps the ECJ might have found cause to re-examine the constitutional foundations of the

---

[36] See Dahl, *supra* n. 28.

[37] Weiler, 'Does Europe Need a Constitution? Reflections on Demos, Telos and the German Maastricht Decision', 1 *ELJ* (1995) 219.

[38] In fact, as an accommodation to the realities of supranational delegation and the challenges of international coordination and cooperation, the Court used a highly relaxed version of the foreseeability test normally applied under Article 80(1). Later, the Court relied on somewhat conventional notions of technocratic expertise, as well as the political incapacities of parliaments, to justify the shift in normative power to the ECB.

Community's normative power in something other than conclusory terms. What is most disturbing about much of the jurisprudence of the European Court of Justice in the 1990s is its singular failure even to discuss, much less appreciate, the continuing dependence of European integration on democratic legitimacy derived from, and mediated through, national constitutional orders. At its worst (*Francovich*) the Court's case-law suggests to some observers that the Member States have been reduced to *mere agents* of the Community (rather than vice versa), a view that Carol Harlow has aptly characterized as 'insulting'.[39]

Only moderately better is the Court's subsidiarity case-law,[40] in which the Court implies, at least by its failure to demand reasons from the Community *législateur* as to the subsidiarity aspects of the Community rules under challenge, that the Community legislative process is somehow worthy of the same deference as a constitutional legislature on the national level.[41] The implication of the Court's treatment of subsidiarity is that the Community now constitutes a federal-type system in which two levels of legitimate constitutional governance—one national, one supranational—interact.[42] This view is entirely consistent with the Court's prior characterization of the EC Treaty as a 'constitutional charter of a Community based on the rule of law',[43] in which the Court itself serves as the ultimate legitimating mechanism. By asserting, however, that the institutional legitimacy of the Community results primarily from forms of mediated *legal* rather than traditionally *democratic* control, the ECJ in fact betrays the weakness of its constitutionalist analogy and points to the administrative character of the Community system.

[39] Harlow, '*Francovich* and the Problem of the Disobedient State', 2 *ELJ* (1996) 199, at 224 (critiquing the interpretation in Steiner, 'From Direct Effects to *Francovich*: Shifting Means of Enforcement of Community Law', 18 *ELJ* (1993) 3, at 16, which in turn draws from the opinion of Advocate General Mischco in *Francovich* itself that the function of national legislatures implementing directives is 'similar to an administration under an obligation to implement a law').

[40] See the Court's judgments regarding the Working Time Directive, 1996 ECR I-5755, and the Deposit-Guarantee Schemes Directive, 1997 ECR I-2405. For a detailed critique, see Lindseth, n. 28 above, at 714–726.

[41] Compare *United States RR Retirement Bd v Fritz* (1980) 449 US 166, 179 ('Where, as here, there are plausible reasons for Congress' action, our inquiry is at an end. . . . [T]his Court has never insisted that a legislative body articulate its reasons for enacting a statute.'), with *Working Time Directive*, 1996 ECR at I-5816 ('[I]t would be pointless to require [that the legislature provide] a specific statement of reasons for each of the technical choices made by it').

[42] Cf. Bermann, 'Taking Subsidiarity Seriously: Federalism in the European Community and the United States', 94 *Columbia Law Review* (1994) 331.

[43] Opinion 1/91, 1991 ECR I-6079, I-6102, para. 21; see also Case C-2/88 Imm., *Zwartveld et al.* [1990] ECR I-3365, I-3373, para. 16; Case 294/83, *Parti écologiste 'Les Verts' v Parliament* [1986] ECR 1339, 1365, para. 23.

The subsidiarity cases of the 1990s were, in fact, a major missed opportunity for the Court to develop a more sophisticated judicial doctrine of mediated legitimacy in the Community's regulatory system. Properly understood, the subsidiarity principle should serve as a delegation constraint on normative autonomy, not to create insurmountable obstacles to supranational delegation, but rather simply to avoid treaty interpretations that amount to democratically problematic, open-ended transfers of normative power to the Community's essentially administrative regulatory system. In this regard, deploying subsidiarity as a delegation constraint would be particularly helpful on questions of institutional balance and legal basis, which can only become more complex and problematic as the Member States broaden the flexibility of Community law through opt-outs, derogation rights, and closer cooperation provisions. The increasing flexibility in Community law merely heightens the risk that two plausible legal bases for Community legislation will exist for any particular piece of legislation, one which may require unanimity or permit an opt-out, and another which demands only qualified- or even simple-majority voting.

The right to derogate from a particular legislative programme inevitably casts doubt on the relative scope of the Community's general legislative competence—in which a Member State may not, in theory, opt out—compared to its more specific competence under the closer cooperation provisions— from which certain Member States have, by definition, chosen not to participate. The evolving flexibility in Community law may simply lay the groundwork for further highly contentious legal disputes over perhaps the most sensitive issue in Community law: the line between national and supranational competence.[44] Using subsidiarity as an interpretive principle— something the ECJ has shown a singular unwillingness to do[45]—should lead to an interpretive presumption in favour of legislative bases that maximize Member State prerogatives (i.e., those which either require unanimity or, more ideally, permit an opt-out), unless there is evidence of a contrary intent on the part of the Member States at the adoption of the provisions of the Treaty in question.

What role should transparency and participation rights play in this scheme? Rather than viewing broader transparency and third-party participation rights as a means of establishing a 'directly-deliberative' democracy at the supranational level (although certainly the deliberative dimension of such rights are worthy of support), one should favour broadening such rights for a different reason: as tools for *national legislatures* to monitor the activities of their national executives and bureaucratic officials as they participate in the

---

[44] See, e.g., the Court's decision regarding the Working Time Directive, 1996 ECR I-5755. These sorts of disputes will become more common not just as European law becomes more flexible, but also as the Community system expands to the east.

[45] For an extensive critique, see Lindseth, *supra* n. 28, at 718–722.

process of supranational regulatory norm-production.[46] Transparency and participation rights are means by which national legislatures can enlist both social interests and the courts in the task of supervising the Community in the exercise of delegated normative power. Within the Community system, these tools could work in conjunction with other mechanisms put into place at both the national and Community levels to increase the involvement of domestic parliaments in supranational decision-making.[47] To achieve this end, however, such rights and duties must be extended to cover the activities of the Council, a body which the ECJ has up to this point largely treated as a 'constitutional' legislature (now together with the European Parliament) and therefore worthy of the broadest possible judicial deference.[48] Moreover, any expansion of transparency and participation rights would require active judicial supervision, to ensure the efficacy and fairness of their application.[49]

The reforms advocated here, I believe, are broadly in line with changes inserted into European public law since 1986—subsidiarity, comitology, the pillar structure and flexibility. The purpose of these changes is, in the absence

[46] The same reasoning of course would—and should—support the expansion of transparency and participation rights at the purely national level as well. From a principal–agent perspective, transparency and participation rights in the administrative sphere can be understood as forms of 'fire-alarm oversight'—that is, as a way in which legislatures enlist private interests and the courts in the broader project of reducing the inevitable agency autonomy which flows from delegation. See McCubbins and Schwartz, 'Congressional Oversight Overlooked: Police Patrols versus Fire Alarms', in M. McCubbins and T. Sullivan (eds), *Congress: Structure and Policy* (1987) 426.

[47] See, e.g., Article 88-4 of the French Constitution, inserted with the adoption of the Maastricht Treaty in 1992, requiring the French government to report proposed Community measures to the French Parliament if those measures would have fallen within the domestic legislative domain. See also Article 23 of the German Grundgesetz, also inserted after Maastricht, requiring notice to the German Bundestag of Community legislation and an opportunity for the Bundestag to take a position. See, finally, the Protocol on the Role of National Parliaments in the European Union attached to the Treaty of Amsterdam, and in particular its preamble, which acknowledges the need 'to encourage greater involvement of national parliaments in the activities of the European Union and to enhance their ability to express their views on matters which may be of particular interest to them'. OJ 1997 C 340/113.

[48] See, e.g., Case C-331/88, *Fedesa* [1990] ECR I-4023, I-4063.

[49] Such judicial involvement, of course, runs the risk of fomenting the sort of 'adversarial legalism' that afflicts the administrative system in the United States. See Lindseth *supra* n. 28, at 693–694. However, it is difficult to imagine an administrative system that will not entail some judicial supervision of expanded transparency and participation rights, particularly when those rights are presented by some as the instruments of 'deliberative democracy' and not merely as tools for achieving better public policy outcomes. If the former is true, then the pressures by outside groups for some kind of judicial protection of those rights will almost certainly be intense. Even if only the latter is the case, however, such judicial review will be essential to maintaining the 'mediated legitimacy' of the regulatory system. For these reasons, I find calls by certain commentators (e.g., Loïc Azoulay in this volume) for a restriction of the judicial role in policing transparency and participation rights in the Community system to be both unrealistic and contrary to aims of legitimation that they also advocate.

of the unworkable national veto, to harness the constitutional legitimacy of national institutions in favour of Europe's denationalized process of economic integration without unduly impeding the process of integration—a tough balancing act to be sure, but a necessary one—in recognition of the still 'mediated' legitimacy of supranational norm-production. In due time, the European Court of Justice may itself recognize a similar need for mediated legitimacy in its institutional (and particularly subsidiarity) jurisprudence.[50] For now, however, as Ellen Vos has pointed out, the Court 'appears to interpret the institutional balance in a purely horizontal manner (a balance between "institutions"), and does not include the Member States within it'.[51] Although such an approach might be justified if the Community constituted an autonomous level of governance in a federal-type system, from the administrative perspective advanced here this horizontal understanding of institutional balance ignores the place of the Member States as the constitutional principals in the Community system. As a consequence, it fails to acknowledge what is arguably the central function of the division of powers at the Community level, which is to address 'the Member States' concerns that the integrity of their own powers be maintained and thus acts as a shield against too great an institutional concentration of powers' at the Community level.[52]

Given the reluctance of the ECJ to factor the Member States into its institutional jurisprudence, Europeans might consider an additional institutional reform to 'manage the democratic disconnect' that is specifically directed at the Court. Because the ECJ's own adjudicative authority is intimately bound up with the administrative character of the Community, I have argued in detail elsewhere that it should not possess exclusive jurisdiction to rule on the extent of the Community's delegated legislative authority, as it has effectively claimed to date.[53] Rather, the Community must develop a system to resolve conflicts between the two orders of jurisdiction (national and supranational) in a manner that respects the legitimate prerogatives of each. I thus propose the establishment of a 'European Conflicts Tribunal' akin to the French *Tribunal des Conflits* to resolve disputes over competences.

Cognizant, however, that 'not all legal problems can be solved legally',[54] I would build an additional, formalized political check into the otherwise essentially judicial conflicts process that I propose. In the event that a dissenting Member State is dissatisfied with a legal decision of the Conflicts Tribunal, it should have the right to appeal the matter to a political body

---

[50] The Court's recent judgment concerning the tobacco advertising directive may suggest a willingness to move in this direction. See Case C-376/98, *Federal Republic of Germany v European Parliament and Council of the European Union* [2000] ECJ CELEX LEXIS 3074.

[51] E. Vos, *Institutional Frameworks of Community Health and Safety Regulation: Committees, Agencies and Private Bodies* (1999), at 88.

[52] Ibid.   [53] See Lindseth, *supra* n. 28, at 726–734.

[54] MacCormick, 'The *Maastricht Urteil*: Sovereignty Now', 1 *ELJ* (1995) 259, at 265.

comprised of the heads of state or government of the Member States, the European Council. If the Member State concerned cannot negotiate a satisfactory political solution within the European Council, then it should have the right—subject to significant procedural conditions precedent—to opt out of the disputed legislation. This sort of opt-out right would be another manifestation of the emerging flexibility in Community law, but more importantly it would reinforce political responsibility at the national level for the normative output of the Community, thus augmenting its mediated legitimacy.[55]

IV. CONCLUSION: DELEGATION CONSTRAINTS IN A SYSTEM OF TRANSNATIONAL ADMINISTRATIVE GOVERNANCE

The idea of the Community as a system of 'transnational governance'—a view that has gained increasing adherents in recent years[56]—provides a promising conceptual terrain on which to develop a sophisticated understanding of the relationship between national constitutional orders and supranational regulatory processes. The transnational interpretation emphasizes the relative autonomy of the Community regulatory system but it also recognizes, as Jürgen Neyer has written, that 'democracy is fundamentally a demos-bound concept (which cannot be easily translated to the European Community)'.[57] It is unclear, however, whether adherents of the transnational interpretation are prepared to accept the full normative implications of this insight, given the seeming attachment of many of them to an understanding of the Community system as enjoying at least a degree of 'weak' constitutional legitimacy of its own.[58]

[55] Undoubtedly, the existence of an opt-out right raises legitimate concerns regarding the incentives given to potentially uncooperative Member States (the hypothetical 'upstream polluter', for example). In my view, however, these objections are not decisive. The choice to opt out would carry significant political costs, and the prospect of incurring these costs may in fact tend toward public-regarding legislation at the Community level rather than against it, while also augmenting the legislation's democratic legitimacy. A decision by a Member State government to opt out, after a very public invocation of the Conflicts Tribunal and reference to the European Council, should be sufficiently controversial as to garner the attention of the domestic press, both specialized and general. The ensuing public debate should in fact reduce the institutional 'slack' that might allow a Member State government to conceal its decision from the broader public. See Levine and Forrence, 'Regulatory Capture, Public Interests, and the Public Agenda: Toward a Synthesis', 6 *Journal of Law, Economics, and Organization* (1990) 167 (Special Issue). For further details, see Lindseth, *supra* n. 28, at 733–734.

[56] See, e.g., the various contributions in C. Joerges and E. Vos (eds), *EU Committees: Social Regulation, Law and Politics* (1999).

[57] Neyer, 'The Comitology Challenge to Analytical Integration Theory', in ibid., at 231.

[58] See Lindseth, ' "Weak" Constitutionalism? Reflections on Comitology and Transnational Governance in the European Union', 21 *OJLS* (2001) 145 (reviewing Joerges and Vos, *supra* n. 56).

Arguably, the recognition that the Member States remain the locus of democratic legitimacy should lead us back, at least in normative-legal terms, to the notion of delegation and the principal–agent relationship that this notion implies. One of the more articulate advocates of the transnational approach, however, has argued that the notion of delegated normative power should be rejected as a legal fiction: 'What is at stake', rather, 'is the emergence of co-operative arrangements which respond to the fact that the bodies legally competent for law production cannot factually cope with their tasks and thus meet their responsibility only formally'.[59] The diffuse and fragmented nature of normative power in the Community system cannot be attributed to some abstract *législateur*, so this argument suggests, and therefore the notion of delegation on which modern administrative law has been built should be avoided in Community public law as empirically unhelpful and even misleading. We are indeed living in a world of 'agents without principals'.

A normatively constitutional theory of transnational governance cannot have it both ways. On the one hand, it cannot concede that the democratic foundations of the transnational system somehow continue to reside in the hierarchical structures of the nation state but on the other hand assert that, because the notion of delegated normative power is a fiction, the transnational system must therefore rely on autonomous 'non-hierarchical' means of democratic and constitutional legitimation. Notions of delegation and agency are intimately connected to prevailing understandings of both democratic and constitutional legitimacy in an era of administrative governance, as this contribution has attempted to show, and thus their normative pull will likely remain strong despite their weak empirical underpinnings. The purportedly fictional quality of delegation within the Community system is merely evidence of what is, in fact, the core challenge of legitimation facing Europe: managing the growing disconnect between structures of governance—which are being progressively denationalized and diffused throughout a complex multi-level system of governance—and the capacity of Europeans to experience those structures as democratically and constitutionally legitimate—cultural ideals still strongly bound to the institutions of hierarchical government at the national level.

Rather than devising ways of legitimizing Community norm-production exclusively or primarily in non-hierarchical terms, therefore, this analysis suggests that the focus of legal integration theory should be on devising ways to balance any such non-hierarchical mechanisms with 'mediated' forms of national legitimation, whether direct or indirect. The challenge now confronting Europe, in other words, is to find ways of legitimizing the novel and denationalized forms of regulatory norm-production in the Community not

[59] Joerges, ' "Good Governance" through Comitology?', in Joerges and Vos, *supra* n. 56, at 329.

merely as *instrumentally necessary* to the construction of an integrated market-polity but also as *recognizably democratic* in light of the historical evolution of administrative governance, both national and supranational. The notion of delegation, whatever its empirical shortfalls, has served as a cornerstone of the constitutional reconciliation of administrative governance and parliamentary democracy. It is my belief that it will almost certainly serve a similar function in reconciling supranational administrative governance with national constitutional orders.

The notion of delegation and the principal–agent relationship that it implies were never intended to deny the fact of normative autonomy in the administrative sphere. This kind of normative autonomy has been, for the last half century, as much a fact of political life at the national level as it now is at the supranational level, flowing both from organizational complexity and, in certain more recent cases, from formal legal right. Rather, the notion of delegation as a normative-legal principle has provided a conceptual foundation for a whole range of substantive and procedural mechanisms (including, most recently, increased direct participation in, and transparency of, regulatory processes), which are designed to manage that autonomy in ways that can be broadly understood as democratic in a historically recognizable sense. If Europeans were to follow the suggestion of some commentators and dispense with the concept of delegation as a normative-legal principle in the Community, they would risk exacerbating the very legitimacy concerns that they seek to address. Abandonment of delegation as a normative-legal principle in the Community system should be disfavoured precisely because it risks also abandoning the heritage of an important constitutional achievement at the national level over the course of the twentieth century—the reconciliation of administrative governance (i.e., normative autonomy) with parliamentary democracy.

SECTION III

ADMINISTERING EUROPE

6

European Administrative Law and the Law of a Europeanized Administration

STEFAN KADELBACH

INTRODUCTION

Administrative law in Europe has developed into three directions so that it consists of three bodies of law. The first set of rules and principles governs the execution of European law by institutions of the Union and, as far as that law takes direct effect, by the Member States. This European administrative law in the genuine meaning of the term has not been codified systematically. It is judge-made law, developed by the European judiciary which drew inspiration from the common legal traditions of the Member States.[1]

The second body of administrative law governs the enforcement of European law by national authorities. Other than European administrative law, those norms are national in origin. But they have been modified in order to adapt the national legal order to the exigencies of European law. That 'Europeanized' administrative law receives guidelines from the European Court of Justice and from legislation which is enacted in order to transform Community law into national law. Whereas European administrative law is genuine law of the Union, Europeanized law comes about as the result of an interaction between the national and the European systems.[2] In Italy, to name an example, there used to be a distinction between two concepts of standing before courts, '*diritto soggettivo*' and '*interesse legittimo*'; whereas an infringement of the violation of a right of the first category entitled the holder of that right to recover damages, this was not true of a violation of legitimate interests.[3]

---

[1] The field is demarcated in J. Schwarze, *Europäisches Verwaltungsrecht* (1988); the English edition was published as *European Administrative Law* (1992); A. J. C. de Moor-van Vugt and E. M. Vermeulen, *Europees Bestuursrecht* (1998).

[2] See J. H. Jans, R. de Lange, S. Prechal and R. J. G. M. Widdershoven, *Inleiding tot het Europees bestuursrecht* (1999), at 19 et seq.; S. Kadelbach, *Allgemeines Verwaltungsrecht unter europäischem Einfluß* (1999).

[3] Cf. S. Cassese, *Le basi del diritto amministrativo* (5th edn., 1998), at 463–469.

A recent decision by the Court of Appeal in a public procurement case reversed this distinction, due to developments in the aftermath of the jurisprudence of the ECJ on Member State liability for violations of Community law.[4]

The third layer of administrative law consists of rules which apply to cases which have no direct relation to EU law. However, there are examples where European administrative law has influenced the national law plane even without there being an underlying legal obligation.[5] In the United Kingdom and Ireland, the principle of proportionality, which had not formed part of the national law before, has apparently been adopted from the European level as a principle also applicable to national cases, although the exact scope of that impact is controversial.[6] By the same token, the continental notions of legitimate expectations, of damages for faults of legislation and the duty to grant interim relief are reported to have modified British and Irish law.[7] In France, the concepts of *services publics* and *contrats administratifs* have come under pressure,[8] and even the instruments of judicial control are expected to change.[9] Adjustments of that kind can in part be characterized as a process of voluntary adaptation, others follow more or less compelling impulses which originate from EU law. Since the intensity of changes not cogently evoked by the Union varies from one Member State to another and does not follow a general pattern, designed by the European legislature or the European judiciary, the sphere of national, but voluntarily Europeanized administrative law will not be dealt with in depth in this chapter.

The suggested categorization may be seen, at first glance, as to contrast sharply with the fact that, in many fields, multi-level co-operation between European, national and hybrid authorities as well as complex networks of

[4] Corte di Cassazione, *Comune di Fiesole v Vitali*, judgment of 22 July 1999, [1999] Foro Italiano, 2487; see annotations by Torchia, *Giornale di diritto amministrativo* (1999), at 843–850; Cassese, ibid., at 1221–1226.

[5] Fenelly, 'Legal interpenetration—Towards freedom of movement of principles', in M. Andenas (ed.), *English Public Law and the Common Law of Europe* (1998) 7, at 12.

[6] De Búrca, 'Proportionality and Wednesbury Unreasonableness: The Influence of European Legal Concepts on UK Law', in Andenas, *supra* n. 5, at 53; Schwarze, 'The Europeanization of National Administrative Law', in J. Schwarze (ed.), *Administrative Law under European Influence* (1996) 789, at 792; Jowell and Birkinshaw, 'British Report', ibid., 273, at 282; Jowell and Lester, 'Proportionality: Neither Novel Nor Dangerous', in J. L. Jowell and D. Oliver (eds), *New Directions in Judicial Review* (1988) 51, at 59 et seq.

[7] For the UK see Craig, 'Substantive Legitimate Expectations and the Principles of Judicial Review', in Andenas *supra* n. 5, at 23; Lewis, 'The Right to an Effective Remedy', in ibid., at 131; Craig, 'Once More unto the Breach: The Community, the State and Damages Liability', in ibid., at 141. For Ireland see G. Hogan and D. G. Morgan, *Administrative Law in Ireland* (3rd ed., 1998), ch. 13.

[8] Flauss, 'French Report', in Schwarze *supra* n. 6, 31, at 46 and 53.

[9] Galmot, 'L'apport des principes généraux du droit communautaire à la garantie des droits dans l'ordre juridique français', 33 *Cahiers de droit européen* (1997) 67.

governance dominate administrative practice rather than the need to define distinct bodies of law and conflict of law rules which resolve collisions between them.[10] Thus, one might presume that there were a demand for a unified administrative law. Sensible as this expectation may be, it does not reflect the jurisprudence of the courts. Whereas European legislation has harmonized policies in several sector-specific areas, general administrative law, being the result of judicial abstraction, develops separately on the Union and state levels.

Therefore, although it is possible that the three layers of administrative law described above will merge one day and form a common administrative law of Europe, they ought to be distinguished.[11] In the following sections, the elements of the European administrative law system (section II) and the conditions of the Europeanization of law (section III) will be dealt with separately. It will be asked what the differences are and whether or not an approximation by general harmonization is likely or even advisable (section IV). But before doing so, in order to distinguish the scope of the two spheres more clearly, it is necessary to take a look at the institutional structure of the administration of Europe.

I. ADMINISTRATION IN THE EUROPEAN MULTI-LEVEL SYSTEM

The reason why European and Europeanized administrative law have developed distinctly lies in the separation of powers between the two levels on which EU law is enforced. Whereas there is a strong demand for autonomy on the state level, the Community has an interest in uniform interpretation and application of EU law.

A. Member State Autonomy

1. Decentralized Administration of EU Law

As far as EU institutions fulfil executive functions, the main actor is the European Commission, but European agencies are playing an increasingly

---

[10] See the contributions in C. Joerges and J. Falke (eds), *Das Ausschußwesen in der Europäischen Union* (2000); E. Schmidt-Aßmann, *Das allgemeine Verwaltungsrecht als Ordnungsidee* (1998), at 318/9 points at the need for 'co-operative administrative law', but rightly stresses that it does not form a fourth category; rather, it resembles elements from different spheres of law.

[11] This is also the scheme followed in M. P. Chiti and G. Greco (eds), *Trattato di diritto amministrativo europeo, parte generale* (1997), at 15 et seq. and 399 et seq., respectively.

important role.[12] Although the instances in which European institutions execute EU law themselves are growing in number and extent, it is primarily the Member States which are entrusted with the task of implementing European policies. The rules which govern the administrative activities of European authorities, consequently, are dispersed and fragmentary. Some areas, such as the common competition policy, the law on state aid and anti-dumping law, are partly guided by primary law and secondary legislation.[13] In other fields the bulk of norms is of a merely internal nature, such as communications, notices, guidelines and Community frameworks.[14] Most of the European agencies do not dispose of a written code on administrative practice.[15] The rules that do have an external effect cover little more than specific subject matters. One of the rare examples of administrative law that applies to all policies alike are the rules on access to institution-held documents.[16]

That state of affairs is a consequence of the merely punctual attribution of administrative powers to the Union. The administration of Europe is decentralized. Although the Commission functions as the guardian of the Treaties (Article 226 EC), the relationship between the Commission, as the central European authority, and the Member State executive is not hierarchical. Unless otherwise provided for by specific EU law, the Commission has no supervisory powers over specific Member State agencies. It has to revert to the responsible government if national authorities violate EU law. Thus, the Member States retain autonomy of organization and procedure. That is why the administration of Europe basically relies on the national legal orders.

Autonomy may, therefore, be considered as a guiding principle of the European multi-level legal system. To be sure, autonomy is not a synonym for sovereignty, but the basis for the national legal orders' ability to define and produce legal norms the Union does not provide and which comply with the purposes of the administrative system of which EU policies form part.[17]

That structural principle of autonomy is reflected in many facets. From the beginning, it was acknowledged by the ECJ as one of the pillars on which

---

[12] Chiti, 'The Emergence of a Community Administration: The Case of European Agencies', 37 *CMLRev.* (2000) 309; Vos, 'Reforming the European Commission: What Role to Play for EU Agencies?', 37 *CMLRev.* (2000) 1113.

[13] Regulation No. 17 on competition procedure, OJ 1962, 204, repeatedly amended; Council Regulation 659/99 of 22 March 1999 laying down detailed rules for the application of Article 93 (now Article 88) of the EC Treaty, OJ 1999 L 83/1.

[14] With respect to state aid, see A. Wagner, *Die Stellung des Wettbewerbers im Beihilfeaufsichtsverfahren der Europäischen Gemeinschaft* (2000) 91.

[15] But see European Environmental Agency, Decision of 20 March 2000 on Good Administrative Practices of the Agency, OJ 2000 L 216/15.

[16] See below, Section II A 5.

[17] For a concept of shared sovereignty see MacCormick, 'Beyond the Sovereign State', 56 *MLR* (1990), 1; 'Sovereignty, Democracy and Subsidiarity', in R. Bellamy, V. Bufacchi and D. Castiglione (eds), *Democracy and Constitutional Culture in the Union of Europe* (1995).

Member State execution of EU law rests. The European Council of Edinburgh in 1992 reiterated that the Member States shall be left as much independence as is compatible with the object and purpose of the Treaties and the safeguarding of Community policies and that the institutional structure and the administrative law of the Member States is to be respected.[18] Since the Maastricht Treaty entered into force, the principle of subsidiarity has expanded the underlying rationale of the vertical distribution of administrative capacities to form a general scheme for the distribution of powers between the European and the state levels. The ECJ characterized the organizational framework as a 'decentralized system of management based on a division of tasks and responsibilities as between Member States and the Commission.'[19]

EU law thus, as a rule, does not interfere with the internal organization of the Member States. Exceptions were rare for a long time. As integration intensified, the implementation of a number of policies required that the Member States provided for a particular organizational structure. The common agricultural policy demands that Member States establish agencies which are responsible for the administration of Community funds.[20] The provisions on public enterprises (Article 86 EC) have a strong impact on areas where the state provides goods and services in the public interest and influence, for example, the French concept of *services publics*.[21] In many instances secondary EU law provides for the participation of the Commission in administrative procedures before national authorities. Examples are customs law, the regulation of genetic engineering and the admission of chemical substances which have a detrimental effect on the atmosphere.[22] Yet other concepts attribute to one state the final decision on certain matters and thus require a waiver of Member State jurisdiction. That is the case with certification of products

---

[18] Conference of 11/12 December 1992, Bull EC No. 12, 1992, 7, at 15.

[19] Case C-478/93, *Netherlands v Commission* [1995] ECR I-3081, at 3109.

[20] e.g., Council Regulation 2262/84 of 17 July 1984 laying down special measures in respect of olive oil, OJ 1984 L 208/1, as amended by Council Regulation 593/92 of 3 March 1992, OJ 1992 L 64/1.

[21] Case C-320/91, *Corbeau* [1993] ECR I-2533; Flauss (n. 8 above), at 53; Rodrigues, 'Prospective du service public en Europe', *Revue des affaires européennes* [1994] 72.

[22] For customs law see Article 52 Council Regulation 918/83 of 28 March 1983 setting up a Community system of relief from customs duty, OJ 1983 L 105/1, in connection with Article 7 Commission Regulation 2290/83 of 29 July 1983 laying down provisions for the implementation of Articles 50 to 59 of Council Regulation 918/83 setting up a Community system of relief from customs duty, OJ 1983 L 220/20; for regulation of genetic engineering see Articles 10–15, 21 Council Directive 90/220 of 23 April 1990 on the deliberate release into the environment of genetically modified organisms, OJ 1990 L 117/15 and Regulation 258/97 by Council and Parliament of 27 January 1997, OJ 1997 L 43/1; for the admission of chemical substances with a detrimental effect on the atmosphere see Articles 3 and 6 Council Regulation 3093/94 of 15 Dec. 1994 on substances that deplete the ozone layer, OJ 1994 L 333/1.

under European product safety law.[23] Even enforcement of administrative powers may transgress the borders so that the territorial state's jurisdiction to enforce is no longer exclusive. Agencies competent for the supervision of banks, insurance companies and the capital market are conferred upon the power to investigate in the foreign branches of resident companies in other Union states.[24]

Other influences on the organizational autonomy are more of an indirect nature. The need to set up a workable system for the distribution of structural funds was not the least important reason for Greece to create a new regional level of administrative authorities.[25] Italy established an environmental authority which is responsible for the implementation of European environmental law.[26]

EU law has a very strong impact on the organization of the states which intend to accede to the Union in the near future. The conditions of accession cover, among other rather economy-related criteria, the administrative structure. Thus, the analysis of the European Commission induced Poland to restructure its internal organization and to reduce the number of '*Woijwodships*' which now form regional level entities.[27]

In general, however, intrusions into the organizational autonomy of the present Member States are punctual. The distribution of administrative powers in the European Union rests on the presumption that EU law is administered by Member States which act autonomously. Interference into that organizational autonomy is either punctual or indirect.

2. Accountability

The structuring of administrative responsibilities thus described corresponds with the institutional architecture of the Union. Notwithstanding the potential of the weapon of censure the European Parliament can launch according

---

[23] H. C. Röhl, *Akkreditierung und Zertifizierung im Produktsicherheitsrecht* (2000), at 23.

[24] Article 15 I Second Council Directive 89/646 of 15 Dec. 1989 on the coordination of laws, regulations and administrative provisions relating to the taking up and pursuit of the business of credit institutions and amending Directive 77/780, OJ 1989 L 386/1; Article 10 Directive 73/239 as amended by Council Directive 92/49 of 18 June 1992 on the coordination of laws, regulations and administrative provisions relating to direct insurance other than life assurance and amending (third non-life insurance Directive), OJ 1992 L 228/1; Council Directive 93/22 of 10 May 1993 on investment services in the securities field, OJ 1993 L 141/27.

[25] Flogaitis, 'Greek Report', in Schwarze, *supra* n. 6, 409, at 427.

[26] Legislative decree 25 July 1994, No. 464; see: Chiti, 'Italian Report', in Schwarze, *supra* n. 6, 229, at 240; see also Franchini, 'L'organizzazione amministrativa italiana', in Chiti and Greco, *supra* n. 11, at 467; Onida and Cartabia, 'Le regioni e la Comunità europea', in ibid., at 605.

[27] Regular report from the Commission on Poland's progress towards accession (1999), at 13, 14, 70.

to Article 201 EC, parliamentary accountability of the Commission, as parliamentary monitoring of the administrative substructure of the executive in general, is relatively weak. The control exercised by the European judiciary and the Court of Auditors obviously has a stronger disciplining effect, as is the case with parallel structures in states.[28]

However, there are conceptual differences between the European and the state levels which relate to the democratic deficit of the Union. In the Member States, the hierarchical organization of the executive branch and political responsibility of the competent minister ensure that parliamentary control of the government, albeit often peripherally, monitors the use of powers by administrative bodies. By contrast, responsibility of the Commission to the European peoples is very rudimentary. The link between the European citizens' vote for the European Parliament and the election of the Commission is weak. The Council derives from the national parliaments a certain degree of democratic legitimacy, but the Commission does not participate in that rooting in the peoples' will in any substantial way.

Therefore, the interrelation between democracy and the rule of law, which is close under state constitutions, is loose on the European level.[29] The system is not well equipped to provide for a systematic administrative law as a legal framework which governs conduct by state authorities vis-à-vis individuals.[30] It makes sense that European administrative law covers above all the activities of European institutions, but those of state agencies only as far as overriding EU policies leave no discretion.

3. National Constitutions

The presumption in favour of the application of Member State administrative law, at first sight, contrasts sharply with the doctrine of supremacy of Community law. Since European administrative law is, for the most part, either not specific or not binding on state authorities, the necessity to enforce EU objectives often collides directly with national administrative law. The long history of the problem of recovery of state aid is illustrative in that respect.[31]

---

[28] See della Cananea, 'L'amministrazione Europea', in S. Cassese (ed.), *Trattato di diritto amministrativo*, tom. II (2000) 1511, at 1541 et seq.; Kadelbach, 'Verwaltungskontrollen im Europäischen Mehrebenen-System', in E. Schmidt-Aßmann and W. Hoffmann-Riem (eds), *Verwaltungskontrollen* (2001) 205.

[29] J. Habermas, *Die Einbeziehung des Anderen* (1996), at 185 et seq.

[30] So far, apart from fundamental rights, the legal framework for administration in the Union has not yet been discovered as an aspect of the debate on the 'constitutionalization of Europe'.

[31] The question is whether an order to recover state aid which was granted contrary to Articles 87 and 88 EC violates legitimate expectations of the recipient company; the German Federal Constitutional Court dismissed a complaint against judgments of the administrative

Whereas national law was not from the beginning modelled after the requirements of EU law enforcement, it is closely linked to the constitutions of the Member States. Many constitutions or constitutional courts formulate reservations to the supremacy of EU law, so that the potential of conflict appears to be more conscious than the common traditions of the Union and its Member States. The constitutions of Sweden and Germany contain provisions which limit the transfer of powers to supranational organizations and thus implicitly restrict the application of EU law.[32] The dominant view in France still holds that the priority of Union law does not derive from its autonomy but from the constitution.[33] In the United Kingdom, the approach apparently is that sovereignty of Parliament is somehow modified by the obligation to give priority to EU law but would prevail in the theoretical case that Parliament expressly decided otherwise.[34] The prevailing opinion on the interpretation of the Portuguese constitution appears to suggest that EU law does not take precedence over the constitution itself.[35] Constitutional or supreme courts in Denmark, Germany, Greece, Ireland, Italy and Spain take a sceptical stand vis-à-vis an unconditional prevalence of Community law.[36]

Thus, the unifying impulse of EU law, however strong it may be, is confronted with strong countercurrents in the state constitutions. Given the dependence of administrative law on the constitutional framework, harmonization of administrative law, from that perspective, does not appear to be a realistic prospect in the near future. It becomes obvious that European administrative law and Europeanized law are necessarily different in nature and origin.

courts which upheld an order of recovery, see order of 17 February 2000, reported in [2000] *Europa-Recht* 257.

[32] See Chapter 10 sec. 5 of the Swedish constitution; Article 23 of the German basic law.

[33] Cf. Oberdorff, 'Des incidences de l'Union européenne et des Communautés européennes sur le système administratif français', 111 *Revue de droit public* (1995) 29, at 38–39.

[34] House of Lords, *Macarthys Ltd v Smith*, judgment of 25 July 1979, [1979] 3 All ER 325, at 329 per Lord Denning.

[35] See Articles 8 (2) and 290 of the Portuguese constitution; cf. Goncalves, 'Quelques problèmes juridiques que pourra poser l'application du droit communautaire dans l'ordre juridique portugais face à la Constitution de 1976', 16 *Revue trimestrielle de droit européen* (1980) 662, at 679; Tavares de Pinho, 'L'application du droit communautaire dans l'ordre juridique portugais', *Revue du marché commun*, (1983) 35, at 38.

[36] Danish Supreme Court, *Carlsen v Prime Minister*, judgment of 6 April 1998, reported in 24 *ELR* (1999) 80; German Federal Constitutional Court, judgment of 12 October 1993, 89 BVerfGE 155, English translation in 33 *ILM* (1993) 388; Greek Council of State, *Diamantopoulos v IKA* decision No. 4674 of 27 November 1998, annotated by Maganaris, 'The Greek Council of State—Europhobic or Simply Over-protective?', 25 *ELR* (2000) 200; Supreme Court of Ireland, *SPUC v Grogan*, judgment of 19 December 1990, *Irish Law Review Monthly* (1990) 443; Italian Constitutional Court, *Frontini v AFS*, judgment of 18 December 1973, [1973] Giur. Cost. 2401, at 2410; *Granital v AFS*, judgment of 5 June 1984, *Giurisprudenza costituzionale* (1984) 1098, at 1116; Spanish Constitutional Court, declaration 108/1992 of 1 July 1992, 135 [1992] *Boletín de jurisprudencia constitucional*, 5.

4. Purity of National Systems

Another factor largely neglected in communitarianist writings that reinforces the resistance of national law against Europeanization is the tendency of courts and authorities to build and elaborate on an existing legal system along the lines of their traditional components rather than to integrate elements from 'outside'. If the German experience is representative for Europe in general, awareness of the impact of EU law and the willingness to adjust well-established patterns of legal thinking to its exigencies cannot always be taken for granted. It takes a long time for the implications of secondary law and the jurisprudence of the European Court of Justice to reach daily legal practice. Some representatives of national administrative law doctrine like to think of their respective home systems as a model code from which the relatively recent discipline of European administrative law ought to learn rather than to depart.[37]

B. Demands of Control on the European Level

In the process of Europeanization, the counterforce to the static element of state autonomy is channelled by the supervisory powers of EU institutions. Disparities with respect to the implementation of EU law are, to some extent, taken into account as a natural consequence of the difference between the various legal systems. However, the internal legal order of a Member State may not be taken as an excuse for failure of implementation.[38] The more the success of EU policies depends on uniform practice, the more there is a need for supervision.

In order to exercise effective control over national administration, the Commission has a number of tools at its disposal to fulfil its task to ensure that measures taken by the institutions are properly applied (Article 211 EC). As has been pointed out above, the Commission does not, as a rule, have the power to give orders to the national administration. The Member States owe defined results to the Union, but usually no specific mode of execution. It is therefore above all the state authorities themselves who are responsible for the proper implementation of EU policies. If it comes to violations of EU law, the Commission, according to Article 226 EC, will initiate infringement procedures by contacting the government of the state concerned which, in turn, will go through the internal administrative hierarchy in order to assess whether the complaint is considered well founded. Supervision by the

---

[37] See T. von Danwitz, *Verwaltungsrechtliches System und Europäische Integration* (1996), at 494 et seq.

[38] Case 49/86, *Commission v Italy* [1987] ECR I-2995, at 3002.

Commission, as it was originally designed in the Treaties, thus largely follows the logic of state responsibility in public international law. It focuses on legality, but does not extend to exigencies of 'good administration', usefulness and efficiency.

However, means have developed which permit a more specific monitoring of state administration. There are several degrees of how the Commission is involved in administrative procedure of state authorities.

The Commission has a right of information, not only against the Member States as a whole under Article 10 EC, but also *vis-à-vis* their competent bodies as soon as the Council will have laid down the pertinent conditions (Article 284 EC). There are many examples for special rights of the Commission to be notified of state measures, such as, for instance, plans to grant aid under Article 88 (3) EC. In other cases the Commission may collect information on its own initiative.[39] Member State bodies are also frequently obliged to consult the Commission before taking a final decision.

In some instances the Commission itself has the final decision in matters administered by state authorities. This may be true of procedures regulated under an exclusive competence of the Community. That is the case, e.g., in customs law and under the common commercial policy.[40] Beyond those areas, as far as such measures intrude into the procedural autonomy of states, the European Court of Justice requires a special justification in the public interest and strict observance of the proportionality test.[41] Among the fields where the Commission may supervise Member State enforcement directly are measures which serve the protection of public health. In the aftermath of the BSE crisis, a general competence of the Commission was created to conduct on-site inspections and to notify to the state authorities which measures have to be taken.[42]

C. The Problem of Dual Loyalty

National authorities are thus subject to two claims to obedience, stemming from two legal orders which are different in origin. They find themselves in a situation where they owe dual loyalty. On one hand, they are integrated in their respective institutional hierarchies. On the other hand, national agencies are responsible for the implementation of EU law and thus function as the

[39] See Article 22 of Council Regulation 659/99 on the application of Article 88 EC, OJ 1999 L 83/1; cf. also Article 35 Euratom.

[40] See Article 236 et seq. of Council Regulation (EEC) 2913/92 of 12 October 1992 establishing the Community Customs Code, OJ 1992, L 302/1.

[41] Case 359/92, *Germany v Council* [1994] ECR I-3681, at 3705.

[42] Commission Decision 98/139 of 4 February 1998, OJ 1998 L 38/10.

substructure of the European institutions.[43] That *dédoublement fonctionnel* may lead to conflicts if state officials receive diverging commands from the two orders.

Since administrative authorities are expected to apply self-executing Union law, including directives,[44] the problem arises to establish its scope, to decide when a legal norm takes direct effect and to foresee the consequences it has on domestic law. If such a norm would be in conflict with national law, the authorities have a problem of choice. To suggest that the doctrine of priority resolves the conflict is to presuppose what is often yet to ascertain, namely that EU law applies directly and has a defined content. Since authorities do not have the option to refer questions to the ECJ, legality of administrative conduct is at risk of becoming selective.[45]

The result is uncertainty, even though it is caused not primarily by EU law but by Member States who fail to live up to their obligations, and it is open to doubt whether such demands enhance demands uniform application of Community law. An example is the implementation of the Directive on the conservation of natural habitat, flora and wildlife[46] which currently troubles state authorities in some European states. It sets up a three-step procedure in which areas that are worth being protected are first nominated by the Member States and then selected by the Commission. Disputes on the qualification of such areas are, in the third phase, settled by special proceedings. That procedure notwithstanding, the directive may take direct effect. The ECJ found that the discretion national authorities have in the nomination of habitats for birds under the migratory bird protection directive could be so restricted by ornithological criteria that nothing but protection complied with EU law.[47] The question is open for discussion whether that also holds true for the habitat directive, possibly even against national measures to the contrary.[48]

There are four possible solutions to the problem of dual loyalty. The first one would be to apply both national and EU law. Although there is precedence for that suggestion,[49] it would not resolve many possible conflicts, particularly those where both standards are contradictory.

A second model grants priority to Community law as a rule, but insists that national law supersedes EU law in cases where the Union has acted beyond its

---

[43] Romano Prodi, '2000–2005: Shaping the New Europe', The President's Speech to the European Parliament, 15 February 2000, Bull EC, Suppl. 1/2000, 21.

[44] Case 103/88, *Fratelli Costanzo v City of Milan* [1989] ECR 1839, at 1871; Case 431/92, *Commission v Germany* [1995] ECR I-2189, at 2198.

[45] Schmidt-Aßmann, 'Zur Europäisierung des allgemeinen Verwaltungsrechts', in P. Badura and R. Scholz (eds), *Festschrift Peter Lerche* (1993) 513, at 526.

[46] Directive 92/43 of 21 May 1992, OJ 1992 L 206/7.

[47] Case 355/90, *Commission v Spain* [1993] ECR I-4221, at 4278 (Santona).

[48] With that tendency see German Federal Administrative Court (Bundesverwaltungsgericht), judgment of 19 May 1998, [1998] Neue Zeitschrift für Verwaltungsrecht 961.

[49] Joined Cases 46/87 and 227/88, *Hoechst AG v Commission* [1989] ECR 2859, at 2928.

powers or where essential components of the constitutions were violated. That approach was followed by some national courts.[50] The problem is, of course, that EU law would be subject to decentral judicial review and its uniform application would be at risk.

The third concept would grant EU law unrestricted priority. The method is simple: conflicting national norms are derogated, and in effect replaced, by EU law.[51] The jurisprudence of the ECJ has repeatedly stressed that no legal norm of whatever nature may compromise directly applicable European law,[52] not even national constitutions.[53] That is acceptable as long as European law provides for norms which fulfil the same function as those which were superseded by national law. Initially this was not the case with fundamental rights. Consequently, the ECJ extended the reach of European fundamental rights not only to measures of European institutions, but also to the administration of EU law by the Member States[54] and to national legislation on a subject covered by EU law.[55] However, priority does not help where there is nothing on the Union level which can compensate for the loss of the norm set aside for the sake of uniform application of EU law. This is usually the situation in administrative law.

Thus, a fourth path must be looked at which is able to achieve both maintenance of national administrative law and implementation of EU policies. The solution is Europeanization of national administrative law.

D. Rules, Principles and their Europeanizing Effects

From a legal theory perspective, Europeanization is a process by which principles of European law govern the application of domestic rules. The standard examples are cases where Community funds were wrongly paid, but tried to be recovered later: the administration of Community funds follows common agricultural policy regulations, which contain no rules on recovery procedures. The authorities have to apply their national laws. Administrative laws of some of the Member States set limits to the revocation of administrative

---

[50] See n. 37 above; as to consequences for administrative law courts see, e.g., Cassia, 'Le juge administratif français et la validité des actes communautaires', 35 *Revue trimestrielle de droit européen* (1999) 409.

[51] Case 184/89, *Nimz v Freie und Hansestadt Hamburg* [1991] ECR I-297, at 321; Case 358/95, *Morellato v Unità sanitaria locale* [1997] ECR I-1431, at 1451.

[52] Case 6/64, *Costa v ENEL* [1964] ECR 1251, at 1270.

[53] Case 11/70, *Internationale Handelsgesellschaft v Einfuhr-und Vorratsstelle f. Futtermittel* [1970] ECR 1125, at 1137–1138; Case 106/77, *AFS v Simmenthal* [1978] ECR 629, at 644.

[54] Case C-2/92, *The Queen v Ministry of Agriculture, Fisheries and Food, ex parte: DC Bostock* [1994] ECR I-955, at 982.

[55] Case 260/89, *ERT v Dimotiki Plioforisis and Sotorios Kouvelas* [1991] ECR I-2925, at 2964.

acts or to the recovery of money received in good faith in order to honour legitimate expectations or legal certainty.[56] Giving effect to the supremacy rule would mean to set aside national administrative law without leaving any margin of appreciation to national authorities. However, this is not the solution the ECJ has found. There is a series of ECJ judgments which stress that, in those cases, national law may be applied, on two conditions: it 'must not have the effect of making it virtually impossible to implement Community regulations and must be applied in a manner which is not discriminatory compared to procedures for deciding similar but purely national disputes'.[57] The Court has referred to these two conditions as the principles of effectiveness and equivalence.[58]

In that jurisprudence the ECJ expressly recognizes that, in the absence of Community law dealing with the matter, such cases must be decided 'by national courts pursuant to their own national law',[59] thus apparently stressing Member State autonomy as an integral part of European administrative law. The way in which the objectives of the common market are integrated into domestic law therefore differs from the way in which priority works. Effectiveness of EU law, in those cases, does not require uniformity, but equivalent conditions of application. It is submitted that the difference relates to the distinction between rules and principles.[60] Whereas rules work in an all-or-nothing fashion, principles require a balancing out of diverging interests and thus allow for flexible solutions.[61] Under the doctrine of priority, Community laws function as rules whereas the principles of effectiveness and equivalence demand that the interests of the Community are fully taken into account, but may be balanced out against interests protected by national law. The condition is that the latter are in principle recognized as legitimate by European administrative law.

In other judgments, the court seemed to leave less space for Member State autonomy. In a series of cases on revocation of decisions granting state aid the ECJ referred to the jurisprudence just mentioned, but reversed the presumption in favour of the application of national law into the opposite.[62] The Court held that undertakings to which aid has been granted may not, 'in

---

[56] See for Germany, Sections 48, 49 *Verwaltungsverfahrensgesetz*; for Spain, Articles 27, 1 and 369 *Ley de Régimen Jurídico de la Administración del Estado* (L.R.J.); Articles 109, 110 *Ley de Procedimiento Administrativo*.

[57] See Cases 205–215/82, *Deutsche Milchkontor v FRG* [1983] ECR 2633, at 2666.

[58] Case C-231/96, *Edis v Ministero delle Finanze* [1998] ECR I-4951, at 4952.

[59] ECJ in *Milchkontor, supra* n. 57, at 2665.

[60] Kadelbach, *supra* n. 2, at 51 et seq.

[61] See generally R. Dworkin, *Taking Rights Seriously* (5th edn., 1987), at 22; with respect to EU law see Allott, 'Parliamentary Sovereignty—From Austin to Hart', 49 *Cambridge Law Journal* (1990) 377, at 379 et seq.

[62] Case C-142/87, *Belgium v Commission* [1990] ECR I-959, at 969; Case C-5/89, *Commission v Germany* [1990] ECR I-3437, 3456.

principle', entertain a legitimate expectation to keep subsidies which had not been properly notified to the Commission as required by Article 88 (3) EC.[63] Consequently, national authorities, as a rule, do not have any discretion regarding the revocation even where provided for by national law.

These judgments, however, do not permit the conclusion that the jurisprudence defines Member State autonomy now more narrowly than it did in cases of the 1970s and 1980s.[64] The two series of decisions concern different cases. Whereas the first series dealt with recovery of Community aid, the second was on state subsidies. Other than Community aid, state subsidies are placed under supervision by the Commission. The Community and the Member States have a parallel interest in recovery of unduly paid Community funds. In state aid cases, by contrast, there are common interests of the beneficiary and the state granting aid. Therefore, in the interest of an undistorted competition, there is need to channel the use of discretion by state authorities. That difference explains why the Court has continuously upheld its jurisprudence on Member State autonomy in Community aid cases.[65]

It follows that Member State autonomy does not reach equally far in all cases. It is an underlying presumption of administrative law in Europe which can be restricted if the public interest of the Community so requires.

E. Conclusion

For a number of reasons, administrative law in Europe is not a homogeneous legal order applying equally to European institutions and to the administration of EU policies by national authorities, at least as long as the latter do not execute directly applicable Union law. On the other hand, there is a need to adapt national law to the standards of effectiveness and equivalence. These requirements are flexible and vary with the weight of the EU interests involved. Member State autonomy forms a part of the system. Although it is more restricted the more uniform application of Community law would be questioned by diverging legal practice, it always retains a certain degree of independence which is due to its origin. Whereas Europeanized administrative law comes about as a result of processes on both the European and the national level, European administrative law receives its authority exclusively from the European institutions. The way in which this difference in law-making is reflected by the contents of the two bodies of law will now be examined.

[63] Case C-24/95, *Land Rheinland-Pfalz v Alcan* [1997] ECR I-1591, at 1616–1619.

[64] See generally Kakouris, 'Do the Member States Still Possess Judicial Procedural Autonomy?', 34 *CMLRev.* (1997) 1389.

[65] Case 366/95, *Landbrugsministeriet-EF-Direktoratet v Steff Houlberg Export I/S u.a.* [1998] ECR I-2661, at 2682.

II. ELEMENTS OF EUROPEAN ADMINISTRATIVE LAW

What are the characteristic features of European administrative law? Following the definition suggested in the introduction, by European administrative law I mean the principles and rules which govern administrative conduct of EU institutions and of national authorities as far as they execute directly applicable Union law. Principles, rights of the individual and judicial remedies as the most elementary components of a public law system will be analysed separately in order to establish a basis for a comparison with the Europeanized sphere of administrative law.

A. Principles of European Administrative Law

European administrative law consists of subject-related legislation, such as the customs code, and general principles developed by the EU courts. Both components draw inspiration from the common traditions of the Member States. But whereas legislation does not depend on Member States' experience alone, judge-made law derives specific legitimacy from the fact that its contents are accepted as elements of domestic legal orders. It resembles most of the principles which guide administrations of Member States as well.

1. Legality

As with any modern legal order, the Union is based on the rule of law.[66] One of the many consequences is the principle of legality which requires that administrative measures are compatible with the legal act on which they are based.[67] The underlying regulations, in turn, are subject to incidental review before the ECJ and may be tested against the standards of European fundamental rights which thus form an essential component of the rule of law.

2. Legal Certainty

Legal certainty is but one facet of the principle of legality. Not only secondary Community law, but also internal measures of transformation have to conform with it.[68] It requires that decisions are sufficiently clear in wording so that the individuals concerned are in a position to determine without any doubt what their rights and obligations are.[69] On the other hand, legal

---

[66] Case 294/83, *Parti Ecologiste 'Les Verts' v European Parliament* [1986] ECR 1339, at 1365; Opinion 1/91, [1991] ECR I-6079, at 6102 (*EEA*).

[67] Dutheil de la Rochère, 'Le principe de la legalité', *L'Actualité juridique—droit administratif* (1996), special number, 161.

[68] Case 77/81, *Zuckerfabrik Franken v FRG* [1982] ECR 681, at 694–695.

[69] Case 354/95, *National Farmers' Union* [1997] ECR I-4559, at 4583; Case 177/96, *Banque Indosuez* [1997] ECR I-5659, at 5669.

certainty may function as an exception to legality if it precludes remedies against decisions after the time limit for instituting proceedings has expired.[70]

3. Legitimate Expectations

The protection of legitimate expectations, a principle which is central to EU administrative law,[71] is closely related to the concept of legal certainty. It deals with the situation that participants in the market trust that a given legal or factual constellation remains the same or develops into a direction provided for by law. Whether or not measures are nullified for an infringement of legitimate expectations depends on two conditions. The first element, defined expectations of citizens, is subjective; the other, legitimacy of such expectations, is of an objective nature. Farmers who trust that a given market order will remain unchanged are thus, as a rule, not protected since the objective test fails.[72]

Under these conditions, it becomes clear that rules that take retroactive effect may violate legitimate expectations. The ECJ has taken a critical stand vis-à-vis rules applying to circumstances which have been concluded before the law enters into force. In some cases, the Court held that retroactive legislation may violate legitimate trust in the continuation of an existing situation. Although it is not altogether excluded that acts take retroactive effect,[73] EU measures may, as a rule, not enter into force at a point of time before they are published in the Official Journal.[74] If the institutions decide to change, for example, agricultural market order regulations, they are under an obligation to respect transitional periods in order to allow market participants to adjust to the new conditions and to avoid undue hardship.[75]

Further illustrative examples for honouring of expectations occurred under the dairy market order.[76] Farmers had successfully applied for a subsidy for not producing milk within a certain period. Upon expiration of the grant, they applied for production quota. The quota was, according to a market regulation, calculated on the basis of a reference period including the time in

---

[70] Case C-188/92, *Textilwerke Deggendorf v FRG* [1994] ECR I-833, at 852; Case 310/97 P, *Commission v Assidomän* [1999] ECR I-5363, at 5365.

[71] Case C-60/98, *Butterfly Music v CEMED* [1999] ECR I-3939, at 3966.

[72] See Case-22/94, *The Irish Farmers Association v Minister for Agriculture, Food and Forestry, Ireland* [1997] ECR I-1809, at 1819.

[73] Case C-331/88, *R v Ministry of Agriculture, Fisheries and Food and Secretary of State for Health, ex parte: Fedesa* [1990] ECR I-4023.

[74] Cf. Case 98/78, *Firma Racke v HZA Mainz* [1979] ECR 69; Case T-167/94, *Nölle v Council & Commission* [1995] ECR II-2589.

[75] Case 133/93, 300/93 and 362/93, *Antonio Crispoltoni a.o. v Fattoria Autonoma Tabacchi and Donatab Srl* [1994] ECR I-4863, at 57.

[76] Case 170/86, *von Deetzen v Hauptzollamt Hamburg-Jonas* [1988] ECR 2368; Case 189/89, *Spagl v Hauptzollamt Rosenheim* [1990] ECR I-4574; Case 217/89, *Pastätter v Hauptzollamt Reichenhall* [1990] ECR I-4589.

which non-production grants were awarded. The authorities therefore denied the quota because the applicants had not produced. Although the jurisprudence on the matter is complicated in detail, the ECJ gave convincing evidence of its willingness to grant effective legal protection and held the mentioned regulation invalid.[77]

In sum, the jurisprudence of the courts demonstrates that legitimate expectations are safeguarded not very differently from the way they are by many Member States.

4. Proportionality

The ECJ recognized proportionality as a general principle of Community law, taking up, it is claimed, a German tradition,[78] long before it was incorporated into the Treaty as Article 5 (3) EC. Legislative measures as well as administrative decisions of the Commission are measured against it,[79] so that it functions as a standard of constitutional law. Proportionality standards also apply to measures taken by the Member States if enacted to implement Community regulations.[80]

Proportionality allows judicial control without interfering too deeply with the administration's power to assess the facts of a case.[81] The ECJ applies a three-tier test that consists of appropriateness, necessity and reasonableness.[82] A legal act is appropriate if it is capable of achieving the goal pursued; the authorities have a wide margin of appreciation in that respect. Secondly, the measure taken has to be the least intrusive means to achieve the indicated objective. As a third step, proportionality requires a reasonableness test which fails if its adverse effects on protected interests go further than can be justified

---

[77] In Case 181/96, *Wilkens v Chamber of Agriculture Hannover* [1999] ECR I-399, a farmer violated his obligation not to market milk, but did not reach the quota he had before he was granted a non-production subsidy. The Court held that he lost the right to be granted a new quota only as far as he had violated his obligations, thereby inflicting upon him a sanction. However, the decision is hard to defend, as Schilling, 'Bestand und allgemeine Lehren der bürgerlichen allgemeinen Rechtsgrundsätze des Gemeinschaftsrechts', *Europäische Grundrechte-Zeitschrift* (2000) 3, at 21–22 rightly observes. The recipient could not reasonably have divided his expectations into two parts so that he was protected with respect to the part of the quota not used.

[78] Koopmans, 'The Birth of European Law at the Crossroads of Legal Traditions', 39 *AJCL* (1991) 493, at 501.

[79] Case 280/93, *Germany v Council* [1994] ECR I-4973.

[80] In the *Zuckerfabrik Franken* case, *supra* n. 68, German law was tested against the European principle of proportionality. Cf. also Case 331/88, *Fedesa v The Queen–Minister of Agriculture* [1990] ECR I-4023.

[81] De Búrca, 'The Principle of Proportionality and its Application in EC Law', *Yearbook of European Law* (1993) 105.

[82] Case 265/87, *Schräder v Hauptzollamt Gronau* [1989] ECR 2237, at 2269.

by the objective pursued. This part of review may, for instance, lead to a check of the amount of fines imposed on individuals.[83]

5. Transparency

According to more recent tendencies in the law of the Union, publicity and transparency is intended to become one of the basic patterns of European administrative law. Article 1 TEU demands that decisions be 'taken as openly as possible', and Article 255 EC created a right of access to all documents, but general principles, limits and procedure are yet to be defined by Council legislation.[84] The motives for that novelty are twofold. The first objective is to strengthen the legitimacy of the Union by enhancing active participation in the building of public opinion. Secondly, to grant citizens a right to monitor administration is hoped to have a disciplining effect on the use of power.

Until further measures are taken, the matter is dealt with in secondary law enacted under the rules of procedure power of the Community institutions. Acting on the recommendation of the Conference and upon preparative work done by the Commission,[85] the Council and the Commission approved a Code of Conduct concerning public access to Council and Commission documents.[86] The Code of Conduct has the character of an interinstitutional agreement and does not confer any rights on individuals. However, it provides the framework for further measures which produce legal effects.[87] In order to implement the Code of Conduct, both the Commission and the Council adopted decisions on public access to documents.[88]

According to the Code of Conduct as adopted by decisions of the institutions, the public 'will have the widest possible access' to documents. However, there are two categories of exceptions to the rule. The first category comprises documents whose disclosure would undermine the protection of public interests such as public security, international relations, monetary stability, court proceedings, inspections and investigations as well as the protection of indi-

---

[83] Case 122/78, *Buitoni v Fonds d'Orientation et de Régularisation du Marché Agricole* [1979] ECR 677, at 685; Case 240/78, *Atalanta v Produktschap voor Vee en Vlees* [1979] ECR 2137, at 2151; Case 181/84, *Man Sugar Ltd v Intervention Board for Agricultural Produce* [1985] ECR 2889, at 2903.

[84] See Commission proposal for a regulation on public access to documents of the European Parliament, the Council and the Commission of 21 February 2000, COM (2000) 30 final/2.

[85] Communication 93/C 156/05 of 5 May 1993, OJ 1993 C 156/5; Communication 93/C 166/04 of 2 June 1993 on openness in the Community, OJ 1993, C 166/4.

[86] OJ 1993 L 340/41.

[87] Case C-58/94, *Netherlands v Council* [1996] ECR I-2169, at 2195.

[88] See Decision 93/731 of 20 December 1993 on public access to Council documents, OJ 1993 L 340/43, repeatedly amended; Decision 94/90 of 8 February 1994 on public access to Commission documents, OJ 1994 L 46/58, as amended by Decision 96/567, OJ 1996 L 247/45; cf. also Decision of the European Parliament of 10 July 1997, OJ 1997 L 263/27.

viduals in general and of privacy in particular, of commercial and industrial secrecy, of the Community's financial interests and of confidentiality, as requested by the person or the Member State who supplied the information. In these cases, Commission and Council are under an obligation to deny access, once the relevant circumstances have been substantiated. The second category, concerning the institution's interest in the confidentiality of its proceedings, is of an optional nature. In these cases, a certain degree of discretion is attributed to the institution from which access to documents is requested.

As of now, the European Court of Justice hesitates to attribute to the transparency policies the character of a general principle of Community law.[89] Such a step might upgrade the present legal basis which still seems to be weakly rooted in legal practice. As to the institutions, both the European Ombudsman and the Committee of Independent Experts which was set up preceding the resignation of the Santer Commission accused the Council and the Commission of being still in a 'tradition of secretiveness'.[90] The amendments to the Amsterdam Treaty and the reform of the Commission in progress[91] is hoped to lead to a further change in mentality.

Also as far as public participation is concerned, the process is still at its very beginning. According to a recent analysis of the Commission, the openness initiatives started so far had relatively little impact on the public.[92] In the cases decided by the CFI and the ECJ until now, the applicants were an environmentalist non-governmental organization,[93] the press,[94] a member of the European Parliament,[95] and persons with a legal interest in the widest sense in the information requested.[96] Citizens rarely go to the Court in order to enforce their right of access to information as a means to participate in the political process.[97] But even with little participation of the public, the courts

[89] Case C-58/94, *Netherlands v Council* [1996] ECR I-2169, at 2195; Case C-174/98 P and Case C-189/98 P, *Kingdom of the Netherlands and Gerard van der Wal v Commission,* Judgment of ECJ of 11 January 2000, nyr.

[90] See Committee of Independent Experts, *Second Report on Reform of the Commission. Analysis of Current Practice and Proposals for Tackling Mismanagement, Irregularities and Fraud* (10 September 1999), Vol. II, para. 7.6.3, referring to an interview of the EU Ombudsman, Mr. Söderman, with *European Voice* (22 April 1999).

[91] *Reforming the Commission,* White Paper, COM (2000) 200 final/2.

[92] See European Commission, Discussion paper of 23 April 1999 on public access to Commission documents, SGC2/VJ/CD D (99) 83.

[93] Case T-105/95, *WWF UK v Commission* [1997] ECR II-313.

[94] *John Carvel and Guardian Newspapers Ltd v Council* [1995] ECR II-2765; Case T-174/95, *Svenska Journalistförbundet v Council* [1998] ECR II-2289.

[95] Case T-14/98, *Heidi Hautala v Council,* judgment of 19 July 1999.

[96] *Interporc Im- und Export GmbH v Commission* [1998] ECR II-231; Case T-83/96, *Gerard van der Wal v Commission* [1998] ECR II-545; Case T-188/97, *Rothmans International BV v Commission,* judgment of 19 July 1999; Case T-309/97, *The Bavarian Lager Company Ltd v Commission,* judgment of 14 October 1999.

[97] An example is Case T 610/97 R, *Hanne Norup Carlsen et al v Council* [1998] ECR II-485.

continuously improved the standard of individual rights safeguards by integrating openness into a concept of effective judicial protection.[98]

6. *Principles of 'Good Administration'*

'Good' or 'sound' administration is a very vague concept frequently referred to by the ECJ. It resembles a number of procedural standards which relate to legal process. The Court held, for example, that to grant access to information was in conformity with good administration. Similar statements are found with respect to the right to be heard and a somewhat ill-defined standard of 'care' or 'diligence' which the administration, in particular the Commission, have to observe while conducting administrative procedure. The common denominator appears to be the duty, for the administrative authorities, to investigate carefully and to give persons involved the opportunity to be heard in order to avoid deficiencies in the course of procedure. Good administration embodies procedural constraints on administrative decision-making.

It has been submitted that all of these components of good administration have developed into different legal concepts of their own.[99] Thus access to documents, as we have seen, is now a subjective right which can be invoked before the European Courts, and the right to be heard is recognized as essential for due process in competition, anti-dumping and customs recovery cases.

B. Rights

From a citizen's perspective, the rule of law has repercussions on rights and protected interests which are subject to very different concepts in the Member States. Whereas some legal systems, such as German administrative law, focus on judicial protection of the individual, others, like the French legal order, stress the legality of administrative process.[100] It is therefore interesting to examine whether European administrative law follows rather a 'subjective' or an 'objective' approach.[101]

The ECJ does not take a clear position on the matter. Its jurisprudence appears to be open to interpretation, and necessarily so since it is continuously changing. After the ECJ had converted obligations of the states which were

[98] Kadelbach, Annotation on Case C-349/99 P, *Commission v ADT Projekt Gesellschaft der Arbeitsgemeinschaft Deutscher Tierzüchter mbH,* Order of the ECJ of 4 Oct. 1999, 38 *CMLRev.* (2001) 179.

[99] Cf. H. P. Nehl, *Administrative Procedure in EC Law* (1999) 13.

[100] Compare Schmidt-Aßmann, *supra* n. 10, at 13 with A. de Laubadère, J. C. Venezia and Y. Gaudemet, 1, *Droit administratif,* (14th ed., 1996), sec. 814, 985, 990.

[101] Schilling, *supra* n. 77, defends the thesis that Community law rights were objective principles, inspired by notions of administrative law which followed the French tradition.

expressly embodied as such in the Founding Treaties into rights of the individual in the early 1960s, the Court began, in the following decade, to develop its fundamental rights jurisprudence which brought about nearly all civil and human rights commonly found in constitutional and conventional catalogues. The final point was the creation of Union citizenship in the Treaty of Maastricht. The principles of free movement of goods, capital, persons and services were thus transformed to a subjective position of common market citizens which, in turn, was later enriched with human rights, including rudimentary rights of political participation, and thus elevated to a constitutional level.

However, substantive rights barely give rise to well-founded challenges of administrative decision-making. By far more important are procedural safeguards derived from due process guarantees, in particular from Article 6 ECHR. In the course of investigations and in order to prepare defence against onerous administrative measures, individuals enjoy the complete set of fair trial rights such as the right to be heard, the right to counsel, the right of privacy and the protection of correspondence.[102]

Against this background the ECJ, on one hand, defined the Community as a legal order which does not only have states but also citizens as its subjects,[103] and thus seems to follow a subjective concept. Undoubtedly, EU law knows subjective rights which are protected by the courts and whose infringement gives rise to claims for damages pursuant to Article 288 EC. On the other hand, the violation of general principles such as those referred to above does not automatically entail responsibility of EU institutions.[104] It therefore seems difficult to ascribe EU law either to a purely subjective or objective notion. It is submitted that one and the same norm may incorporate both, objective principles and subjective rights. The positive effect of this hybrid character is that subjective rights thus also have objective elements against which legal acts can be measured, even if no individual applicant claims undue interference with rights or legitimate interests.[105] Fundamental rights and freedoms set up negative powers for the executive in that they limit the discretion of authorities.

C. Remedies

The ECJ has repeatedly stressed the importance of effective remedies for a viable administrative system, for there can be no rule of law without judicial

---

[102] See Lenaerts and Vanhamme, 'Procedural Rights of Private Parties in the Community Administrative Process', 34 *CMLRev.* (1997) 531.

[103] Opinion 1/91, n. 66 above, at 6102.

[104] See, e.g., Cases 116–124/77, *Amylum and Tunnel Refineries v Council and Commission* [1979] ECR 3497.

[105] Case C-280/93, *FRG v Council* [1994] ECR I-4973.

protection.[106] With respect to the safeguarding of individual rights, the concepts which the various systems of administrative law follow are very different. In order to appreciate the characteristics of the European judicial system appropriately, four criteria may be employed: standing, scrutiny, preliminary protection and extra-contractual liability.

1. Standing

The concept of standing reflects the subjective/objective law dichotomy which has been alluded to above.[107] A subjective notion equates substantive rights and standing before administrative courts. It will tend to define the right in question in abstract legal terms as clearly as possible. From the perspective of the claimant seeking judicial protection, standing is a question of how to substantiate a pre-defined type of claim and thus a matter of facts to be brought forward. Again, German administrative law is the prototype of such a concept. For an objective system, by contrast, an individual claim is but an occasion for review of administrative conduct and, if the challenged measure proves illegal, to restore legality. Under systems of that kind, standing is defined in rather vague terms. For that notion, the French concept of '*interêt à agir*' is representative.

For a complaint for illegality brought by natural or legal persons to be permissible, Article 230 (4) EC demands that the measure appealed against is 'of direct and individual concern'. A complaint for failure to act under Article 233 (3) EC requires that the measure to be taken must be one 'addressed' to the applicant. In other words, a certain factual relation between the conduct complained of and the legal interests of the applicant must be shown. The description which the ECJ and the CFI give of 'individual concern' is quite restrictive. In order to qualify for admission, the applicant must be either the addressee of the challenged measure or his or her interests must be interfered with in a comparable way. It does not suffice that the private individuals potentially concerned are identifiable. It is necessary that all persons whose interests are affected be known. No individual concern, for instance, was recognized for persons whose particular situation was not taken into account at the time the measure was taken.[108] The CFI also denied protection for those who might suffer personal harm from atomic testing if such harm is inflicted upon all persons living in a particular area alike.[109] These observations alone do not allow a reliable qualification with respect to the 'subjective' or 'objective' nature of the system. It appears that the Court does not dispose of dis-

---

[106] Case 222/86, *Heylens v Unectef* [1987] ECR 4097, at 4117; Case 393/96, *Antonissen v Council & Commission* [1997] ECR I-441, at 456.

[107] For the distinction between *contentieux subjectif* and *contentieux objectif* see L. Duguit, *Traité de droit constitutionnel*, vol. II (3rd ed., 1928) 435, at 459–480.

[108] Case T-321/95, *Greenpeace Council v Commission* [1998] ECR II-1651, at 1652.

[109] Case T-219/95, *Danielsson v Commission* [1995] ECR II-3051, at 3072.

tinctly defined categories of rights as they are typical for a subjective system. On the other hand, it did not develop an overly inclusive approach with the purpose to review legality of administrative conduct on a larger scale. The European Courts are less generous in granting standing than, for instance, the French administrative courts. In sum, they appear to be about as strict as the German system,[110] without, however, adopting the approach of defining categories of rights in an abstract way.

2. The Level of Scrutiny

Apart from standing, the most crucial point for the character of legal protection is the level of scrutiny applied by the courts. A system in which standing is generously granted but which leaves a wide margin of discretion to the authorities may, seen from a citizen's perspective, prove less effective than a concept with a narrow definition of a right to sue which applies a strict level of scrutiny to all acts under review.

The question is, therefore, to what extent the European judiciary recognizes a margin of appraisal and corresponding limits of judicial review. Practice seems complex since it varies with the subject matter. As a rule, the ECJ and the CFI leave broad margins to the Commission as far as the substance of decisions is concerned. In competition and subsidies law, for instance, the Commission has an acknowledged area of economic expertise with which the judiciary does not easily interfere.[111] Similarly, complex technical issues such as, for example, the assessment of the scientific value of imported goods which must be verified for a waiver on customs duties are left to the Commission's discretion.[112] Also in other areas like public service law, the courts display considerable self-restraint,[113] provided that the principle of proportionality is observed.[114]

---

[110] Cf. the analyses by Ehlers, 'Die Klagebefugnis nach deutschem, europäischem Gemeinschafts- und US-amerikanischem Recht', 84 *Verwaltungs-Archiv* (1993) 139, at 156; Canedo, 'L'interêt à agir dans le recours en annulation du droit communautaire', 36 *Revue trimestrielle de droit européen* (2000) 452. Such conclusions are difficult to verify since EU court jurisprudence is casuistic and the pre-conditions of standing in the systems do not correspond.

[111] Cases 56 and 58/64, *Consten and Grundig v Commission* [1966] ECR 321, at 396; Case C-355/95 P, *Textilwerke Deggendorf v Commission* [1997] ECR I-2549, at 2576.

[112] Case 269/90, *Hauptzollamt München-Mitte v Technische Universität München* [1991] ECR I-5469, at 5499.

[113] Case 74/77, *Allgeyer v European Parliament* [1978] ECR 977, at 985; Case 280/80, *Bakke d'Aloya v Council* [1981] ECR 2887, at 2898; cf. also Kirschner, 'Die Kontrolldichte bei der Überprüfung der Entscheidungen der Kommission durch das Gericht erster Instanz der Europaeischen Gemeinschaften', *Zentrum für Europäisches Wirtschaftsrecht Bonn* (1996), Vorträge und Berichte, no. 61.

[114] The ample discretionary powers thus acknowledged by the courts may be interpreted as an expression of the high level of expertise some authors attribute to the Commission, see G. Majone, *Regulating Europe* (1996); Lindseth, 'Democratic Legitimacy and the Administrative Character of Supranationalism', 99 *Columbia Law Review* 628. If technical expertise is

Rather than restricting margins of appreciation, the Courts place a high value on procedural safeguards. The exigencies of due process and of 'good administration' in general have been mentioned above. In particular, regarding the use of discretionary powers, the courts developed rich case-law on two requirements; the principle of care and the obligation to give reasons have emerged.

Taking a discretionary decision means to make a choice out of two or more options, all of which are, at first glance, equally feasible. In order to produce the correct outcome, the acting authority has to assess the facts properly. Therefore, in all legal systems which allow for a wide margin of appreciation, the administration is under a duty to investigate the factual basis carefully.[115] It is therefore a corollary of the judicial self-restraint displayed by the EU courts in the evaluation of the facts assessed that their jurisprudence, at the same time, requires a certain level of diligence for the collection of relevant data for which there can be no discretion.[116]

The essential counterpart to the level of care guarded by the Courts is the obligation to give reasons (Article 253 EC).[117] The obligation to give a reasoned decision has a strong tradition in the Netherlands and in Germany, but is comparatively new in France and the UK.[118] The requirement has a dual rationale: without a detailed statement on the factual and legal grounds on which the decision rests, the courts are not able to test it against the standard of care, and the private party concerned is not in a position to foresee whether remedies promise success.[119] To set aside the decision for failure of a proper statement of reasons gives the authority from which it originates the opportunity to assess the matter anew, without there being a need, on the part of the courts, to go into the considerations on merit.

---

considered as a source of legitimacy, margins of discretion are an essential component of the system.

[115] Kahn, 'Discretionary Power and the Administrative Judge', 29 *The International and Comparative Law Quarterly* (1980) 521, at 526.

[116] See the thorough analysis of the relevant case-law by Nehl, *supra* n. 99, at 127 et seq.

[117] Dubouis, 'A propos de deux principes généraux du droit communautaire (droit au contrôle juridictionnel effectif et motivation des décisions des autorités nationales qui portent atteinte à un droit conféré par la règle communautaire)', *Revue française de droit administratif* (1988) 691; Schockweiler, 'La motivation des décisions individuelles en droit communautaire', 25 *Cahiers de droit européen* (1989) 1.

[118] See, for the Netherlands, Widdershoven and de Lange, 'Dutch Report, in Schwarze *supra* n. 6, 529, at 600; for Germany see Badura, 'Das Verwaltungsverfahren', in H. U. Erichsen (ed.), *Allgemeines Verwaltungsrecht* (11th edn., 1998) 463, at 521 et seq.; for France see G. Braibant, *Le droit administratif français*, (4th edn., 1998), at 246; for the UK see D. Foulkes, *Administrative Law* (1995), at 327.

[119] See Case C-350/88, *Delacre v Commission* [1990] ECR I-395, at 422; Case T-85/94, *Branco v Commission* [1995] ECR II-45, at 57; Case T-105/95, *WWF UK v Commission* [1997] ECR II-315, at 346.

3. Preliminary Measures

As the ECJ has stressed in the *Antonissen* case, effective interim relief is a necessary component of the guarantee of judicial protection.[120] The EC Treaty can be read as an effort to strike a balance between legitimate interests of the claimant party and the exigencies of a workable administration.[121] Article 242 EC excludes that actions brought before the EU courts have suspensory effect and lays down that the application of the contested act depends on a court order. Preliminary judicial protection requires two elements, one legal and one factual. As to the facts, the applicant is expected to substantiate the urgency to avoid grave and irreparable harm and the necessity to suspend execution of the contested act. With respect to the legal requirements, the EU courts undertake a preliminary evaluation of the action on merit. Regarding the level of individual rights protection, although a comparison of the EU court practice and the jurisprudence of Member States is difficult to draw, the concept as spelled out by law and court decisions corresponds with the average standard of interim protection in Europe.[122]

4. Liability

Extra-contractual liability of the institutions, according to Article 288 EC, should by definition follow a common European standard. The pre-condition is the violation of a European norm which confers subjective rights on individuals.[123] If the norm infringed upon grants discretion to the competent body, the violation must be of a qualified character.[124] Finally, the act complained of must have inflicted harm on the individual.[125] Special conditions must be met if a legislative measure is alleged to have caused unlawful damage.[126] The norm breached must be of a fundamental character, and the authorities must be responsible for an obvious and severe fault in using discretionary powers. The group of persons concerned must be clearly defined, and the harm done has to go beyond the risks typical for participation in the market. Recently, the CFI began to elaborate on rules governing the compensation for harm done by lawful, but particularly onerous conduct,[127] as

---

[120] *Supra* n. 106.

[121] Tesauro, 'Les mesures provisoires dans le système communautaire', *Homenaje Díez de Velasco* (1993), at 1241.

[122] S. Lehr, *Einstweiliger Rechtsschutz und Europäische Union* (1997), at 98.

[123] Cases 5, 7 and 13–24/66, *Kampffmeyer et al v Commission* [1967] ECR 331, at 354.

[124] Case 5/71, *Zuckerfabrik Schöppenstedt v Council* [1971] ECR 975, at 985.

[125] Joined Cases 29, 31, 36, 39–47, 50 and 51/63, *des Laminoirs v High Authority* [1965] ECR 1197, at 1234.

[126] Case 238/78, *Ireks-Arkady v Council and Commission* [1979] ECR 2955, at 2972.

[127] Case T-184/95, *Dorsch Consult v Council* [1998] ECR II-667; as to the situation before see Bronkhorst, 'The Valid Legislative Act as a Cause of Liability of the Communities', in

they exist in some of the national systems. It appears fair to conclude that these standards are in harmony with the law of most of the Member States.[128]

D. Conclusions

European administrative law consists, on the one hand, of an unsystematic patchwork of highly specific rules, and on the other hand of a set of general principles. Those principles are very abstract in character as far as they are purely 'objective' and have no implication for individual rights. However, many facets of these principles reflect a comparably high degree of concern for citizens' interests. For the purposes of judicial protection the Community courts have brought about specific jurisprudence, which has proceeded from rather general requirements of good administrative conduct to an ever more precise standard of procedural safeguards. Although the concept of standing before the courts is rather narrow and the authorities are permitted to act within a wide margin of appreciation, the level of procedural diligence demanded by the courts is able to ensure fairly effective judicial protection. The concepts of interim relief and of liability may not seem over-protective, but, it is submitted, the basically comply with what is granted in most of the Member States.

III. THE LAW OF A EUROPEANIZED ADMINISTRATION

In this section, the framework for Europeanized administrative law will be examined. That sphere of law is governed by specific EU policies, such as state aid, public procurement, environmental law or the common agricultural policy, and, as has been pointed out above, principles like effectiveness and equivalence which channel their modes of implementation. The very elements already found on the level of European administrative law are also valid on the domestic plane. Here, in turn, they are subject to modification in the public interest of the Community. It will be seen whether the standards on both levels tend to approximate one to another.

H. G. Schermers, T. Heukels and P. Mead (eds), *Non-contractual Liability of the European Communities* (1988) 13, at 20.

[128] Schockweiler, Wivenes and Godard, 'Le régime de la responsabilité extra-contractuelle du fait d'actes juridiques dans la Communauté européenne', 26 *Revue trimestrielle de droit européen* (1990) 27, at 62.

A. Principles of Europeanized Administrative Law

1. Legality

From the Community's perspective, the principle of legality can only be of interest with respect to compliance of domestic law with the Community's legal order. The infringement and preliminary reference procedures under Articles 226 and 234 EC, respectively, serve this objective. Other than in conflicts of secondary law with primary EU law, the conflicting domestic norm may not be declared null and void if municipal law does not so provide. Thus, the principle of legality, as between the two levels, is compromised by the autonomy of national law.

An answer to the threat to uniform application of law ensuing from that vertical separation of powers would, of course, be harmonization, as it is usually realized where the EU has an exclusive competence. The Customs Code is a rare, if not the only, example where the Community did not only set up a uniform substance law, but also enacted procedural rules and harmonized even a certain type of decision-making, the customs decision under Article 4, no. 5 of the Code.[129]

EU courts may not declare national administrative acts invalid. Thus, they are not competent to resolve a conflict of laws by imposing legal consequences on illegal national measures. But there are examples where the ECJ seized the opportunity to declare that national courts and authorities may be obliged to deny unlawful acts any legal effect. Thus, decisions granting state aids without prior notification to the Commission under Article 88 (3), last sentence EC, must be held to be invalid in order to offer to competitors the certain prospect that all necessary inferences will be drawn as regards the recovery of supports and possible interim measures.[130] The Commission's final decision, accordingly, 'does not have the effect of regularizing *ex post facto* the implementing measures which were invalid' because they had been taken in breach of the Treaty provisions governing state aid.[131]

2. Legal Certainty

Legal certainty, as a necessary corollary to legality, in European administrative law means that law has to be as clear as to allow everyone to notice what his or her rights and obligations are. In the Europeanized sphere, a similar requirement applies to legal acts which transform directives into internal law. Generally speaking, the transposition of a directive into domestic law does not require formal and specific legislation, provided the full application of the directive is ensured in a sufficiently clear and precise manner. As the ECJ has

---

[129] Regulation 2913/92 of 12 October 1992, OJ 1992 L 392/1.
[130] Case C-354/90, *Fénacomex v France* [1991] ECR I-5505, at 5528.
[131] Ibid., at 5529.

repeatedly held, a general legal context may be adequate for that purpose.[132] Yet if directives are intended to create individual rights for citizens, the persons concerned must be in a position to ascertain the full extent of their rights and duties. It follows that administrative circulars of a technical nature do not suffice if those norms do not take external effects such as to allow individuals to rely on them before courts.[133] The principle of certainty thus, on the Europeanized plane, takes the shape of a prohibition of certain types of decision-making in certain cases. However justified that result may be, it remains to be noted that the national administrations are under stricter constraints in their freedom to codify practice than are the European authorities.

The other aspect of legal certainty considered above is the necessity of time limits to law suits for the sake of reliability of expectations. In the famous *Emmott* case, the plaintiff invoked a non-discrimination directive in social law affairs that had not been transformed into Irish law.[134] She relied on the directive, but the suit was dismissed because the time limit to bring proceedings had expired. The ECJ held that the period of time could not start to run before the directive was transposed into internal law. The useful effect of Community law could be impaired if time limits could preclude an action even before the beneficiaries had the opportunity to know their rights.[135] In this case, *effet utile* and subjective rights overruled legal certainty. The Court later clarified that the rule developed in *Emmott* applied only if the time limit in question deprived the applicant party of any opportunity to bring the claim.[136] This jurisprudence holds that only if the right is not introduced into the domestic legal order at all may time limits not preclude action. In other cases, suits may be dismissed on grounds of expiration so that national rules on legal certainty are given effect.

---

[132] Case 102/79, *Commission v Belgium* [1980] ECR 1473, at 1486; Case 29/84, *Commission v Germany* [1985] ECR 1661, at 1673; Case 322/86, *Commission v Italy* [1988] ECR 3995, at 4007.

[133] Case 363/86, *Commission v Italy* [1987] ECR 1733, at 1740; Case C-339/87, *Commission v Netherlands* [1990] ECR I-851, at 880; Cases C-361/88 and C-59/89, *Commission v Germany* [1991] ECR I-2567, at 2602 and I-2606, at 2631; Cases C-13/90, C-14/90 and C-64/90, *Commission v France* [1991] ECR I-4327, I-4331 and I-4335.

[134] Case C-208/90, *Emmott v Minister for Social Welfare* [1991] ECR I-4269; in Case C-312/93, *Peterbroeck et al v Belgium* [1995] ECR I-4599, at 4622/3 the Court banned time limits for invoking EU legal rights before national courts, even though national courts are not under an obligation to draw the attention of the parties to favourable EU law *ex officio*, see Cases C-430–1/93, *van Schijndel Stichtings Pensioenfonds voor Fysiotherapeuten* [1995] ECR I-4705.

[135] *Emmott, supra* n. 134, at 4298.

[136] See Case 338/91, *Steenhorst-Neerings v Bestuur van de Bedrijfsvereniging voor Detailhandel* [1993] ECR I-5475, at 5502; Case 410/92, *Johnson v Chief Adjudication Officer* [1994] ECR I-5483, at 5510; Case 188/95, *Fantask v Industriministeriet* [1997] ECR I-6783, at 6837.

There is yet another example where legal certainty was compromised in the European public interest. Under German domestic administrative procedure law, and similarly in other legal orders, the authorities may revoke unlawful administrative decisions within a time limit of one year after the relevant circumstances are known. The Court held in the *Alcan* case that a decision to grant state aid has to be recalled even after the end of the relevant period of time. The principle of legal certainty, the argument runs, could not preclude repayment, for otherwise recovery of unduly paid amounts would be rendered practically impossible.[137] The principle of effectiveness thus, once again, superseded a general principle of national administrative law. As opposed to that judgment, legal certainty in European administrative law cases, it appears, has been applied very strictly.

3. Legitimate Expectations

The ECJ's decisions on the revocation of public grants paid unlawfully established ample jurisprudence on legitimate expectations.[138] The lengthy debate it provoked shows that this is one of the topics which gave rise to the very idea of Europeanization. As has been pointed out earlier, two major categories of cases ought to be distinguished, recovery of Community aid and of state aid. The common point of departure is the principle that the conditions of recovery are, without any harmonization of the matter, governed by national law. Since its application is conditioned by the principles of effectiveness and equivalence, domestic provisions which leave a certain margin of discretion to the authorities must be applied in a manner such as not to render recovery virtually impossible. The public interest protected by EU law must be fully taken into account.

Those guidelines lead to different solutions. With respect to EU subsidies, domestic law may bar a recall of the administrative act by which the sums were granted if the circumstances justify legitimate expectations of the recipient.[139] State aid, by contrast, is incurably illegal from the start, if the national authorities either failed to notify the intended payment or proceeded before the Commission had taken a decision.[140] The central argument is that there can be, in principle, no trust in measures which are contrary to EU competition law.

In state aid cases, legitimate expectations may only be invoked successfully before national courts in exceptional cases. In the normal conduct of

---

[137] Case C-24/95, *Land Rheinland Pfalz v Alcan* [1997] ECR I-1591, at 1619.

[138] Case 14/81, *Alpha Steel v Commission* [1982] ECR 749, at 786; Case 15/85, *Consorzio Cooperative d'Abruzzo v Commission* [1987] ECR 1005, at 1036/7; Case 223/85, *Rijn-Schelde-Verolme Machinefabrieken en Scheepswerven NV v Commission* [1987] ECR 4617, 4659; Case 310/85, *Deufil v Commission* [1987] ECR 901, at 927; Case C-5/89, *Germany v Commission* [1990] ECR I-3437, at 3456/7.

[139] See *Milchkontor, supra* n. 57.　　　　　　[140] *Fénacomex, supra* n. 130.

procedure, a complaint based on that ground can only be raised against the Commission. The recipient may appeal against the order to recall the amount addressed to the competent Member State if that decision violated legitimate interests.

National concepts of legitimate expectations, in the cases at issue, are dominated by European public concerns as specified in the Treaty. But it should not be concluded from those judgments, which relate to a very particular context, that the Europeanized concept of legitimate expectations is less favourable to individual rights concerns than the corresponding notion in European administrative law.

4. Proportionality

As far as the principle of proportionality plays a role on the national level, it has not been modified in its contents by the jurisprudence of the EU courts. It is interesting to note, however, that the principle applies also to national legislation, namely where measures were taken in order to restrict basic freedoms in the overriding interest of public policy. A recent analysis of ECJ case-law suggests that the level of scrutiny applied in these cases was stricter than in cases where the validity of EU acts was at issue.[141] If that contention is true, it fits into a general pattern that can be observed also with respect to other general principles: the interest of the Union in uniform application of its laws reduces the autonomy of Member States' bodies. Hence it appears that principles present on both the European and the Europeanized levels differ in scope.

5. Transparency

Other than for the European institutions, there is no general policy of freedom of information regarding documents held by national authorities. However, there are traces of the underlying concept of transparency in the Europeanized sphere. The ECJ continuously holds that directives have to be transformed by a formal act which is legally binding as far as its provisions create individual rights.[142] Other trends with a view at more transparency in national law are set by EU legislation. In environmental law, the principle of openness has a special significance. Public participation is a prerequisite in planning and admission procedures with respect to certain projects. That notion received particular attention in the directive on the environmental impact assessment.[143] Some years after that directive was passed, the concept

---

[141] Kinggreen and Störmer, 'Die subjektiv-öffentlichen Rechte des primären Gemeinschaftsrechts', *Europa-Recht* (1998) 263, at 278.

[142] See, e.g., Case C-361/88, *Commission v Germany* [1991] ECR I-2567, at 2601.

[143] Council Directive 85/337 of 27 Jun. 1985 on the assessment of the effects of certain public and private projects on the environment, OJ 1985 L 175/40 as amended by Directive 97/11 of 3 Mar. 1997, OJ 1997 L 73/5.

of openness was expanded by the directive on access to information concerning the environment.[144] Pursuant to that directive, everyone has a right of insight into all data national authorities hold on the condition of the environment, without having to substantiate a special legal or economic interest.[145] Whereas freedom of information for some states like Sweden, Finland and the Netherlands is a familiar notion, for others, such as Germany and the UK, it is comparatively new if not unknown so that it induces major changes in legal thinking.

Certainly, the rationales of transparency on the EU level hold equally true on the state level. But the Community does not intend, and does not have the power, to create a new fundamental right of openness in the Member States. The justification of, and the idea common to, the jurisprudence on the quality of acts of transposition and the environmental law directives is that individual interests, which run parallel to public policy of the EU, may serve as an effective means to enhance the implementation records of Member States.

B. Rights

The doctrine of direct effect gave to the citizens of the European Community the opportunity to invoke rights before national courts which were initially designed as state obligations. Behind that judicial transformation of Treaty provisions, decisions addressed to states and directives into domestic law stands a threefold rationale. The first is the consideration that, in any legal order, individuals are natural holders of rights and obligations. Subjective rights belong to the normal condition of a modern legal system.[146] Secondly, direct application of EU law replaces transformation and promotes uniformity and effectiveness of EU law on the domestic sphere.[147] The third reason for direct effect is that states should not profit from their unlawful failure by invoking EU law against private parties for whose benefit those rights were created.[148] Thus, individual rights serve not only the interests of the citizens, but also as a means for the decentral enforcement of EU law.

The instrumental component of individual rights is not found in many legal orders, particularly not in those which made the protection of individual rights

---

[144] OJ 1990 L 158/56.

[145] As to the contents of the right of access to information see Case C-217/97, *Commission v Germany* [1999] ECR, (9 Sept. 1999).

[146] Case 26/62, *Van Gend en Loos v Netherlands Finance Administration* [1963] ECR 1, at 25; Cases C-6/90 and 9/90, *Francovich et al v Italy* [1991] ECR I-5357, at 5414; Opinion 1/91, [1991] ECR I-6079, at 6102 (EEA).

[147] *Van Gend, supra* n. 146.

[148] Case 148/78, *Ratti* [1979] ECR 1629, at 1642; see also Green, 'Directives, Equity and the Protection of Individual Rights', 9 *ELR* (1984) 295, at 304 et seq.

their very core. However, systems referred to above as 'objective' have related elements; for even if subjective rights are not situated in the centre of the system, complaints filed by private parties give rise for review. The EU system has elements of both subjective and objective systems.

Another typical feature of entitlements under EU law is a comparatively strong emphasis on procedural rights. The example of public participation rights in environmental impact assessment procedures has already been mentioned. Similarly, the law of public procurement enacted under the internal market power of the EU heavily relies on procedural rights.[149] In principle, any undertaking which answered on an invitation to tender has a right that the submitted offer is at least considered.[150]

The useful effect of the strengthening of procedural rights is, again, that the administration is monitored by those whose interests are specially affected which, in turn, is supposed to give an additional incentive for lawful conduct. The principle of transparency thus functions as a corollary to, and the extension of, the reliance on procedural rights.

C. Remedies

The Member States are under an obligation to secure effective remedies against violations of rights based on Community law. The ECJ bases that duty on constitutional traditions and, in particular, on Articles 6 and 13 ECHR.[151]

---

[149] Council Directive 93/36 of 14 June 1993 coordinating procedures for the award of public supply contracts, OJ 1993 L 199/1; Council Directive 93/37 of 14 June 1993 concerning the coordination of procedures for the award of public works contracts, OJ 1993 L 199/54; Council Directive 93/38 of 14 June 1993 coordinating the procurement procedures of entities operating in the water, energy, transport and telecommunications sectors, OJ 1993 L 199/84; Council Directive 92/50 of 18 June 1992 relating to the coordination of procedures for the award of public service contracts, OJ 1992 L 209/1; Council Directive 89/665 of 21 December 1989 on the coordination of the laws, regulations and administrative provisions relating to the application of review procedures to the award of public supply and public works contracts, OJ 1989 L 395/33; Council Directive 92/13 of 25 February 1992 coordinating the laws, regulations and administrative provisions relating to the application of Community rules on the procurement procedures of entities operating in the water, energy, transport and telecommunications sectors, OJ 1992 L 76/14.

[150] Case 76/81, *Transporoute v Ministère des travaux publics* [1982] ECR 417, at 426 et seq.; Case 31/87, *Beentjes v Netherlands* [1988] ECR 4635, at 4662/3; *Fratelli Costanzo*, n. 44 above, at 1870; Case C-433/93, *Commission v Germany* [1995] ECR I-2303, at 2317/8; Case C-54/96, *Dorsch Cunsult v Bundesbaugesellschaft Berlin* [1997] ECR I-4961, at 4997/8.

[151] Case 222/86, *Heylens v Unectef* [1987] ECR 4097, at 4113; see also Case 152/84, *Marshall v Southampton and South-West Hampshire Area Health Authority* [1986] ECR 737, at 748.

1. Standing

From the effective remedy guarantee follows the obligation for the national courts to give full effect to all rights created by the Treaty and by secondary law. Since subjective rights show a close connection with the doctrine of direct effect which, in turn, serves not only the interests of citizens but also fosters uniform application of European law, the concept of standing is inseparably intertwined with the scope of substantive rights. Consequently, standing before national courts follows the requirements of direct effect. The norm invoked must be unconditional and specific so that it allows direct application.

For those countries in which legal protection is based on more specific notions of subjective entitlement, which is the case in Austria, Germany and Italy, the administrative courts are confronted with the task to integrate two different concepts.[152] For legal orders which demand nothing more than a legal interest, the difference might be less obvious. Arguably, the concept of standing prescribed by the doctrine of direct effect displays some similarities with the French procedural requirement of '*intérêt pour agir*'.

Likewise, the marked emphasis EU law places on active participation in administrative procedure should induce new orientation in some legal orders. In many systems, rights of that kind are ancillary to substantive rights and can be invoked only if the underlying legal interest is violated.

Compared to the criteria of 'direct and individual concern' which apply to law suits against the Commission under Article 230 EC, the effective remedy guarantee incumbent on the Member States demands a more generous practice from national courts.

2. The Level of Scrutiny

As we have seen, EU authorities dispose of a relatively wide margin of assessment of facts. Here, again, EU law seems to follow the French tradition where authorities enjoy the power of discretion, but have certain procedural obligations which encourage self-control.[153] Not quite the same holds true when it comes to the execution of EU law by national authorities. In theory, the Union is likely to have a defined interest in control of the proper appreciation of its interests in the process of assessing the facts relevant for decision-making.

Case law points towards that direction. As far as EU directives confer rights on individuals, transposition may not be left to the independent will of administrative authorities. Transformation by statutes which delegate wide discretionary powers to authorities may run counter to the principles of legal

---

[152] F. Schoch, *Die Europäisierung des verwaltungsgerichtlichen Rechtsschutzes* (2000), at 27 et seq.
[153] See J. Rivero and J. Waline, *Droit administratif* (1998), at 259 et seq.

certainty and openness.[154] Once transforming legislation is enacted, EU interests may still reduce authoritative discretion.[155] In customs law, one and the same EU regulation may be read as to grant to the Commission more flexibility than to national customs offices. Even in domestic law which grants discretionary powers to the national administration those powers may be reduced when overruled by dominant interests protected by EU law.[156]

It seems fair to assume that the principle of uniform application generally reduces discretionary competence of state authorities. Consequently, the level of scrutiny for judicial review of administrative decisions is stricter *vis-à-vis* the Europeanized administration than in European administrative law.

3. Interim Measures

The duty to grant effective remedies was, for a long time, not regarded as a minimum standard, but as a prohibition of discrimination. Accordingly, the Member States were not obliged to set up new remedies for the protection of EU rights.[157] As is well known, this jurisprudence was overturned by the first *Factortame* case.[158] Judicial protection consists, according to more recent judgments, of mandatory elements which make up a minimum standard of judicial protection in Europe. An essential element is the obligation to give interim relief in order to secure EU rights before domestic courts.

However, judicial protection is not an overruling policy. It is to be balanced out against the effectiveness of EU law. That is why complaints against administrative measures have no suspensory effect, even if so provided by national law, if the applicant challenges the validity of the underlying regulation.[159] According to the Court, national law may not order automatic non-application of EU law, not even preliminarily. Instead, the Court held that interim relief, also before national courts, has to follow Articles 242 and 243 EC. The Court later clarified that the same reasoning holds true if the plaintiff does not appeal an administrative act for invalidity of EU law, but also applies to claims to favourable decisions which are alleged to be precluded because of an unlawful Council regulation.[160]

This was, at the time the *Zuckerfabriken* decision was taken, a unique example for court-made harmonization of national procedural law. However, as

---

[154] Case 131/88, *Commission v Germany* [1991] ECR I-825, at 870, 876.

[155] Case 72/95, *Kraaijeveld v Gedeputeerde Staten van Zuid-Holland* [1996] ECR I-5403.

[156] See *Land Rheinland-Pfalz v Alcan*, supra n. 63; but see Case 120/97, *Upjohn* [1999] ECR I-223.

[157] Case 131/88, *Rewe v Hauptzollamt Kiel* [1981] ECR 1805.

[158] Case 213/89, *The Queen v Secretary of State ex parte Factortame* [1990] ECR I-2433.

[159] Cases 143/88, 92/89, *Zuckerfabriken Suederdithmarschen und Soest v Hauptzollamt Itzehoe und Paderborn* [1991] ECR I-415.

[160] Case 465/96, *Atlanta v Bundesamt für Ernährung und Forstwirtschaft* [1995] ECR I-3761.

pointed out earlier, the level thus found by and large complied with what is common ground in European legal orders. The result is the more justified since co-operative decision-making is increasing so that it may at times be difficult to select the competent judiciary.[161] It would be unfortunate if the level of judicial protection depended on the authority against which action must be brought.

4. Liability

ECJ jurisprudence concerning the liability of Member States for failure to implement EU law is based on two considerations: to find an effective sanction for misconduct of the Member States and to complete the legal remedies of which individuals may avail themselves in order to enforce rights created by EU law. Beginning with a judgment on a Member State's failure to transpose a directive which was intended to afford support to workers whose employer had become insolvent,[162] the concept was later expanded to all types of violations of subjective EU law. In the *Brasserie* judgment, the conditions on which Member States can be held responsible for breaches of Union law were harmonized with the guidelines governing extra-contractual liability of EU institutions according to Article 288 EC.[163]

In effect, both claims appear to be somewhat asymmetric as far as liability for faulty legislation is concerned. The ECJ acknowledges that the institutions, in their capacity as legislature, have a broad margin of discretion. By contrast, such discretion is by definition narrow for Member State legislation, which transposes EU directives. But this discrepancy does not prove much more than that Member State parliaments are not fully sovereign any more if it comes to areas where the EU has jurisdiction to legislate. This should not obscure the fact that, as is the case with interim judicial protection, liability in Europe is governed by common standards of public liability. Anything but that outcome would have been surprising since Article 288 EC expressly refers to the common traditions of the Member State legal orders. Here, the circle has been closed: elements from national law compose the principles governing the responsibility of the Community which, in turn, influence domestic law.

D. Comparison with European Administrative Law

European and Europeanized administrative law adhere to the same concepts, but fill them often with different contents. Whereas European administrative

---

[161] Case 68/95, *Port v Federal authority for agriculture and food* [1996] ECR I-6065: no relief before national court if not national authorities, but the Commission is authorized to grant what plaintiff sought.

[162] Cases C-6/90 and C-9/90, *Francovich v Italy* [1991] ECR I-5357.

[163] Cases C-46/93 and C-48/93, *Brasserie du pêcheur v Germany* [1996] ECR I-1029; see also van Gerven, 'European Standards for Civil Liability of the State', in J. A. E. Vervaele (ed.), *Compliance and Enforcement of European Community Law* (1999) 335, at 340 et seq.

law has developed a specific version of the rule of law, the concept of legality within Member States lies beyond the reach of European institutions. However, the requirements of priority and direct effect force Member States to integrate an additional layer of law into their respective concepts of legality. Legal certainty is conceived strictly on the European level, but subject to modifications in Europeanized national law. Similarly, legitimate expectations are honoured on the European plane, but Europeanized in internal law with the effect that the concept must be balanced out with the interests of the Union. As to state aid, legitimate expectations are virtually harmonized under the influence of Article 88 (3) EC. Subjective rights, on the European level, are construed more narrowly than subjective rights created by EU law against the Member States. The principle of proportionality as well as the level of scrutiny demanded from courts in general constitute a stricter yardstick for national measures tested against EU law by national courts than they are when it comes to review of Union acts by the European judiciary.

Preliminary judicial protection and liability, by contrast, are largely identical both in scope and consequences on the two levels. Whereas in the case of interim relief the ECJ, under certain conditions, declared the Union's model as compulsory for judicial protection before national courts, the solution found for public liability is a consequence of the mandate for comparative analysis given to the EU courts in Article 288 EC.

It is obvious that the need for effective implementation of EU law makes the difference. Not only does it ensure changes to the national administrative law systems, it also modifies principles and institutions as such. The continuous process of balancing out the effectiveness of EU policies against counterprinciples derived from the rule of law and the exigencies of individual protection brings about a trend towards approximation on the national level. Even the harmonization of interim judicial protection is due to the necessity to find a compromise between the unity of EU law and the safeguarding of fundamental rights. Since the motive to ensure uniform application is less dominant in European administrative law, the question arises whether European and Europeanized law ought to, or can at all, be merged into a single common administrative law of Europe.

IV. CONCEPTS

In a theoretical world which does not know of syncretistic concepts, three positions may be taken with respect to the harmonization of administrative law in Europe. One view, called 'pluralist' in the German discussion, would stress that systems of domestic administrative law should be left untouched and that the diversity of national systems was a value in itself.[164]

---

[164] See M. Kaufmann, *Europäische Integration und Demokratieprinzip* (1997), at 108 et seq.

A second view, which might be referred to as 'functionalist', would consider the European integration as restricted to special policies, but regard the Member States as the most important players in the system. Proponents of that perspective may advocate in favour of sector-specific administrative law, but do not necessarily have to, and in fact will not, demand an elaborate European system. The question is rather where to draw the line between the two spheres. The most that would be needed, therefore, are rules to resolve conflicts of laws.

The third position, as it were, a 'federalist' approach, would be more inclined to support suggestions with a view to harmonizing administrative law. For this view, the question arises as to which method of harmonization should be followed.

A. Pluralist Approach: Preserving the National Systems

Defenders of the pluralist approach insist that the national systems were more elaborate and more experienced than a newly-born European law. Indeed, the components of the national systems are well adapted to each other whereas the experimental character of a new legal order is under a suspicion to provoke instability which the domestic legal orders seek to avoid. Pluralists therefore tend to question already the present state of European legal integration.

It does not come as a surprise that the main argument of pluralist administrative lawyers is that the Union lacks the power to regulate in that field. That part of the debate is typical for a considerable proportion of German administrative law scholarship in the 1990s. The proposal is to define a clear catalogue of powers for the EU in order to avoid what proponents of that view consider as dysfunctional intrusions into grown legal cultures.[165] Thus, the reaction to the changes described above is plain repulsion rather than an effort to integrate the requirements of EU policies. The objection thus provoked is that this view misses reality. It cannot explain, for example, how to live up to the rules of undistorted competition if legitimate expectations can be invoked as a means to prevent revocation of state aid by the very authority that granted unlawful payments. To deny to the Union's institutions the power to regulate and to adjudicate in that field would mean to question the Common Market. The alternative to the Union, however, is not non-cooperation, but, given the interdependence of the economies, another kind of intergovernmental co-operation which would be much farther away from constitutional traditions than the structure of the Union.[166]

---

[165] Von Danwitz, *supra* n. 37, at 431 et seq.
[166] P. Craig and G. de Búrca, *EU Law* (2nd edn., 1998), at 155 et seq.

Plurality and diversity of legal cultures are certainly a common value of the nations assembled in the Union. Bringing state law back in, however, is not a viable option. On the contrary, Europeanization has left its irreversible traces. The question can only be whether the process should be left to sector-specific law and the judiciary or whether it ought to be monitored by European legislation.

B. Functionalist Approach: Conflict of Laws Concepts

Many different approaches are summarized as 'functionalist'. The main stream of those theories, which characterize the Union as a special purpose organization ('*Zweckverband*'), do not necessarily have to take a stand vis-à-vis the question of harmonizing administrative law.[167] The need for enacting administrative law rules depends on the tasks with which the Union is entrusted and varies with the state of integration. The possibility of codified administrative law cannot be ruled out from that standpoint. But much can also be said in favour of a codification of merely sector-specific rules or even no codification at all.[168]

For a position of that kind, the present legal situation might need punctual improvement, but the system as such may remain as it is. The advantages are that case law developed by the Union courts is flexible and facilitates further development. Integration is an ongoing process, and codification might quickly be out of date. For codifying European administrative law, the differences between the national systems might be too significant.

This position characterizes the present majority opinion in the Member States on the matter. The prospects of such a leave-it-as-it-is approach are not absolutely clear. One outcome appears to be further Europeanization of national administrative laws, irrespective of the future attitude of the European Court of Justice. As the examples given in the introduction indicate, the cross-influences between the European and the national levels have reached a state in which the development partly proceeds without obligations of European law to that end.

Whether the result will be a common law of Europe in the long run is a question for the prophets. For the time being, the existing tripartite system will be further developed, consisting of European administrative law and two spheres of national administrative orders, composed of the Europeanized and the national bodies of law.

---

[167] Cf. H. P. Ipsen, *Europäisches Gemeinschaftsrecht* (1972), sec. 8, note 28; see also Majone and Lindseth, *supra* n. 114; Everson, 'Administering Europe?', 36 *JCMS* (1998) 195.

[168] See, for instance, Jans, de Lange, Prechal and Widdershoven, *supra* n. 2, at 370 et seq.

C. Federalist Approach: Codifying Administrative Law?

Codified European administrative law would fit into concepts which regard the European Union as a federal system or even as the predecessor of a federal state. From a pragmatic point of view, such a step would do away with disparities in the execution of EU law which create problems of inequality as between citizens of different Member States. It may also be inferred that it is the task of the legislature, not of courts to make rules.

On a more conceptual basis, it may be argued that where there are common constitutional values there has to be a common administrative law which is, according to the continental traditions, but a more concrete form of constitutional guarantees. Codified law would enhance legal certainty and transparency since judge-made law is not easily accessible. Codification could give a signal to the European executive to adhere strictly to the rule of law and enhance the awareness that its acts are subject to review. It could also serve as a means to reduce widespread citizens' distrust in 'Brussels' and thus have a positive effect on public opinion.

From the present legal situation it appears doubtful if the founding treaties grant the power to the EU to enact a comprehensive codification of administrative law.[169] All that can be said is that specific powers as in the fields of agriculture, customs and environmental policy certainly comprise the implied powers for administrative rules which are necessary to pursue those Treaty objectives. The question whether the internal market power (Article 95 EC) or even the subsidiary competence of Article 308 EC may be used to that end is open for further discussion.

The debate is not as theoretical as it appears. Under the auspices of the Council of Europe, there are several proposals under discussion which aim at framing conventions in the field of administrative law such as the status of public officials in Europe[170] and alternatives to litigation between administrative authorities and private parties.[171] Depending on the success of initiatives of the kind, comparable projects might as well appear on the EU agenda.

Since the present legal situation is at least ambiguous and given the constitutional implications of the subject matter, a comprehensive codification of general administrative law should not be treated as an annex to economic or environmental powers of the Union. The preferable solution is an

---

[169] Cf. Kahl, 'Hat die EG die Kompetenz zur Regelung des Allgemeinen Verwaltungsrechts?', *Neue Zeitschrift für Verwaltungsrecht* (1996) 865.

[170] 'The Status of Public Officials in Europe', Council of Europe Publishing, Strasbourg, November 1999.

[171] 'Alternatives to Litigation Between Administrative Authorities and Private Parties', Proceedings, Multilateral conference Lisbon 31 May–2 June 1999, Council of Europe Publishing, Strasbourg, March 2000.

amendment to the Treaty. Objections based on the constitutions of the Member States would be less fundamental since necessary adjustments could be made in the process of ratification.

This suggestion still does not even come close to a proposal on the subject matter. Many questions are to be answered. Some of the Member States do not dispose of codified administrative law, and other legal systems have a long history of judicial development before the first statutes on general administrative law were considered. Even if they were inclined to give an affirmative answer, the scope of such a project is yet to be determined: should harmonization only cover European administrative law in the meaning introduced above? Or should such a project include indirect enforcement of Union law, in other words, the Europeanized sphere of national law? Should it focus on administrative procedure or also include judicial protection? Should codification extend to principles such as legal certainty, legitimate expectations and proportionality which, in some of the Member States, are enshrined in the constitution? Beyond the issue of EU powers in that field, the discussion has not yet begun.

As the debates on the need for a fundamental rights catalogue and a European Constitution demonstrate, initiatives which aim at defining the legal identity of the Union are topical. European administrative lawyers ought to engage in such a debate in time. Administrative law scholarship must become international, and thorough comparative analysis is crucial. This is the pre-condition for a substantial discussion on the feasibility of codification initiatives of any sort. It would be unfortunate to leave the issue to more or less accidental future proposals of Member State governments or the EU institutions, which means primarily the Commission, alone. The executive should not be the main player when it comes to the development of rules which are designed to govern its own conduct.

7

Misfits: EU Law and the Transformation of European Governance

RENAUD DEHOUSSE

INTRODUCTION

The analysis of European integration is informed by deeply-anchored views of the ways in which public policy unfolds at the European level. The interpretation of the treaties, shaped by decades of decisions of the European Courts, has given birth to a kind of *vulgata* that is rarely called into question. Interaction among the main institutional players—the Commission, the Parliament and the Council—is held to be the key element in the decision-making process. Hence, inter alia, the importance of the concept of 'institutional balance' (discussed in the contribution of Lenaerts and Verhoeven in this volume). Adoption of legislative instruments is the integration technique *par excellence*: it was through the 300 or so directives contained in the 1985 White Paper on the Single Market that barriers to intra-Community trade were to be dismantled and, even today, legislative activity is the main parameter by which we measure the growth in the scope of EU activities.[1] Implementation of EU policies is constrained by choices made in the legislative phase; it is thus perceived to be of secondary importance and generally receives less attention. Classical views about institutional balance simply stress that, in theory, the implementation of EU policies remains in the hands of national administrations.[2]

This legislative bias is equally pervasive in normative assessments of EU policies. One generally discusses legitimacy issues in relation to legislative activities: the classical description of the 'democratic deficit' rests entirely on the role played by legislative assemblies in decision-making procedures.[3] The

[1] Pollack, 'The End of Creeping Competence? EU Policy-Making since Maastricht', 38 *JCMS* (2000) 519.

[2] See the submissions of the German government in Case C-359/92, *Germany v Council* [1994] ECR, p. I-3681.

[3] Resolution of the European Parliament on the Democratic Deficit OJ C 87/89 of 18 July 1988.

European Court of First Instance has also made the clear suggestion that alternative forms of legitimization—such as the participation of management and labour representatives in decision-making processes—mattered only 'in the absence of the participation of the European Parliament in the legislative process'.[4]

However, a gradual shift has occurred in European governance in the wake of the single market programme. The European Union has assumed new tasks that are largely linked to what is increasingly referred to as 'risk regulation'; that is, the assessment and management of risks that may result from natural events or human activities.[5] It has also become apparent that—unlike the mere removal of trade barriers—managing a single market entails a degree of positive action that does not always fit within the neat legal categories inherited from the past. New actors have emerged, such as European administrative agencies; and others, such as intergovernmental committees, have seen their roles deeply transformed. Scientific expertise has acquired an unprecedented level of importance. Traditional legal categories have therefore ceased to reflect adequately the actual operation of the EU's machinery. How should one react to this mismatch between law and reality? Should one return to the purity of the classical model? Or has the time come to envisage a paradigmatic shift?

This contribution tries to address these issues. It is organized as follows. Section I highlights the main transformations occurring in European Union governance. The next sections try to demonstrate the growing gap that has emerged between new patterns of governance and traditional legal analyses. It does this by focusing on three sets of issues: comitology (section II); the powers that can be conferred on specialized European agencies and other bodies whose existence was not contemplated by the EC Treaty (section III); and the role of scientific expertise (section IV). Section V returns to the discrepancy between legal perceptions and functional realities.

I. THE TRANSFORMATION OF EUROPEAN GOVERNANCE

The past fifteen years have seen a deep transformation in the way in which the European Union functions. Some elements affect the whole range of European activities, albeit to different degrees. A good example is the emergence of the European Parliament as a key actor in European policy-making. Other transformations can be seen as the result of a shift in the kind of tasks undertaken by the European Union.

While European integration has long been associated with market unification, there has been a significant expansion in the nature of EU activities. The EU has moved beyond the realm of economic regulation into areas such as

---

[4] Case T-135/96, *UEAPME v Council* [1998] ECR II-2335, at 89.
[5] S. Breyer, *Breaking the Vicious Circle. Towards Effective Risk Regulation* (1993).

environmental and consumer protection, and health and safety issues. Although this expansion process was initially founded on a rather tenuous legal base, it has been ratified by successive Treaty changes: the Single European Act and the Maastricht and Amsterdam Treaties consolidated European intervention in the area of social or risk regulation.[6] First, they explicitly recognized the competence of the European Community to deal with these issues, and second, they brought about a gradual shift to qualified majority voting that simplified decision-making. The reasons for this gradual Europeanization of regulatory policies are simple. The division of labour outlined in the Treaty of Rome—with the European Community focusing on economic integration while social regulation remained primarily under the Member States' control—resulted in de-regulatory pressures as the EC set out to dismantle non-tariff barriers to trade. It therefore emerged that the only way to reconcile market integration with ambitious social regulation programmes, and to thus avoid trade distortions, was to develop such programmes at the European level. Combined with the fact that European firms often prefer to comply with a single European rule rather than fifteen different rules, this element generated growing pressures in favour of the development of European regulation.

This transfer of powers from the national to the European level has been accompanied by a transformation in the conduct of European policies. The prototype of European interventions were primarily of a legislative kind; the 'approximation of laws' contemplated in the EC Treaty. Yet the classic dichotomy between legislation (assumed to deal with broad principles) and implementation (understood as the mere application of those principles) is particularly ill-suited to activities undertaken by public authorities in a risk regulation framework. By their very nature, the problems dealt with in such a framework cannot all be anticipated in the legislative phase; the precise nature of the hazards, the likelihood that they will materialize, and the kind of response they will require are often fairly uncertain. Not only will the technical nature of the likely problems require use of expert knowledge at various stages of the process but, equally importantly, implementation decisions often acquire a significant political salience. Consumers are more likely to show interest in an administrative decision about whether or not to authorize the marketing of Viagra, than in a decision about the adoption of broad (legislative) principles spelling out the safety and efficacy conditions that a pharmaceutical product must satisfy before it can be licensed. In other words, risk regulation has led to the development of a new kind of function—'political administration'[7]—that is not easy to fit into the classic categories of public

---

[6] The phenomenon has been analysed in G. Majone, *Regulating Europe* (1996).

[7] Joerges, ' "Good governance" through Comitology?', in C. Joerges and E. Vos (eds), *EU Committees: Social Regulation, Law and Politics* (1999) 309, at 322, referring to the work of Rudolf Wiethölter.

law. In an integrated market, this function must clearly be exercised in a uniform—though not necessarily centralized—fashion, lest dismantled legislative barriers are replaced by newly emerging administrative obstacles. At the
very least, a convergence of scientific risk assessment and administrative practices is required.[8]

Interestingly, the years following the completion of the single market programme have seen a marked decline in the volume of primary legislation (that
is, of new legislative initiatives) adopted by European institutions, as is
demonstrated by Figure 1. Although the total number of directives and regulations has remained fairly stable, this is largely due to the fact that implementation decisions—the functional equivalent to delegated legislation at the
European level—often have the same form as primary legislation because
Community law ignores any clear hierarchy of norms. The data shown in
Figure 1 can therefore be read as confirming that a large number of EU decisions are now being made in the post-legislative phase.

This shift is far from being merely formal. It suggests that important decisions are now taken by other actors—technocrats (be they bureaucrats or

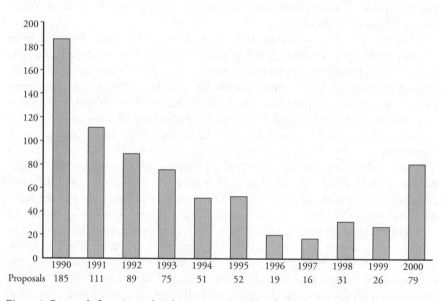

	1990	1991	1992	1993	1994	1995	1996	1997	1998	1999	2000
Proposals	185	111	89	75	51	52	19	16	31	26	79

Figure 1 Proposals for primary legislation introduced by the European Commission

Sources: Reinforcing Political Union and Preparing for Enlargement, Commission Opinion for the
Intergovernmental Conference 1996, 1995, p. 87, for years 1990–1995; COM (95) 512 final for year
1996; SEC (96) final for year 1997; http://europa.eu.int/comm/off/work/1998 for year 1998; http://
europa.eu.int/comm/off/work/1999 for year 1999; http://europa.eu.int/comm/off/work/2000 for year
2000.

[8] See Dehousse 'Regulation by Networks: The Role of European Agencies', 4 *JEPP* (1997)
246 et seq. for further developments.

scientific experts) instead of politicians—and according to procedures that do not necessarily allow for the degree of transparency or citizen participation required by a democracy. The problem is compounded at the European level by the fact that risk regulation is at the crossroads between national and EU competencies, and intermediate structures had to be established in order to bridge the gap between the two levels. The evidence suggests that the importance of these structures is growing: ten European agencies have been created over the last decade[9] to connect national administrations with a (modest) European structure, and the frequency of committee meetings appears to be increasing.

Europe is therefore confronted with a phenomenon akin to the emergence of what some American authors have described as a technocratic 'fourth branch of government'.[10] There are clear differences between the two shores of the Atlantic: in the EU, the distinction between legislative and executive functions is far from being as clear-cut as that in the United States (where each function is given to a different branch of government).[11] Similarly, US administrative law has struggled to define the proper status of *federal* agencies whereas European technocratic structures have a clear *multi-level* character, given their role as a connecting device between the EU and national administrations. Notwithstanding these differences, the growing importance of technocratic governance has given rise to serious legitimacy concerns in both cases. It has also represented an analytical challenge for legal systems that were accustomed to regard administrative decision-making as necessarily constrained by the will of the legislator.[12] The *aggiornamento* is still to be done in the EU context: legal treatment of technocratic governance structures remains informed by a somewhat dated view of their role, as we shall now see.

II. COMITOLOGY: INTERGOVERNMENTAL CONTROL OR DELIBERATIVE NETWORKS?

A. Government by Committees and Institutional Politics

The body of literature looking at the role of intergovernmental committees in the EU system has expanded significantly in recent years.[13] It is therefore

---

[9] Majone, 'The New European Agencies: Regulation by Information', 4 *JEPP* (1997) 262.

[10] Strauss, 'The Place of Agencies in Government: Separation of Powers and the Fourth Branch of Government', 84 *Columbia Law Review* (1984) 573.

[11] See the contribution by Lenaerts and Verhoeven in this volume.

[12] As regards US administrative law, the *locus classicus* is Richard Stewart, 'The Reformation of American Administrative Law', 88 *Harvard Law Journal* (1975) 1667.

[13] Joerges and Vos, *supra* n. 7; G. Pedler and G. F. Schäfer (eds), *Shaping European Law and Policy: The Role of Committees and Comitology in the Policy Process* (1999).

sufficient to highlight a few elements of relevance to the overall argumentation of this contribution.

The Treaty of Rome was fairly elliptic with regard to the implementation of Community measures: Article 155 contemplated the possibility that the Council of Ministers would delegate to the Commission the right to adopt implementation measures. However, national governments have been wary of granting too much discretionary power to the Commission, and they have often obliged the latter to consult a committee of national representatives prior to making a decision.

Whereas the procedures regulating relationships between the Commission and those committees have varied a lot, there is broad agreement on a number of points. First, committees are viewed as a mere *control* device and are deprived of their own decision-making powers: the final word rests either with the Commission or, more rarely, with the Council. This enabled the Court to rule that the management procedure was not contrary to the institutional balance established by the Treaty.[14] Second, committees are widely seen as the instrument of a principal–agent relationship between the Council and the Commission. In the same ruling, for instance, the European Court of Justice argued that '[t]he function of the management committee is to ensure permanent consultation in order to guide the Commission in the exercise of the powers conferred on it by the Council and to enable the latter to substitute its own decision to that of the Commission.'[15] Finally, clear limits are supposedly assigned to committees' powers: according to the procedures established by the Treaty, 'basic elements' of the matter to be regulated must be decided by the Council itself. The committees are supposedly confined to implementation issues.[16]

Such a view is symptomatic of a traditional understanding of the dynamics underpinning the integration process. Not only does it hold legislative procedures to be the most legitimate form of decision-making, but it attaches great importance to the necessity of achieving a balance of power between the Commission and national governments (which are implicitly regarded as unitary actors acting in a cohesive fashion).[17]

Institutional politics have shown that this view was shared by almost all of the actors that are active on the European scene. The Commission has long

[14] Case 25/70, *Einfuhr—und Vorratstelle für Getreide und Futtermittel v Köster* [1970] ECR 1161, at 9.

[15] Ibid.; see also the Conclusions by Advocate-General Jacobs in Case C-212/91, *Angelopharm* [1994] ECR I-171, at para. 38, where an intergovernmental committee is described as 'a control mechanism'.

[16] Case 25/70, *supra* n. 14, at para. 6.

[17] See e.g. Vos, 'EU Committees: The Evolution of Unforeseen Institutional Actors in European Product Regulation', in Joerges and Vos, *supra* n. 7, at 34, who argues that committees may be viewed as a way to protect the institutional balance against the growth of the EU, and ultimately of Commission powers.

fought against the most restrictive of the committee procedures, notably the *contre-filet* variant of the regulatory committee procedure, which it regarded as a burdensome interference in its implementation powers. The Single European Act's failure to simplify comitology procedures was one of the main reasons for the Commission's initial reservations concerning that Treaty.[18] During the Delors years, the Commission made no secret of its loathing for comitology. For its part, the European Parliament has repeatedly declared its aversion to a system that it perceived to be an undue restriction of the Commission's regulatory powers.[19] Of course, this position was largely explained by the fact that it enjoys more influence over the Commission than over the Council of Ministers. Thus the Parliament has frequently used its powers in co-decision procedures to oppose overly stringent procedures: the first instance in which the Council's common position was rejected arose because of a dispute over the proper implementation procedure. Similarly, in the post-Maastricht years the European Parliament brought several cases before the Court of Justice when it deemed its prerogatives to be threatened by decisions of other institutions.[20] Conversely, the Member States' frequent insistence on imposing stricter procedures, notwithstanding their own commitment to favour advisory committees for internal market legislation,[21] illustrates their unwillingness to give free rein to the Commission. Thus, all the main institutional actors appear to agree on a vision of comitology as a rather traditional mechanism of intergovernmental control.

Yet, turning to the actual operation of the system, there is no shortage of evidence to present a radically different picture of the very same phenomenon. While official discourse would lead one to expect systematic confrontations over the proper role of committees, day-to-day reality seems to have been much more consensual. Of the thousands of opinions submitted by committees in the period between 1993 and 1995, only six cases were referred back to the Council, and none of these led to a failure to decide.[22] Moreover, accounts of committee members suggest that voting tends to be a rare event, and that the Commission—which chairs committee meetings—exerts considerable influence over their work.[23] This might explain why the Commission has often been prepared to agree with the Council on the procedure to

[18] Ehlermann, 'The Internal Market following the Single European Act', 24 *CMLRev.* (1987) 361.

[19] On the European Parliament's position, see generally Bradley, 'The European Parliament and Comitology: On the Road to Nowhere?', 3 *ELJ* (1997) 230.

[20] See e.g. Cases 302/87, *Parliament v Council* [1988] ECR 5615 and C-156/93, *Parliament v Commission* [1995] ECR I-2019.

[21] Declaration on the implementation powers of the Commission, annexed to the Single European Act.

[22] SEC (95) 731 final, para. 52.

[23] Buitendijk and van Schemedelen: 'Brussels Advisory Committees: A Channel for Influence?', 20 *ELR* (1995) 37.

be chosen, notwithstanding its proud declarations to the contrary.[24] Empirical works have depicted committees as peer structures in which the quest for consensus is a prevailing concern. In a now famous contribution, Joerges and Neyer have suggested a radically new vision of comitology as a forum for 'deliberative politics' in which all participants engage in the search for the common good.[25]

Interestingly, there has been a change of attitude in recent years, even among European institutions. Once so critical of committees, the Commission has now adopted a more conciliatory tone.[26] In its proposal for a new framework decision on comitology following the Treaty of Amsterdam,[27] the Commission deliberately omitted any provision aimed at enhancing the transparency of comitology proceedings, lest (it was said) this might alter the quality of interaction with national officials.[28]

B. Who watches the Watchmen? The Need for New Legal Constructs

The consensual nature of the exercise undoubtedly has positive aspects, if only because it lessens the risk of institutional conflicts and provides for the smooth functioning of the EU regulatory system. Yet it brings its own set of problems. In a period of widespread mistrust of technocratic structures of all kinds, consensual deliberations between well-intentioned experts who meet behind closed doors to avoid unwanted interference may easily be resented as collusion between technocrats. If intergovernmental control mechanisms no longer fulfil the task for which they have been established, and if comitology has indeed evolved into a freewheeling transnational structure, the key question becomes: who controls this structure, and how? Hence, inter alia, a request for more transparency and for participatory rights in committee procedures.[29]

[24] Dogan, 'Comitology: Little Procedures with Big Implications', 20 *West European Politics* (1997) 31.

[25] Joerges and Neyer, 'From Intergovernmental Bargaining to Deliberative Political Processes: The Constitutionalization of Comitology', 3 *ELJ* (1997) 273.

[26] See its submissions in view of the 1996 Intergovernmental Conference, *Reinforcing Political Union and Preparing for Enlargement*, Brussels, 1995.

[27] Proposal for a Council decision laying down the procedures for the exercise of implementing powers conferred on the Commission, OJ 1998 C 279/5.

[28] Surprisingly enough, such a provision was introduced by the Council of Ministers in the final version. See Article 7 of Council decision 1999/468 of 28 June 1999 laying down the procedures for the exercise of implementing powers conferred on the Commission, OJ 1999 L 184/23.

[29] Dehousse, 'Towards a Regulation of Transnational Governance? Citizens' Rights and the Reform of Comitology Procedures', in Joerges and Vos, *supra* n. 7, at 109; Bignami, 'The Democratic Deficit in European Community Rulemaking: A Call for Notice and Comment in Comitology', 40 *Harvard International Law Journal* (1999) 451.

Problems arise at different levels. The rather poor transparency of the committee procedures 'makes it difficult to discern the part played by the committees in the formulation and eventual adoption of measures'.[30] It also tends to complicate judicial review of committees' work as they are deprived of decision-making powers of their own. True, the validity of the decisions eventually adopted by the Commission or the Council at the end of a comitology procedure can always be challenged: in recent years, the European Court of Justice has indeed started to look more closely at the functioning of committees, particularly when their procedural rules were allegedly violated.[31] Needless to say, the indirect character of the review process, compounded by the more general difficulty experienced by private parties seeking annulment of Community decisions, reduces incentives to rely on litigation to ensure the proper functioning of committees.

Similar concerns have led to a gradual shift in judicial perceptions of the legal status of committees. This is exemplified by the *Rothmans* case. Under the access rule contained in Decision 94/90, a well-known cigarette manufacturer had requested of the Commission the minutes of the Customs Code Committee.[32] The reasons for the application were simple: like all 'comitology' committees, this one did not have its own administration, budget, archives or premises, nor an address of its own (as the Court of First Instance subsequently noted). It therefore appeared natural to turn to the only permanent member of the network—the Commission—which chairs the Committee and performs secretarial duties. Yet Decision 94/90 provides that applications must be sent 'direct to the author'. The Commission thus rejected the application, arguing that it could not be regarded as the author of the minutes 'in the intellectual sense' because it was subject to the Committee's control even though, in practice, it held the pen for the Committee.

Although the Commission's decision merely reflected the traditional construction of comitology's role, it gave rise to an embarrassing situation. Committees are supposed to be an emanation of the Council, which does not generally hold copies of Committee documents. Thus, in practice, the Commission's conclusion amounted to an exclusion of comitology from the scope of rules regarding access to Community documents.

In such conditions, adherence to the traditional view of committees would have ended up frustrating the principle of transparency to which European institutions have given so much importance in recent years,[33] as Sweden, a

---

[30] De Búrca, 'The Institutional Development of the EU: A Constitutional Analysis', in P. Craig and G. de Búrca (eds), *The Evolution of EU Law* (1999) 55, at 77.

[31] See e.g. Case C-263/95, *Germany v Commission (Construction Products)* [1998] ECR I-441.

[32] OJ 1994 L 46, at 58.

[33] Curtin, 'Democracy, Transparency and Political Participation', in V. Deckmyn and I. Thomson (eds), *Openness and Transparency in the European Union* (1998) 107.

notoriously transparency-minded government, promptly argued before the Court. Thus the Court preferred to rule that 'for the purposes of the Community rules on access to documents, "comitology" committees come under the Commission itself, . . . which is responsible for rulings on applications for access to documents of those committees.'[34] In order to avoid a situation in which it would be nearly impossible to hold the actual authors of a decision accountable, the Court of First Instance decided to adopt a radically new reading of the role of committees. A stroke of the pen transformed them from control bodies into structures subordinate to the very institution they were supposed to control.

Rothmans is an interesting ruling in several respects. First, it is symptomatic of the paradigmatic shift in the perception of committees. The Court was faced with a tension between classical constructions in which committees are viewed as a control device, and the actual operation of the bureaucratic machinery where the dividing line between the various actors is somewhat fuzzy. Second, it illustrates a difficulty inherent in the emergence of transnational bureaucratic structures at European level: keeping them under control is made more difficult by the discrepancy between their legal status and their actual role. To avoid creating a black hole in which important decisions could be made without any control, the Court had no choice but to opt for an innovative reading of the situation, in which 'comitology' committees and the Commission are depicted as forming part of the same network-like structure. This concession to pragmatism is noteworthy as, in other areas, traditional legal constructs have stood in the way of an acknowledgement of the changing conditions in which European governance structures now operate.

III. EUROPEAN AGENCIES: DELEGATION VERSUS ACCOUNTABILITY?

A. The Growth of European Agencies

Quantitatively and qualitatively, the mushrooming of specialized European agencies is one of the most interesting developments in the functioning of EU bureaucracy in the post-Maastricht years.

To better illustrate this, a general remark is in order. The Commission is by far the largest sector of the EU's administration: in 1999, the number of authorized staff totalled 21,438 persons (including temporary agents), compared to 4,102 in the European Parliament and 2,671 in the Council of Ministers.[35] However, the staffing of both the Council and Parliament—

---

[34] Case T-188/97, *Rothmans v Commission* [1999] ECR. II-2463, at para 61.
[35] Source: Final budget of the European Community, OJ L 39, 12 February 1999.

although starting from a much more modest base—recently appears to have grown at a faster rate than that of the Commission.[36] This is noteworthy, given the expansion in the scope of EU policies registered at Maastricht and Amsterdam. As indicated above, the growing role of the EU in the field of risk regulation does not merely entail the adoption of legislative rules; it also requires an elaborate apparatus for scientific assessment, as well as decisions about risk management that must be taken at the European level. One might thus have expected this evolution to be reflected in a sizable growth of the Commission, but this does not appear to have been the case. Between 1995 and 2000, Commission staff (including clerical and logistical support staff, as well as translators) increased from 15,836 to 17,087. In roughly the same period, ten European administrative agencies with a total staff of 1,045 were created. These covered areas ranging from the environment, or health and safety at work, to racism and xenophobia, and reconstruction in Kosovo. These figures provide a simplistic, yet arguably telling, picture of the contradictory trends at work. On the one hand, national governments keep enlarging the range of missions entrusted to the Union; on the other hand, they are reluctant to accept parallel growth in the means with which the Commission (symbol of the loathed Brussels Eurocracy) is endowed. It is known that the tension between these two logics has resulted in the managerial inadequacies—massive outsourcing, absence of control, and ultimately corruption—depicted in the report of the independent experts that prompted the resignation of the Santer Commission.[37] However, beyond these pathological episodes, the same structural contradictions have also played a key role in the emergence of some kind of functional decentralization within the EU bureaucracy.

Most of the agencies created in recent years appeared as responses to the growing need for administrative assistance in the preparation of EU policies and their implementation. The existing agencies can be grouped in three broad categories:[38]

(1) *information agencies*,[39] whose main function is to gather information and to liaise between national authorities and EU administrations;[40]

---

[36] A. Stevens (with W. Stevens), *Brussels Bureaucrats? The Administration of the European Union* (2001) 15.

[37] Committee on Independent Experts, 'First Report on Allegations Regarding Fraud, Mismanagement and Nepotism in the European Commission', 15 March 1999, <http://www.europarl.eu.int/experts/en.default.htm/>.

[38] A general description of EU agencies' tasks can be found in Kreher, 'Agencies in the European Community: A Step towards Administrative Integration in Europe', 4 *JEPP* (1997) 246; see also Chiti, 'The Emergence of a Community Administration: The Case of European Agencies', 37 *CMLRev.* (2000) 309.

[39] The expression is borrowed from Majone, *supra* n. 9.

[40] This is e.g. the case of the European Centre for the Development of Vocational Training (Council Regulation 337/75, OJ 1975 L 39/1), the European Foundation for the

(2) *implementation agencies*, entrusted with the duty of implementing the EU regimes in highly specialized areas such as trademarks or plant variety rights;[41]

(3) *management agencies*, which assist the Commission in the management of EU programmes.[42]

The trend towards the establishment of specialized administrative structures seems to have been encouraged by the criticisms levelled at the Commission's managerial capabilities in recent years. The establishment of agencies for food safety,[43] aviation safety[44] and maritime safety[45] is currently contemplated, and others are said to be following. This might be seen as an indication that the evolution towards a greater devolution of administrative responsibilities to European structures is fairly uncontroversial. However, the situation is more complex.

Following the lead of Majone, some scholars have been arguing that the establishment of specialized agencies was a positive development in its own right, likely to improve the effectiveness and the credibility of European regulatory policies.[46] However, reactions within the relevant policy communities have shown far less enthusiasm. Commission officials have warned against a development that might lead to the establishment of rival structures and that they thus view as a threat to their institution. Commission President Romano Prodi was most explicit in this respect. In a speech before the European Parliament on 3 October 2000, he made a vibrant plea in favour of the necessity of preserving the Commission's authority over specialized agencies.[47] On their side, national administrations have often insisted on retaining a measure of control over the work of agencies.

All this has led to the establishment of a system of checks and balances aimed to ensure that agencies will not emerge as structures that are likely to be too autonomous in their operations. All existing agencies are therefore

Improvement of Living and Working Conditions (Council Regulation 1365/75, OJ 1975 L 139/1) as well as the European Environment Agency (Council Regulation 1210/90, OJ 1990 L 131/1, amended by Council Regulation 2063/94, OJ 1994 L 216/9).

[41] Office of Harmonization in the Internal Market (OHIM), Council Regulation 40/94, OJ 1994 L 11/1; Community Plant Variety Office, Council Regulation 2100/94, OJ 1994 L 227/1.

[42] European Training Foundation Council Regulation 1360/90, OJ 1990 L 120/1.

[43] COM(00)716 of 8 November 2000.   [44] COM(00)595 of 27 September 2000.

[45] COM(00)802 of 6 December 2000.

[46] Majone, *supra* n. 6; Majone and Everson, 'Institutional Reform: Independent Agencies, Oversight, Coordination and Procedural Control', in O. De Schutter, N. Lebessis and J. Paterson (eds), *Governance in the European Union* (2001); Vos, 'Reforming the European Commission: What Role to Play for European Agencies', 37 *CMLRev.* (2000) 1113; Kelemen, 'The European "Independent" Agencies and Regulation in the EU', CEPS Working Document no. 12, 1997.

[47] Speech 00/352 of 3 October 2000.

governed by administrative boards composed of national representatives, to which an expert appointed by the European Parliament is occasionally added. Great care has also been taken to ensure the smooth cooperation of European agencies with their national counterparts, particularly for those agencies that enjoy autonomous decision-making power (such as the Trademark Office) or that are entrusted with the responsibility to prepare decisions to be made by the Commission, as is the case for the European Agency for the Evaluation of Medicinal Products (EMEA).[48] Last, but not least, agencies' powers have generally been defined fairly strictly. Most of them have been denied any decision-making power of their own. The regulation establishing the Lisbon Drug Monitoring Centre made it explicit that '[t]he Centre may not take any measure which in any way goes beyond the sphere of information and the processing thereof'.[49] Whereas the Commission's initial proposal foresaw the possibility that the EMEA would make autonomous decisions about certain procedural matters—such as the format of the application for marketing authorizations[50]—the regulation that was ultimately adopted denied the Agency even this limited degree of autonomy.[51] Even the above-mentioned 'implementation agencies', which were given narrowly-defined executive powers to implement specialized EU regimes, are subject to a legality control by the Commission.[52]

A more relaxed attitude seems to have emerged in recent times. Council Regulation 2454/1999 of 15 November 1999[53] has granted to the European Agency for Reconstruction in Kosovo wide powers to manage external aid programmes, which appears to encroach upon the Commission's budgetary powers ex Article 274 EC. The Commission proposal for the establishment of a European Aviation Safety Agency also envisages the possibility that the latter might adopt non-binding 'guidance material';[54] coupled with the power to issue individual decisions, this comes close to an independent regulatory power, as has been shown by the Commission's experience in the field of competition policy. Recent proposals also suggested that the administrative boards of yet-to-be-created agencies might not include representatives of all Member

---

[48] See Dehousse, *supra* n. 8, at 256–257, for a detailed analysis.

[49] Art. 1(4) of Council Regulation EEC 302/93, OJ 1993 L 36/1.

[50] Art. 13(2) of the amended Commission proposal for a regulation establishing a European Agency for the Evaluation of Medicinal Products, OJ 1991 C 310/7.

[51] See Art. 6(5) of Council Regulation 2309/93 of 22 July 1993 establishing a European Agency for the Evaluation of Medicinal Products, OJ 1993 L 214/1.

[52] See e.g. Art. 44 of Regulation 2100/94 on Community Plant Variety Rights, *supra* n. 41. A similar control is foreseen in the regulation establishing other agencies. See e.g. Art. 18 of the regulation establishing the Centre for the Development of Vocational Training, *supra* n. 40.

[53] OJ 1994 L 46, at 58.

[54] See Art. 13(b) of the Commission proposal, *supra* n. 44.

States. This seems to reflect a hope that the credibility of these new bodies will thereby be strengthened.[55]

Notwithstanding these signs of greater openness, a strong anti-delegation bias seems to prevail. The explicit conferral of regulatory powers on autonomous agencies is perceived to be encroaching on the Commission's own implementation powers. Even more symptomatically, although Commission President Romano Prodi had initially called for the establishment of a 'strong' regulatory body at the EU level in the wake of manifold food scares, the Commission's own proposal did not even suggest providing the European Food Authority with autonomous power to adopt individual decisions.[56]

B. *Meroni* and the Non-Delegation Doctrine

This reluctance to delegate decision-making powers to decentralized bodies is allegedly based on the rather restrictive case law of the European Court of Justice. As early as 1958, the Court's famous *Meroni* ruling set out a series of conditions that had to be met if delegations of power were to be admissible. The Court admitted that it 'cannot be excluded' that power might be delegated to bodies whose existence was not contemplated by the Treaties, if doing so appears compatible with the regulatory powers conferred on the institutions (in the case at hand, the High Authority of the Coal and Steel Community). However, the ruling also specified that such delegation is permissible only when 'it involves clearly defined executive powers the exercise of which can, therefore, be subject to strict review in the light of criteria determined by the delegating authority', whereas delegation of 'a discretionary power, implying a wide margin of discretion', is to be excluded in all cases.[57] The Court justified this restrictive position by stressing that the balance of power between European institutions is 'a fundamental guarantee granted by the Treaty in particular to the undertakings and associations of undertakings to which it applies'.[58] It added that the delegating authority could not confer any powers other than those that it had itself received under the Treaty. Delegated powers are thus to be subject to the conditions that would have

---

[55] See Art. 24 of the proposal for a Regulation establishing the European Food Authority, n. 43 above, and Art. 11 of the proposal concerning the European Maritime Safety Agency, *supra* n. 45.

[56] Proposal for a Regulation of the European Parliament and of the Council laying down the general principles and requirements of food law, and laying down procedures in matters of food safety, COM(00)716 of 8 November 2000.

[57] *Meroni v High Authority* [1957–58] ECR 133, at 151–152.

[58] Ibid.

applied if the delegation had not taken place; treaty rules on publicity, the giving of reasons, and judicial review cannot be evaded by transferring powers to outside bodies.[59]

Although given in the framework of the ECSC Treaty, this ruling is generally considered to be valid within the wider Community legal order.[60] However, this view appears to neglect the important differences that exist between the institutional settings created by the various treaties establishing the European Communities. The Coal and Steel Community was a largely integrated system in which the High Authority had been endowed with important regulatory powers. In contrast, the Treaty of Rome is regarded to be a mere 'framework agreement' that establishes a system in which broad objectives are to be reached gradually through legislative decisions. These basic elements are important in order to assess the relevance of the *Meroni* precedent in the context of what is now the European Community.

The factual situation that gave rise to the *Meroni* dispute is worth recalling. Article 53 ECSC confers power upon the High Authority to make financial arrangements common to several undertakings. On that basis, the High Authority adopted a decision establishing a financial arrangement for ensuring a regular supply of ferrous scrap. The implementation of this agreement was entrusted to two private law funds established in Brussels, which enjoyed broad autonomy in the operation of the equalization scheme. The Court therefore concluded that the High Authority had delegated a power it enjoyed by virtue of the Treaty. Situations of this kind are rather rare in the EC context, where decisions taken by the European institutions are usually to be implemented by national administrations. Assuming implementation powers are to be given to some administrative agency, those powers would rarely be taken away from a Community institution; they would instead be removed from national administrations. Indeed, prior to the establishment of EMEA or OHIM, marketing authorizations for medicinal products were delivered, and trademarks registered, by national bodies rather than the Commission.

The concept of delegation is therefore quite ill-suited to such situations; as the Court pointed out in *Meroni*, such a concept makes sense only in relation to powers 'which the delegating authority itself received under the Treaty'.[61] *Europeanization* would be a better description of a process in which powers are transferred vertically (from the national to the EU level) rather than horizontally (from Community institutions to specialized agencies).

---

[59] *Meroni v High Authority* [1957–58] ECR 133, at 149–150.

[60] See e.g. Lenaerts, 'Regulating the Regulatory Process: "Delegation of Powers" in the European Community', 18 *ELR* (1993) 22, at 41.

[61] *Meroni, supra* n. 57, at 150.

Yet it is through the prism of delegation that the legal community has examined the legality of European agencies.[62] This may be partly due to the problem of making sense of a novel type of structure that is difficult to frame within existing categories because of its network-like character.[63] But less innocent interpretations are also possible. The alleged inflexibility of the legal system has often been invoked—not least by the Commission and its legal service—against any attempt to confer autonomous powers on specialized agencies, regardless of how limited this delegation might be.

The example of the EMEA is again quite significant. Even though Regulation 2309/93 entrusted the Agency with the management of some procedures for the authorization of pharmaceuticals, its powers stop short of actual decision-making. The measures to be adopted in this framework must therefore be taken by the Commission acting under the supervision of two 'comitology' committees (the Committee for Proprietary Medicinal Products and the Committee for Veterinary Medicinal Products). This limitation is largely viewed as a consequence of the non-delegation principle defined in *Meroni*. Decisions about whether or not to grant a marketing authorization for a given pharmaceutical are indeed complex; they involve difficult choices and a balance must be found between a variety of objectives ranging from health and safety to industrial concerns. As such, they clearly fall into the category of 'discretionary decisions' contemplated in *Meroni*. But even in this case, the *Meroni* precedent is not as restrictive as one might have thought, for it explicitly contemplated the possibility to 'grant agencies the power to draw up resolutions the application of which belongs to the High Authority, the latter retaining full responsibility for the same'.[64] The Court argued that in such a case there is actually no delegation because the High Authority remains in charge. Thus, a system in which the EMEA would have been granted the power to adopt marketing authorizations would have been perfectly in line with the *Meroni* doctrine, provided that the Commission retained the power to disallow those decisions.[65] In other words, even accepting that the *Meroni* precedent was relevant for the new agencies—a questionable view, as has been seen—other control devices that are more respectful of agency autonomy

---

[62] See Chiti, 'The Emergence of a Community Administration: The Case of European Agencies', 37 *CMLRev.* (2000) 309; Lenaerts, *supra* n. 60; Everson, 'Independent Agencies: Hierarchy Beaters', 1 *ELJ* (1995) 180; and E. Vos, *Institutional Frameworks of Community Health and Safety Regulations: Committees, Agencies and Private Bodies* (1999), at 200–3 and 241–248.

[63] Dehousse, *supra* n. 8, and Ladeur, 'Towards a Legal Concept of the Network in European Standard-Setting', in Joerges and Vos, *supra* n. 7, at 151.

[64] *Supra* n. 57, at 147.

[65] In *Meroni*, the Court of Justice clearly indicated that a system in which decisions may be subordinated to the approval of the High Authority, as was envisaged in Arts 8 and 9 of Decision 14/55 ECSC, cannot be assimilated to a delegation since the final say (implicitly or explicitly) remains with the High Authority.

might have met the demands of the Court of Justice. Another option was chosen nonetheless. This clearly suggests that, in addition to legal concerns, considerations of political opportunity obviously played a role in the definition
of agencies' power.

The difference between the current system, in which decisions are prepared
by the agency and formally adopted by the Commission, and the kind of
delegation contemplated here, might appear tenuous. Yet keeping an arm's
length between agencies' operations and the Commission might offer advantages of two kinds.

First, it would significantly increase the transparency of the system.
Although all marketing authorizations are Commission decisions under the
present rules, the Commission systematically rubber-stamps EMEA recommendations—apparently without even discussing them, since a written procedure is followed. Thus, while EU institutions appear, in principle, to stick
to a very strict non-delegation doctrine, in practice, they have been content
to adopt a far more relaxed attitude. This is easily understandable: given the
technical character of the decisions in question, the Commission is naturally
inclined to follow expert advice. But why portray a substantively expert decision as a 'political' decision? Wouldn't the situation be clearer if the respective
responsibilities of scientists and politicians were more clearly delineated? The
Commission appears to fear the emergence of potential competitors.
However, it should appreciate that the present situation's ambiguity creates
risks. One day the Commission might be called upon to bear the responsibility for decisions in which it played a merely formal role. The risk is not simply political. Risk regulation and litigation have developed in parallel in
several countries, as citizens aggrieved by decisions of public authorities tend
to bring the matters before administrative or even criminal courts. Politicians
and public officials are increasingly being sued for their alleged wrongdoings.
It would therefore be in their interest to assist in the clarification of everyone's
responsibilities.

Second, a clearer delegation of authority to agencies might have the advantage of reducing the risk of undue political interference in what constitutes
primarily technical decisions. This does not mean that all political considerations should be precluded. Indeed, many scientific decisions do involve political dimensions: a decision about whether or not to authorize the
morning-after pill will necessarily entail ethical considerations in addition to
efficacy concerns. Other decisions will have distributive implications that are
not for experts to determine. But a clearer demarcation between these two
kinds of logic would make it more difficult for all kinds of economic interests
and political concerns to hide behind pseudo-scientific arguments, as frequently happens. Of course political bodies would retain the right to disallow
the experts, but they would be forced to do so openly. This would force them
to give reasons for their deeds. Paradoxically, the development of delegation

might therefore enhance accountability, instead of reducing it as is often feared.

IV. STRUCTURING THE INTERFACE BETWEEN SCIENTIFIC EXPERTISE AND POLITICAL DECISIONS

One of the peculiarities of risk regulation is that it often requires decisions to be made in a context of uncertainty. The problem is not merely that those decisions will have to be based on the recommendations of experts who are expected to master the technical complexity of the issues. The very nature or extent of the risk will sometimes be disputed: it has taken long debates for the existence of a greenhouse effect to be accepted by experts. In other cases, the controversy will concern the kind of measures to be adopted in order to tackle a given problem. Political leaders are usually unlikely to be confronted with undisputed recommendations by the scientific community. Hence the question: how is the interface between scientists and policy-makers to be structured?

A. Giving Science a Say

The most obvious response to this question takes the form of a mandatory requirement to consult experts before a decision is made. The Treaty of Amsterdam's insertion of a provision obligating the Commission to 'tak[e] account of any new development based on scientific facts' in its harmonization proposals[66] can easily be construed as an obligation to consult scientific experts. Similarly, even before this provision was adopted, the European Court of Justice had declared in a widely noticed ruling that:

[t]he drafting and adaptation of Community rules governing cosmetic products are founded on scientific and technical assessments which must themselves be based on the results of the latest international research ... Since the purpose of consulting the Scientific Committee is to ensure that the measures adopted at Community level are necessary and adapted to the objective, pursued by the Cosmetics Directive, of protecting human health, consultation of the Committee must be mandatory in all cases.[67]

While the innovative character of this ruling has been challenged,[68] its objective is beyond dispute: it is meant to enhance the quality of Community

---

[66] New Art. 95(3) of the EC Treaty.

[67] Case C-212/91, *Angelopharm GmbH v Freie und Hansestadt Hamburg* [1994] ECR I-171.

[68] See Bradley, 'Institutional Aspects of Comitology: Scenes from the Cutting Room Floor', in Joerges and Vos, *supra* n. 7, at 71.

rule-making through procedural requirements. This would initially appear to be compatible with a classic view of the division of labour between policy-makers and scientists: the former are supposed to make the best possible decisions on the basis of the evidence they have at their disposal, while the latter must assist them by giving advice. This basic distinction has influenced much of the current thinking about risk regulation at the EU level. Thus, in its recent proposal for the establishment of a Food Safety Authority, the European Commission insisted on the necessity of drawing a clear line between risk assessment (a scientific task to be carried out by the Authority) and risk management (which must remain in the hands of the Commission because it entails policy choices).[69]

However, the boundary between scientific arguments and political concerns is not always easy to draw in decisions entailing very complex technical assessments, particularly those involving scientific controversy. Policy-makers will sometimes come under attack simply for having followed experts' recommendations. For instance, in the *Bergaderm* case, the Commission was taken to court for a decision to ban an allegedly carcinogenic substance on the basis of a scientific committee's controversial assessment.[70] At other times, scientific evidence might be biased by the experts' national origins. Thus, in its report about the European Union's handling of the BSE crisis, the European Parliament's inquiry committee drew a rather bleak picture of the functioning of the Scientific Veterinary Committee. It noted *inter alia* that '[the] preponderance of UK scientists and officials . . . meant that the SVC tended to reflect current thinking within the British Ministry for Agriculture, Fisheries and Food.'[71] Neither the efficiency nor the fairness of the policy process can therefore be guaranteed by a mere consultation mechanism. Like it or not, it is necessary to open the black box and look at the way in which scientific deliberations are organized.

B. Structuring Scientific Deliberations

The very importance of scientific assessments in contemporary public policy means that scientific deliberations cannot be left to develop in an autonomous fashion. The 'benign neglect' with which this crucial phase of the policy process was considered largely stemmed from a tendency to regard science as a universal, boundary-free world that was entirely governed by the quest for

[69] Proposal for a Regulation of the European Parliament and of the Council laying down the general principles and requirements of food law, establishing the European Food Authority, and laying down procedures in matters of food safety, COM(00)716 of 8 November 2000, at 13–14.

[70] Case T-199/96, *Bergaderm and Goupil v Commission* [1998] ECR II-2805.

[71] EP Doc A4-0020/97/A, at 10.

the truth (in contrast to policy processes dominated by sectoral interests of various kinds).[72] The reality is somewhat more complex. We have seen that scientists can be 'captured' by sectoral interests. More fundamentally, science is controversial, by definition. Whereas policy-makers expect scientific assessments to provide them with clear-cut answers, we have known since Karl Popper that there is no such thing as a stable and definitive truth in scientific discussions. More often than not, policy-makers will be confronted with conflicting views and uncertainty. The quality of scientific deliberations therefore assumes an enhanced level of importance. The legitimacy of scientific assessments will ultimately depend on the way in which those deliberations are organized. How have the various 'experts' been selected? What measures have been taken to ensure their independence or the pluralism of the debate? Have the different views expressed in the deliberation process been given adequate consideration?

The 1997 reform of scientific committees operating at the EU level made some important steps in that direction.[73] The selection procedure has been tightened by setting up a Scientific Steering Committee that is vested, inter alia, with the power to ensure the selection of the 'most suitable candidates' for all scientific committees.[74] Scientific experts are to operate with absolute independence and are to declare all possible conflicts of interests.[75] Rules of procedures, agendas, minutes and opinions of the scientific committees must be made publicly available. To avoid some of the deviations noticed in the functioning of the Standing Veterinary Committee during the BSE crisis, provision is also made for minority views to be included in the minutes.[76] These are all welcome developments because they foster the transparency of the debate, thereby improving the credibility and the legitimacy of scientific assessments.

However, one might wonder whether this suffices. Given the importance assumed by scientific assessments in many decision-making processes, it might be argued that it is crucial to the quality and the fairness of those processes that adequate consideration be given to the widest possible range of views. The Court of Justice has previously ruled that 'respect for the rights guaranteed by the Community legal order in administrative procedures is of

---

[72] The contrast is addressed in Joerges, 'Scientific Expertise in Social Regulation and the European Court of Justice: Legal Frameworks for Denationalized Governance Structure', in C. Joerges, K.-H. Ladeur and E. Vos (eds), *Integrating Scientific Expertise into Regulatory Decision-Making* (1997) 295.

[73] Commission Decision 97/404/EC of 10 June 1997 setting up a Scientific Steering Committee, OJ 1997 L 169/85 and Commission Decision 97/579/EC of 23 July 1997 setting up Scientific Committees in the field of consumer health and food safety, OJ 1997 L 237/18, both amended by Commission Decision 2000/443/EC of 18 May 2000, OJ 2000 L 179/13.

[74] Article 3(4) of Decision 97/404.   [75] See e.g. Article 4 of Decision 97/404.

[76] Article 7 of Decision 97/404.

. . . fundamental importance' where the Community institutions are engaged in complex technical evaluations. Among these guarantees, the Court mentioned 'the duty of the competent institution to examine carefully and impartially all the relevant aspects' of the issue, and 'the right of the person concerned to make his view known and to have an adequately reasoned decision'.[77] This ruling applied to an individual decision and not to rule-making activities, yet the clear rationale was that the quality of experts' deliberations is of crucial importance when European institutions tend to follow experts' recommendations mechanically. 'In those circumstances, the court noted, the group of experts cannot properly carry out its task unless it is composed of persons possessing the necessary technical knowledge . . . or the members of that group are advised by experts having that knowledge.'[78] Moreover, the Court made it clear that the debate had to address all relevant issues; this is why 'the person concerned must be able to explain his position to the group of experts or to comment on the information before the group'.[79] While some of these guarantees may be better adapted to the level of risk management than to risk assessment, they also appear to be relevant to the latter. The same ethos should lead one to conclude that scientific bodies are subject to a 'duty of care' in their operations that should lead them to give adequate consideration to all of the views put forward. In any event, the Court of Justice made it very clear that the need for legal guarantees did not apply merely to the 'political' level of the regulatory process, but also to preparatory stages.

V. CONCLUSION: LOST BOUNDARIES

EU law remains influenced by a fairly traditional view of the way in which the integration process unfolds. EU policies are still largely seen as an exercise in international diplomacy in which the convergence between would-be 'national' interests—expressed by national governments and mitigated by the influence of enlightened technocrats (the Commission)—plays a key role. They carry a somewhat dated vision of public policy: the legislative stage is supposed to be decisive, and the control of elected representatives is expected to be the main way in which to ensure the legitimacy of policy choices.

These assumptions are being shaken by the evolution of European governance. The boundaries between law-making and implementation, or between scientific advice and policy-making, have become difficult to discern. The point is not that these classical concepts have become entirely obsolete, but that they are no longer sufficient to make sense of the way things work, let

---

[77] Case C-269/90, *Hauptzollamt München-Mitte v Technische Universität München* [1991] ECR I-5495.

[78] Ibid., at 22.   [79] Ibid., at 23.

alone to regulate the policy-making process. Functional needs have led to the emergence of new actors—scientists, bureaucrats, interests representatives—whose influence is often essential. Decision-making processes have evolved. The idea that a clear-cut response can be given to the problems faced by modern society is increasingly challenged by the technical complexity of the issues to be addressed. Those are mighty problems for any society; at the European level, they are compounded by the necessity to involve a plurality of actors—national and European—at all stages of the policy process.

In combination, these trends have led to the emergence of transnational bureaucratic networks and to a strengthening of the administrative stages of the decision-making process at the expense of the legislative component. Constitutional principles have often been invoked as a brake in this process. The European Court of Justice has tried to preserve the primacy of legislative procedures by assigning limits to what can be delegated to technocratic bodies such as 'comitology' committees or specialized agencies. Basic principles (such as the concept of 'institutional balance') have been instrumentalized by those who tried to oppose the above-mentioned trends, not least in the European Commission. The stubborn insistence on a non-delegation doctrine has often been presented as a defence against a technocratic drift, and an attempt to preserve the 'political' character of basic decisions against the evils of technocracy. However, the reality is somewhat more complex. The EU's legislative processes are heavily technocratic. Moreover, despite many protests to the contrary, one has accepted—in fact, if not in law—that basic decisions are made by technocratic bodies of various kinds, the choices of which are duly rubber-stamped by the 'political' powers that be. EU law is then used as a façade to hide a reality that is deemed to be unacceptable.

Law is said to protect normative values. Are these better served by this exercise in camouflage? It seems hard to believe. Are decisions that are made (de facto) by committees and agencies more amenable to judicial or parliamentary control simply because they are formally attributed to the European Commission? Hardly so. On the judicial plane, the rule of law ethos that led the European Court of Justice to declare itself competent to review the legality of decisions taken by the European Parliament (at a time this was not foreseen by the Treaty)[80] would lead it similarly to accept jurisdiction to review the acts of any delegated body.[81] For its part, the European Parliament has given ample evidence of its ability to transform its budgetary powers as an instrument of political control, even in areas in which it was granted no formal powers. Specific mechanisms of parliamentary oversight can also be established.

Given the technical complexity of the decisions that are taken by delegated bodies, it is unlikely to be of much help to advocate a return to the *status quo*

---

[80] Case 294/83, *Parti écologiste 'Les Verts' v European Parliament* [1986] ECR 1339.
[81] As was for instance suggested by Lenaerts, *supra* n. 60.

ante. Indeed, insisting on a principle of non-delegation ill-serves exactly the constitutional principles it is supposed to assist; hiding the identity of the organization actually responsible for decisions will sooner or later give rise to delicate liability issues. Those who are attached to the primary rule of constitutionalism—according to which all powers must be controlled—would be better inspired to acknowledge the evolution that has taken place. This is not tantamount to granting *carte blanche* to experts. Political institutions would still retain the right to define the basic objectives to be reached and the means to be used for that purpose. As indicated above, they might be given the power to overrule decisions that they deem to be incompatible with those objectives. However, the formal recognition of the role played by experts would enable one to insist on the necessity of consolidating the basic guarantees that surround decision-making at their level. Ensuring transparency, participatory rights, the pluralist character (and therefore the quality) of scientific deliberations, and fair behaviour on the side of public authorities, are all essential elements in the construction of a legal order that tries to reconcile the functional necessities of our time with individual rights and democratic principles. Important steps have already been made in this direction in the new framework decisions on comitology,[82] and on the codes of conduct to be adopted by all EU bodies, following the Ombudsman's initiatives on transparency. With their rulings on transparency and principles of good administration, the European Courts have also actively promoted higher control standards.[83] This trend could be strengthened by a clearer recognition of the transformations that have taken place within European governance.

[82] Council Decision 99/468/EC, OJ 1999 L 184/23.
[83] See the analysis of H. P. Nehl, *Principles of Administrative Procedure in EC Law* (1999).

8

The Crisis of Indeterminacy: An 'Equitable' Law of 'Deliberative' European Market Administration?

MICHELLE EVERSON

INTRODUCTION

Increasingly, the administration of the internal market, and the law which governs/structures that administration, is being called upon to integrate non-economic (social/ethical) concerns within its workings. Few markets, it would seem, can operate in full isolation from the wider society in which they are embedded. The European market is no exception. In particular, regulatory instruments such as competition law which may impact upon social arrangements and structures that mimic the institutions of the market (for example, mutual insurers) have drawn the 'social' into the ambit of the European market. Equally, however, even the most commonplace of regulatory activities (combating market failure and the like) may bring a rationalizing economic administration into conflict with social interests seeking to redefine the underlying institutions and structures of the market in order to embed their values within the economic sphere. In an uncertain post-national political setting,[1] the ability of the European market administration and its law to respond to the social will largely determine its long-term success or otherwise: in the absence of on-going political direction, the 'technocratic' needs must be administratively balanced against the 'ethical', whilst the 'economically rational' must be weighed against social demands within the administrative process.

The socialization of the European market and its administration is an imperative demand to which law must respond. Nonetheless, being concerned more with the integrity of the 'law' writ large than with social organization in general, the following chapter does not entail a direct attempt to

---

[1] Perhaps better phrased as an 'incomplete' post-national political setting, where the line of political direction to the market administration remains blurred.

address the issue of socialization. Instead, but still with this issue in mind, it seeks very tentatively to tackle the issue of what, if anything, makes or can make the law of European market administration an authoritative legal order. Here, the starting point for analysis is accordingly a perceived crisis of indeterminacy within the law of European market administration, whereby certain liberties have been taken with the term 'indeterminacy'.[2]

In other words, the initial contention is one that the law-led process of economic integration within Europe has exposed the inherent 'meaninglessness'—lack of pre-political authority—of the substantive provisions of the European market order to public gaze. Meanwhile, the currently fragmented and highly pluralist make-up of an indeterminate European polity furthermore determines that the law of European market administration must now find new means of establishing its authority within each (political) process of adjudication between the various political, social, ethical, economically-rational, national, European, public and private interests, values and mores that revolve around and struggle to determine the predominant meaning of the institutions and law of market administration.

As noted, the study is a tentative one: the endeavour to evolve new forms of legal legitimation in the absence of clear constitutional settlement is necessarily a slow and experimental process. Accordingly, the following pages, with their corollary search for a means legitimately to 'socialize the European market sphere', are limited in scope (only one case study on adjudication is offered) so that the conclusions reached are perhaps best understood in terms of an agenda for future research.

I. THE NATURAL ASCENDANCY OF
THIRD-PARTY DISPUTE RESOLUTION?

In a recent essay, Martin Shapiro seeks to explain the unexpected story that is the success of an activist European Court of Justice in the more general terms of an increasing global recourse to bodies that exercise judicial review functions.[3] The argument is Madesonian in inception, drawing its inspiration from the 'Marshallian' consolidation of the US Supreme Court and that body's historical self-nomination as the final institutional organ of dispute res-

---

[2] Although linked to the problem of indeterminacy identified by scholars of the critical legal studies movement in relation to the inherently political character of judicial pronouncements of individual rights, the crisis of indeterminacy pinpointed in this chapter concerns a more general malaise within the various bodies of national and European law that are charged with overseeing the workings and administration of the European market in the absence of any clear pre-determined scheme of adjudicatory authority (or formal constitution).

[3] Shapiro, 'The European Court of Justice', in P. Craig and G. de Búrca (eds), *The Evolution of European Law* (1998).

olution within the US Constitution: under conditions of political pluralism and split sovereignty, so it is asserted, the institutional independence and apparent political neutrality of bodies of judicial arbitration mark them out as the obvious 'third-party' to which to turn in the endeavour to resolve intractable disputes between equally authoritative centres of political power. At the same time, the privileged interpretational scope afforded constitutional and 'constitutional-like' courts likewise furnishes them with adequate room for judicial adjudicatory manoeuvre in the tricky matter of identifying an 'appropriate' solution which might overcome persistent deadlock within the pluralist political process.

Thus, just as the partial and highly controversial codification of international trade relations within the WTO is increasingly finding its third-party dispute-resolving counterpart in the enhanced status of WTO Panels, the historical yet continuously contested[4] commitment to the establishment of a consolidated European trading bloc had as its immediate corollary the growth and (far more importantly) the *acceptance* of the authoritative activism of the European Court of Justice. The seemingly natural outcome of the reapportionment of political-economic powers of initiative between the Member States and the institutions of the Communities was therefore an ECJ that:

(1) might extend its adjudicational efforts far beyond the accepted bounds of the literal, schematic, analogous and teleological tools of conventional legal reasoning[5] in order to champion its determinative authority through the purposive interpretational *succubae* of *effet utile* and the need to ensure the overall 'effectiveness' of the European legal order; and that

(2) was adept at the creative application of a supposedly neutral (economic) rationale within the 'constitution-like' treaties that brooked no argument whatsoever with the national political processes within which the economic regulation of the Member States was embedded:

> Community law does not . . . make the implementation of Articles 85 and 86 [now 81 and 82] of the EEC Treaty dependent upon the manner in which the supervision of certain areas of economic activity is organised by national legislation.[6]

This final stark quotation from the Court's mid-1980s jurisprudence—a rejection of the German government's assertion that it should be free to regulate the actuarially-sensitive area of fire insurance through the legislative toleration of private, industry-maintained, premium 'cartels'—is thus perhaps the best proof of the underlying assertion that it is not the absence, but the proliferation of politics that has led to the elevation of courts to instances of

---

[4] At least as to the meaning of the term 'common market'.

[5] i.e., the conventional tools of civil law reasoning.

[6] *Verband der Sachversicherer e.V. v Commission of the European Communities* [1987] ECR 405, at para. 23.

last 'substantive' decisional resort in the battle to reconcile the irreconcilable: to whit, the struggle definitively to master the opposing views and interests of centres of political power that possess—in self-referential terms at least—their own, normatively and logically-derived, basis for legitimate political action. Accordingly, in the setting of the European common market, a potentially fatal political impasse between the 'equal' claims of the German legislature to political-economic self-determination and of the European institutions to treaty-derived (economically-rational) managerial supremacy over the regulatory framework of the European market found itself channelled into the adjudicatory machinery of the European Court of Justice; a constitutional-like court that was able—by dint of interpretational sleight of hand—to dilute conflict, taking care both to secure the supremacy of the European legal order and to ensure the (in effect) substantive supremacy of rationalized economic reasoning through the apparently procedurally-formalist notion that Articles 85 and 86 [now 81 and 82] simply did not admit of more traditional forms of co-operative public/private economic regulation at the national level.

However, notwithstanding the fact that this fait accompli supremacy of the ECJ and the European legal order was clearly necessary in order to secure the *telos* of the Common Market—and was surely accepted by all concerned only upon those terms—it may nonetheless be doubted whether comparative explanatory analyses that draw so heavily on the *simple fact* of the historical success of the US Supreme Court are fully complete. More specifically, one may wonder whether a simple faith in the 'natural' authority of bodies of third-party dispute resolution (courts) is now an adequate mechanism to ensure the consensual management/administration of a 'completed' common market.

II. POLITICAL PLURALISM AND THE CRISIS OF INDETERMINACY

Returning briefly to the sad case of the unacceptable insurance cartel and the corollary demise of German legislative self-determination, it at once becomes apparent that the actions of an unruly European Court of Justice must nonetheless be distinguished from those of the historical US Supreme Court, however unbridled it was betimes by judicial convention.[7] Certainly, we are reminded that the US is a political-constitutional system 'apart';[8] a system in which the simple sovereignty apportioning phrase 'We the People' retains a continuous constitutive character and finds its institutional counterpart in the

---

[7] See Shapiro, *supra* n. 3.

[8] Not least by notable political commentators of the past, see H. Laski, *A Grammar of Politics* (1967) ch. 1.

refusal to endow any single political institution with a decisive measure of transferred popular sovereignty. President, Congress, Senate, state governments and a host of federal and state agencies must all—in the service of the Madesonian principle that the 'People's' enduring constitutive sovereignty is best preserved by the distribution of operative sovereignty amongst as many political institutions as possible—curb and tailor their activities in line with the competing sovereignties of their institutional/political bedfellows. Nonetheless, the pluralist distinction from the formally-constituted 'la Republique' or 'Parliamentary Sovereign' still finds its own unitary limits in the self-evident truths of an overarching and common Constitution: a Constitution that, reaching beyond the analytical to the level of the normative, is embedded within the operations of each and every centre of political sovereignty, so that—indeterminate as its provisions may very well be[9]—the adjudicational efforts of the Supreme Court possess a truly *organic* claim to allegiance.[10]

It is instead within the parameters of the European Common Market that the notion of pluralism (political and legal) casts off all unifying restraints and gives rise to a level of legal indeterminacy, which, when seen through the eyes of a cautious lawyer concerned with the integrity of 'law', might be termed a crisis. Thus, in its dealings with fire insurance cartels and various other manifestations of national regulatory preferences, the European Court of Justice of the 1980s, its essentially operational (Article 234 based) claim to an 'organic' presence within the legal orders of the Member States notwithstanding,[11] was adjudicating upon conflict within a normative void. Granted, its status as a third-party resolver of disputes was assured for reasons of political stability. Nonetheless, shorn of the usual props of judicial constitutional authority—its supremacy was declared by itself and not by its constituents[12]—its role of conflict resolution boiled down to one of ensuring the predominance of its own legal and political order above all others through quasi-formalist modes of Treaty interpretation that could still not disguise the unpalatable fact that, in the absence of explicit constitutional settlement, provisions of putative higher law (treaty-based or otherwise) are no more than indeterminate shells awaiting 'political' substance: Articles 85 and 86 (now 81 and 82) could not admit of alternative modes of—democratically-determined—economic organization and the ECJ, in so declaring, had ceased to be a neutral and independent resolver of 'third-party' disputes, becoming

---

[9] The indeterminacy of the provisions of the US Constitution being a point highlighted by the American Critical Legal Studies Movement.

[10] In that the Court is explicitly afforded authority over the actions of all centres of political power by the Constitution.

[11] I.e., the European Court of Justice was inserted by the Rome Treaties into the legal systems of the Member States, see J. Shaw, *The Law of the European Union* (2000).

[12] Cf. *Van Gend en Loos* [1963] ECR 1.

instead the partisan champion of the 'rationalizing' political-economic authority of the European Communities.

The failure of the historical European Court of Justice—dedicated disciple-like to the propagation of the Community's economically rationalizing philosophy—to maintain its legal authority as the common market neared its completion is now a simple matter of historical record and is well documented:

(1) by the ECJ's own—often somewhat difficult to grasp in purely legal terms[13]—doctrinal efforts to put a brake on its inexorable jurisdictional *aggrandisement* through the *Keck* line of cases; and

(2) by the revolt of various national constitutional jurisdictions; a revolt most eloquently given voice by the *Bundesverfassungsgericht.*[14]

Consequently, it is not the fact of the ECJ's partisanship as such that forms the critical focus of this essay: after all, the Court of the 1980s was arguably merely engaging in the selfsame form of self-referential jurisdiction-securing exercise that any conventional lawyer (national or otherwise), concerned with the consolidation of the legal order within which he or she operates, performs daily. Instead, this chapter is concerned with what the jurisprudence of the ECJ has revealed about the nature of 'law' in general and about the legal exigencies of the common market and its administration in particular.

As noted, in the absence of an overarching constitutional settlement and corollary unbridled pluralism—(i) political pluralism, as (at its most simple level[15]) the Member States struggle with Community institutions in the effort to ensure the ascendancy of their values and interests; and (ii) legal pluralism as national and European legal orders seek to ensure the predominance of their own ('equally') legitimized governmental and political institutions—the indeterminacy of law, or, in quasi-realist terms, its inherent 'meaninglessness' is fully exposed to the critical public spotlight. Prised out of the post-war (national) constitutional settlement, which—albeit perhaps only ever figuratively—squared the positivist circle between the necessary maintenance of an autonomous and thus 'pre-political' law[16] and the all-pervading need for 'real-world' political (democratic) legitimation,[17] the *substance* of 'the law' can no longer lay claim to an inherent moral authority. Equally, modern lawyers suddenly find themselves faced with the selfsame *procedural* conundrum that

[13] *Keck & Mithouard* [1993] ECR I-6097, presenting the world with a curious distinction between product regulation and somewhat difficult to identify 'selling arrangements' in order to delineate the scope of Article 28 EC.

[14] *Brunner v European Union Treaty* [1994] 1 *CMLRev.* 971, dealing with the constitutionality within Germany of the TEU.

[15] For details of the far greater degree of complexity of pluralist interaction at EU level, see Section III below.

[16] I.e., free from social or political influences.

[17] Providing a constantly *democratically* legitimated *Grundnorm* for the law.

was as an old, if prickly, friend to their pre-Peace of Westphalia counterparts: the requirement that law must (re)establish its factual, logical and moral authority in each and every adjudicational operation in order to lay claim to continuing allegiance.

Distilling down to the more substantive issue of the management and administration of the internal market, this crisis of legal indeterminacy thus determines that—beyond the current struggle to soften the consequences of legal pluralism by means of a process of 'shared-values' and 'discourse'-based mutual recognition between national and European legal orders[18]—'the law' within Europe is faced with the further challenge of daily giving authoritative and generally-accepted meaning to its provisions. In an area of governance marked by the presence of diverse and conflicting national interests, scientific concerns, technocratic interests, private values, public morality, social stakes and European economic goals, law must adjudicate, at one and the same time:

(1) freeing itself of any recidivistic tendencies to appeal to a natural past for its authority since a 'scientific age' has but little time for a mysticism within a law that appeals for its authority to acts of faith in quixotic sagas;[19]

(2) maintaining its own discipline-internal—i.e., repellent of partisan foreign interests—logical structures and 'pre-political' autonomy; and

(3) establishing the vital link to the real-world social and political values that underpinned the post-war constitutional settlement and allowed for fifty unbroken years of morally authoritative legal development.[20]

III. THE MODERN CONTOURS OF POLITICAL PLURALISM: A SOCIALLY-EMBEDDED MARKET POLITY?

Clearly then, this essay entails a plea for the evolution of a form of superannuated proceduralism within the law and, more particularly, within the European and national law concerned with the management of the common market: a plea that is realist in its acceptance (under conditions of political pluralism) of the vital function of the courts and law as 'third-party' dispute-resolution mechanisms; yet normatively-founded in its assertion that disputes cannot simply be resolved through unthinking 'substantive' adjudication, and must instead—for the sake of the integrity of legal development as a whole—

---

[18] See Section IV below.

[19] i.e., it will not 'venerate where it cannot comprehend', V. S. Dicey, *The Law of the Constitution* (8th ed., 1926) 11.

[20] The three categories of factual, logical and moral authority are distilled from Harald Laski's analysis of the crisis within the 1930s nation state and its law, more particularly the law's failure to free itself of dangerous mythology and its concomitant inability to establish a linkage to prevailing social values whilst retaining logical coherence, see *supra* n. 8.

be structured, tackled and overcome within an authoritative legal framework that pays due regard to the continuous (re)establishment of the factual, logical and moral legitimacy of the law.

Equally, however, along with realism and normativity, the argument concedes the analytical point that any legal effort to master unbridled political pluralism can only succeed where comprehensive preliminary stock is taken of the full array of the interests, values and concerns that characterize the management and administration of the internal market.

In other words, European political pluralism must not be viewed as a finite value of its own: current pluralism within the European market is sharply distinguished from any Madesonian scheme of the parcelling of operative sovereignty between various identified institutions in the service of the preservation of the constitutive sovereignty of a finite polity. Instead, the institutions of European market management and administration—Articles of the European Treaty (such as the four freedoms and Articles 28 and 30 (ex 30 and 36)), the comitology decision and the various scientific, regulatory and interest committees gathered under the Commission's supervisory umbrella, the various regulatory and policy-forming agencies, as well as the more informal networks of scientific, epistemic, market-based and single-issue opinion—are themselves little more than value-neutral (on occasion, even *ad hoc*) shells around which the various public and (liberated by the process of market integration itself) private actors engaged within the market revolve in the effort to make their value and interest-laden voices heard in the process of market administration.[21]

Accordingly, the form of superannuated proceduralism advocated here cannot simply consist of an enhanced balance of powers doctrine—à la *Meroni*[22]—which takes the fact of pluralism as a sovereignty-preserving value in its own right and subsequently attempts to secure it through the requirement that each and every institution act only within its own stipulated competences. Certainly, notions of *ultra vires* may play their own procedural part in a scheme of 'legalized' market administration, allowing for the control of acts of gross illegality and for the judicial review of the argumentative bases for economic regulatory action. However, in an unconstituted and thus logically indeterminate (infinite) polity the procedural act of policing the boundaries of stipulated competences cannot of itself be argued to serve the preservation of a popular sovereignty that remains ever elusive and might instead be argued simply to reward and consolidate the transitory interests,

---

[21] For a more detailed enumeration of the institutions of European Market Management, see Everson, 'Hierarchy Beaters', *JCMS* (1998) 195.

[22] The initial European case establishing a 'balance of powers' between the institutions laid down in Article 7 EC (ex 4) and determining that each must exercise its authority within the limits laid down by the Treaties, *Meroni v High Authority* [1962] ECR 73.

values and concerns that have conquered any particular institution at any one time.[23]

To restate: political pluralism within the common market is a simple fact that the law must respond to—it is the 'troublesome' subject of adjudicational procedure, not its guiding rationale. On the analytical level, and in common with all markets,[24] the common market remains unconstituted and so lacks the vital sovereign indicator—unitary, parcelled and distributed, or otherwise—around which a pre-determined, 'holistic', scheme of higher governing law might be built.[25] Nonetheless, the European market is still a recognizable polity, no longer being characterized by a neo-liberal economic philosophy or by an ordo-liberal commitment to the creation of a juridified, de-politicized sphere of socially-autonomous market action.[26] Instead:

(1) the reintroduction of regulative limits to the jurisdictional reach of Article 28,[27]
(2) the rejoined battle for the soul of Article 49 (ex 59) and for the identification of the true meaning of concepts such as 'the freedom to provide services',[28]
(3) the struggle to balance the technocratic philosophy inherent in agency-based economic management against the ethical and social concerns raised in comitology proceedings,[29] as well as
(4) the 'networked' regulatory appeal to private strains of market-oriented and social opinion,

all readily demonstrate that 'the market' does not operate in a social vacuum, but is characterized by, even created by, *political* processes.

Equally importantly, however, as a further enduring legacy of the process of judicialized market integration, the political exchanges that constitute the European market as a polity, embedding it firmly within the societal substrata of the Community and its Member States, have no set boundaries. Forcibly divorced from their natural national channels of legislative expression, private fire insurance cartels and their market counterparts elsewhere were understandably drawn to attempt to make their voices heard at the European

---

[23] Thus, for example, the simple judicial preservation of the (currently minimal) regulatory prerogatives of the various agencies that are so beloved of current economically rationalizing approaches to market administration, may yet serve to hinder the review of supposedly rational market management as changing social and scientific circumstances so dictate.

[24] S. L. Elkin and K. E. Soltan, *The New Constitutionalism* (1993).

[25] I.e., markets cannot entertain a *Grundnorm*.

[26] In other words, neither is the European market regarded as a neo-liberal entity, nor is it deemed to be an area that is wholly protected from political intervention by law in the manner promoted by German ordo-liberals led by Ernst Joachim Mestmäcker (for the latter's analysis of the current lack of legitimacy of the European market administration, see 'On the Legitimacy of European Law', 54 *Rabels Zeitschrift* (1994) 614.

[27] Keck, *supra* n. 13.   [28] *Alpine Investments* [1995] ECR I-1141.

[29] See Everson, *supra* n. 21.

level.[30] Similarly, such groups have been gathered—along with more socially-oriented rather than market-based interests—into the welcoming arms of European institutions which, with a keen eye to the efficiency and legitimacy gains to be gleaned from heterarchical styles of economic management, have been eager to bind private, non-governmental, views within the process of market administration.[31]

The sum total of the process of European market integration is thus the emergence of a 'market' that does not stand in isolation from the social and political processes of the Member States and Community, but which is, instead, 'embedded' within those processes to the degree that the meaning of its constitutive institutions—the institutions that, in administering and regulating the market, determine its underlying structures and operations—are fought over by national, European, public and private interests.[32] Equally, this 'socially-embedded market polity' exhibits a degree and intensity of modern political pluralism that extends far beyond an 'original' uncertainty as to which of the conflicting interests, values and concerns of the (in their own self-referential terms) 'equally' legitimated European institutions and Member States would determine the outcome of Europeanization. Instead, the socially-embedded market polity encompasses a sphere of diffuse political processes that are anchored both within European and within national society and are also contributed to by various self-nominating groups and interests whose values and concerns are not created through formalized structures.[33]

IV. THE CHALLENGE OF LEGAL PROCEDURALIZATION

The characterization of the political processes that centre on the European market and the institutions of its administration as a 'socially-embedded market polity' is once again a clear indicator of the very particular challenges of modern legal proceduralization. Most strikingly, the liberation of private, non-formalized interests and concerns, as well as their deliberate (heterarchi-

---

[30] In the case of insurance cartels, by lobbying for a wide-ranging reading of exemptions given by the Commission under Article 81(3) EC.

[31] See Kreher, 'Agencies in the European Communities—a Step Towards Administrative Integration in Europe', 4 *JEPP* (1997) 225 for an analysis of the interaction of European civil servants and private firms in the field of operations of European agencies and networks. Also, Ladeur, 'Towards a Legal Theory of Supranationality: The Viability of the Network Concept', 3 *ELJ* (1997) 33, on the general concept of hierarchical government.

[32] For a full investigation of the concept of the socially-embedded market polity, see Everson, 'The Constitutionalisation of European Administrative Law: Legal Oversight of a Stateless Internal Market', in C. Joerges and E. Vos (eds), *European Committees* (1999) 281, at 287–289.

[33] Ibid., for the 'indeterminacy' of that polity.

cal) integration within the process of market management, determines that
proceduralized law might not simply be founded upon traditional, or even
more innovative, conflict of law mechanisms. Whilst the interests and concerns of the Member States and Community institutions are established in
line with their separate, yet formalized (self-referential), structures and procedures of governance, and so lend themselves more or less readily to an adjudicational process based upon the co-operative interweaving and mutual
recognition of identifiable governmental competences, the non-formalized
status of private interests nonetheless determines that conflict of laws mechanisms alone cannot comprehensively regulate the socially embedded market
polity.

To be sure, the exact same processes of economic spill-over that precipitated the crisis of indeterminacy within the law of the European market have
also irrevocably blurred a once clear-cut distinction between national and
European economic jurisdictions and so have largely precluded any simple
procedural recourse to conflict norms founded in the blanket notion of the
given equal validity of self-legitimating governmental systems. Nonetheless,
as the on-going process of value and discourse-based mutual recognition
between European and national legal systems indicates,[34] more subtle conflict
norms, founded in the established 'normative' equivalence of formally legitimated systems of governance, may yet play their proceduralized part in the
administration of a pluralist European market economy: the concept of the
'open' constitution (or 'permeable self-referential normativity'), found within
recent judicial debate,[35] hinting strongly at dual horizontal processes of
'freely' ceded competences—from the nation state to Europe and vice versa—
as the immediate circumstances so dictate and where the normative standards
of distinct governance systems are deemed (by lawyers) to be equivalent.[36]

However, the presence of liberated private interests within the political
processes of market regulation necessarily set the limits to proceduralism
based upon normative permeability, defying—by simple virtue of their *ad hoc*
and informal nature—any adjudicational effort to avoid direct substantive
judgement on individual interests through demands for normative equivalence in the process of interest formation. As the unbridled pluralism of the
socially-embedded European market polity extends to encompass a series of
social, ethical or market-oriented interests, concerns and opinions formed

[34] See, for example, the writings of Justices of the German Constitutional Court: Kirchhof,
'The Balance of Powers Between National and European Institutions', 5 *ELJ* (1999), with particular mention of the concept of the 'open constitution'.

[35] Thus, the final message of *Brunner, supra* n. 14, was that the German Constitutional system would cede its sovereignty in line with the European legal system's development of standards of democratic legitimation that might be deemed equivalent to those found within the
Federal Republic of Germany.

[36] Ibid.

'outside' the conventional national and European policy-making processes, so too must the law concerned with the regulation of the market polity occasionally step 'beyond' conflict norms grounded in presumed or established systemic normative equivalence.

Accordingly, in addition to concerning itself with the values that characterize (and legitimize) the governance systems that surround the European market polity, the law of that market must similarly pay attention to the legitimizing values of law itself. To reiterate: the challenge of legal proceduralization within the European market relates primarily to the challenge of the continuous establishment of the factual, logical and moral authority of the law itself. As noted, in adjudicating between diverse interests, values and concerns, the regulatory law of the European market must rise above its own inherent indeterminacy—or any unthinking substantive decision-making—and instead structure, address and overcome disputes between diverse political interests within a framework that daily gives authoritative meaning to its provisions.

Initially, however, such a challenge is perhaps best framed in the negative; the demand that law be factually, legally and morally authoritative providing a firm indication of what superannuated legal proceduralization should *not* consist of.

A. Factual Authority

Whilst largely seen as a historical concern of a modernized secular law that sought to liberate itself from legitimating roots founded in extra-legal religious thought or historical mythology, the effort to establish 'real-world' legal authority nonetheless retains a modern relevance:

(1) where the 'modern religions' of 'science' and 'rationality' attain a metaphysical status within the law and are no longer subject to ceaseless review,[37] or

(2) where 'modern mythologies'—more particularly, wholly rhetorical human rights discourses—are accepted by law as legitimate substitutes for real-world political debate.

As individual components of the socially-embedded market polity, science and economic rationality remain relevant and must be duly regarded as such within the process of the administration of the market. Nonetheless, as 'individual components', they must likewise always establish their precedence above competing social or political interests. Similarly, human rights are still best to be understood simply as the vital pre-condition for and not as a substitute for legitimating political discourse.

[37] For a passionate denunciation of the 'new religion' of rationality, see U. Beck, *What is Globalization?* (2000).

B. Logical Authority

A primary cornerstone of the law's claim to on-going allegiance remains its societal independence, or ability to shield itself from undue influence from non-legal interests through its adherence to its own discipline-internal logic. In this sense, 'the language of law', or the dense and formulaic series of tools of reasoning (civil law), precedents (common law) and procedures which constitute the distinct and self-contained grammar and semantics of law and so structure and constrain the process of adjudication, must never lose its particularism-repelling role. However, in the setting of a common market that is both freed from the national constitutional settlement and is the host to a plurality of legal languages that are every bit as diverse as French, German or Swedish, law's doctrines must, at one and the same time, be tailored to facilitate the on-going process of mutual judicial translation and dialogue and be made sufficiently socially-receptive to allow for the establishment of the 'moral' authority of law.

C. Moral Authority

The 'real-world' status of law and its ability to reflect and promulgate the predominant bundle of social and political values that mark societal interaction (materialized law) remains the most elusive of legal competences. Standing in a necessarily contradictory relationship to the 'pre-political', discipline-internal and particularism-repelling grammatical/semantic (logical) authority of law, the demand that law nonetheless be morally-receptive[38] finds its most recent historical genesis in the failings of twentieth-century legal positivism and its most compelling modern challenge in the dissolution of a circle-squaring national constitutional settlement.[39] Accordingly, in the context of the European market, on-going legal materialization and the continuous process of the authoritative re-anchoring of law within societal discourse attains a determinative status for the legitimation of law in its character as an authoritative regulator of social relations; which status—if the renewed temptation to make recourse to ill-defined concepts of the legitimating radiative effects of, say, the *Zeitgeist* upon law is to be effectively avoided[40]—is initially best sought in an examination of the degree to which legal grammars and

[38] Or, be able to give voice to social values.

[39] Or, the lack of direct political legitimation for strictures of supranational law that reach deeply into national legal orders.

[40] Note in this regard, Harald Laski's teasing of Dean Pound's well-meaning, but ultimately 'diffuse' attempts to describe the manner in which realist law responded to social values, see H. Laski, *supra* n. 8.

semantics within the European market (doctrine) remain receptive to social and political concerns.

V. CHALLENGES TO CORPORATISM, PLURALIST LEGAL LIBERATION AND THE RESPONSE OF LAW: A CASE STUDY

A. *Albany* and the Challenge to Collective Bargaining Arrangements

Perhaps one of the greatest *bête noirs* tackled by the process of European economic integration has been the continuing reliance of European governments upon models of market governance that have built explicitly upon the 'corporatist' interweaving of private and public interests in order to regulate a particular economic sector with an eye not only to immediate technical issues of market correction, but also to the furtherance of more general economic or social goals. Prima facie distorting of competition within the European market, semi-official regulatory arrangements such as the German fire insurers' premium-setting association[41] were thus the primary targets of negative integrationist moves and were quickly set aside during a period of heightened European judicial activism.

However, the economically rationalizing strategy of the European Court of Justice (and of the European Communities as a whole) nonetheless found its necessary limits in those sectors of the national economy where corporatist arrangements were designed to serve particular universal aims, such as a measure of 'social justice'. Accordingly, although the seemingly 'pure' economic interests that marked legislative tolerance for fire insurance cartels were early victims of neo-liberal legal assaults, the widespread national practice of ensuring universal occupational pensions provision through the enforced and market-distorting affiliation of private economic entities to sector-wide, solidarity-based insurance schemes was not to receive explicit European judicial attention until the 1999 case of *Albany International v Stichting Bedrijfspensioenfunds Textielindustrie*.[42]

An eagerly awaited case on the legitimacy of the Dutch government's legislative support for compulsory occupational pension schemes (under Articles 82 and 86(2) EC), as well as the acceptable scope of operations of such schemes (under Articles 81 and 82 EC), *Albany* proves to be an invaluable starting point for this analysis of the ability of law to retain its authority in the process of European market administration. Three particular issues mark its importance.

[41] *Supra* n. 3: the legislative tolerance of the cartel within Germany arguably also serving a wider economic goal of capital retention within the Federal Republic, see Everson, 'The Federal Supervisory Authority for Insurance', in G. Majone (ed.), *Regulating Europe* (1996) 202.
[42] Case C-67/96, Judgment of the Court, 21 September 1999.

1. The Insurance Interface

The operations of Stichting Bedrifspensioenfunds Textielindustrie, an occupational pension fund for the Dutch textile industry that was established through a collective bargaining agreement between unions and management and to which the affiliation of private textile companies operating in the Netherlands was made compulsory by the Dutch government in 1975, thus lie within a corner of the European market where public and private interests, economic and social values and private market/public economic logics are inexorably intertwined.

The long-standing European tradition of meeting the social need for pensions provision through the establishment of bodies that resemble commercial insurers in their character as 'private' corporations, yet differ starkly from them by virtue of their application of the solidarity-based principle (universal coverage) rather than actuarial mode (coverage in line with individual risk) of insurance provision, has as its primary consequence the reorganization and subjection of private market logic to mores and rationales derived from a non-market social sphere. Solidarity-based and actuarial insurers accordingly compete for clients at an 'insurance interface' where governmental regulation requiring the affiliation of private individuals and firms to solidarity-based insurance schemes secures the latter's ability to survive and compete in a market economy sphere in which they would otherwise necessarily fail.[43]

In other words, where a commitment to social values is traditionally pursued through quasi-market mechanisms which require—so as to ensure that *all* individuals will receive affordable insurance coverage—that the logic of the private market be altered in order to accommodate them, then the law charged with the administration of the market is required to step beyond any simple application of technical economic values. In a very real sense, the affiliation requirement is a signal that 'continuous market failure' has been accepted (by virtue of the obvious social gains) as the status quo to which law must adapt itself. As a consequence, the law of the market must learn to distinguish between economically-rational regulation and economic administration that legitimately alters private market logic in the light of social values. Accordingly, the underlying legal issue is not one of ensuring the ascendancy of rational economic regulation, but is instead one of determining the legitimate limits to economic rationality.

---

[43] Where the true measure of individual risk is not accounted, an insurance fund will only survive where it derives sufficient continuous income from a large and growing body of insureds in order to offset its outgoings.

2. National and European Competences and the Dialogue Between National and European Law

In the matter of the identification of the legitimate limits to economic rationality, however, the case of *Albany* contains an added complication arising out
of the European Communities' restricted competence in the area of collective
bargaining schemes and the provision of occupational pensions. Granted, as
the ECJ itself notes,[44] Articles 136–143 EC (ex 117–120) signal a nascent
European interest in the issue of social provision based upon collective bargaining agreements; requiring the Commission to foster dialogue between
unions and labour at the European level and likewise making provision for the
introduction of collective agreements to improve working conditions at
European level. Nonetheless, such corporatist awakenings within the
Communities remain (as yet) marginalized. Pertaining simply to the encouragement of management–labour dialogue at European level, they do not constitute a European competence to harmonize national occupational pensions
provision across the European board.[45]

Accordingly, the distinction between economically rationalizing regulation
and market administration based upon the (market-distorting) perpetuation
of legitimate social values was one to be made across systems of national and
European law: the legitimate limits to the economic rationality found within
the EU Treaty scheme of Articles 81, 82 and 86 were to be found, not simply
within explicit Treaty exemptions such as Article 86(2),[46] but mainly within
the normative governance order encapsulated by Dutch law.[47]

3. Pluralist liberation

Equally, however, as a further confirmation that the degree of pluralism
within the European market extends far beyond a relatively simple inter-
change between European and national interests, *Albany* again confirmed that
the creation of a European market has given rise to new and self-defining
'European' private interests that may challenge both the national constitutional settlement and the European legal order in their search for a new form
of post-national expression. Precipitated by an individual textile producer's
Articles 49 and 56 (ex 52 and 59) EC Treaty-based quest for the right to with-

---

[44] *Albany, supra* n. 42, para. 56.

[45] Indeed, the most compelling criticism of *Albany* made amongst labour lawyers was the
ECJ's over-eager approach to Articles 136–143 of the EC Treaty and its preparedness to infer
a Europe-wide pensions competence from them; see S. Vousden, Case Note, *ILJ* (2000) 181.

[46] Or the European legal order's recognition that state aids may serve social goals.

[47] In particular, the normative governance order encapsulated by that national legal order
within the context of its 'interconnectedness' with European law (via, say, the Article 10 EC
duty of co-operation and solidarity with the European legal order).

draw from the (seemingly poorly administered)[48] collective, solidarity-based pensions fund and enter (far better-yielding)[49] actuarially-accounted pension schemes across national borders, the case of *Albany* similarly entailed the self-assertion of novel private European interests.

These interests (encapsulated by the textile-producing firm of Albany) accordingly challenged both the pensions' providing collectivity of the Dutch textile sector—as well as the underlying national legislative collectivity from which it drew its prescriptive powers—and the European legal order's reading of its own economic rationality in the light of its application of competition and state aids law to collective bargaining agreements; reminding the ECJ that, by virtue of the existence of European (economic) rights, it must also answer to its own private European constituency when weighing up the relationship between economically rational (European) regulation and market administration based upon legitimate (national) social values.

In sum total then, the law of the European market was faced in *Albany* with a multi-layered questioning of the 'meaning' of EC Treaty Articles 81, 82 and 86. On the one hand, the parties to the debate on that meaning (or the socially-embedded market polity) were not simply the readily identifiable and formally-constituted nation state and the institutions of the EU, but also encompassed private actors given voice within judicial debate by European rights. On the other hand, the very law of the European market lay within two rather than one legal orders: the meaning of the governing institutions of the European market (Articles 81, 82 and 86 EC) could not be found within one legal logic but was instead to be identified in a process of dialogue between two systems of law.

Seen in this light, the essential question to be asked of the law of the European market within *Albany* is thus one of whether it was in a position to overcome indeterminacy, identifying the meaning of the institutions of European market governance whilst at the same time maintaining its own factual, logical and moral authority.

B. The Proceduralist Requirement for Deliberative Debate

At an initial level, the judgment of the European Court of Justice displays a fairly high degree of authority.

Granted, the four freedoms of the Treaty had given Albany a right to enter into European debate and demand the review of the textile industry's collective bargaining agreement and its resultant occupational pension fund in the light of the rationalizing economic criteria of the EC Treaty. Nonetheless, neither Albany's 'right' nor the rationalizing philosophy (science of the EU

---

[48] See n. 56 below.   [49] Ibid.

Treaty) were to be elevated to a determinative modern religion within the judgment. Certainly, it was 'beyond question that certain restrictions of competition are inherent in collective agreements between organizations representing employers and workers (paragraph 59)'. However, the operations of the pensions fund lay within that area of the market economy where economic rights of expression and the economically rationalizing philosophy of the market must, on occasions, take second place to social values.

Not only was the provision of additional pensions via collective and competition restricting agreements a long-standing part of the traditions of various Member States[50]—designed to improve 'employment and working conditions'—but, such a tradition was now also finding its nascent place within the European legal order (Articles 136–143). Accordingly, and with an added eye to Europe's growing commitment to the evolution of social policy alongside the market economy (Articles 3(1)(g) and (j)):

[I]t therefore follows from an interpretation of the provisions of the Treaty as a whole *which is both effective and consistent* that agreements concluded in the context of collective negotiations between management and labour in pursuit of such objectives must, *by virtue of their nature and purpose*, be regarded as falling outside the scope of Article 85(1) of the Treaty.[51]

Economic rights and economic rationality were a part of the Treaty but were also always to be balanced with social goals and needs that might—through on-going process of the interpretation of the appropriateness 'of their nature and purpose'—be progressively included within the socially-embedded market polity.

Similarly, the internal grammar and semantics of European law (legal logic) precluded recourse by the European Court of Justice to the most immediate mode of avoiding any judgement on the issue of the acceptability of competition-distorting collective bargaining agreements under EC competition law: the simple restriction of the European jurisdiction. Both the wording of the Treaty itself and a long line of cases suggested that—non-profit-making status and application of the solidarity principle of insurance notwithstanding— such pension funds were 'undertakings' within the meaning of EC law since they competed directly with private insurers.[52]

However, the vital link to the moral authority of national and European political debate was also to be established within the reasoning of law since Article 82 read in conjunction with Article 86(2) allowed for the governmental underpinning of the dominant position of a private enterprise where the

---

[50] See, for comprehensive comparative analysis of national traditions (including US traditions), the opinion of Advocate General Jacobs delivered on 28 January 1999 (not yet reported in the ECR).

[51] Para. 60 (emphasis added).   [52] Paras. 71–87.

vital social functions pursued by that enterprise could not otherwise be fulfilled. Here the Court was perhaps unwise not to follow the reasoning of the
Advocate General that a decision on the admissibility of such an exemption
would be best left to a national court operating within the normative governance order that chooses to pursue social goals through semi-private market
structures.[53] It was nonetheless to prove itself adept in rehearsing the justificatory arguments found within national and European debate on the issue:

(1) At the time of the European hearing, Stichting Bedrifspensioenfunds
    Textielindustrie provided an occupational pension of 70 per cent of final
    salary after forty years of service, which was the norm in the Netherlands
    and indicated that it was not abusive of its dominant position.
(2) Equally, and far more importantly, the danger of destructive 'cream-
    skimming' on the part of a private industry that would be unwilling to
    provide affordable coverage for individuals with poor risk profiles was
    such as to justify compulsory affiliation:

> . . . [I]f the exclusive right of the fund to manage the supplementary pension
> scheme for all workers in a given sector were removed, undertakings with young
> employees in good health engaged in non-dangerous activities would seek more
> advantageous insurance terms from private insurers. The progressive departure
> of 'good' risks would leave the sectoral pension fund with increasing responsi-
> bility for an increasing share of 'bad' risks, thereby increasing the cost of pensions
> for workers, particularly those in small and medium-sized undertakings with
> older employees engaged in dangerous activities, to which the fund could no
> longer offer pensions at a reasonable cost.[54]

Accordingly, although the ECJ failed to recognize that the limits of economic
rationality in the area of social policy lay mainly within the national normative governance order (the legislative decision to pursue social values through
the insurance interface with the private market) and so—as a simple matter
of logic—required that the national legal order judge upon their legitimacy, it
nonetheless delineated the scope of the meaning of Articles 81 et seq EC and
so concurrently opened up European law to the predominant themes of
national political debate, albeit through the mouthpiece of the ECJ itself.[55]

The final conclusion of the Court that EC law did not preclude national
governments from requiring the affiliation of private entities to pension funds

---

[53] *Supra* n. 50, the exact reasoning being that the decision on whether such an arrangement
is in fact necessary is a highly complex one.

[54] Para. 108.

[55] This is an important criticism, especially when seen in the light of the nation state's current need to react in an innovative manner to very new forms of work and working conditions
(atypical work). The assumption of the ECJ of the direct competence to review the political
justification for measures such as affiliation requirements may thus hamper speedy national
responses to changing social conditions, see Vousden, *supra* n. 45.

established through collective bargaining agreements would seem to confirm the ability of the law of the European market authoritatively to adapt the logic of an essentially economically rational market administration to accommodate permanent market failure, or the inclusion within the market of social values.

However, in the final and somewhat surprising analysis, the case of *Albany* finds its most compelling source of legitimacy, not in the ECJ's careful amelioration of the potentially socially divisive effects of the rational European legal order, but in the ECJ's and referring national court's (proceduralist) recognition and accommodation of the truth of the private challenge to:

(1) the corporatist collectivity which gave birth to Stichting Bedrifspensioenfunds Textielindustrie,
(2) the national collectivity which gave it prescriptive force, and
(3) a reading of European competition law that would give all such arrangements blanket legitimacy.

Here, immediate attention is drawn to the simple fact that *Albany* did give voice to the view that something was rotten both within the corporatist management of social values within the Dutch textile sector and within Dutch law governing collective bargaining agreements within the Netherlands. Granted, at the time of the European hearing, Stichting Bedrifspensioenfunds Textielindustrie did provide a final pension in line with the norm offered within the Netherlands. However, at the time that Albany chose to join a private fund in 1981, its services were far from optimal with the fund yielding only a pro rata pension of 200 Dutch Guilders following fifty years of service.[56] Similarly, Dutch law on the administration of funds grounded in collective bargaining agreements had proven to contain various vital *lacunae*, the most pressing of which was the fact that although companies that had established a pensions fund six months prior to the establishment of a collective fund were granted an automatic right of exemption from the affiliation duty, firms who wished to leave the fund after that date might do so only at the discretion of the management of the fund. Equally, although the Dutch Insurance Board played a major part in overseeing the competence and business-worthiness of such funds and was likewise called upon to give an opinion in the event of a proposed withdrawal, its decisions in the latter case were not binding upon the fund.

Accordingly, Albany's challenge originated in the 1989 decision of the fund not to allow a withdrawal by Albany, notwithstanding the Dutch Insurance Board's opinion that, in view of the long-standing benefits Albany now enjoyed in its private insurance relationship, withdrawal should be allowed even in the event of a reorganization of the solidarity-based fund.

---

[56] See opinion of the Advocate General at para. 33.

Seen in this light, the inspiring legal moments in the judicial process surrounding Albany's claim are to be found:

(1) in the referring Dutch Court's statement that relations between a sectoral pension fund and its members are governed by requirements of 'reasonableness' and 'equity' as well as by the general principles of sound administration, so that 'considerable' weight should be given to the opinions of the statutorily appointed Insurance Board on exemptions;[57] and

(2) in the ECJ's sting in the tale stipulation that:

> ... national courts adjudicating, as in this case, on an objection to a requirement to pay contributions must subject to review the decision of the fund refusing an exemption from affiliation, which enables them at the least to verify that the fund has not used its power to grant an exemption in an arbitrary manner and that the principle of non-discrimination and the other conditions for the legality of that decision have been complied with.[58]

In other words, the inspirational power of *Albany* lies in a process of judicial dialogue between national and European courts that is facilitated by the existence of individual European rights and by the underlying rationalization demands of a European market order and which allows for a process of individual challenge of societal and national collectivities.

Interestingly, the language of the process of judicial dialogue is constituted by the shared and ancient legal grammar and semantics of 'reasonableness', 'equity', 'non-discrimination' and the demand that authoritative decision-making never be 'arbitrary'. In this regard, it is the 'original' language of law which gives voice to 'true' pluralist interests and allows them to challenge inert, unthinking and overly-complacent collectivities, not through the promotion of positive and at times socially destructive individual rights,[59] but through legal pre-conditions, or stipulations for the manner in which debate between competing interests and values is to be conducted in a civilized and deliberative manner.

VI. CONCLUSION

The tentative conclusion reached by this study of whether the law of the European market might retain its authority during the process of adjudication between the social, economic and political interests and values that revolve around the institutions of European market administration is thus the somewhat surprising one that true strength may be drawn by judicial institutions

---

[57] Found in para. 35 of the ECJ's Judgment.
[58] Para. 121 of the ECJ decision.
[59] That is an absolute right of economic autonomy that continues to contain a potential to undermine universal values.

from ancient legal dogmas. Granted, the process of adjudication within the European market is a highly complex one and must be based on a careful, case-by-case weighing up of rationality and social values, an on-going respect for consistent legal logic and a continuous process of the linkage of law to social and political debate. However, in the context of a liberating demand for rational review of the workings and values of national and societal collectivities, a process of dialogue between national and European courts on the contours of good administration within the European market may yet gain the major part of its authority from concepts of reasonableness and equity.

Granted, such supposedly 'legal' terms may themselves be socially and politically loaded so that further research on the exact usage of such notions within a national–European dialogue is required. Nonetheless, where, as would seem to be the case in *Albany*, the grammar and semantics of reasonableness and equity are used to ensure that the values and views of individual or self-appointed groups might not be simply overlooked or ignored in the process of the administration of the market, traditional legal values may prove to be the most authoritative basis upon which to build the administration of the European market. Where the rallying call of national collectivities was once 'no taxation without representation', the inspirational focus of the law of the European market may very well now be the notion of 'no governance without deliberation'.

9

The Juridification of Uncertainty: Observations on the Ambivalence of the Precautionary Principle within the EU and the WTO

JOANNE SCOTT and ELLEN VOS*

INTRODUCTION

Few legal concepts have achieved the notoriety of the precautionary principle. Praised by some, disparaged by others, the principle is deeply ambivalent and apparently infinitely malleable. The principle has found its way from national (German) law to transnational law, and from statute book to high politics.[1] It is with this principle that this chapter is concerned. It explores it in a context of risk regulation, against a backdrop of integrating markets, and within a framework of multi-levelled, overlapping, governance. It highlights the ambiguities inherent in the principle, both in terms of legal status and substantive application, and the tensions to which it gives rise in the legitimation of power. Seized upon of late as an instrument of reconciliation between popular and expert government it becomes apparent that the principle may operate to conceal rather than resolve such tensions.

* We would like to thank the British Council and the Nederlandse Organisatie voor Wetenschappelijk Onderzoek/Netherlands Organisation for Scientific Research for financial assistance granted to us pursuant to their UK–Dutch Joint Scientific Research Programme. It is as a result of the grants which they made available to us that we were able to pursue this collaborative research. Thanks also to Christian Joerges for his helpful comments on an earlier draft.

[1] By way of example see the recent Council Resolution on the Precautionary Principle at: Council Resolution on the Precautionary Principle at <http://europa.eu.int/council/off/conclu/dec2000/dec2000_en.pdf>. The European Council explicitly emphasizes the importance of this principle. See point 35 of the Presidency Conclusions, 10.

I. THE STATUS OF THE PRECAUTIONARY PRINCIPLE IN COMMUNITY LAW

Article 174(2) EC identifies a number of principles upon which Community environmental policy is to be based. Included among these is the precautionary principle. This first part of this chapter is concerned to explore the legal status of this principle in Community law, and the circumstances in which it may be invoked against (or by) the Community institutions and/or the Member States.[2]

It is well established that Article 174 (ex Article 130r) EC lays down the general objectives of Community environment policy, and that responsibility for deciding upon the action to be taken is conferred upon the Community legislature.[3] The Court has insisted that 'in view of the need to strike a balance between certain of the objectives and principles mentioned in Article 130r [now 174] and of the complexity of the implementation of those criteria, review by the Court must necessarily be limited to the question whether the Council . . . committed a manifest error of appraisal regarding the conditions for the application of Article 130r [now 174]'.[4] As such, recourse to the Article 174 principles as a 'sword' with which to challenge the legality of Community acts is constrained by virtue of the broad discretion enjoyed by the Community's legislative organs, and by the 'light touch' approach to judicial review adopted by the Court. There is, as yet, no case in which the Court seeks specifically to assess the legality of a Community act on the basis of its failure to conform to the demands of the precautionary principle.[5]

On the contrary, in so far as this principle has been invoked by the European Court, it has tended to use it as a 'shield' to justify the actions of the Community institutions. Recently, for example, in *Alpharma*[6] the Court of First Instance (CFI) emphasized that the requirements of public health must take precedence over economic considerations,[7] and that the Community institutions may take protective measures without having to wait until the reality and seriousness of the relevant risks become fully apparent.

---

[2] It should be emphasized that the matter under discussion here is the status of the precautionary principle arising under Article 174 EC. Specific legislation may explicitly invoke this principle, thus leading to a change in the status of the principle in a given instance.

[3] Case C-379/92, *Peralta* [1994] ECR I-3453.

[4] Case C-341/95, *Gianni Bettati v Safety Hi-Tech Srl* [1998] ECR I-4355, para. 35.

[5] However, the Court may be expected to do so in Case C-3/00, *Denmark v Commission* (2000) OJ C 122/6. In this case Denmark claims, inter alia, that the Commission has misapplied the principle of proportionality in relation to the Danish measures on nitrites and nitrates as it did not allow Denmark to adopt a precautionary approach.

[6] Case T-70/99R [1999] ECR II-2027.

[7] See also joined Cases T-125/96 and T-152/96, *Boehringer Ingelheim Vetmedica GmbH and Boehringer Sohn v Council and Commission* [1999] ECR II-3427, para. 102.

Similarly, and in a dramatically more high-profile setting, the European Court[8] upheld the validity of a Commission Decision adopting emergency measures to protect against BSE on the basis of reasoning which is thoroughly infused (though not explicitly) with the language of precaution.

We will return in the next section to consider the substance of the precautionary principle as applied by the European courts in these, and other, cases. For now, however, it is sufficient to note that the principle is binding upon the Community institutions, and that it may be invoked against them as a sword, or by them as a shield.

The above case law is significant in another respect. There is only one explicit reference to the precautionary principle in the Treaty establishing the European Community, namely that in Article 174 where, as noted above, it is included as one of the principles upon which Community environmental policy is to be based. Nonetheless, it is apparent from the cases here discussed that the European Court does not conceive that the application of the principle is limited to this sphere, but sees it rather as applying also in the area of public health.[9] This is a view shared by the European Council,[10] and by the Commission, the latter arguing instead that it:

... covers those specific circumstances where scientific evidence is insufficient, inconclusive or uncertain and there are indications through preliminary objective scientific evaluation that there are reasonable grounds for concern that the potentially dangerous effects on the environment, human, animal or plant health may be inconsistent with the chosen level of protection.[11]

It offers by way of justification two references. The first is to the integration obligation in Article 6 EC. This provides that environmental protection requirements be integrated into the definition and implementation of Community policies and activities referred to in Article 3 EC, in particular with a view to promoting sustainable development.[12] In so far as the

---

[8] Case C-180/96, *United Kingdom and Northern Ireland v Commission* [1996] ECR I-3903. See also Case C-157/56, *R v MAFF ex parte the National Farmers' Union and Others* [1998] ECR I-2211.

[9] Also the Court of First Instance has recognized the use of the precautionary principle outside the field of the environment, see Case T-199/96, *Laboratoires pharmaceutiques Bergaderm SA and Goupil v Commission* [1998] ECR II-2805, para. 66, citing the ECJ ruling in the BSE case.

[10] See para. B of the Council Resolution on the Precautionary Principle, n. 1 above, which emphasizes that the principle is also applicable to human health, as well as to the animal health and plant health sectors. It explicitly asks, in the subsequent paragraph, whether it might be useful to consolidate the principle in this respect, by amending the Treaty provisions concerning health and consumer protection.

[11] COM(2000) 1 *Communication on the Use of the Precautionary Principle*, 10.

[12] While this was introduced in Article 6, the integration obligation itself is not a new one, but stems rather from the Single European Act, being strengthened in turn by the Maastricht and Amsterdam treaties.

precautionary principle is one of the core principles of Community environmental policy, as established by Article 174 EC, it does not demand a great
leap of faith to conclude that it must be integrated in this way, as appropriate,
into other Community policies. The Commission's second reference offered
by way of justification for the more expansive reach of the precautionary principle is Article 95(3) which provides that the Commission, in its proposals
concerning health, safety, environmental protection, and consumer protection, will take as a base a high level of protection taking account in particular
of any new development based on scientific facts. The relevance of this is less
certain. However, in so far as a precautionary approach may be viewed as an
indispensable element of a 'high level of protection' it too offers some textual
basis for the Court's practice of applying the precautionary principle beyond
the environmental sphere, in the realm of the protection of public health. The
Court itself has exhibited no such textual scruples, albeit that while it has in
practice endorsed a precautionary approach in the area of public health, it has
desisted from referring explicitly to the precautionary principle, other than
with regard to environmental protection.

Turning now to the legal status of the precautionary principle vis-à-vis the
Member States, it is clear that this principle has served them in seeking to
defend themselves against allegations that they have breached Community
law. This is apparent both in the context of Article 95 EC derogations, and
in respect of the free movement of goods case law. A single example will suffice in respect of each. As regards the former, one may look to the decision
of the Commission as regards the Danish prohibition on the marketing and
use of creosote.[13] Here the Commission endorsed the national measures on
the basis of the precautionary principle, and by virtue of their compliance
with the concept of proportionality.[14] As regards the latter (free movement
of goods) the recent judgment of the Court in *Toolex* is indicative.[15] While
not explicitly endorsing recourse to the precautionary principle, the Court
emphasizes the scientific uncertainty surrounding the threat posed to human
health by the substance concerned, and concludes that 'taking account of
the latest medical research on the subject, and also the difficulty in establishing the threshold above which exposure to trichloroethylene poses a serious risk to humans, given the present state of research, there is no evidence
in this case to justify a conclusion by the Court that national legislation such
as that at issue in the case in the main proceedings goes beyond what is
necessary to achieve the objectives in view'.[16] Again the principles of pro-

---

[13] Commission Decision 1999/835/EC of 26 October 1999 OJ 1999 L 329/82.

[14] See para. 110 for an explicit reference to the precautionary principle.

[15] Case C-473/98, *Kemikalieinspektionen and Toolex*, [2000] ECR I-5681. See also Case
C-2/90, *Commission v Belgium* [1992] ECR I-4431, in which the Court had regard to the
principle that environmental damage as a priority be rectified (remedied) at source.

[16] *Toolex*, ibid., para. 45.

portionality and precaution are inextricably bound up together in their application.

Relevant also to this analysis is the judgment of the Court in the *Greenpeace* GMO case.[17] Here Greenpeace applied to the Conseil d'Etat to have a domestic law decree authorizing the marketing of seeds of certain varieties of genetically modified maize annulled. Greenpeace argued that the decree had been adopted following an irregular procedure and that it infringed the precautionary principle. The Conseil d'Etat referred a number of questions of interpretation to the European Court concerning Council Directive 90/220/EEC[18] on the deliberate release into the environment of GMOs. The judgment is, as a whole, infused with the language of precaution, and application of this principle has an immediate bearing upon the Court's construction of the provisions of the directive. Thus the Court observes that the precautionary principle is reflected in a variety of its provisions, including the right of Member States provisionally to restrict or prohibit the use and/or sale on its territory of a product which has received consent where it has justifiable reasons to consider that this constitutes a risk to human health or the environment.[19] More controversially, and critical to the case at hand, the Court accepts on this basis that Member States cannot be obliged to give consent to the release of GMOs, 'if in the meantime it has new information which leads it to consider that the product for which notification has been received may constitute a risk to human health and the environment'. This remains so even where the Member State concerned had originally been favourable to the release, and where neither the Commission nor any other Member State has raised an objection pursuant to the procedure laid down in the directive.[20]

Moving on, one final issue remains in considering the status of the precautionary principle in Community law, and this issue is both immensely significant and far from being resolved. It relates to the enforcement of the principle as a 'sword' against the Member States.[21] In what circumstances (if at all) is it possible to invoke this (or other) principles of Community environmental law to challenge the legality of acts of the Member States?

While at first glance, in the light of *Peralta*,[22] it would seem unlikely that the Article 174 principles are binding on the Member States, in the sense of

---

[17] Case C-6/99 [2000] ECR I-1651.   [18] OJ 1990 L 117/15.

[19] *Supra* n. 17, para. 44.

[20] Ibid. In this event the Member State concerned would be obliged to immediately inform the Commission and the other Member States about the new information in order that a decision may be taken in accordance with the procedure provided for in Article 21 of the directive.

[21] See in this respect the recent European Council Resolution on the Precautionary Principle, n. 1 above. Para. 2 of this provides as follows: 'Considering that the precautionary principle applies to the policies and action of the Community and its Member States and concerns action by public authorities both at the level of the Community institutions and at that of the Member States . . .'.

[22] *Supra* n. 3.

imposing upon them a duty to act in a manner which is consistent with them, recent case law and other developments militate against such a simple conclusion. One case of some significance in this respect is that of *Standley and Metson*.[23] Here a number of questions were put to the European Court concerning the validity of the Community's nitrates directive.[24] Put simply, the applicants in question, comprising farmers and their trade union, argued inter alia that the directive infringed the 'polluter pays' principle and the principle that environmental damage as a priority be rectified at source (the proximity principle); these, like the precautionary principle, being principles laid down in Article 174 EC. Their argument was based principally on the fact that 'farmers alone bear the cost of reducing the concentration of nitrates in waters to below the threshold of 50 mg/l even though agriculture is acknowledged to be only one of the sources of those nitrates, while the other sources escape all financial burden'.[25]

The judgment of the Court in this case does not address squarely the question of the binding effect of the Article 174 EC principles vis-à-vis the Member States. The focus of the judgment is on the application of the proportionality principle; a general principle of Community law which is binding on the Member States when they act within the scope of Community law, including when they are implementing Community law.[26] In this respect the Court accepts that the contested directive is sufficiently flexible in its substantive scope to enable 'the Member States to observe the principle of proportionality in the application of the measures which they adopt', it being for the national courts to ensure such compliance.[27] It goes on to conclude that 'the polluter pays principle reflects the principle of proportionality on which the Court has already expressed its view',[28] and that 'the arguments of the applicants in the main proceedings [regarding breach of the proximity principle] are indissociable from their arguments relating to breach of the principle of proportionality'.[29] Thus these principles are not deemed, per se, to bind the Member States in implementing Community law, but to do so indirectly in so far as they constitute expressions of the proportionality principle which self-evidently does. This equation between proportionality and proximity is merely stated, not explained, by the Court. As regards the polluter pays principle, the Court conceives it as implying an obligation on the Member States not to impose on farmers costs of eliminating pollution that

---

[23] C-293/97 [1999] ECR I-2603.
[24] Council Directive 91/676/EEC OJ 1991 L 375/1.   [25] *Supra* n. 23, para. 43.
[26] See, for example, Case C-5/88 *Wachauf* [1989] ECR 2609, in the context of the general principle relating to the protection of fundamental human rights. Member States are also bound by the Community law general principles when they are seeking to derogate from one of the internal market fundamental freedoms.
[27] *Supra* n. 23, para. 50.   [28] Ibid., para. 52.   [29] Ibid., para. 53.

are unnecessary. Recourse to the language of necessity is resonant of proportionality and thus the basis for the equation is established.

While the reasoning of the Court in *Standley and Metson* remains enigmatic, it is nonetheless important. At the very least it hints at the possibility that the principles contained in Article 174(2) EC may enjoy a status vis-à-vis the Member States which is comparable to that of Community law general principles. That is to say that Member States are bound to comply with these principles in implementing Community law, on the basis that where they cannot interpret or apply the Community law in a way which is compatible with these principles, grounds may be disclosed affecting the validity of the Community law in question. Thus the obligation on the part of the Member States to respect these principles reflects the obligation of the Community institutions to do so. It would simply not make practical sense, in a complex system of multi-level governance, based upon interlocking and overlapping legal orders, for these obligations to cease to bite at the door of the Member States.

This conclusion, tentatively put forward on the basis of the judgment in *Standley and Metson*, gains credibility in the light of a more recent decision of the Court. In *Fornasar*[30] the Court explicitly characterizes Article 4 of the Waste Framework Directive,[31] as intending to implement both the precautionary principle and the principle that preventive action should be taken.[32] On this basis, the Court provides that '[b]y virtue of those principles, it is for the Community *and the Member States* to prevent, reduce, and, in so far as is possible, eliminate from the outset, the sources of pollution or nuisance by adopting measures of a nature such as to eliminate recognised risks . . .'.[33] The precise wording of the judgment is important. If, as would appear to be the case, it is *by virtue of* these principles that Member States are bound to a given course of action in implementing a Community law directive, there can be little doubt that these principles are binding on the Member States in this setting.

If the recent case law of the Court is such as to lend support to the argument that the Article 174 EC principles are binding on Member States, at least when they are implementing Community environmental law, one further development outside the doors of the European Court militates further in favour of this, or perhaps even in favour of an even broader conclusion.

---

[30] Case C-318/98, *Criminal proceedings against Giancarlo Fornasar, Andrea Strizzolo, Giancarlo Toso, Lucio Mucchino, Enzo Peressutti and Sante Chiarcosso* [2000] ECR I-4785.

[31] Council Directive 75/442 OJ 1975 L 194/39 (as amended by Council Directive 91/156/EEC OJ 1991 L 78/32).

[32] *Supra* n. 30, para. 37.

[33] Ibid. (emphasis added). The 'in so far as is possible' in that quotation refers specifically to the duty to eliminate pollution or nuisance from the outset, and not to the duty to prevent or reduce sources of pollution or nuisance on the basis of the application of the precautionary principle and the principle that preventive action should be taken.

This takes the form of the Article 6 EC integration principle discussed above. As noted, this demands that environmental protection requirements be integrated into the definition and implementation of other Community policies. Thus, in so far as Member States are implementing other Community policies they are bound to integrate environmental protection requirements including, it seems legitimate to assume, the principles underpinning Community environmental policy, and hence the precautionary principle. In so far as the Member States would then appear to incur an obligation to apply the precautionary principle in respect of measures implementing other Community policies, this would in turn imply that such an obligation must also persist in respect of the implementation of that policy—environmental policy—in respect of which application of the principle was first conceived in Community law, and in respect of which even today the only explicit EC Treaty reference is to be found.

II. THE PRECAUTIONARY PRINCIPLE BEFORE THE EUROPEAN COURT AND THE EUROPEAN COMMISSION

A. The Precautionary Principle Before the European Court of Justice

1. National Provisions

Much litigation arising in the context of Article 28 EC has concerned controversies about the degree of risk inherent in certain products and the need to adopt specific protective measures.[34] In these cases the Court has applied a test to national provisions restricting trade, examining whether these are necessary, proportionate and the least trade restrictive means available to achieve the objective in question. Difficulties, however, arise in applying this test in a context of scientific uncertainty. How, in such a case, can the necessity or sufficiency of a measure be authoritatively assessed or, in the case of conflicting evidence as to the existence or magnitude of risk, might the proportionality of a measure be evaluated? That said, the Court itself has never expressed disquiet in the application of this test. In many cases, it has refrained from going into scientific detail, preferring simply to confirm Member States' powers to decide the level of protection 'in so far as uncertainties persist in the present state of scientific research' of the products concerned or that risk assessment procedures exist.[35] Member States have always been allowed considerable dis-

---

[34] See in general Joerges, 'Scientific Expertise in Social Regulation and the European Court of Justice: Legal Frameworks for Denationalised Governance Structures', in C. Joerges, K.-H. Ladeur and E. Vos, *Integrating Scientific Expertise into Regulatory Decision-Making: National Traditions and European Innovations* (1997).

[35] See, among others, Case 227/82, *Van Bennekom* [1983] ECR 3883 and Case 174/82, *Sandoz BV* [1983] ECR 2445.

cretion 'in [the] absence of harmonisation',[36] whilst the Court has clearly been hesitant to identify situations in which the relevant Community measures are such as to regulate exhaustively the area at hand.[37] However, Member States' discretion is not absolute: they must always have regard to the requirements of free movement. Thus, the Court has insisted that the burden of proving that national measures hindering trade are necessary for the protection of human health and/or the environment rests with the Member State concerned.[38] In the face of scientific uncertainty it is clear, however, that the evidential stringency declines, although the Court continues to insist that Member States give, as a minimum, evidence of scientific uncertainty, although this may be different in the case of Article 226 proceedings.[39]

In *Kaasfabriek Eyssen* for example, the Court had to consider whether a Dutch prohibition on the use of an antibiotic, nisin, as a preservative in processed cheese was justified on the ground of health protection.[40] The Court established that the addition of nisin to processed cheese was not uniformly regulated in all Member States: some Member States had issued a total prohibition, whilst others permitted its use without restriction. The Court considered that serious doubts as to the risk associated with the consumption of products containing nisin had led to international organizations, such as the FAO and the WHO, undertaking scientific research on the risk of ingestion, not only from cheese but from all sources. Even though these studies had not (yet) established with absolute certainty a maximum quantity of this substance which a person might consume daily without serious risk to his or her health,[41] the Court accepted that in view of the scientific uncertainties prevailing in the various countries on the maximum level of nisin to be

---

[36] See, among others, already Case 104/75, *De Peijper* [1976] ECR 613, Case 132/80, *NV United Foods and PVBA Van den Abeele v Belgian State* [1981] ECR 995, Case 272/80, *Biologische producten* [1981] ECR 3277, *Sandoz*, ibid., *Van Bennekom*, ibid., and more recently, Case C-293/94, *Brandsma* [1996] ECR I-3159, Case C-400/96, *Harpenies* [1998] ECR I-5121 and Case 55/99, *Commission v France*, judgment of 14 December 2000.

[37] See the refinements made by the Court in *Motte* (Case 247/84 [1985] ECR 3887 at 3903) where it held that 'it is only when Community directives make provision for the full harmonisation of all measures needed to ensure the protection of health and institute Community measures to monitor compliance therewith that recourse to Article 36 ceases to be justified'. See more recently, also Case C-400/96, *Harpenies*, ibid. On the inconsistencies in the Court's case law in this respect see Scott, 'Trade and Environment in the EU and the WTO', in J. H. H. Weiler (ed.), *The EU, the WTO and the NAFTA: Towards a Common Law of International Trade* (2000), and Dougan, 'Minimum Harmonization and the Internal Market', 37 *CMLRev.* (2000) 853.

[38] e.g., *Van Bennekom*, n. 35 above, Case 304/84, *Muller* [1986] ECR 1511 and Case 178/84, *Commission v Germany (Reinheitsgebot)* [1987] ECR 1227.

[39] See below.   [40] Case 53/80, *Kaasfabrick Eyssen* [1981] ECR 409.

[41] This was principally due to the fact that the risk assessment connected with the consumption of nisin by a person without serious risk to his or her health depended on several variable factors such as the dietary habits of each country.

prescribed in relation to each preserved product intended to satisfy the various dietary habits, the prohibition on the use of nisin in cheese by the Dutch legislation in question appeared to be in conformity with the proportionality principle.[42]

The Court has built on this ruling in its subsequent case-law. In *Van Bennekom* the Court ruled that national authorities must demonstrate in each case that their rules are necessary 'to give effective protection to the interests referred to in Article 36 (now Article 30) of the Treaty and, in particular, to show that the marketing of the product in question raises a serious risk to public health'.[43] In this context the famous *Reinheitsgebot* case is particularly interesting.[44] Four points seem important here. First, referring to its judgments in *Sandoz, Muller* and *Motte,* the Court confirmed its earlier interpretation of the proportionality principle and held that the prohibitions concerning the use of additives in foodstuffs must be restricted to what is actually necessary to secure the protection of public health. Second, in assessing the risk presented by additives, national authorities must, on the one hand, take account of the results of international scientific research and in particular the work of the Community's Scientific Committee on Food, and on the other hand of the particular eating habits prevailing in the country concerned. According to the Court, an additive must be authorized if in view of the scientific research and the particular eating habits that additive does not present a risk to human health and it meets a real need, especially a technical one. Third, the Court viewed it as essential, on the basis of the proportionality principle, that Member States must establish an easily accessible administrative procedure for companies seeking a general authorization for the use of specific additives, and it must be open to such parties to bring an action before the courts in the event of a refusal to grant authorization.[45] Fourth, the Court refused to allow for a general ban on additives based on a general preventive policy. The Court observed in the latter context first that the German rules result in the exclusion of all the additives authorized in other Member States and not the exclusion of just some of them for which 'there is concrete justification by reason of the risks which they involve in view of the eating habits of the German population'. In order to prove the harmfulness of additives, the German authorities referred to the risks inherent in the ingestion of additives in general, basing this claim on expert reports. They maintained that for reasons of general preventive health protection, there was a need to avoid excessive use of additives and to prohibit their use in beer, which was a substance consumed in large quantities. As it appeared that some of the additives

---

[42] See *Eyssen, supra* n. 40, at 422.   [43] *Van Bennekom, supra* n. 35, para. 47.

[44] *Supra* n. 38.

[45] See generally *Toolex, supra* n. 15, and *Motte, supra* n. 37, for an insight into the crucial importance of such a system.

authorized in beer by other Member States were also authorized under German law for use in virtually all other beverages, the Court found that these arguments were not sufficient to justify the imposition of stricter rules on beer.

It is notable that, although the Court (as in its other case-law[46]) emphasized the importance of the eating habits of a country for the presence of risk, it remained unimpressed by the appeal of the German authorities to the scale of consumption of beer in Germany.[47] Foremost this might be explained by the Court's demand for evidence of the specificity of the risk and its refusal to allow a general ban on additives based on a general preventive approach. The Court demands, particularly where German law authorized some additives in the case of other beverages, that the relevant authorities come up with more specific scientific evidence than that constituted by a mere reference to the potential risks of the ingestion of additives in general, and to the large quantities of beer consumed.[48]

The ruling of the Court in *Reinheitsgebot* must in fact be contrasted with its findings in other cases, where the Court did allow Member States to adopt a general preventive approach. Here it seems to distinguish between measures prohibiting the use of substances which can be harmful when consumed in certain quantities, and measures prohibiting the use of substances of which 'it is not disputed that [they] constitute a major risk to human and animal health and the environment'.[49] In *Albert Heijn* therefore the Court, considering that pesticides were such substances, ruled that Member States could regulate the presence of residues of pesticides on foodstuffs taking account of climatic conditions, the normal diet of the population and their state of health. In this respect, and contrary to its later ruling in *Reinheitsgebot*, the Court ruled that

---

[46] e.g. *Eyssen*, *supra* n. 40 and *Motte*, *supra* n. 37.

[47] According to the German authorities, when allowing additives in beer, certain persons might consume 300 to 350 litres of beer containing additives. See report for the hearing in Case 178/84, *supra* n. 38, at 1241.

[48] On the other hand, in view of its consistent case-law allowing to take particular account of the national eating habits, it is tempting to assume that the Court shared the view of Advocate General Slynn who put Germany's invocation of the German drinking habits into ridicule and who, although considering the factors invoked by Germany (among others the need to avoid excessive use of additives) legitimate, asserted that: 'it seems to me disproportionate to seek to justify rules which exclude the whole of society from beer other than nationally produced beer because some additives may constitute a risk for a person who drinks in excess of 1,000 litres of beer a year or for an alcoholic already suffering from cirrhosis of the liver. Accepting that such persons may need protection there are other ways of achieving it, medical advice as to quantum and self-restraint to name only two'. Opinion to Case 178/84, n. 38 above, at 1257.

[49] In relation to pesticides, see e.g. Case 94/83, *Albert Heijn NV* [1984] ECR 3263 and Case 54/85, *Mirepoix* [1986] ECR 1067. See also the Court's approach to biocidals in *Brandsma* and *Harpenies*, *supra* n. 36.

national rules could be part of a general preventive policy designed to prevent the presence of pesticides residues on foodstuffs.[50]

Furthermore, it is notable in the *Reinheitsgebot* case that the Commission explicitly viewed the German authorities as bearing the burden of proving that beers with additives constitute a danger to public health. Although the Court did not explicitly address this issue, it appears from the Court's reasoning that it implicitly shared this view.[51] In its more recent case-law, however, the Court seems to have taken a different approach. In Case 55/99 *Commission v France*,[52] for example, the Court was asked to consider, inter alia, whether a French law requiring a registration procedure for all medical reagents constituted an unjustified barrier to trade. It is important to note that this case, like the German *Reinheitsgebot* case, concerned an Article 226 EC direct action in which the Commission challenged the French authorities for having failed to fulfil their obligations under Article 28 EC. Recalling its consistent case-law that with respect to products liable to create a danger to human health, in the absence of harmonization, it is for the Member States to decide the level of protection, the Court first established that Member States had the power in principle to introduce a prior authorization procedure for reagents which may, if only indirectly, endanger human health. The proportionality principle, however, required the Member States to limit their action to what is necessary to achieve the objective of health protection. The Court subsequently affirmed that:

In proceedings for failure to fulfil an obligation, it is for the Commission to prove the allegation that the obligation has not been fulfilled and to place before the Court the information needed to enable it to determine whether the obligation has not been fulfilled.[53]

Importantly, the Court rejected the Commission's complaint in this respect, since the Commission had not put before the Court evidence from which it could conclude that the registration system for reagents under the contested decree is disproportionate. Thus, here the Court seems to accept that the initial burden rests with the Commission upon whom it is incumbent to demonstrate the existence of an infringement of Community law.

It appears therefore that in cases of scientific uncertainty, Member States have considerable discretion in deciding to err on the side of caution. They

---

[50] *Heijn, supra* n. 49, para 17.

[51] Although it is true the Court explicitly stated that in the context of court proceedings involving a refusal to grant authorization Member States bear the burden of proof to demonstrate that the prohibition of additives was justified on grounds of health protection. Case 178/84, *supra* n. 38, para. 46.

[52] *Supra* n. 36.

[53] Ibid., para. 30. See already Case C-159/94, *Commission v France* [1997] ECR I-5815, para. 102.

must, however, deliver some evidence of scientific uncertainty. They must adduce evidence of a specific, concrete risk and not merely of potential risks based on a general preventive approach. The specificity of risk must be assessed in view of the specific eating habits of a country. Yet, in Article 226 proceedings in which the Commission challenges national measures aimed at health protection on the basis of their incompatibility with the free movement rules, it seems that the initial burden rests upon the Commission.

2. Community Provisions

In applying the proportionality principle the Court generally examines whether the means applied by a Community measure correspond to 'the importance of the aim, and . . . whether they are necessary for its achievement'.[54] However, where Community institutions possess wide discretionary powers, as is often the case, the Court has consistently applied a somewhat deferential proportionality test, and solely examined whether the relevant Community measure is vitiated by manifest error, misuse of powers, or a clear case of *ultra vires*.[55] In *BSE* therefore, the Court held that the legality of the Commission's emergency decision to ban live animals, bovine meat and derived products adopted in the exercise of its discretionary power on agricultural policy could be affected only if the measure was manifestly inappropriate in relation to its aim. Pointing to the great uncertainty as to the risk posed by live animals, bovine meat and derived products to human health, the Court held that the Community institutions were allowed to take protective measures without having to wait for the risk to become fully apparent.[56] Of importance is that the Court inferred this approach from Article 130r (1) (now Article 174 (1)) EC and Article 130r (2) (now Article 174 (2)) EC. It is somewhat peculiar, however, that the Court in this context did not refer to the precautionary principle laid down in the latter, but to the principle that preventive action should be taken and to the integration obligation.[57] Evidence of scientific uncertainty is found by the Court in the reports of the Community's scientific veterinary committee, and those of the UK committee, SEAC. It is by reference to such scientific uncertainty that the Court concluded that the ban on the export of live animals, bovine meat and derived products could not be regarded as manifestly inappropriate, and that the Commission by adopting the ban had not infringed the proportionality principle. An important element in the evaluation of the Court seems to be the

[54] See, for instance, Case C-118/89, *Lingenfelser* [1990] ECR I-2637; Case C-155/89, *Philipp Brothers* [1990] ECR I-330.
[55] See, for instance, Case C-331/88, *The Queen v The Minister for Agriculture, Fisheries and Food and the Secretary of State for Health, ex parte: Fedesa and other (Fedesa)* [1990] ECR I-4023; Case C-405/92, *Établissements Armand Mondiet SA v Armement Islais SARL (Mondiet)* [1993] ECR I-6133; Case C-280/93, *Germany v Council* [1994] ECR I-4973.
[56] *Supra* n. 8.   [57] Ibid., para. 100.

fact that the Commission's decision was an emergency decision and there was, as the Commission's decision itself acknowledged in the preamble, a need to review the contested decision following an overall examination of the situation.

In *Bergaderm*, the Court of First Instance affirmed the Court's ruling in *BSE*.[58] In this case the CFI was to decide upon a request for compensation under Article 288 (2) EC, in respect of damages suffered by Bergaderm as a result of an investigation conducted by the Commission. The case concerned the setting of a maximum level on the use of a substance 'psoralens' in sun products, pursuant to the Commission adapting the cosmetics directive. Bergaderm produced a sun oil containing this substance; the Commission's decision ultimately led to its liquidation. In determining whether the Commission had acted in breach of the proportionality principle, the CFI considered that there was nothing in the documents submitted to it to make it believe that the Commission had misunderstood the scientific arguments concerning the extent of the risk involved in the use of sun oil containing psoralens. The Court continued by arguing that the protection of health is one of the objectives of the cosmetics directive and asserted that 'the Commission is not in a position to carry out itself the scientific assessments needed to further that objective'[59] and that the Scientific Committee on Cosmetology was entrusted with the task of assisting the Community authorities on scientific and technical issues in order to enable them to adopt, in full knowledge of the facts, the necessary measures. The Court therefore considered that

... in the light of those factors, the Commission cannot be criticised for placing the matter before the Scientific Committee or for complying with that body's opinion, which was drawn up on the basis of a large number of meetings, visits and specialists reports.[60]

In this context the CFI referred to the *BSE* ruling that in cases of scientific uncertainty the institutions may take protective measures without having to wait until the reality and seriousness of those risks becomes fully apparent. In such circumstances the Court concluded that the Commission's conduct, and the measure adopted by it, could not be regarded as vitiated by manifest error or assessment, or as disproportionate. *Bergaderm*, however, also invoked procedural irregularities *inter alia* in relation to the rights of defence. In line with the Commission's submissions, however, the Court rejected the presence of such irregularities. Important in this respect is the fact that the Commission withdrew its proposed measures in the light of the views of the national representatives of the Standing Adaptation Committee on Cosmetics, and that

---

[58] Case T-199/96, *supra* n.9.

[59] Ibid., para. 64. The CFI referred hereby to Case C-212/91, *Angelopharm* [1994] ECR I-171.

[60] *Bergaderm*, *supra* n. 9, para. 65.

Bergaderm had had ample opportunity to express its views to the members of the Scientific Committee and to the Commission, and that they were allowed access to the ad hoc group of experts.

B. The Precautionary Principle before the European Commission

The precautionary principle is explicitly referred to by the Commission in its decisions responding to requests by Member States to 'opt out' from a harmonization measure. The heavily debated possibility of 'opting out' with respect to internal market measures was introduced by the Single European Act and counterbalanced by the introduction of qualified majority voting in harmonization measures under the former Article 100a (4) EC. Amended by the Amsterdam Treaty, new paragraphs (4) and (5) of Article 95 EC first make a distinction between national measures which exist at the moment of adoption of a harmonization measure (new paragraph (4)) and national measures which are introduced after the adoption of a harmonization measure (new paragraph (5)). Paragraph (4) retains the criteria for the possibility of maintaining the already existing national measures unaltered: the protection of the interests laid down in Article 30 EC and the protection of the environment or working environment. It is not possible under Article 95 (4) to maintain national provisions which are less protective than the provisions laid down in the Community harmonization measure.[61] Stricter limitations are posed on the introduction of national measures after harmonization. Paragraph (5) allows Member States to adopt new national measures only where these are based on new scientific evidence relating to the protection of the environment or the working environment, on the grounds of a problem specific to that Member State which has arisen after the adoption of a harmonization measure.[62] Where a problem relating to health protection is raised by a Member State in a field which is subjected to prior harmonization measures, it needs to bring this matter to the attention of the Commission which shall immediately examine whether it is necessary to propose appropriate measures to the Council (paragraph (8)). The instrument of introducing new unilateral measures therefore does not seem to apply to health protection.

In its ten decisions[63] issued up to now, the Commission has submitted the

---

[61] *Supra* n. 13.

[62] See generally for a discussion of the difficulties of interpretation to which this gives rise Sevenster, 'The Environmental Guarantee After Amsterdam: Does the Emperor Have New Clothes?', in H. Somsen (ed.), *The Yearbook of European Environmental Law: Volume One* (2000).

[63] Commission Decision 94/783/EC concerning the prohibition of PCP notified by Germany, OJ 1994 L 316/43; Commission Decision 96/211/EC concerning the prohibition of PCP notified by Denmark, OJ 1996 L 68/32; Commission Decision 1999/5/EC on the

national derogations to a test similar to the test carried out by the ECJ in relation to Article 30 EC. However, in its assessment the Commission formally carries out its analysis in four steps, examining:

(1) need,
(2) absence of arbitrary discrimination,
(3) absence of a disguised restriction on trade, and
(4) absence of an obstacle to the functioning of the internal market.

Both in the first and fourth steps, the Commission examines the proportionality of the measures, examining whether they are excessive in relation to their aim[64] (first step) and whether they are not disproportionate obstacles to the functioning of the internal market in relation to the pursued objective[65] (fourth step). As with resort to Article 30 EC and the rule of reason, the burden of proof lies on the Member State wishing to derogate.

The existing Commission decisions concern requests for derogation from the common Community approach in favour of a stricter national approach on PCP, creosote, mineral wool, food colourings and sulphites and nitrites and nitrates used in foodstuffs. In its set of decisions issued in October 1999, the Commission explicitly applied for the first time the precautionary principle. Of particular interest are the Commission's observations concerning creosote. This substance, which is principally used as a wood-preserving agent, is a complex mixture of over 200 chemical compounds. Directive 94/60/EC put specific limits on the use and marketing of creosote.[66] Yet four countries (the Netherlands, Germany, Sweden and Denmark) wished to maintain their own stricter national provisions for reasons of protection of health and the environment. Although only the Dutch authorities had succeeded in demonstrating the presence of a situation specific to their country, the Commission considered that, taking the scientific uncertainties concerning exposure into account,

Swedish request for derogation on the use of certain colours and sweeteners in foodstuffs, OJ 1999 L 3/13; Commission Decision 1999/830/EC on the Danish request for derogation on the use of sulphites, nitrites and nitrates in foodstuffs, OJ 1999 L 329/1; Commission Decision 1999/832 concerning the Dutch request for derogation on the use of creosote notified, OJ 1999 L 329/25; Commission Decision 1999/833/EC concerning the German request for derogation on the use of creosote, OJ 1999 L 329/43; Commission Decision 1999/834/EC concerning the Swedish request for derogation on the use of creosote, OJ 1999 L 329/63; Commission Decision 1999/835/EC concerning the Danish request for derogation on the use of creosote; Commission Decision 1999/831/EC concerning the prohibition of PCP notified by The Netherlands, OJ 1999 L 329/15; Commission Decision 1999/836/EC concerning the German request for derogation on the use of mineral wool, OJ 1999 L 329/100; Commission Decision 2000/509/EC concerning the Belgian request for derogation, OJ 2000 L 205/7.

[64] See Commission Decision 1999/830/EC on the Danish derogation concerning the use of sulphites, nitrites and nitrates in foodstuffs, OJ 1999 L 329/1, para. 44.
[65] See inter alia Commission Decision 1999/835/EC, n. 63 above.
[66] Directive 94/60/EC amending Directive 76/769/EEC, OJ 1994 L 364/1.

. . . national measures aiming at reducing the probability of prolonged dermal exposure to creosote, either through direct contact with creosote or wood treated with creosote, are justified in the light of the precautionary principle.[67]

Resort to the precautionary principle by the Commission in these decisions is interesting from a variety of perspectives. First, it is notable that it is the Commission, and not the Member States, which relies on the precautionary principle to justify the national derogations. Herewith the Commission arguably gives the Member States both a sword against Community decisions based on Article 95 EC, and a shield to justify their own national legislation at the same time. This principle is now in fact invoked by Denmark as an argument (albeit still in the context of the proportionality principle) for annulment of the Commission's refusal to grant its derogation request for its stricter national provisions on the use of nitrites and nitrates in foodstuffs.[68]

Second, whilst the ECJ and the Member States (i.e., Denmark in its recourse against the Commission's refusal to grant derogation) still derive the precautionary principle from the proportionality principle, the Commission seems to be beginning to treat the precautionary principle somewhat separately from the proportionality principle. It evaluates the precautionary principle in considering justifications for the national measures, which in turn need to be in conformity with the proportionality principle. As such the Commission seems to be prepared to promote the precautionary principle as an independent principle also for human health protection.[69] This may be explained within the context of its new general approach to the precautionary principle and risk regulation.[70]

Third, and this is not new, the Commission bases its considerations in applying the precautionary principle foremost on the scientific advice delivered by the Community's scientific committees. In addition, it also resorts to external expertise, e.g., in the PCP and creosote cases. The committees generally are asked to examine the scientific evidence submitted by the national authorities, as well as, in the case of creosote, the external scientific evidence prepared upon the request of the Commission. The enormous influence these committees have on the Community's decision-making process may be clear: the Commission generally follows almost 'blindly' the opinion of the scientific committees.[71] In the case of most requests to 'opt out', the Commission

---

[67] *Creosote, supra* n. 13, para. 110. The other decisions contain similar phrasings.

[68] *Supra* n. 5.

[69] On the other hand, in its Report to the European Council 'Better Lawmaking 2000', the Commission refers to the precautionary principle as part of the proportionality principle, see point 1.2. of the Report, COM(2000) 772 final.

[70] See its Communication on the precautionary principle, n. 11 above. See also Section IIIB below.

[71] This also appears in the Commission's practice in the authorization procedures on the placing of the market of GMOs or novel food.

first makes use of external scientific advice which it subsequently submits to the scientific committees for evaluation. Hence, in contrast to the evaluation underpinning the Commission's PCP decisions, where it relied only on ad hoc external advice, the Commission turns to the precautionary principle on the basis of the scientific advice obtained from the Community's scientific committee, the Scientific Committee for Toxicology, Ecotoxicology and the Environment (CSTEE), after having commissioned on its own initiative (immediately after the adoption of the relevant Community directive) a new carcinogenicity study by an external German research institute, the Fraunhofer Institute of Toxicology and Aerosol Research. Relying primarily on this new study, the CSTEE concluded that there was sufficient scientific evidence to support the opinion that there was a cancer risk to consumers from creosote or wood treated with creosote containing less than the limit set by the Community directive. Furthermore, the Commission considers of particular significance the fact that the scientific evidence delivered by the Member States contains new information. Failure to deliver, in the eyes of the Commission, new scientific evidence which was not already considered at the time of the adoption of the relevant Community provision is bound to lead to a rejection of the derogation request.[72]

Fourth, in its evaluation, the Commission seems to be influenced by the nature of harmfulness of the specific substances: PCPs and creosotes are recognized as dangerous ('per se' dangerous) substances,[73] whilst colourings and sweeteners are not, presenting 'merely' potential allergy risks for specific groups of persons. In the case of dangerous substances, the Commission seems more willing to allow the Member States to adopt a precautionary approach although national measures need still to be in conformity with the general proportionality principle. The Commission, however, requires Member States herein to be consistent. Inconsistency, for example a prohibition on the use of additives in one foodstuff, but not in another, is punished by the Commission with a refusal to allow a Member State to opt out.[74] Moreover, particular—but not always decisive (for example, in the case of creosote)—weight seems to be placed on the presence of specific circum-

---

[72] In the context of the Danish derogation request in respect of nitrites and nitrates, it is interesting that in relation to their measures setting stricter levels to the use of nitrites, the Danish authorities referred to scientific evidence produced by the SCF in 1995 after the adoption of the Community directive, which concluded that if the levels of nitrite residues were as high as those authorized by the Community directive, the ADI would be exceeded. The Commission, however, found that evidence referred to by the Danish authorities did not contain any new evidence, as the 1995 opinion of the SCF repeated the same conclusion which it had pronounced before the adoption of the Community directive.

[73] See the submissions by the German and Dutch authorities in *Heijn* where they used this terminology of dangerous substances *per se* in the context of pesticides, *supra* n. 49, at 3279.

[74] See the Commission's decision on the Danish request for derogation on the use of nitrites and nitrates in foodstuffs, *supra* n. 63.

stances in a given country, taking into account, for example, genetics, environment or food habits, and its causal link with the national measures and the existence of a specific health risk in contrast to general prevention. If Member States cannot prove that they are in a particular situation in comparison with the other Member States, the Commission is generally likely to refuse to sanction the national measure. In line with the Court's case-law, the Commission requires that national measures should respond to the existence of a specific risk and not merely make part of a general preventive policy.[75]

It may be concluded that generally the Commission allows Member States to rely on the precautionary principle only when the scientific committees consider the scientific evidence delivered by the Member States to be justified in the light of new scientific evidence, or by the particular situation of the Member States. Yet, as we noted in the context of the Court's case-law, Member States are increasingly distrustful of the findings of the Community's scientific committees and seek increasingly to adhere to the findings of their own national bodies to support national protective measures.

Examples of conflicts between scientific findings may be found within the context of safeguard clauses invoked by Member States. Safeguard clauses are included in virtually all directives concerning the protection of human health (see Article 95 (10) EC).[76] They commonly allow Member States temporarily to restrict or prohibit the use of products on their territories, where they, as a result of new information or a re-assessment of existing information, have detailed grounds for considering that the use of the product in question, though complying with the relevant Community directives, endangers human health or the environment.[77] Such national measures are, however, subject to a Community control procedure, which requires Member States to immediately notify the Commission of any stricter national provision which they want to maintain or adopt, specifying the reasons for their decisions. As soon as possible, the Commission must examine the evidence and consult the relevant standing committee, composed of national representatives. On the basis of a positive opinion of this committee, the Commission takes the appropriate measures.[78] If this committee, however, adopts a negative opinion or fails to adopt one, the Commission must refer the matter back to the

[75] See the Commission's decision on the Swedish request for derogation, n. 63 above.

[76] Similar, though not identical, problems arise in the environmental sphere given that in this sphere Community measures are by definition minimum harmonization measures according to Article 176 EC, and thus Member States may take stricter protective measures so long as these are compatible with the Treaty and especially Articles 28–30 thereof.

[77] For example, Article 12 of the Novel Food Regulation (97/258 OJ 1997 L 43/1); Article 16 of the GMO directive (90/220 OJ 1990 L 117/15). Similar clauses are laid down in Community decisions on food and other issues touching upon human health and safety.

[78] These cases too generally lead the Commission to consider whether a revision of the relevant provisions in the harmonization measure is necessary.

Council.[79] If the Council does not act, the Commission may adopt its draft measures; if the Council opposed the Commission draft measures, the Commission must re-examine the matter.[80]

Although safeguard clauses must have been invoked in the past, recently more information on Member State recourse to them has been made public, by means of the publication of the records of meetings, and the opinions of the Community's scientific committees. We thus learn that Austria, Luxembourg, Germany and Italy have invoked the safeguard clauses laid down in both the genetically modified organisms (GMOs) Directive[81] and the Novel Food Regulation[82] in order to block the circulation of genetically modified maize within their territories. Recourse on the part of these countries to the safeguard clauses does not come as a complete surprise, as the approval of specific genetically modified maize products and products derived from genetically modified maize had proved particularly controversial for them, and notwithstanding objections by several Member States, the Commission had approved four GM maize products and swede rape product.[83]

Also in these cases, the Commission submits the scientific evidence delivered by the Member States to the Community's scientific committees. Although the countries concerned all delivered scientific evidence of the harmfulness of the genetically modified maize earlier approved by the Commission to human health and the environment (e.g., Austria claimed adverse effects of this product to the Monarch butterfly), the relevant scientific committees concluded that the information submitted by the countries did not constitute new significant information that was not already considered in their original risk assessment and opinion[84] or that it did not contain detailed scientific grounds for considering that the use of these products

[79] Although the Comitology Decision 1999/468/EC (OJ 1999 L 184/23) provides for a special procedure which may be applied for safeguard measures, virtually no use is made of this procedure in the food sector. Instead, resort is made to the regulatory committee procedure. See e.g. Article 12 of the Novel Food Regulation, *supra* n. 77.

[80] See for more details, Article 5 of the Comitology Decision, ibid.

[81] Directive 90/220, *supra* n. 77.

[82] Regulation 97/258, *supra* n. 77.

[83] See Commission Decision 97/98/EC concerning herbicide-tolerant GM maize produced by Ciba-Geigy (now Novartis), OJ 1997 L 31/69; Commission Decision 98/292/EC concerning grains of GM maize produced by Novartis, OJ 1998 L 131/28; Commission Decision 98/293/EC concerning seeds and grains of GM maize produced by AgrEvo, OJ 1998 L 131/30; Commission Decision 98/294/EC concerning herbicide-tolerant GM maize produced by Monsanto, OJ 1998 L 131/32 and Commission Decision 98/291/EC concerning GM spring swede rapes produced by AgrEvo, OJ 1998 L 131/26.

[84] In case of the Austrian invocation of Article 16 GMO directive in respect of the Monsanto GM maize, see Opinion of the Scientific Committee on Plants of 24 September 1999, <http://europa.eu.int/comm/food/sc/scp/out49_en.html>.

endangered human health.[85] Although such conclusions were sufficient for the Commission to propose a negative decision in these cases, it appeared to be extremely difficult to reach agreement on these issues with the national representatives within the context of the regulatory committee procedure. Hence, whilst the Commission reconsidered the matter in the context of its overall strategy on GMOs, Member States were allowed to adhere to their own more restrictive national provisions.[86]

The increasing frequency of scientific conflicts between the Community's scientific committees/authorities and national bodies/authorities would appear to be one of the most urgent and striking tensions in the governance of the internal market. Evidently, basing the precautionary principle purely on the scientific advice produced by the Community's committees will, and already does, raise problems. Therefore, the Community is currently seeking a solution to this issue (see below).

III. THE APPLICATION OF THE PRECAUTIONARY PRINCIPLE IN RISK REGULATION

A. The Precautionary Principle and the WTO

The European Union's commitment to, and application of, the precautionary principle is currently facing a new challenge in the shape of the WTO. One important aspect of this challenge is the lack of clarity surrounding WTO norms, and uncertainty as to the extent to which a precautionary approach will be accommodated within the framework of the WTO's multilateral trading system. The precautionary principle finds expression only once in the entire WTO Agreement. Article 5:7 of the Agreement on Sanitary and Phytosanitary Measures provides:[87]

In cases where relevant scientific evidence is insufficient, a Member may provisionally adopt sanitary and phytosanitary measures on the basis of available pertinent information, including that from the relevant international organizations as well as that from sanitary or phytosanitary measures applied by other Members. In such circumstances, Members shall seek to obtain the additional information necessary for a

[85] In case of the Italian invocation of Article 12 Novel Food Regulation in respect of the use of GM maize in general, see Opinion of the Scientific Committee on Food of 7 September 2000, <http://europa.eu.int/comm/food/fs/sc/scf/out66_en.pdf>.

[86] On 21 March 2001 the European Parliament and the Council adopted a new Directive on GMOs, see OJ 2001 L 106/1.

[87] The scope of such measures is defined in Annex A to the Agreement. They are concerned with the protection of the life or health of animals, plants or humans, from the sources identified in the Annex. These include pests and diseases, as well as additives, contaminants, toxins or disease-carrying organisms in foods, beverages or feedstuffs.

more objective assessment of risk and review the sanitary and phytosanitary measures accordingly within a reasonable period of time.

This expression of the precautionary principle has not yet fallen for interpretation before the WTO dispute settlement bodies. In the beef hormones 'case',[88] Article 5:7 was not invoked by the European Community, and the Appellate Body shied away from elaborating upon the status of this principle in international law.[89] The Appellate Body restricted its observations to two remarks. It observed first that the principle has not been written into the SPS Agreement as a ground for justifying SPS measures that are otherwise inconsistent with the obligations of Members set out in particular provisions of that Agreement. Second, the Appellate Body noted that it need not be assumed that Article 5:7 exhausts the relevance of the precautionary principle, it being 'reflected' also in further parts of the Agreement, including Article 3:3 and its preamble. Finally, the Appellate Body observes, in its discussion of the precautionary principle, and in assessing whether 'sufficient scientific evidence' (Article 3:3) exists to warrant an SPS measure, that a panel should bear in mind that 'responsible, representative governments commonly act from perspectives of prudence and precaution where risks of irreversible, e.g., life-terminating, damage to human health are concerned'.[90]

The Appellate Body builds upon these observations regarding prudence and precaution in its reading of Article 5:1 of the SPS Agreement which requires that SPS measures are to be 'based on' risk assessment. Article 5:1 is construed as requiring that 'the results of the risk assessment must sufficiently warrant—that is to say reasonably support—the SPS measure at stake'.[91] To put it differently, 'there must be a rational relationship between the measure and the risk assessment'.[92] The Appellate Body goes on to observe:

We do not believe that a risk assessment has to come to a monolithic conclusion that coincides with the scientific conclusion or view implicit in the SPS measure. The risk assessment could set out both the prevailing view representing the 'mainstream' of scientific opinion, as well as the opinions of scientists taking a divergent view .... In most cases, responsible and representative governments tend to base their legislative and administrative measures on 'mainstream' scientific opinion. In other cases, equally responsible and representative governments may act in good faith on the basis of what, at a given time, may be a divergent opinion coming from qualified and respected sources. By itself, this does not necessarily signal the absence of a reasonable relationship between the SPS measure and the risk assessment, especially where the risk involved is life-threatening in character and is perceived to constitute a clear and imminent threat to public health and safety. Determination of the presence or

---

[88] *EC Measures Concerning Meat and Meat Products (Hormones)* AB-1997-4, Report of 16 January 1998. This can be found in the 'Documents' section of the WTO website: <http://www.wto.org/>.

[89] Ibid., paras 120–135.   [90] Ibid., para. 124.   [91] Ibid., para. 193.
[92] Ibid.

absence of that relationship can only be done on a case-to-case basis, after account is taken of all considerations rationally bearing upon the issue of potential adverse health effects.[93]

That the Appellate Body, nonetheless, ruled against the Community in this 'case' is indicative of two crucial factors. First, in so far as the panel had been presented with 'divergent' scientific opinions evidencing the existence of a risk to human health, these were dismissed as not 'sufficiently specific to the case at hand'. They took the form of 'general studies', but did not 'address the particular kind of risk here at stake'.[94] Second, the Appellate Body endorsed the finding of the panel that 'theoretical uncertainty' arising because 'science can never provide absolute certainty that a given substance will not ever have adverse health effects' is not the kind of risk to be assessed under Article 5:1 of the Agreement.[95]

It is clear from the above that recourse to concepts of 'reasonableness' and 'rationality' in the context of risk assessment leaves scope for the pursuit of a broadly precautionary approach to risk regulation. Nonetheless, the reasonableness or rationality of a given measure will be assessed on a case by case basis, with little guidance being available as to the nature of, or relationship between, those considerations which will be relevant to any such assessment. Thus, for example, it is not clear to what extent the intensity of the putative harm associated with any given risk is relevant in determining the reasonableness of a measure, and in particular the threshold of 'possibility' which must be transcended. Is it the case that the more dreadful the possible harm, the less certain of it we need be in order to take steps to guard against it?[96]

This would appear to be the implication of the Appellate Body's observations in 'hormones', in the paragraph cited above, concerning the life-threatening

---

[93] Ibid., para. 194. See also the panel report in *European Communities—Measures affecting asbestos and products containing asbestos* (DS135/R) and (DS135/R/Add.1), Report of 18 September 2000. See WTO website at: <http://www.wto.org/>. The panel observes, in the context of the application of the GATT Article XX exception, that 'the evidence before it tends to show that handling chrysotile-cement products constitutes a risk to health rather than the opposite. Accordingly a decision-maker responsible for taking public health measures might reasonably conclude that the presence of chrysotile-cement products posed a risk because of the risks involved in working with these products' (para. 8.193). On this basis the panel accepted that the EC had made a prima facie case regarding the existence of a health risk, and that Canada had failed to rebut this. See also the report of the Appellate Body in this case where the panel's finding that the measure protects human life or health within the meaning of Article XX(b) was upheld, as was the conclusion of the panel that there was no reasonably available alternative to the contested asbestos ban. *European Communities—Measures Affecting Asbestos and Asbestos-Containing Products* WT/DS135/AB/R report of 12 March 2001, para. 172.

[94] *Supra* n. 88, para. 200.   [95] Ibid., para. 186.

[96] Or alternatively, where the degree of harm envisaged is small, might it nonetheless be legitimate to act on the basis of precaution where the likelihood of that harm transpiring is more clearly established on the basis of scientific evidence, albeit that some doubt remains?

nature of the harm risked.[97] Confusingly, however, in the same paragraph the Appellate Body speaks of a 'clear and imminent threat' and does so in the context of the legitimacy of upholding minority scientific opinion. This makes sense only if the Appellate Body is assessing clarity and imminence on the basis of the minority opinion concerned. In the asbestos 'case', similarly, the panel, in assessing the adequacy of less trade restrictive measures in protecting public health, emphasizes both the severity of the risk (lung cancers and mesotheliomas which are still difficult to cure or incurable), and the large numbers potentially exposed.[98] The Appellate Body, in its *Asbestos* report, emphasized too that the more vital or important the common interests or values at stake, the easier it is to accept the measures as 'necessary' within the meaning of GATT Article XX(b).[99] Not only did the Appellate Body conclude that it is 'perfectly legitimate for a Member to seek to halt the spread of a highly risky product while allowing the use of a less risky product in its place', even where the less risky product is not demonstrated to be risk free,[100] but also it accepted the European Communities' proposition that there was no reasonably available (less trade restrictive) alternative to the contested asbestos ban. In reaching this conclusion the Appellate Body placed emphasis upon the fact that:

France could not reasonably be expected to employ *any* alternative measure if that measure would involve a continuation of the very risk that the Decree seeks to 'halt'. Such an alternative measure would, in effect, prevent France from achieving its chosen level of health protection. On the basis of the scientific evidence before it, the Panel found that, in general, the efficacy of 'controlled use' remains to be demonstrated . . . Moreover, even in cases where 'controlled use' practices are applied 'with greater certainty', the scientific evidence suggests that the level of exposure can, in some circumstances, still be high enough for there to be a 'significant residual risk of developing asbestos-related diseases'.[101]

If there remains considerable doubt as to the positioning of the thresholds for the application of a precautionary approach to the protection of public health in the WTO, this is doubly so as concerns social regulation more generally. We saw above that, in the context of Community law, the precautionary principle first emerged in the sphere of environmental policy, later to be transposed to the area of public health. In the context of the WTO the environmental dimension is clearly relevant. This is most immediately apparent within the framework of GATT, Article XX, particularly in respect of paragraph (g) thereof, concerned with the conservation of natural resources. It is relevant too in the application of the Agreement on Technical Barriers to Trade, Article 2:2 of which provides that '. . . technical regulations shall not be more trade-restrictive than necessary to fulfil a legitimate objective, taking

---

[97] *Supra* n. 88. [98] Ibid., paras 8.200 and 8.201. [99] Ibid.
[100] Ibid., para. 168. [101] Ibid., para. 174.

account of the risks that non-fulfilment would create. . .'. A non-exhaustive list of legitimate objectives is added, and these include protection of animal or plant life or health, and protection of the environment. In view of the breadth of the definition of technical regulations,[102] the willingness of the dispute settlement bodies to extend to the environmental sphere their endorsement in principle of a precautionary approach, even when applying a WTO norm which is not explicit in its reference to the principle, is of crucial importance.

While the above merely alludes to the considerable uncertainty underpinning the scope of application and substance of the WTO conception of precaution, it highlights the all-important issue of thresholds, both individually, and in terms of the relationships between the different threshold parameters applying. It reminds us, moreover, that there is much to play for in the WTO system. This novel order is just beginning the task of articulating the concepts which will govern the relationship between trade and social regulation. It is against this backdrop that the EU's relatively recent communication on the precautionary principle should be viewed.[103]

B. The Commission's Communication on the Precautionary Principle

The communication makes no secret of this background, stating that, inter alia, it 'seeks to provide an input into the ongoing debate on this issue, both in the Community and internationally'.[104] It goes on to observe that:

the Commission considers that the Community, like other WTO members, has the right to establish the level of protection—particularly of the environment, human, animal and plant health,—that it deems appropriate. Applying the precautionary principle is a key tenet of its policy, and the choices it makes to this end will continue to affect the views it defends internationally, on how this principle should be applied.[105]

There is much in the Commission's communication which is helpful in thinking about the precautionary principle. Notable in this respect is its attempt to break down the principle into two constituent parts. First there arises a political decision to act, or not to act, and second is the decision relating to how to act. The first is observed to be linked to factors triggering recourse to the

---

[102] Annex 1, para. 1 of the TBT Agreement defines a technical regulation as a '[d]ocument which lays down product characteristics or their related processes and production methods, including the applicable administrative provisions, with which compliance is mandatory. It may also include or deal exclusively with terminology, symbols, packaging, marking or labelling requirements as they apply to a product, process or production method'.

[103] *Supra* n. 11.   [104] Ibid., para. 2 of the Summary.

[105] Ibid., para. 3 of the Summary.

precautionary principle, and the second to the nature of the measures resulting from the application of this principle.[106] While it may not always be possible in practice to separate a decision to act from a decision as to how to act,
this distinction is useful in forcing a careful consideration of which factors and
thresholds may be relevant at which stage of analysis.

There is, in addition, much in the Commission's communication which is
resonant of the approach of the Appellate Body in the hormones 'case'. In this
sense the communication may be seen not only as a contribution to the ongoing debate at international level, but also as a public relations exercise
designed to calm the fears of those who perceive that the precautionary principle serves, in the case of the EU, to legitimate decisions which are irrational,
other than in terms of their capacity to serve protectionist goals. Thus, the
centrality of scientific evaluation is emphasized again and again; this being
posited as an indispensable prerequisite for triggering a decision to invoke the
precautionary principle. Nonetheless, the Commission, like the Appellate
Body, insists that due account should be taken of minority scientific views,
provided the credibility and reputation of the minority faction is recognized.[107]

Alongside this emphasis upon the scientific basis of decision-making is an
insistence that the precautionary principle should not in any sense be used to
justify the adoption of arbitrary decisions.[108] Again this is resonant of the
Appellate Body's emphasis upon reasonableness and rationality. Related to
this is the Commission's insistence that application of the precautionary principle, at the stage of determining the nature of the measures to be enacted,
offers no excuse for derogating from general principles of risk management,
and specifically from the principles of proportionality, non-discrimination,
consistency, examination of the benefits and costs of action or lack of action,
and examination of scientific developments. Without assessing the
Commission's understanding of these principles in any detail (and in fact the
level of detail put forward is not great), it is important to note the existence
of a fundamental tension—unacknowledged and unresolved—between this
emphasis upon non-arbitrary, rational decision-making on the one hand, and
transparency, participation and responsiveness to public opinion on the
other.[109] Whereas the former lays emphasis upon the value of coherence and
consistency, emphasizing objective criteria of assessment, the latter is concerned with social acceptability and the quelling of public fears. Thus, non-
discrimination means, the Commission tells us, that comparable situations
should not be treated differently, unless there are objective grounds for so

---

[106] *Supra* n. 11, para. 5.   [107] Ibid., para. 6.2.   [108] Ibid., para. 5.1.

[109] This tension is evident too in the recent European Council Resolution on the
Precautionary Principle, n. 1 above, which similarly places emphasis not only upon scientific
assessment of risk and the consistency of measures adopted, but upon transparency, the
involvement of civil, and the addressing of public concerns regarding risk.

doing. Consistency means that measures should be of comparable scope and nature to those already taken in equivalent areas. Cost-benefit analysis encompasses not only an evaluation of the costs 'to the Community' (!) of action or lack of action, but also includes non-economic considerations such as acceptability to the public.

This latter point is interesting. Here, and it seems only here, the Commission has sought to integrate social acceptability into the core risk management concept; in this case cost-benefit analysis. In this way, what is adjudged to be efficient will depend, inter alia, upon public sentiment as to the acceptability of the risk. So little detail is given that it is impossible to assess the weight to be given to public opinion, or the methodological basis according to which this will be determined. Nonetheless, conceptually this is important in that it seeks to define the concept in such a way as to reflect the quest for social legitimacy among decision-makers. There is no suggestion that public opinion is to impact similarly upon conceptions of the rational, or upon assessments of proportionality. There is no suggestion even that divergent public opinion will serve to distinguish risks which are otherwise represented as comparable, thus serving to justify differential treatment in a manner which is nonetheless consistent with the Community's stated commitment to coherence and consistency. Yet perhaps this is precisely the challenge facing the Community. It is vital that it operates mechanisms for the application of the precautionary principle which are confident not only in their assertion of the scientific basis for decision-making, but which also articulate a defined role, and defined limits, for public opinion, and for considerations of social acceptability. One specific point may be made in this respect, though it is an issue to which we will return in our concluding comments.

As noted above, the WTO Appellate Body concluded in the hormones 'case' that theoretical risk, arising by virtue of the impossibility of ever proving a product or substance completely safe for all time, is not the kind of risk to be assessed under Article 5:1, and that consequently risk regulation measures taken pursuant to this kind of risk cannot be said to be 'based on' a risk assessment within the meaning of the SPS Agreement. Less clear is the issue of whether theoretical risk of this kind may legitimately form the subject of provisional regulation adopted under Article 5:7, this constituting a specific enunciation of the precautionary principle. Whereas this speaks of the insufficiency of scientific evidence, this tells us nothing about the threshold to be applied. Certainly if the provision is to be meaningful the threshold must operate at a level which is lower than those prevailing elsewhere in the Agreement. Nonetheless, it is by no means certain that it will be set at the level of theoretical risk of this kind. And yet this has the most profound implications from the perspective of social legitimacy. It may be that a society, or societies, confronted with the emergence of new technologies will choose to restrain their development, even where the risks associated with them are no more than theoretical, until such a time as it is accepted by them that the benefits which will potentially ensue are such as to render any risk, even theoretical, worth enduring. This would be especially the case where, as in 'hormones', there is deemed to be no more than a theoretical risk even though the substances in question are demonstrably dangerous, but in respect of which there is no specifically focused scientific research evidencing a risk associated with a specific given application. It seems clear that, from a perspective of social legitimacy, the more than 'merely' theoretical risk threshold is one which is woefully misconceived.

C. The Precautionary Principle and Food Regulation

The communication on the precautionary principle is, however, of a general scope and is, as the Commission itself admits, a starting point which requires further study of the conditions of risk assessments, management and communication.[110] It is therefore of great interest to examine how the Commission will elaborate its position on the precautionary principle in the specific policy fields. In November 2000, the Commission proposed to apply the precautionary principle in risk management decisions on food issues,[111] applying its communication for the first time.[112] The Commission's proposal to apply the precautionary principle to food safety does not come as a surprise and must be viewed against the background of the BSE crisis. The BSE crisis of 1996 clearly demonstrated that where important political interests are at stake, the Commission's former ad hoc approach to food regulation was not sufficient to guarantee an effective and legitimate food safety policy, or decision-making free from manipulation and capture. In response to the BSE crisis, the Commission sought to present a more coherent approach to food safety based on true 'principles' of a separation of responsibility for legislation and scientific advice, a separation of responsibility for legislation and inspection, and greater transparency and information throughout the decision-making and inspection processes, whilst disciplining the production of scientific advice by means of the principles of excellence, independence and transparency. In its White Paper on Food Safety of 12 January 2000 the Commission proposes to refine and reinforce these principles,[113] which are

[110] Communication, *supra* n. 11, at 22.
[111] Proposal for a European Parliament and Council Regulation laying down the general principles and requirements of food law, establishing a European Food Authority and laying down procedures in matters of food safety, COM(2000) 716. Recently, the Commission presented its amended proposal. See COM(2001) 475 final.
[112] See also in the context for the Community's fisheries policy: Communication from the Commission to the Council and the European Parliament—Application of the precautionary principle and multiannual arrangements for setting TACs, COM(2000) 803 final.

further elaborated in the Commission's recent proposal for a general food law.

Of importance for our analysis, and new in the history of Community food legislation, is the proposal's explicit reference to the precautionary principle. In the explanatory memorandum to the proposal, the Commission recognizes the precautionary principle as 'an option open to risk managers when decisions have to be made to protect health or the environment but scientific information concerning risks is inconclusive or incomplete in some way'.[114] Paragraph (1) of Article 7 of the amended proposal therefore stipulates that:

In circumstances where, following an assessment of available information, the possibility of harmful effects has been identified but scientific uncertainty persists, provisional risk management measures necessary to ensure the high level of health protection chosen in the Community may be adopted, pending further scientific information for a more comprehensive risk assessment.

Paragraph (2) of this Article subsequently stipulates its commitment to the principles of proportionality and least restrictive means, and requires that account be taken of technical and economic feasibility and other factors 'regarded as legitimate to the matter under consideration'. It commands that the measures thus taken should be 'reviewed within a reasonable period of time, depending on the nature of the risk to life or health identified and the type of scientific information needed to clarify the scientific uncertainty and to conduct a more comprehensive risk assessment'.

This phrasing of the precautionary principle is important in that it seems to allow it to be invoked both by the Community and the Member States, although always within the limits of the proportionality principle. It also indicates that the measures taken must be of a temporary nature until further scientific information for a more comprehensive assessment is available. Yet the wording can be criticized in that it does not determine when the scientific information is sufficiently uncertain to adopt provisional measures, and who will establish that scientific uncertainty exists (national or Community authorities), allowing for provisional measures. Disputes on these issues are hence likely to arise.

The Commission sets high store on the quality of scientific information, in its eyes essential to restore consumer confidence in food regulation. To this end, the Commission proposes to create a European Food Authority (EFA). This body is to replace and absorb the Community's system of scientific committees. The EFA, supported by the European Council of Nice,[115] will be entrusted with the task of providing the Community institutions with 'first class, independent scientific opinions',[116] the gathering and analysis of

---

[113] COM(1999) 719 final.   [114] *Supra* n. 111, point 1.5, at 9, initial proposal.
[115] Presidency Conclusions, n. 1 above, para. 36.
[116] *Supra* n. 111, point 2.1, at 13, initial proposal.

information, management of the Community's rapid alert system and the communication of risk. In addition, it will play a key role in the management of crisis situations falling within the sphere of the Commission's responsibilities. The EFA would have to demonstrate the highest level of independence, of scientific excellence and of transparency in its operations and would be at the centre of a network of scientific contacts, namely, national scientific agencies and institutions. In cases in which consultation of the EFA is not compulsory, the European Parliament and the Member States, as well as the Commission, may address requests to the EFA for a scientific opinion. The EFA may also issue an opinion on its own initiative. Although it goes beyond the scope of this chapter to discuss the proposed EFA in detail, two points must be highlighted.

First, two particular proposals seem to put the Community's commitment to both science and transparency, participation and social acceptability into practice to some extent. Important and new is its proposal to introduce into the composition of the EFA's management board four representatives of consumers and industry designated by the Commission, in addition to four representatives appointed by the Council, four appointed by the Commission and four representatives appointed by the Parliament.[117] This, in the Commission's view, will serve to facilitate 'the involvement of EFA's many and diverse stakeholders, independence from external pressures, transparency and accountability to the democratic institutions'.[118] The EFA is furthermore charged with the task of communicating on food issues falling within its competence, although the Commission remains responsible for communication on risk management decisions. The EFA must thus ensure that the public and any interested party are rapidly given 'objective, reliable and easily understandable information'.[119] Although these proposals are clearly far from resolving the tension between scientific reason and the reason of non-expert participants in food regulation, they might be viewed as a first attempt to release this tension.

Second, and very interesting, is the Commission's proposal in relation to situations of diverging scientific opinion between national and Community bodies. As we noted above, such situations are increasingly likely to occur. The most manifest example of this tendency has been the conflict between France, the UK and the Commission on the refusal by France to allow British beef into their market in 1999. In this case, on the basis of the opinion of the Scientific Steering Committee, the Community decided to lift the ban on the export of British beef under a specific export scheme as from 1 August 1999. France, and later also Germany, however, refused to lift the ban, as according to its own *Agence Française de Sécurité Sanitaire des Aliments*,[120] the beef still constituted a danger to human health. The Commission made several efforts

---

[117] Ibid., Article 25, amended proposal.   [118] Ibid., point 2.3, at 15.
[119] Ibid., Article 39.   [120] See its dossiers on <http://www.afssa.fr/>.

to reach a solution that was consistent with Community law and satisfied the parties concerned. Yet, on 4 January 2000, disappointed with the slow results, the Commission decided to bring France before the ECJ.[121]

In its proposal, the Commission nonetheless peeks to overcome the political impasse and endeavours to enhance the confidence of both Member States and European citizens in its system of risk assessment, and to strengthen the participation of Member States (and their competent authorities) in it. In this context, again new in the history of Community legislation, the Commission proposes that the EFA play an important role in anticipating conflicts between Community bodies or scientific committees between themselves and between the EFA and national bodies. Very wisely, the Commission does not empower the EFA to act as a final, scientific arbitrator in such cases. Instead, it introduces an obligation to co-operate.[122] In the event of a substantive divergence over scientific opinions, this body will be obliged to co-operate with the Community and national bodies and either resolve the divergence together or to present a document clarifying the contentious scientific issues. Such an obligation to co-operate might indeed work as an 'early warning' system and envisage a kind of 'learning process' analogue to the process foreseen in the Information Directive,[123] while also serving as a source of innovation through sharing and learning. Even were the EFA not able to resolve such scientific conflicts, this procedure would in any event provide the Commission with a clear understanding of the underlying scientific conflict and areas of contention. It may be clear that whenever scientific opinions continue to diverge, or where scientific opinion and public opinion diverge, this will result in a deadlock, thus again necessitating a solution which is conceived in a setting which looks beyond the merely scientific.

IV. CONCLUSIONS

Recent events in the EU and the WTO have highlighted the limits of science as an arbiter of international disputes, and the futility of looking exclusively

---

[121] Case 1/00, pending. Also France brought a case before the ECJ to challenge a statement of Commissioner Byrne. This case has, however, been declared inadmissible by the ECJ. Case C-514/99, *France v Commission* [2000] ECR I-4705.

[122] *Supra* n. 111, Article 30 (3 and amended proposal). Although the Commission does not make any reference, such an obligation could be seen in the light of Article 10 EC.

[123] Directive 98/34/EC (OJ 1998 L 204) consolidates Directive 83/189/EEC, as amended principally by Directives 88/182/EEC and 94/10/EC. For an analysis of the operation of this directive see Weatherill, 'Compulsory Notification of Draft Technical Regulations: The Contribution of Directive 83/189 to the Management of the Internal Market', 16 *YEL* (1996) 129 and Pelkmans, Vos and di Mauro, 'Reforming Product Regulation in the EU: A Painstaking, Iterative Two-level Game', in G. Galli and J. Pelkmans (eds), *Regulatory Reform for the Better Functioning of Markets* (2000).

to science in a bid to transcend politics in the management of globalizing markets. In the face of scientific conflicts, often at different levels of governance, and disparities in scientific and public opinion, it is all too apparent that scientific truth will in itself serve neither to quell public fears, nor to distinguish the acceptable from the unacceptable in terms of restrictions on trade. Never has this been clearer than in our age of precaution. Application of this principle demands that thresholds be identified and set, and that costs and benefits be articulated and evaluated. It is this task of setting parameters for the application of this principle which has, of late, preoccupied the Community institutions; the Commission, the European Council, and the courts. Much of interest is emerging, both conceptually and practically, in thinking about evolving institutional frameworks for the application of the principle. Nonetheless, profound tensions remain as the institutions continue to dodge the very grave difficulties, and especially those associated with the integration of expert and non-expert perspectives into decision-making. It is, however, clear that this integration will never be achieved until these difficulties are acknowledged and confronted. The Commission's spoken commitment to science in risk regulation, alongside transparency, participation and social acceptability, may be laudable, but in so far as the tensions lurk unacknowledged it remains unconvincing. One of the principal difficulties associated with a commitment to the democratization of risk regulation lies with the task of gauging public opinion(s). In our 'vote, shut up and obey' democracies, the links between parliaments and peoples are often tenuous in the extreme. As such, while the opinions of national and European parliaments may be relevant to an assessment of social acceptability, it might be that further evidence from a diverse range of sources may be required before public opinion can be allowed to play a role in justifying restrictions on imports predicated upon the risks which these goods or services present or are seen to present. In *Fedesa*, in assessing the validity of the Community's hormones directive, the European Court observed that:

. . . the Council remained within the limits of its discretionary power in deciding to adopt the solution of prohibiting the hormones in question, and respond in that way to the concerns expressed by the European Parliament, the Economic and Social Committee and by several consumer organizations.[124]

As such the Court looked beyond formal parliamentary structures to other government committees, and to non-governmental organizations. In so doing, however, it did not specify clearly the status or precise relevance of these viewpoints. Nor did it explore the basis of the opinions put forward by these bodies, either in terms of their substantive premises, or in terms of the procedures which led to their articulation. The Court did not engage critically

---

[124] Case 331/88, *R v MAFF ex parte Fedesa and Others* [1990] ECR I-4023, para. 9.

with the statements put forward. It did not seek to examine or assess the context in which these opinions were formed, or the nature of the procedural mechanisms according to which they were received or articulated. Important in this respect is the issue of whether the viewpoints were passively received and aggregated, or whether they took shape within a framework of discursive and critical engagement, and openness to arguments from competing positions and perspectives. These, however, are difficult issues to assess.

What lies behind these comments is an awareness of the profound difficulties associated with arguing that public opinion as to the acceptability of risk, fickle as it is, might legitimately serve to justify restrictions on trade. It creates an apparently open door whereby mere reference to public opinion will tend to undermine free trade. Equally, however, as is recognized by both the Commission and the European Council in their respective contributions on the precautionary principle, to exclude public opinion from risk assessment/management, and from questions of market access for particular goods and services, must surely be unthinkable in a world in which the contingency of knowledge is accepted and the concept of objective—even scientific—truth denied.

In a sense then, what is being hinted at here is the idea that in the same way as states must adduce evidence of the scientific basis of risk, so too they must be required to adduce evidence of the strength of public opinion as regards particular decisions in risk regulation. Such evidence may be quantitative or qualitative; the latter referring not to the proportion of the public so concerned (minority public opinion should be allowed to play a role alongside minority scientific opinion) but to the 'quality' of that opinion.

Quality in this sense may be concerned with more than merely the accuracy of the way in which the relevant viewpoints have been represented, but also with the way in which, and the institutional framework within which, these viewpoints have been formed. Relevant in this respect perhaps would be the question of exposure to competing arguments, and apparently conflicting information, including, crucially, viewpoints representing interests and perspectives from outside that state. It might be, in keeping with the current penchant for deliberative democracy, that emphasis would be placed upon the dialogic process, and upon the fact of argument and exchange. No single institutional blueprint would be advocated, states being free to experiment with new models of governance which are such as to allow for the expression of public opinion, and which facilitate the integration of these viewpoints. Thus, in a manner not dissimilar to the Appellate Body, with its emphasis upon the centrality of transnational negotiation and respect for due process, or the European Court, with its insistence upon the existence of open and accessible procedures which allow traders to seek an exemption from a given import restriction, the argument is that it is process along with substance which might serve to distinguish the legitimate from the arbitrary in the context of considerations of the social acceptability of risk. In the same way as science was formerly used to rubber-stamp decisions in the context of risk, with little or no assessment of the basis of the scientific claims, so too considerations of social acceptability with their roots in democracy are too important to be abused by states at their convenience rather than at the convenience of their more or less risk-averse publics. In a context of globalizing markets the authenticity of public opinion needs to be demonstrated, and not assumed to coincide with the (predominantly economic) interests of the state concerned.

SECTION IV

GOOD GOVERNANCE AND DEMOCRATIC THEORY

10

Directly-Deliberative Polyarchy:
An Institutional Ideal for Europe?

OLIVER GERSTENBERG and CHARLES F. SABEL*

INTRODUCTION

The continuing effort to harmonize the laws of the Member States of the European Union and the prospect of extending membership in the Union to new states intensifies the debate already underway in the Atlantic political community about the connections between democracy and the nation state as we know it since the time of the French and American Revolutions. Attention focuses on three concerns.

The first, particularly acute among European social democrats, is that the heterogeneous polity of the new Europe will undermine the political basis for a new European welfare state, even as the dominance of market-making (the negative integration that removes barriers to trade) over market-correcting (the positive integration of policies and regulations that protect citizens against market outcomes that might otherwise overwhelm them) destroys the basis of the existing national ones. Put another way, the creation of a common market leads to a loss of national boundary control, while the political decisions at the European level that might compensate are easily frustrated because of differences of interest or institutional obstacles.

The second concern regards a tension between the problem-solving capacities of and the possibilities for democratic participation in the system of multi-level governance (MLGS) emerging in the formal and informal

* For comments we would like to thank Gráinne de Búrca, Joshua Cohen, Michael Dorf, Klaus Günther, Christian Joerges, Frank Michelman, Andrew Moravcsik, Patrizia Nanz, Fritz Scharpf, Joanne Scott and Jonathan Zeitlin—and the participants of the AEL Course. For help with the manuscript we would like to thank Monika Hobbie (ZERP). As the title suggests, this essay develops arguments in 'Directly-Deliberative Polyarchy' (with Joshua Cohen), 3 *ELJ* (1997) 313. For the background conception of the new class of institutions, such as the Open Method of Coordination, discussed below, see Sabel, 'Learning by Monitoring: The Institutions of Economic Development', in N. Smelser and R. Swedberg (eds), *Handbook of Economic Sociology* (1994) 137.

interplay of Member States, European Commission, European Parliament, Council of Ministers and European Court of Justice (ECJ). The worry is that the sheer complexity of this MLGS, and especially its reliance on technocratic deliberation, renders implausible even the most modest assumption of effective political oversight by an informed citizenry. Excluded from politics, the best citizens can get from their democracy—the reward as it were for their acquiescence in decisions they can scarcely influence—is a responsive administration or 'good governance'.

The third concern, less salient to citizens, more to constitutional theorists, is captured in the question, Why does the 'higher', but 'weakly legitimated', European law in fact increasingly trump the 'strongly legitimated' law of the nation states? On the one hand, political authority in the MLGS remains based on international treaties, which rest in turn on the sovereignty of the Member States. On the other hand, however, there is de facto within the MLGS a substantial accretion of authority by supranational institutions such as the ECJ and Commission. The EU is thus no longer merely an instrument of the will of the Member States.[1] On the contrary, European law possesses a primacy over the law of the Member States, but it is also directly applicable to the citizens. Indeed the doctrine of direct effect makes citizens in many circumstances the addressees of binding and coercive law, tenuously derived from the (democratically elected) national governments, rather than originating from the united citizens of Europe themselves.

These three concerns, and the accompanying sense of narrowing political possibilities, are European in their cadences and references. But they reflect a deeper antinomy within contemporary democratic and constitutional theory between two lines of thought we will call the personificationist thesis and the non-demos or reasonable-pluralism thesis.

The personificationist thesis, associated we will see with authors as different as Habermas and Dworkin, holds that any egalitarian notion of democracy, including especially those built on some combination of solidaristic redistribution and the requirement that law be justified by reasons acceptable to all as free and equal citizens, depends in principle on the existence of a demos or 'political community personified', capable of harnessing preexisting commonalities for the creation of a collective identity above the level of primary groups. In practice this political community is the nation state, with its self-evident identity, arising from the spontaneous mutuality and transparency of its citizens, and its insistence on the distinction between members and non-members of the relevant collectivity for purposes of defining whose welfare is to be counted in the distributive process.

---

[1] 'The community constitutes a new legal order . . . for the benefit of which the states have limited their sovereign rights, albeit within limited fields, and the subjects of which comprise not only Member States but also their nationals.' Case 26/62, *van Gend en Loos* [1963] ECR 1.

The non-demos or reasonable-pluralism thesis asserts that under conditions of modernity actual political communities do not have the demotic characteristics that the personificationist thesis requires of them. In the European legal disputes this thesis has been reduced to a syllogism by the *Bundesverfassungsgericht.* Only a demos meeting the conditions of self-evidence and mutual transparency that mark a personified citizenry can make law for itself; Europe, being a composite of nations, has no such European demos; there can be no general European law with the legitimacy of national, demotic law.

Among constitutionalists on both sides of the Atlantic the same concern with the heterogeneity of the modern polity is expressed as recognition of the fact of 'reasonable pluralism'. Citizens of the same polity view the world, or the good life, in fundamentally different ways despite continuing, good-faith efforts to arrive at common understandings. These differences undermine the legitimacy of the higher, constitutional law as an expression of just such commonalities, and so limit its power to protect minorities against the predations of bigoted or selfish majorities.

The clash of the personificationist and reasonable-pluralism theses produces a new appreciation, bordering on nostalgia, for the nation state as necessary to the political expression of solidarity. The reaction is all the more poignant in just those quarters that traditionally regarded the Romantic identification of the citizens as a people bound together by ties of language and history as, at best, a latent threat to the ideal of an inclusive polity, at worst, a standing invitation to war.

This essay argues that the opening boundaries of the modern polity, the undeniable increase in heterogeneity that follows, and the manifold institutional responses that these changes in turn provoke are better seen as creating the occasion for, indeed in part anticipating, a radical re-definition of our democratic and constitutional ideals, rather than as signs of a democratic declension. Our core claim is that the exploration of difference, as it may occur in choosing among diverse solutions to the pressing problems of everyday life (the task of harmonization most broadly conceived), can provide the basis for protection for the economically vulnerable and the politically disdained that may become as effective under emerging conditions as the policies of redistribution and judicial determination of rights were in the world that is passing.

The institutional armature of this new principle of differential, democratic problem-solving we will call experimentalism or directly-deliberative polyarchy. In a deliberative polyarchy local-, or, more exactly, lower-level actors (nation states or national peak organizations of various kinds within the EU; regions, provinces or sub-national associations within these, and so on down to the level of whatever kind of neighbourhood the problem in question makes relevant) are granted autonomy to experiment with solutions of their own devising within broadly defined areas of public policy. In return they furnish central or higher-level units with rich information regarding their goals as well as the progress they are making towards achieving them, and agree to respect in their actions framework rights of democratic procedure and substance as these are elaborated in the course of experimentation itself. The periodic pooling of results reveals the defects of parochial solutions, and allows the elaboration of standards for comparing local achievements, exposing poor performers to criticism from within and without, and making of good ones (temporary) models for emulation. We call this system directly-deliberative because it depends crucially on the exploration of possibilities, and the discovery of unsuspected ones, that occur when actors come to grips with their differences in the course of solving common problems that none can resolve alone. The contrast is with the notion common to theories of civic republicanism and other discursive ideas of democracy of deliberation at a distance, by an administrative or political elite that defines the public good in abstraction from everyday immediacies. We call the emergent form of democracy polyarchic to emphasize the permanent dis-equilibrium created by the grant of substantial powers of initiative to lower-level units. No sooner do promising solutions emerge in one place than they are being re-elaborated through adaptation to different circumstances elsewhere.

We assume as a background condition a world of radical indeterminacy or complexity, in which actors at all levels cannot solve their own problems without continuing collaboration with others whose experiences, orientations and even most general goals will differ from their own. The need for such connections can arise from any of several causes: because each actor's solutions require complementary ones that cannot be identified precisely in advance of actually undertaking the project; or because each solution generates externalities that can only be detected and mitigated with the co-operation of others. Put another way, in a world of radical indeterminacy, or because the costs of exploring the most promising potential solutions would over-burden the most capable actor, and therefore even the strongest favour some division of investigative labour to incurring the risks of choosing and executing a solution alone. In such a world—to whose verisimilitude the creation and continuing elaboration of the EU bears witness—the constant testing and re-examination of assumptions and practices that results from permanent, polyarchic dis-equilibrium will itself provide a powerful motive for jurisdictions of many kinds to participate in the problem-solving and information-pooling that experimentalism requires. Insofar as homogeneity is more nearly a curse than a blessing in such a world, and openness to difference, paradoxically, a pre-condition for preservation of identity we can think of de-nationalization or the end of the Romantic identity of people and state as a pre-condition and consequence of directly deliberative polyarchy.

To respond fully to the most pressing fears of the social democrats and constitutionalists we would have to extend this sparest sketch of directly-deliberative polyarchy in two directions, and show the empirical plausibility of both extensions. We would have to show, first, how, beginning with engagement with currently pressing problems such as, for example, the harmonization of the laws of EU Member States, the emergent regime could reasonably be expected to provide a web of protective rules and related services that together afforded citizens of the Union protections against untrammelled market operations arguably equivalent to those enjoyed under the welfare state. A starting point for this argument would be the idea of radical indeterminacy itself, and in particular its implication that, in a complex world, 'strong' actors cannot rule out the possibility that they will come to depend on solutions discovered by 'weak' ones. Then we would have to demonstrate how this link or entanglement leads not to the recognition of a solidarity of sentiment, but to an institutional acknowledgement and commitment to sustain a commonality of capabilities—especially the ability to engage, as citizens, in common forms of problem-solving that underpin, and render mutually intelligible, the efforts dedicated to separate projects. The resulting web of connections might (indeed very probably would) have the consequence of redistributing resources from one group to another; but redistribution would be the consequence of a solution adopted first and foremost to address broad common problems (above all, the problem of maintaining the ability to address together, as a democracy, unforeseen problems), not correct social or economic imbalances. Standards requiring that citizens be provided with 'adequate' environmental protection, employment policies, workplace health and safety, and education and vocational training, where 'adequate' is continuously redefined in the light of experimental advances in the respective areas, would have this result.

We would have to show, second, how, using the information about intentions and results provided as a matter of course in these experimental efforts, courts could frame background rules of constitutional order precise enough to provide the securities of citizenship to even disadvantaged groups, yet open enough to permit—indeed require—citizens, using the possibilities for directly-deliberative elaboration of norms afforded by the new architecture of democracy, to actively explore and redefine the meanings of constitutional norms in everyday life. Agreement on constitutional essentials might, indeed very probably would, result from this collaborative interpretation. Such agreement would resemble in its texture, though not the degree of its entrenchment, more the open-ended and self-questioning results of (subconstitutional) legal or regulatory harmonization than the strictures of constitutional law that are displayed today as the tenants of a people's integrity or the purified postulates of justice itself. We will see how the *Bosman* and other[2] decisions of the ECJ, as well as developments in the harmonization of EU

[2] Case C-415/93, *Union royale belge des sociétés de football association ASBL et al. v Jean-Marc Bosman* [1995] ECR I-4921. As to other cases, see n. 88, n. 89 and n. 94 below.

contract law, provide models for how this shift from a vertical conception of constitutional jurisprudence might be accomplished.

Judged with respect to these goals, this essay, conceived as the exploratory opening of a larger programme of enquiry, pursues more modest ambitions. Though we will be mindful throughout of the large burdens that our claims regarding the potential of a directly-deliberative alternative to representative democracy impose, we concentrate here on tracing the often paradoxical origins of the constitutionalists' and social democrats' fears; showing that these fears are empirically unfounded; and that the evidence against them, together with other circumstances, strongly suggest that the emerging legal integrity of the contemporary Europe is the outcome and expression of the new architecture for democracy.

Section I shows how, confronted with the fact of reasonable pluralism, constitutional theory in the US and Europe discovered itself to be founded not on principle but on *patria*. In Section II we observe a related set of debates played out among social democrats and economic liberals: both agree that the fundamental dichotomies are those of market and politics, egoism and visceral solidarity. They agree further that the globalization of markets undermines the nation-state foundations of politics. Hence the social democrats' nostalgia for the nation and the liberals' jubilation at the prospect of a world economy without politics.

In Section III we argue that the circle of discussion is wider, and the horizon of possibilities it reveals broader and more promising than the initial survey suggests. Two overlapping lines of research and discussion are especially important correctives to the constitutionalist and social-democratic views. The first is a series of careful investigations of the progress and outcome of efforts to harmonize EU regulations in areas such as consumer protection against dangerous products, workplace safety, environmental protection, financial regulation, and transportation policy. Many of these studies were prompted by social-democratic concerns with the threat to the welfare state supposedly inherent in harmonization; and the expected outcome was, accordingly, a race to the regulatory bottom in each area. In the event the results rarely, if ever, confirmed the hypothesis. In most cases the outcome was more nearly a race to the top—the elaboration through the process of harmonization itself of a regulatory regime that is more demanding than that in place in most, sometimes all, the EU Member States. Of course theoretical anomalies can always be explained as exceptional cases, arising under conditions outside the domain covered by the theory; and some social democratic writers have not hesitated to provide the requisite emendations to their original propositions. Others, sensing that the exceptions now overwhelm in number and importance the ruley results, are beginning to treat them not as aberrations but rather as the expressions of a systematic, if ill-understood form of public governance: the 'substitute' democracy of the new Europe.

A second line of research, concerned with 'comitology'—the networks of expert and interest-group committees to which the Commission entrusts elaboration of its regulatory initiatives—arrives at a strikingly similar conclusion. The research accepts the lay view that comitology is so opaque in its operations and removed from the normal controls of democratic oversight as to have the aspect of a nearly conspiratorial convocation of insiders against the public interest. But closer investigation shows that, appearances notwithstanding, comitology, like the regulatory processes of which it is a part, is not an engine for converting pressure-group interests into policies, and still less for driving a downward spiral of deregulation. Rather, as an institution it proves capable of practical, problem-solving deliberation, and so of producing results which arguably embody the public interest in novel ways precisely by exploring the differences in current understandings of it. Hence there is an interpretation of comitology as a kind of 'deliberative supranationalism', a clique of experts owing allegiance to their professional honour, not any sovereign state or domestic interest, that conspires for, not against the international public of the new Europe. So despite its resemblance to the cosmopolitan officialdom of the cameralist bureaucracies of the late Absolutist states, comitology too can be thought of as a 'substitute' democracy.

Critics are understandably quick to point out that these interpretations give little reason to view the institutional innovations that make Europe work as a 'substitute' democracy—or, more exactly, a variation on familiar democratic institutions—rather than simply and ominously as a substitute for democracy. But this criticism itself supposes, without pausing to say why, that the only alternative to the democracy we know is none at all.

Section IV challenges that supposition conceptually and empirically in interpreting the EU as an emergent directly-deliberative democracy. First it provides the conceptual rudiments for experimentalist polyarchy by contrasting its assumptions to those of the social democrats, constitutionalists, and the exponents of a 'substitute' democracy. Notice in all of these discourses the unbridgeable gulf between effortless and complete mutual understanding founded on identity, and selfish, incommunicable and uncomprehending solipsism. *Either* (in the social-democratic view) the citizens are a nation, in which case they are transparent to one another, and generous because palpably similar; *or* they pursue their self-interest without regard to other. *Either* (in the constitutional view) the citizens will share constitutional fundamentals, and therefore can agree to accord one another extensive rights to mutual regard; *or* they do not share them, and only inertia can shelter them from the ravages of their differences. *Either* (in the 'substitute' democracy view) decision-making is entrusted to experts, able to deliberate practically because of the professionalism that binds them together even as it sets them off from the citizens; *or* the latter are left to their own devices and to disarray. Drawing on familiar and influential arguments in variants of pragmatist philosophy associated with Davidson[3] and others, we will argue in contrast that understanding within a language—more difficult and fraught with ambiguity than these juxtapositions suggest—is itself a kind of translation among the local languages of particular speakers, and translation between languages is therefore a possibility, being in fact an extension of just the kind of work native speakers must accomplish to grasp one another's meaning. From this vantage the exchange of ideas among those with differing views of the world is a condition of self-understanding, not a feat of transcendence. Identities and interests are emergent, not fixed. Jurisdictional boundaries are not fixed limits and reminders of identity, but rather the starting points for problem-solving investigations which entertain the possibility, among other things, of revising the boundaries along with the conceptions they mark. The polity, no longer personified, itself gives meaning to the frameworks it adopts, and need no longer delegate this task to a separate administration of experts. Formulations of this sort raise at once the suspicion that we intend only to reverse the sign of familiar debates and make society, suddenly discovered to be self-regulating, its own immediate and exclusive sovereign. To avoid misunderstanding we therefore contrast our view with two schools of thought which do exalt society in this way: the social law of Gourvitch,[4] which (as heir to the Durkheimian tradition) sees a spontaneous mutualism of the social parts, owing to (their recognition of) the natural division of labour among them and the related idea of autopoesis, in which each participant takes account of the activities of the other, while remaining within a conceptual world all its own.

The second step of the argument is to show how this alternative characterization of the relation of ambiguity and idiom is reflected in the institutions of directly-deliberative polyarchy in general, and emergent features of the EU in particular. Here we show how the very institutions that produce a permanent dis-equilibrium in rules enable a continuing discussion of differences that clarifies as much what each entity does alone as what it does with the others. Then we show how continuing clarification opens the way to an upward drift of regulation which can be understood as a harbinger of the more encompassing and constitutional connections we envisage.

I. FALSE DICHOTOMY: MARKET VERSUS 'POLITICAL COMMUNITY PERSONIFIED' (DEMOS)

In contemporary European constitutional debate constitutionalism and democracy have become antagonists, with the survival of the one seeming to require

---

[3] D. Davidson, *Inquiries into Truth and Interpretation* (1984).
[4] G. Gurvitch, *L'idée du droit social* (1931).

sacrifice of the other. Authors in the tradition of economic liberalism celebrate the Europeanization process because it seems ultimately to disconnect constitutionalism from democratic practice and to firmly entrench a logic of market evolution that marginalizes politics. Social democrats have come to believe that democracy can only flourish if the solidary politics of the nation retains its sovereignty against cosmopolitan, 'constitutional' intrusions from without. In this section we examine this antagonism from both perspectives, emphasizing the commonalities that join the views despite their manifest differences.

The liberal view proceeds from the idea that the true function of constitutionalism is to protect a set of well-circumscribed private rights from the vicissitudes of pluralist politics, placing them beyond the reach of majorities by establishing them as legal principles to be applied by the courts. Constitutionalism, in such a world, provides the integrity and fidelity to principle that democratic politics, given the inevitable pluralism of incorrigible, pre-political identities and interests, inherently lacks. This framework suggests that even if democratic politics lingers on in the Member States of the EU, the economic rights and liberties of the market citizen are supposed to constitute the true higher law of the Union. It is the task of the Community to implement and protect a system of open markets and undistorted competition, while the Member States retain those legislative powers that prove compatible with open markets.[5] The chain binding law and democratic politics breaks. European law comes to have a distinctive legitimacy, derived from utilitarian consideration and independent of democracy. The very rationale and goal of the European Community is to separate economics and politics as far as possible.

The ideas of the feasibility of an 'economic integration without political integration', of 'carefully' keeping the 'economic and the political tracks . . . separate', and of a '[d]epoliticization of European policymaking'[6] stand, for example, behind Majone's argument that the legitimacy of the European integration process should not be assessed by standards appropriate for the nation state. His whole argument depends on the distinction, well-known from legal theory, between efficiency-oriented and distribution-oriented standards of legitimacy. The latter belong to the world of bargaining, preference aggregation and majoritarianism. Decisions involving significant redistribution of

[5] Mestmäcker, 'On the Legitimacy of European Law', 58 *RabelsZ* (1994) 615, at 633. The German version is even more straightforward, idem, 'Zur Wirtschaftsverfassung in der Europäischen Union', in R. H. Hasse, J. Molsberger and C. Watrin (eds), *Ordnung und Freiheit*. Festgabe für Hans Willgerodt zum 70. Geburtstag, 263, at 274. It runs: 'Aufgabe der Gemeinschaft ist es bei dieser Betrachtung, die wirtschaftlichen Freiheitsrechte, den Binnenmarkt und das System des unverfälschten Wettbewerbs mit Vorrang vor dem Recht der Mitgliedstaaten zu gewährleisten. Den Mitgliedstaaten bliebe es überlassen, die demokratische Legitimation beanspruchenden, diskretionären Politiken in eigener Zuständigkeit, aber unter den Bedingungen offener Märkte zu betreiben.'

[6] Majone, 'Europe's "Democratic Deficit": The Question of Standards', 14 *ELJ* (1998), at 17.

resources from one group to another cannot, Majone says, legitimately be delegated to some independent experts, but must be taken by elected officials or
by administrators directly responsible to elected officials. They carry with
them the relatively low rationality-presumptions of strategic politics, and the
concept of democracy is identified with the majority principle. Efficiency-
oriented standards in contrast are geared towards the correction of market
failures and towards the increase of the efficiency of market transactions
(problem-solving).[7] A pre-condition of the accountability of decision-making
in the realm of efficiency-oriented standards is that they be taken in greatest
possible isolation from the pressures and distortions stemming from the
world of strategic/distributive politics. Majone recognizes that 'regulatory
policies, like all public policies, have distributive consequences'.[8] But he
believes nonetheless that it is possible to identify a class of (predominantly)
efficiency-oriented decisions or policy areas, with regard to which a 'delegation' to independent institutions is democratically justifiable as a method of
achieving credible policy commitments. By contrast, where distributive concerns prevail, accountability is 'political' and legitimacy can be ensured only
by majoritarian means. Thus, as it turns out, in the case of efficiency-oriented
standards the decision-makers' independence and democratic accountability
are complementary and mutually reinforcing rather than antithetical values.
Majone also suggests that we should think of there being a 'right to exercise
public authority' and that this 'right' is conceivable of in terms of a 'political'
property right which can be allocated to actors in more or less efficient ways.
Delegation, in this perspective, amounts to a 'transfer of political property
rights in a given policy to decision-makers who are one step removed from
election returns'.[9] Moreover, 'the stronger the legal basis of independence, the
better defined are the rights of the new "owners" '.[10]

Three important consequences follow. First, this view leads to an understanding of the EU as a device for firmly entrenching 'political property rights'
as a defence against 'democracy' as a world of purely strategic interaction,
majoritarianism and preference-aggregation. The logic which drives the
European integration process, from this perspective, is to strengthen—to
'constitutionalize'—the 'legal basis of independence' of a realm of de-
politicized processes of decision-making, hived off from the contingencies of
strategic politics and faithful to efficiency-oriented standards. Accordingly,
the normative standards for evaluating the EC institutions should essentially
be efficiency-oriented rather than distribution-oriented. Hence the claim that
the apparent European 'democracy deficit' is, at a deeper level, 'democratically
justified'[11] as a legitimate way of respecting the epistemological and normative differences between different realms.

---

[7] Notice the trenchant criticism by Duncan Kennedy in *A Critique of Adjudication* (1997).
[8] Majone, *supra* n. 6 above.   [9] Ibid.   [10] Ibid.   [11] Ibid., at 7.

Second, the distinction between efficiency-oriented and distributive standards, and the 'de-politicization' of European policy-making that comes with it, has the consequence (as Majone himself asserts) of largely preserving national sovereignty intact. This implies on the one hand that EC institutions must be thought of as a regulatory branch of the Member States, as a fourth branch of government within a total complex comprising the EU and the Member States. The nation states here are the principals and the supranational European institutions are the agents. Delegation becomes the crucial device of achieving political accountability and legitimacy in a de-nationalized setting. National policy-makers alone would lack credibility both domestically and in the eyes of policy-makers from other Member States. Furthermore, national capacities to monitor international agreements in areas where regulatory discretion is unavoidable are low. The 'deep cleavages'[12] within the EU—linguistic, economic, the division between large and small Member States—make rule-making by majoritarian procedures unlikely. Hence the way to address trans-boundary problems that leave room for substantial regulatory discretion is to delegate regulatory decision-making to politically independent agencies on two conditions. The first is that they reduce the possibilities of abuse ex ante by institutionalizing reason-giving requirements and rules 'defining the rights of various groups to participate directly in the decision-making'. The second is that they ensure ex-post monitoring through legislative and executive oversight, judicial review and attention to citizens' complaints. Not only do economic and political integration—as Majone says—proceed 'at different speeds', but they 'also follow different principles'[13]—supranationalism in the first case, intergovernmentalism in the second case.

But third, the kind of delegation needed to mediate and ensure solidarity among strangers in a de-nationalized setting characterized by 'deep cleavages' breaks with the traditional understanding of the concept as expressed in the familiar *Meroni* doctrine of the ECJ.[14] According to this doctrine, delegation is only feasible and legitimate when in some sense it is not needed: when, that is, the delegating authority is sufficiently knowledgeable about future states of the relevant world-segment to anticipate and control consequences and side-effects of the regulatory process. One sign of this capacity is the ability to distinguish clearly between the generation and application of a rule. Contrary to

---

[12] Ibid., at 11.　　　　[13] Ibid., at 14.

[14] Case 9/56, *Meroni & Co. Industrie Metallurgiche S.p.A. v High Authority of the ECSC*, [1958] ECR 133; Case 10/56, *Meroni & Co. Industrie Metallurgiche S.p.A. v High Authority of the ECSC*, [1958] ECR 157. The core of the *Meroni* doctrine is:

The Commission may not delegate more extensive powers than it enjoys itself. The delegation may only be in relation to the preparation or carrying through of decisions. The Commission may not delegate a latitude for judgment or discretion. The delegated competence must remain under the control and responsibility of the Commission. The institutional balance between the EC institutions may not be distorted.

this traditional understanding, Majone emphasizes the independence of agencies, the impossibility of exercising control from any fixed place in the system, and the need therefore to establish accountability ex ante, for example by linking the grant to reason-giving requirements.

The upshot is an irreconcilable conflict within this school of thought itself. The traditional form of delegation, based on confidence in technical logic, is needed to legitimate the EU. The non-traditional form of delegation, based on the recognition of technical ambiguity (or rather the impossibility of distinguishing cleanly between the political and the technical in the first place), is required to make the EU work. Students of US administrative law will find nothing novel in this conceptual tension except, perhaps, the confidence that it will somehow prove more amenable to resolution in the EU's adaptation of US practice than it has in its homeland.

By contrast, the social democrats fear above all that this emergent form of transnational governance will undo such progress as pluralist democracies have made towards the redistributive welfare state. Consider the defensive turn of the European social democrats in response to the construction of the EU. This line of argument is best seen as a chastened emendation of Marshall's theory of the social evolution of citizenship rights, one of the most influential formulations of the claim that reform, not revolution, is the telos of historical progress. Marshall defined social policy as the use of 'political power to supersede, supplement or modify operations of the economic system in order to achieve results which the economic system would not achieve of its own, . . . guided by values other than those determined by open market forces'.[15] He claimed further that in modern nation states citizenship tends to progress from the economic right to enter markets and contract to the political right to participate in democratic governance and on to the social right to a decent material existence, regardless of market vicissitudes.[16]

The core of the 'neo'-Marshallian, social democratic position is the conviction that this learning process cannot be expected to spill over to, and to unfold on, the Community level. This being so, further progress toward an 'ever closer union' in Europe is an undesirable, perhaps (given the tenuous democratic underpinnings of EU law) an illegitimate political goal.[17] While the problem-solving capacity and the democratic legitimacy of national governments are being weakened, the loss is not—as the protagonists of this view argue—fully 'compensated' at the European level. Accordingly (and paradoxically), on this view, the scope of national policy choices should be enlarged.[18] There are two mutually reinforcing types of arguments for this position: argu-

[15] T. H. Marshall, *Social Policy* (1975), at 15.
[16] T. H. Marshall, *Class, Citizenship and Social Development* (1977).
[17] So explicitly F. Scharpf, 'Democratic Policy in Europe', 2 *ELJ* (1996) 136; idem, *Governing in Europe, Effective and Democratic?* (1999).
[18] Ibid.

ments concerning the normative pre-conditions of the democracy principle, and arguments concerning the effectiveness of political choices.

The normative argument, as recently advanced by Scharpf, is as follows: redistributive democracy is premised upon cultural identity and upon the public-interest orientation of citizens. When we speak of democratic legitimation, we refer to arguments that establish a moral duty to obey collectively binding decisions even if these conflict with our individual preferences. Without a collective identity, however, citizens would not be prepared to treat their fellow citizens' interests in regard to particular issues as (equal to) their own. Redistributive democracy thus presupposes boundaries as a condition for or expression of the distinction between members and non-members of the relevant collectivity. To drive his point home, Scharpf distinguishes between a (procedure-oriented) 'input-legitimacy' and a (substance-oriented) 'output-legitimacy'. The argument is that while shared national identity is a nearly self-evident condition for 'input-legitimacy' (who, after all, would we be apart from our mutual knowledge of who we are?), it proves to be a condition of the apparently less demanding 'output-legitimacy' as well.

Without a common identity requirement, Scharpf maintains, we risk regression to a crude, pluralist democracy, which offers no warrant that the majority will take into consideration the interests of the minority. 'At bottom . . . notions of democracy that rely exclusively on the "will of the people" as a source of political legitimacy must assume conditions of a strong collective identity that overrides concerns based on divergent preferences and interests.'[19] The strong collective identity requirement (CIR) is thought to be necessary in order to provide a foundation for constitutional guarantees and rights—conceived as external constraints on the democratic process—and, above all, to ensure the possibility of market-correcting redistribution. Put another way, the CIR is thought to be necessary in order to justify the citizens' trust that the welfare of the minority figures as an argument in the preference function of the majority.

The argument can, moreover, be extended from re-distributive to deliberative democracy. Public deliberation, Scharpf observes, creates its own constraints: certain arguments will simply count as unacceptable in a public setting. These constraints, however, can only be made operative if arguing is defined in relation to the reference group whose collective interests would be affected by the policy options discussed. Appeals to shared criteria of justice, in turn, are premised upon the CIR. In sum, only when participants have already internalized criteria of justice and thus share a national identity is it possible to reach outcomes that regard the public interest from the

[19] F. Scharpf, *Interdependence and Democratic Legitimation*, Cologne, Max Planck Institute for the Study of Societies, <http://www.mpi-fg-koeln.mpg.de/pu/workpap/wp98–2/wp98–2. html>. Similar ideas are also expressed in Scharpf, *Governing in Europe*, *supra* n. 17.

un-compelled preferences of the citizens. This requirement of a substantive solidaristic bond based on cultural homogeneity cannot, however, be met on the European level, given the fact of the ethnic, cultural, linguistic and economic heterogeneity of the EU. Any step towards further integration would therefore not be politically desirable—it would alienate us from our democratic commitments, destroy (contrary to the principle of subsidiarity) local autonomy and in the end would subordinate cultural identity to an unattractive mixture of bureaucracy and the market. The only possible answer to the legitimation problem is therefore (in this view) the revitalization of the nation state and its democratic process.

The argument for an increase in national authority as a condition for effective democratic politics on the European level focuses on locational competition, and especially the conflict between the more highly industrial and the less developed members of the European Union. Countries of the former group can impose high wages and high social and environmental costs on firms—and will yet remain successful in European competition because of their high labour productivity. Countries of the second group, which have a far lower average productivity, cannot. Unitary European social or environmental regulations would destroy the competitiveness of the countries of the second group. Moreover, locational competition makes joint deregulation, via races to the bottom, more likely. The way out seems to be to strengthen the capacity of the nation states to deal with social and environmental issues.

However, faced with evidence that we will consider in a moment, Scharpf has had to amend his argument to include the possibility that regulatory competition does not inevitably set off a race to the bottom or 'Delaware effect'. (The name derives from the alleged preference of US corporations for legal domicile in Delaware over other, more demanding states.) Instead it may even produce a race to the regulatory top or 'California effect'. (California regulation is said to attract corporations because it imposes disciplines to which they would like to be subject but cannot impose on themselves.) The California effect prevails, in this view, if regulatory competition is on 'regulatory quality' rather than simply on the costs. This will be the case, for example, when national regulations serve as a trust-enhancing certificate of superior product quality that is rewarded by the market. Under such circumstances, it is likely that high levels of regulation may create a competitive advantage for the firms subjected to them, and thus exert a competitive pressure on other governments to raise their own levels of regulation. Therefore negative or market-making integration may not affect national product regulations and, when it does, need not induce a race to the bottom.

However, this qualification of the argument has in turn been qualified. While national product-related standards may induce a race to the top, this is unlikely to be the case with standards which concern the social background conditions of industrial production. Examples are regulations concerning, for example, air pollution, work safety, sick pay, minimum wages as well as taxation, i.e., environmental process regulations and social policy measures. These areas are not characterized by a common interest in coordination but by competitive or even conflicting interests. Since none of these regulations affect the products themselves, and since (as Scharpf believes) these standards cannot easily be 'translated' back into a self-interest of consumers—i.e., into a consumer preference for goods and services produced under more stringent process regulations—regulatory competition under conditions of transnational mobility will generally exert downward pressures on national regulations. So, qualified qualifications notwithstanding, the argument reverts to the initial claim of a link between de-regulation at the EU level and locational competition.[20]

Accordingly, for Scharpf, the central place for democratic self-government remains the *national* policy discourse. Moreover, even within the nation state the scope of democratic self-government is rapidly decreasing given the fact that the national policy discourses have to stay attentive to the constraints imposed by supranational law (such as GATT rules, EC law, interventions by the WTO, decisions by the ECJ, etc.). In the end, therefore, Scharpf opts for elite-led national policy discourses as the proper—and only—place for deliberative democracy. 'It is in such elite-led, but nevertheless public discourses that policy choices must be explained and justified in ways that can be challenged by counter-elites, and in terms that can also be understood and judged by (interested) non-elites as well.'[21] These national policy discourses must be guided by an awareness of the limitations of the national problem-solving capacities to meet the requirement of output-legitimacy—and thus avoid any illusion of (as Scharpf puts it) 'omnipotence'. Furthermore, the national policy discourses must develop reflexive capacities concerning the interests of other nation states—that is, they must be 'informed by an empathetic understanding of the preferences, worldviews and capabilities of the other countries involved'.[22] In this case, these discourses can, as Scharpf believes, provide a link between on the one hand efficiency- or feasibility-oriented legitimation criteria, and on the other hand input-oriented criteria that remain sensitive to 'the perceptions and preferences of non-elites'.[23] Thus, the normative perspective is one of enlightened nationalism, but not one of transnational democracy.

Hugh Collins presents a variant of this argument in challenging the project of a common European private law.[24] Collins' point is that the creation of a common European private law would also lead to excessive centralization, and the corresponding destruction of the cultural identity of the Member

---

[20] Ibid.   [21] Ibid.   [22] Ibid.   [23] Ibid.
[24] Collins, 'European Private Law and the Cultural Identity of Member States', 3 *ERPL* (1995) 353.

States. According to Collins, private law systems can be regarded as the language of a society. Suffused by its characteristic principles of distributive justice a society's private law expresses its *cultural identity*. For the way a society draws the boundaries of commodification and of market-alienability articulates its defining commitments and social values. The fusion of private law systems and the substantive goals of the political community is seen as a historical triumph of each and every nation state over the abstraction and formalism of modern private law. From this perspective, the creation of a single European market disrupts the precarious balance between markets and the cultural identities of the Member States. The social democrats fear that the victory of EU regulation will lead to the dominance of the market over the solidary polity. Collins fears that, within the market itself, the victory of European economic law will lead to the dominance of the 'unencumbered self':[25] the un-situated, striving individual who 'displays impatience with the ties of the community, and seeks to invent himself and his environment through rational choice'.[26]

Carried to its limit the social democratic view issues in sociological theories of identity that highlight the ultimate dependence of democracy and constitutionalism on the nation or the group as a pre-political condition. The theory turns sociological when stable territorial boundaries and a shared political culture and history are not just seen as a *supplément*, but as the pivotal pre-political conditions of democracy. Offe's recent work on 'democratic impossibilities'[27] goes this further step. His central argument is that democratic politics cannot determine the constituent features of a state; a state must always already be in place before a constitutional democracy can possibly begin to operate. The claim is that democracy cannot be brought into being by democratic means. He identifies four democratic impossibilities: 'matters which, by their very logic, cannot be resolved in democratic ways'.[28] First, there must be a pouvoir constituant 'prior to and unconstrained by the democratic principles which govern in a democratic society once established'—'the initial framework in which democratically legitimated power is to be created is not enacted democratically'.[29] Second, it is 'democratically impossible for the people to decide or (re)define who belongs to the people (as opposed to who is to be enfranchised within an existing people)'.[30] Third, 'territorial borders cannot be changed in obviously democratic ways'.[31] Fourth, as to democratic agenda-setting, 'the citizenry of a democracy cannot decide on the issues the citizens are to decide on'.[32]

---

[25] On the 'unencumbered self', see M. Sandel, *Liberalism and the Limits of Justice* (1982).
[26] Ibid., at 353.
[27] Offe, ' "Homogeneity" and Constitutional Democracy: Coping with Identity Conflicts through Group Rights', 6 *The Journal of Political Philosophy* (1998) 113.
[28] Ibid., at 115.   [29] Ibid.   [30] Ibid.   [31] Ibid.   [32] Ibid.

Accordingly, the very possibility of democratic self-government comes to depend upon what Offe calls 'reflexive homogeneity'.[33] Homogeneity is 'reflexive', because it offers a real-world grounding for mutual trust between citizens and for solidarity—both pre-conditions, as in Scharpf's argument, for stable, mutual obligations among citizens that ban the Hobbesian spectre of a world of self-interest, and give a motivational foundation to the modern welfare state. Clear territorial boundaries are the 'decision points' that define whose welfare is to be counted in the distributive process and whose resources are to be equalized with regard to which reference group. The ultimate remnant of constitutional democracy, in Offe's case, becomes a *pre-democratic decision*—and consequently all interpretative efforts of this reconstructive project are directed toward assuring us that at least *this* foundational decision is removed from the endangering and de-solidarizing sway of strategic politics under conditions of globalization, precisely because it is 'pre-political'—that is, *intrinsically* sundered off from and stabilized against the vicissitudes of the political process, as a matter of sociological faith. Democratic constitutionalism recedes into a decisionism that recalls Carl Schmitt—our friends and our enemies are just who they are, because we are who we are.

Ultimately then, both the social democratic and the liberal-constitutional views describe the European integration process as an accommodation between European economic law and the political sovereignty of the nation states.[34] In both views political autonomy remains locked into the nation state. While the former—libertarian—approach celebrates integration as securing the primacy of economic rights and liberties over the political rights firmly in place on the national level, the second approach criticizes integration as *alienating* European societies from their basic democratic commitments. The second approach is sensitive to the deficiencies of the libertarian approach, but has, in its emphasis of the nation state, only a deeply ambivalent option to offer. The supranational primacy of European law over national law appears from this perspective as a dangerous anomaly in constitutional theory: the more law that has neither democratic pedigree nor warrant in tradition overrides the law with both.[35]

So tight is the grip of this dichotomy on constitutional thought that even the most deliberately innovative proposals for reform in the EU aim at the recombination of the contrary elements, not a reconceptualization of the system of categories by which they become antithetic. A prominent example is

[33] Offe, 'Demokratie und Wohlfahrtsstaat: Eine europäische Regimeform unter dem Streß der europäischen Integration', in W. Streeck (ed.), *Internationale Wirtschaft, nationale Demokratie. Herausforderungen für die Demokratietheorie* (1998) 99, at 112.

[34] See Streeck, 'From Market Making to State Building? Reflections on the Political Economy of European Social Policy', in S. Leibfried and P. Pierson (eds), *European Social Policy Between Fragmentation and Integration* (1995) 389.

[35] So explicitly Scharpf, 'Democratic Policy in Europe', 2 *ELJ* (1996) 136, at 149.

Weiler's proposal to conceive of the constitutional structure of the European Union in terms of a variable geometry of romanticism and enlightenment. Weiler calls his 'a politically conservative view since it insists not simply on the inevitability of the nation state but on its virtues'.[36] Weiler's aim is to find an alternative to outright rejection of European citizenship (given his empirical assumption that there is no demos 'out there': 'no demos thesis') and reduction of European integration process to (higher-level) nation-building. His project is at the same time motivated by the insight that the nation state has lost its presumption of innocence:

A central plank of the project of European integration may be seen . . . as an attempt to control the excesses of the modern nation state in Europe, especially, but not only, its propensity to violent conflict and the inability of the international system to constrain that propensity.[37]

Given the modern nation state's historical propensity to dangerous excesses of nationalism, it would be, Weiler notes, 'more than ironic if a polity set up as a means to counter the excesses of statism ended up in coming round full circle and transforming itself into a (super) state'. So Weiler's project is to join what he takes to be the virtues of the nation state with an idea of European constitutionalism. 'Nationhood' is associated with 'Belongingness and Originality' as a 'framework for social interaction', 'statehood' with 'the organizational framework within which the nation is to realize its potentialities', and 'supranationalism' 'is about affirming the values of the liberal nation state by policing the boundaries against abuse', it 'aspires to keep the values of the nation state pure and uncorrupted by . . . abuses . . .', it 'does not reject boundaries: it guards them but it also guards against them'; it is not meant 'to eliminate the national state but to create a regime which seeks to tame the national interest with a new discipline'.[38]

The idea of supranationalism, with its focus on individual rights to non-discrimination or free movement, is on the one hand 'to control at the societal level the uncontrolled reflexes of national interest in the international sphere', and on the other hand to protect the nation against abuses by the state. Weiler thus offers a kind of 'quasi-Kantian' *Zwei-Reiche-Lehre*. The supranational level is the realm of 'liberal notions of human rights', of criticism and of 'civilization' (the 'intelligible world'). The national level is the realm of the good, of identification and of 'Eros' (the 'empirical world'). This model allows for 'a European civic, value-driven demos . . . side by side with a national organic cultural one'. It is designed 'to re-establish a new framework for a new epoch in the life of the European nation state, and, at the same

---

[36] See Weiler and Trachtman, 'European Constitutionalism and its Discontents', *Northwestern Journal of International Law and Business* (Winter-Spring 1996–1997) 354.

[37] J. H. H. Weiler, *The Constitution of Europe* (1999), at 341.

[38] Ibid.

time, give legitimacy to the normative claims of European constitutional-ism'.[39]

Moreover, rights-based supranationalism and organicist national citizen-ship are, according to Weiler, mutually supportive and correcting. Together they offer 'a structured model of critical citizenship'. European rights-based 'civilization' may—as Weiler believes—lead to destructive abstraction from concrete forms of life: to an 'increased bureaucratization', to 'commodifica-tion . . . through competitive structures of mobility', and to 'centralization of power', in short, to 'the angst of modernity'. This propensity to 'alienation' has to be counter-balanced by the nation state, because 'the nation and the state, with their organizing myths of fate and destiny, provide a captivating and reassuring answer to many'. Thus European citizenship 'could be regarded as emblematic of that new liberal effort which seeks to preserve the Eros of the national while holding its demonic aspects under civilizing con-straints and to bestow on the Union a legitimacy which acknowledges the constitutive elements of democracy and demos without compromising its Community non-statal telos'.[40]

Weiler believes that the strength of his view is to conceive of the Treaties (of Maastricht and of Amsterdam) as a social contract among the nationals of the Member States rather than an agreement among the States themselves. Yet the thrust of his approach is to contain and domesticate rather than valorize and foment this incipient transnational political dialogue and the novel forms of citizenship to which it might lead. It (further) constitutionalizes the national constitutional democracies through the affirmation of 'supranationalism' without envisaging European constitutionalism as an instrument for actively advancing innovative projects among citizens creating new forms of solidar-ity, trust and reciprocal recognition *beyond the nation state*.

II. COUNTERFACTUALS: DEMOCRATIC EXPERIMENTATION AND THE 'BURDENS OF JUDGEMENT'

The consensus informing this line of argument is all the more striking because it echoes an earlier, surprising turn in a leading school of constitutional the-ory associated with Dworkin, Habermas, Michelman and Rawls. That school was long committed to the claim that the possibility of constitutional demo-cracy does not depend on the (allegedly) pre-political cultural homogeneity and self-evidence of a demos. A central feature of these 'middle-ground' approaches has been to insist that democratic self-government is not thwarted by, but rather benefits from, the heterogeneity of participants: that the 'diversities of experience and vision and the thousand shocks to which

---

[39] Ibid.   [40] Ibid.

human judgement is heir'[41] favour rather than impede democratic experimentation.

The highest goal of theories of this kind of democratic constitutionalism was the reconciliation of two apparently contradictory ideas. The first is 'democracy', meaning political self-government: the people deciding for themselves the contents of the laws that organize and regulate their political association. The second is 'constitutionalism', meaning the containment of politics, and not least the sovereignty of the demos, by a 'higher law' or law of law-making that controls which laws can be made and by what procedures. At its most ambitious, the aspiration of constitutional theory was to show that democracy as the recognition by each citizen of the others as free and equal beings would give rise to a kind of constitution of reason. This constitution of reason effectively becomes the highest law, guiding such reform in the procedures and substance of democracy that in time the people's constitutional and political choices are as one. The aspiration of constitutional theory, accordingly, was to show that democracy is not simply about individual interests and their aggregation, but about the discovery of collective courses of action that can be mutually justified among free and equal citizens in the light of collectively shared understandings of constitutional principles.

But even those sophisticated normative theories have withdrawn to incantation of a shared constitutional identity as a basic condition (and last resort) of democracy in a context of deep cleavages. Habermas—who evidently knows when he is playing with fire—calls this shared identity 'constitutional patriotism'. The underlying fear is that pluralism 'at all levels' will affect the higher law or constitutional essentials of a complex society, endangering the very possibility of integration through law. Given this danger the practical success of constitutional justification unexpectedly turns out to depend on what Dworkin calls the 'structural conditions of democracy':[42] the stable territorial boundaries, shared political culture central to social democratic nostalgia for the nation.

Before going into details, it may be helpful to have a look at the overall structure of the original argument. The starting point for this constitutional theory was the fundamental question, how can the exercise of political power, which is always coercive power, be rendered 'justifiable to others as free and equal'?[43] The answer comprised three elements in constant tension with each other. Specific exercises of coercive political power are justified, when:

(1) they are validated by a set of constitutional essentials,
(2) everyone can see that everyone affected has reason to accept in the light of his or her own interests,

---

[41] F. I. Michelman, *Brennan and Democracy* (1999), at 28.
[42] R. Dworkin, *Freedom's Law: The Moral Reading of the American Constitution* (1996), at 24.
[43] J. Rawls, *Political Liberalism* (1993), at 217.

(3) sharing the commitment to conduct political argument on common ground (the 'desire to honour fair terms of cooperation'[44]), the sundry causes of disagreement about normative questions (the 'burdens of judgement'[45]) notwithstanding.

These three elements were supposed to reconcile pluralism with the constitution of reason. The guiding idea is that the principles for the constitution of a law-making system can be—and indeed must be—cast in terms sufficiently removed from the immediate everyday conflicts of interest and vision in order to allow for reasonable acceptability of a set of principles to everyone concerned. But this accommodation of the idea of political justification to the fact of pluralism depends on the weak motivational presupposition expressed in (3): the presupposition that actors understand themselves as participants in a joint project of searching agreement on fair terms of cooperation within a shared social space.

The problem with this way of accommodating pluralism emerges when, in the process of self-government, reasonable disagreement is unavoidably re-iterated 'all the way up' into the realm of constitutional interpretation. To the extent that the higher-law core is affected by reasonable disagreement, the constitution becomes untenably unstable. On the one hand, it itself becomes an object of reasonable disagreement. On the other hand, such disagreement notwithstanding, its content must at any given moment be determinate enough to guide a programme of constitutional reform that increases the security of disadvantaged groups.

In this situation, however, the initially weak motivational presupposition (3) seems to become stronger and stronger—to the point of becoming the sole and crucial warrant of the very possibility of a meaningful process of interpretation of constitutional principles. Consider three routes to this retreat to personification.

The first is Dworkin's synthesis of constitutionalism and democracy—better known for the rights it promises to vindicate than the national ties that it supposes. Indeed, Dworkin is often read, correctly, as arguing that an ethically coherent community is in some important sense a political construct: that, *pace* Schmitt, the community supposes the polity at least as much as the other way around. Dworkin's project is to specify those conditions that must be fulfilled in order for politics not to be a usurpation but an exercise of the citizens' special responsibility for their own lives.

How, he asks, can collectively binding decision-making be made consistent with the people's ethical responsibility to lead their own lives? He rejects a social contract as a useless fiction: not as a pallid contract, but as no contract at all. He also rejects a consensus to agree on constitutional essentials while abiding disagreement on comprehensive notions of the good life (the

---

[44] Ibid., at 54–58.   [45] Ibid.

Rawlsian overlapping consensus). For this kind of constitution of convenience divorces justice from ethical ideals related to concrete forms of life. Rather, democracy can become an authentic form of self-government only if it allows people, one by one, to take control over their own lives. If the political structure in which disagreement persists is, in this sense, truly democratic; if it is, as Dworkin says, a partnership among equals, then it is fair to enforce collective decisions even on those who oppose those decisions.

This partnership is in turn realized if three 'relational conditions' of communal—as opposed to simply 'statistical'—democracy are met: fair and equal access to the process of public will-formation; an equal measure of concern for the interests of each in decisions of public policy; and the mutual recognition of the moral independence of each citizen as a person who can take personal responsibility both on questions of the good life and on issues of justice—i.e., about how competing interests of all citizens should be accommodated. The political community's observance in its law-making acts of these relational conditions provides each individual with reason to identify his or her political agency with the law-making acts of collective institutions.

But Dworkin realizes that the very general rights that secure the relational conditions of communal democracy are, by their very generality, too indeterminate to themselves compel resolution of the actual controversies that come before tribunals in complex societies. To close the gap between rights and controversies Dworkin appeals to what he calls a 'moral reading' of the constitution. This reading 'presupposes that we all—judges, lawyers, citizens—interpret and apply these abstract clauses on the understanding that they invoke moral principles about political decency and justice. . . . The moral reading therefore brings political morality into the heart of constitutional law.'[46]

The background conditions that make possible this moral reading, however, require in effect that the political community be personified before it can be constructed. Thus Dworkin writes: 'Political integrity assumes a particularly deep personification of the community or state.' He instructs judges 'to identify legal rights and duties, so far as possible, on the assumption that they were all created by a single author—the community personified—expressing a coherent conception of justice and fairness'.[47] Political community is explicitly conceived as a 'moral agent', acting above the heads of the real citizens, as 'some special kind of entity distinct from the actual people who are its citizens'.[48] Or, as he puts the point elsewhere: 'The political community must be more than nominal: it must have been established by a historical process that has produced generally recognized and stable territorial boundaries.'[49] And he insists 'that the members of a genuine political community must share a cul-

---

[46] Dworkin, *supra* n. 42.   [47] Ibid., at 168.   [48] Ibid.
[49] Ibid., at 24.

ture as well as a political history: that they must speak a common language, have common values, and so forth'.⁵⁰ In the end, then, the citizens' relation to democracy via the state is abstract, while their relation to one another via the community is visceral.

Not the least of the ironies of this personification of the political community is its surprising—because wholly unintended—affinity with the legal positivism that Dworkin originally intended to overcome. A core tenet of legal positivism is that we need a master rule of recognition that marks legitimate commands of the sovereign as such. Without such a pedigree we cannot distinguish the command of a sovereign, which is obeyed because it is the legitimate sovereign who issued it, from the orders of a gunman, which are obeyed because of the threat of violence. Of all law only the one not legitimated in this way was thought to be the rule of recognition itself, unavoidably based on the brute fact of social acceptance as a natural substratum.

Dworkin challenged this picture by showing that it leaves no place for principles within argumentative games. Principles, as Dworkin argued, do not apply, as rules do, in all-or-nothing fashion. Instead they incline a decision in one way or other, stay intact if they do not prevail, and are linked to general notions of fairness. There is no positivist test of pedigree tying legal principles back to acts of legislation. Principles are controversial, they are part of a (dialogic) process of interpretation, with regard to which Hart's sharp distinction between acceptance and validity does not hold. Arguing about principles, Dworkin says, 'introduces a note of validity into the chord of acceptance'.⁵¹ So, after all, there is no ultimate master rule of recognition relating principles to acts of legislation; and the neat distinction between fully conventionalized rules and background culture—a distinction which leaves no space for the practice of deliberative justification itself—collapses.

Yet a consequence of Dworkin's insistence on a moral reading of the constitution and his specification of the conditions making this possible seem to root the dialogic practice of constructivist constitutional justification in the factual existence of a sovereign (people) reminiscent of positivism. Or put in Dworkin's own language, his solution to the problem of applying principles to controversies under conditions of diversity introduces a note of acceptance in the chord of validity. The 'ethical grounding' of democratic politics points to the pre-political as surely as did the social democratic concern for the social conditions of re-distribution.

The second trajectory is that of Habermas. His efforts are directed towards the reconstruction of a universalizing, or at least transatlantic, idea of democratic constitutionalism that abhors the parochialism of nation political cultures. Rather than securing the convergence and legitimating force of democratic law-making in advance by tying it back to a (supposedly)

---

⁵⁰ Ibid.   ⁵¹ R. Dworkin, *Taking Rights Seriously* (1977), at 41.

pre-existing substantive ethical consensus of a political community, Habermas argues that it is the 'democratic procedure for the production of law' itself, which is the only 'postmetaphysical source of legitimacy' of coercive law.[52] There are four aspects to this idea.

First, the idea of a legitimacy-conferring democratic procedure builds on the idea that only those laws are legitimate which might claim the agreement of all citizens in a discursive process equally open to all. Encapsulated within the democratic procedure—and 'transmitted . . . to the complex and increasingly anonymous spheres of a functionally differentiated society'[53] through law—is a 'discourse principle (D)', according to which 'only those norms of action are valid to which all possibly affected persons could assent as participants in rational discourses'.[54] And Habermas emphasizes that only the actual discursive engagements among citizens over the contents of their country's constitutive laws—as opposed to hypothetical agreement—can confer legitimacy upon a legal order. Only a process of actual dialogic encounter with the full range of affected others can reliably appraise the rational acceptability of proposed fundamental laws to all those who stand to be affected by them.

Second, the emphasis on the actual democratic-procedural provenance of constitutional law goes hand in hand with what Habermas calls a proceduralist paradigm of law, which introduces his version of the idea of a non-court-centred understanding of constitutional interpretation. The proceduralist paradigm of law is directed against a legalist self-understanding of law which maintains that equal rights as moral rules are already 'there' in some sense and can be 'applied' by some elitist institution—a constitutional court, both removed from and standing for the people—thus restricting the very scope of democratic discourse itself. The proceduralist paradigm expresses the idea that the resolution of divisive political conflicts cannot be pictured as a simple integration of morality—of procedure-independent standards of rightness—into the law by judicial acts of pure practical reason. Relatedly, against Rawlsian political constructivism Habermas objects that from the perspective of a philosophically elaborated and judicially enacted theory of justice the act of founding the democratic constitution cannot be repeated under the institutional conditions of an already constituted just society. If the results of the theory are already sedimented in the constitution, the citizens cannot conceive of the constitution as a project. Establishing a substantive political conception of justice would in the end amount to usurping the prerogatives of free democratic discussion and to anticipating, in the wrong way, its outcomes.

Third, the proceduralist paradigm of law aims to vindicate the idea that citizens and social actors themselves, acting as societal law-makers, decide how

---

[52] J. Habermas, *Between Facts and Norms: Contributions to a Discourse Theory of Law and Democracy* (1997), ch. 3.

[53] Ibid., at 318.   [54] Ibid.

they must fashion the rights that give the discourse principle legal shape as a principle of democracy. The citizens themselves, through the continuous exercise of political autonomy, have to apply the discourse principle to the legal form over and over again in an ongoing process yielding a system of equal rights which in turn offers a moral constraint upon the law-making process. Thus, Habermas says, a legitimate legal order is 'one that has become reflexive with regard to the very process of institutionalization'; only those laws can be legitimate that can gain assent in a procedure that has itself been legally constituted. 'The idea of the rule of law sets in motion a spiralling self-application of law.'[55]

Fourth, this practice of (constitutional) law-making, Habermas insists, cannot be assimilated to a 'hermeneutical process of self-explication of a shared form of life or collective identity' or to the 'clarification of a collective ethical self-understanding'.[56] Rather, the very point of constitutionalism is to institutionalize 'the communicative presuppositions that allow the better arguments to come into play in various forms of deliberation'.[57] From a discourse-theoretical point of view the 'self' of the self-organizing legal community 'disappears in the subjectless forms of communication that regulate the flow of deliberations in such a way that their fallible results enjoy the presumption of rationality'.[58] Ethical questions are 'subordinate' to questions of justice which concern matters to be regulated in the 'equal interest of all' and which are 'not related from the outset to a specific collective and its form of life'.[59] The politically enacted law of a 'concrete legal community' must—in order to be legitimate—'at least be compatible with moral tenets that claim universal validity going beyond the legal community'.[60]

Two changes undercut this Habermasian proceduralism. One is the retreat of popular sovereignty into subjectless democratic procedures (which, Habermas says, in a denationalized context must 'catch up' with globalized markets[61]). The other is the divorce of claims to unconditional moral rightness from the citizens' ethical outlooks. Under these conditions, the legitimacy-conferring force of Habermasian proceduralism comes to depend on constitutional patriotism as an empirical warrant or moral substratum. It alone bridges the conceptual gap between hypothetical consent and actual democratic practice. The practical pursuit of the idea of universalizing political justification becomes contingent upon the community's concrete ethical character, as the substance of constitutional patriotism unavoidably involves identification with an actual historical community. The emphasis shifts from

---

[55] Ibid., at 39.
[56] Habermas, 'Three Normative Models of Democracy', in S. Benhabib (ed.), *Democracy and Difference. Contesting the Boundaries of the Political* (1996).
[57] Ibid., at 32.   [58] Ibid., at 29.   [59] Ibid., at 25.   [60] Ibid.
[61] Habermas, 'The European Nation State and the Pressures of Globalisation', 235 *The New Left Review* (1999) 46.

universalist striving for transcendence from within, born of a discontent with
the exceptionalism of national experience, back to historically shared values—
and to the idea that '[d]ie Nation oder der Volksgeist . . . versorgt die rechtlich
konstituierte Staatsform mit einem kulturellen Substrat'.[62] ('The nation or
the spirit of the people provides the legally constituted form of the state with
a cultural substratum'—our translation.)

Thus, both Dworkinian and Habermasian constitutionalism leave us with
a world in which normativity—the warrant of the legitimacy-conferring character or 'persuasiveness' of democratic politics under conditions of reasonable
pluralism—is always where we are not. The choice is either between grounding the principle-guided 'moral reading' of constitutionalism in the
hermeneutic self-explication of shared value orientations, or of grounding it
in a generic, quasi-transcendental consensus on communicative presuppositions—with each position unavoidably and continuously collapsing into its
respective opposite, and no hope of conceptual closure.

These criticisms parallel Michelman's recent attempt to resolve what he
calls the 'paradox of democracy'. In his criticism of Dworkin's theory,
Michelman points out that in reducing self-government to identification,
Dworkin mistakes a state of mind or an attitude for a case of agency and of
dialogue. Identification with a result is evidently not the same as actual participation in a jurisgenerative process, not self-rule actually carried out—with
'a reference to something that someone *does*'.[63] But democracy at the same
time requires, Michelman argues, a pre-inscription—itself not politically 'up
for grabs'[64]—into the 'higher law' of law-making of whatever substantive
constraints on subsequent political action are necessary to maintain 'demo-
cracy-constituting conditions of equality, independence, freedom and security'[65]—and which 'place government under reason expressed as law'.[66] It is
therefore, Michelman argues, 'absolutely . . . not possible to appoint democracy to decide what democracy is' and what 'democracy means and
requires—as a matter of "logics" '.[67] Democratic commitment, therefore,
contains (on this view) a fundamental paradox. On the one hand, democratic commitment means concern with actual self-rule—with the 'individualis-
tic notion of "everyone's" political self-government'[68] as the source of valid
law. On the other hand, the concern with substantive, democracy-constitut-
ing conditions—procedure-independent standards of rightness—generates
an 'irrepressible impulse to exclude basic law-determinations from the procedural purview of democracy',[69] which bars democracy from a decision-space
'where it would seem urgently and rightly to want to go, that of deciding the
contents of the . . . laws of lawmaking'.[70]

[62] J. Habermas, *Die Einbeziehung des Anderen* (1996), at 135.
[63] Michelman, *supra* n. 41, at 24.   [64] Ibid., at 33.   [65] Ibid.
[66] Ibid., at 50.   [67] Ibid., at 34.   [68] Ibid., at 14.   [69] Ibid., at 34.
[70] Ibid., at 34.

Michelman shows that any purely procedural resolution of the paradox of democracy would simply re-instantiate it, because any procedural standard—such as equal and unrestricted access to public discourse—is, in turn, 'hooked on substance'. Nor would a purely 'substantive' resolution be possible. Citizens, Michelman argues, cannot simply put aside those differences of comprehensive outlook that make for reasonable pluralism when they turn to matters of constitutional interpretation. Indeed, suppose citizens could somehow put their reasonable differences aside and agree on uncontroversial constitutional essentials, on the contents of 'the really high law'.[71] Application of those—inevitably abstract and broad—essentials to any particular problem would themselves require interpretation and further specification; this process, however, opens the constitution to divisive, eventually destructive, conflict. Given deep disagreement over the application of constitutional essentials, and in order for disagreement to remain within the realm of the reasonable, the only hope—'the only remaining possibility for self-government in politics'[72]—lies in the shared insight into (and citizens' loyalty to) the ethical bases of democracy—constitutional patriotism. Constitutional patriotism, Michelman (taking up a Wordsworthian trope) writes, 'recovers and explains the possibility of moral reasons and of moral experience, but at the same time it shows them to be reasons and experience into which we always enter not in entire forgetfulness but trailing clouds of culture from our particular national home'.[73] Michelman's own project directs all its energies to showing how constitutional practice is contingent upon constitutional patriotism as a protective ethical base.

Constitutional patriotism transforms disagreements over the interpretation of constitutional essentials into a difference over a community's political self-understanding, that is, into a difference which remains always already internal to a collectively shared constitutional project. Thus, constitutional patriotism makes it possible for citizens to accept disagreement over the application of shared constitutional principles, without loss of confidence in the univocality of these principles themselves (think of it in terms of '*Frustrationstoleranz*')—it envisions constitutional justification as a process which requires 'conscious reference by those involved to their mutual and reciprocal awareness of being co-participants not just in this one debate, but in a more encompassing form of life, bearing the imprint of a common past, within and from which the arguments and claims arise and draw their meaning'.[74]

As we will see below, democratic experimentalism/DDP will take a different route in order to reconcile the commitment to constitutional justification

---

[71] Ibid., at 50. [72] Ibid., at 51.

[73] Michelman, 'Morality, Identity and "Constitutional Patriotism" ', 14 *Ratio Juris* (2001) 268.

[74] Michelman, 'Law's Republic', 97 *Yale Law Journal* (1988) 1493, at 1512.

with the burdens of judgement. Herein lies, as we will see below, the challenge the recent developments in Europe pose for the very idea of democratic constitutionalism. Rather than seeking refuge in supposedly stable, pre-deliberative 'external' certainties (hoped to confer 'persuasiveness' upon the process of constitutional justification)—observable preferences, fixed identities, the boundaries of a political community personified—the aim of the alternative view is to defend a radically internalist view of constitutionalism: to spell out the normative and institutional infrastructure of a constructivist jurisgenerative process in which reasons and boundaries, rights and identities, actors and procedures, principles and practices, mutually transform and 'educate' one another in the light of new experience. This jurisgenerative process is 'hooked' neither on the hermeneutical self-explication, nor on the citizens' generic agreement on the communicative presuppositions of discourse, but blurs this distinction. Initially shared forms of discourse, as the mutual exploration of difference proceeds, become themselves stakes in political deliberation—signs, which are not just vehicles of political contention, but at the same time crucial objects of contention. These signs, on the one hand, reflect (and are motivated by) diverse perceptions of interest and situation, of need and possibility; and on the other hand, anticipate common ground. By the same token, they are also tendentiously oppressive—and need destabilization through exposure to difference. Thus, in this alternative view, the polyarchical dispersion of sovereignty and legal pluralism are seen not as an evacuation of the practice of constitutional justification, but rather as an innovative way, open to modern denationalized societies, of self-consciously vindicating the original idea that democratic self-government and constitutional justification are not thwarted by, but rather benefit from the heterogeneity of participants—thrive, that is, from the very 'diversities of experience and vision and the thousand shocks to which human judgement is heir'.[75]

These ideas are closely related too, and develop certain implications of what Frank Michelman calls 'romantic constitutionalism'.[76] Michelman's argument is that no elaboration of principle or recourse to perfected procedures can fully reconcile the requirements of constitutional democracy that the people be self-governing and that the higher law guaranteeing the democratic character of law-making itself be subtracted from popular control and reposed, for example, in a judiciary not accountable to the electorate. We cannot accept constitutional democracy as a legitimate embodiment of the true principles of a democracy because, even if we agreed on those principles, their interpretation would be controversial, and we have no uncontroversial principles for deciding the procedures by which those controversies would be decided. A purely procedural solution, along the lines of a government equally responsive to the concerns of each of us, fails because every procedure embod-

---

[75] Michelman, *supra* n. 41, *passim*.   [76] Ibid., *passim*.

ies certain principles, and these, or the principles governing controversies aris-ing under them, are controversial. Nonetheless, recognizing our limits as indi-viduals and as members of large decision-making bodies we might agree 'epistemically' that a constitutional democracy is legitimate if it embodies the best possible interpretation of our understanding of democracy ('our right to be treated as equal', for example) *and* if those empowered to interpret the higher law—the constitutional judiciary—expose themselves and other insti-tutions to the 'full blast' of opinions and interests in society. The first condi-tion allows us to identify with our democracy, the latter allows us a measure of participation in its actual law-making. The constitutional judge will exer-cise her powers most in conformity with these commitments when she embraces what Michelman calls romantic constitutionalism: the view that individuals can transcend the limits of their personality if society will make the social contexts that both shape and obstruct the flourishing of their iden-tity susceptible to revision. Toleration for the clash of principles and for the jostling of competing designs for living is both a sign and an instrument of this heightening of revisability. Justice Brennan embodies the type of the romantic constitutionalist in his willingness to give room to dissident, even offensive views in his interpretation of the right of free speech; in his willing-ness to allow minorities to pursue remedies through courts or expressive boy-cotts that they might have pursued through political parties, circumstances allowing; and in his unwillingness to defer to official claims of expertise in dis-putes between citizens and bureaucrats.

So far Michelman's view. The question arises, can romantic constitutional-ism itself be institutionalized in the sense of embodied in systematic changes in the relations between the branches of government, judiciary included, and civil society that better serve its animating value of more democratically legit-imating constitutional democracy? The earlier discussion suggests a limit to such improving institutionalization. No set of procedures can 'finally' resolve the tensions of constitutionalism and democracy. Still, the limit is not the whole story. Many if not most of the changes wrought by the romantic con-stitutionalist judge are institutional innovations. Think of Brennan's support for expressive boycotts. Surely it must be possible to link decisions of this kind and think of them as a programme of institutional change in the service of romantic constitutionalism? And just as surely, some programmes could be judged better than others by the lights of romantic constitutionalism itself. Our claim is that the standard-based reforms, because of the way they link local action to the revision of the frameworks of social action, have a privi-leged place in the family of romantic constitutionalist programmes, despite its origins elsewhere. Indeed, seeking to normalize insurgency standards-based reform might be thought to capture the essence of romantic constitutional-ism. Still, the enthusiasm may not be mutual. Advocates of romantic consti-tutionalism may suspect (incorrectly, in our view) that the reforms discussed here aim at a managerialist domestication of the conflict and so suffocate the struggles that permit and give meaning to the transcendent recreation of identity.[77]

There is, as Michelman in his rejoinders to Habermas observes, 'no real-life disentangling of the call of unconditional rightness from the call of integrity or self-constituency, of loyalty to the best one can make of one's own and one's community life history and self-understanding'.[78]

III. COUNTERTHEORETICALS: TRANSNATIONAL INSTITUTIONS—MANAGERIAL INFORMALISM OR INCREMENTAL CONSTITUTIONALISM?

The horizon of transformative possibilities, however, is broader than this normative debate suggests. A new round of investigations into decision-making in the EU—growing originally out of concern with the threat to the welfare state supposedly inherent to harmonization—dis-confirms claims of a race to the bottom and points, if anywhere, to a spiralling trudge upwards. By the same token, these studies show that de-regulation through extension of the four freedoms has not simply resulted in an expansion of the private and the market to the detriment of the public and the 'forum', as originally expected. Rather, de-regulation has been accompanied by re-politicization (and 're-regulation') through the emergence of new transnational governance structures with the explicit capacity to take into account diversity. Of these new forms of governance the most important and often remarked is 'comitology': the web of committees, chaired by representatives of the Commission, which assist the latter in the implementation of Community legislation. This it does chiefly by determining the terms under which social actors—'private' standard setting entities very broadly conceived—will give content to particular framework rules. These committees are variously composed of representatives of the Member States, economic interest groups, scientific experts and advocacy groups of many stripes. They explicate and scrutinize heterogeneous interests and vocabularies—national, governmental, sectoral, technical, or self-avowedly public regarding. They are designed not to reflect and aggregate self-interest, but rather to use the initially parochial and sectarian perspectives to foster mutual learning, and eventually the transformation of preferences as part of the elaboration of shared interpretations. Within this new institutional architecture, innovation—the resetting of the very conceptual frameworks and political conflict lines which gave form to the initial discussion—becomes a condition of bureaucratic and political success.

---

[77] Michelman, *supra* n. 41.   [78] Ibid., at 51.

Despite broad agreement that the new empirical findings will not support the conclusions of the market-demos debate canvassed above without substantial qualification, there is nothing approaching a consensus regarding what to make of these facts. One tendency, best exemplified in the work of Weiler, is to see the new institutions as a colonialization of political sovereignty through managerial informalism. As the contrast between definition and execution of tasks softens, society's fundamental distributive questions will be decided by actors and processes so removed from the standard institutions of representative democracy as to be politically invisible and therefore unaccountable.[79] The contrary tendency, exemplified in the work of Joerges,

---

[79] J. H. H. Weiler, *The Constitution of Europe. 'Do the New Clothes have an Emperor?' and Other Essays on European Integration* (1999). Weiler argues that comitology—originally meant to remove crucial risk-related and distributive decisions to non-court-centric politically accountable forms of decision-making—has resulted in disastrously undermining the fundamental constitutional value of accountable political decision-making. He points out that comitology remains 'outside the classical parameters of constitutionalism' (343) and fears that there is (and will be) no robust substitute: '. . . we should not hide the utilitarian or social engineering dimension of this governance choice and it hardly provides a basis for a generalized normative model' (349).

Weiler points out that, within the setting of the comitology procedures, actors may, in a formal sense, be representatives of the Member States or of organized sectorial interests, but '[i]n substance they socialize into an independent identity' (342). Actors develop their own self-standing 'constructivist identity and culture (or subculture)' (342), which helps them to neutralize (one-sided) national interests and sectorial pressure. Committees 'composed of mid-ranking officials have long lost their allegiance to their controllers and work very much within their own universe for what they perceive as their function and task' (342). By generating its own universe, comitology transcends (and operates alongside) the intergovernmental/supranational divide and becomes paradigmatic for what Weiler dubs 'infranationalism'.

But the more comitology generates its own distinct, discretionary, value-driven and self-standing constructivist identity and culture, the more—Weiler says—it unavoidably defies and escapes 'the normal constitutional categories laboriously constructed in the context of a supranational understanding of the Community' (346). Weiler elaborates the failure of the conventional judicial strategies to constitutionalize comitology: a judicial strategy which constructs committees in terms of 'juridical subjects, to which . . . powers may (or may not) be delegated', would, by presupposing 'a subject-subject relationship between, say, Council and committee', camouflage comitology's constructivist autonomy and be blind to problems of unequal access and privileged sectorial influence. An—amended—second strategy, premised on the belief in the ability to assign 'certain functions and powers to the sharply defined subjects' (343) would fail for related reasons. The idea of committees fulfilling clearly delineated tasks and functions—set out in advance—diverts attention from the fact that 'committees *do* exercise considerable political and policy discretion without adequate political accountability' (345) and, as one might add, redefine these very tasks—if not the whole *raison d'être* of comitology itself—in the ongoing and self-sustaining process of executing these tasks. In the end, comitology/infranationalism inevitably undermine the normative circularity between law and politics—between the 'political process explaining and conditioning legal structure and legal structure conditioning and explaining political process'—the price of infranationalism being: the triumph of the managerial and expertocratic over the spontaneous and the public where ideological choices expose themselves to a process of public scrutiny, argument and debate; the

is to see the results as a potentially promising novelty requiring 'a shift of paradigmatic dimensions in the legal conceptualization of European governance'[80] or a 'new conceptual analysis'[81] that reaches beyond the legal to the political and constitutional. Yet a third tendency, manifest in the work of Heritier,[82] is to register the developments and limit commentary to the observation that the new processes and actors fill the void left by the deficiencies of the familiar ones. So long as they decide questions that representative democracy used to, but no longer can resolve, and those decisions are accepted, the new institutions amount to a 'substitute democracy', regardless of whether they claim any legitimacy beyond acceptance.

However, there is a tendency for the tendencies to shade into each other. Those concerned with the dangers of managerial informalism are not blind to the innovative character of developments, nor closed to the possibility of beneficent effects. Those drawn to the novelty and the conceptual innovation it apparently demands are for their part attracted to the idea that the innovations may accomplish the familiar ends of administration by new means. In particular they may improve government performance and renovate the role of the bureaucrat and expert without much changing the role of the citizen.[83]

concern with stability, efficiency and growth at the expense of redistributive politics and dialogue; the rise of informalism in policy-making which renders actors invisible and eludes those fixed procedural and substantive guarantees and framework-conditions which protect debate from deformations through external or internal coercion (power).

[80] Joerges, 'Bureaucratic Nightmare, Technocratic Regime and the Dream of Good Transnational Governance', in C. Joerges and E. Vos (eds), *EU Committees: Social Regulation, Law and Politics* (1999) 3; Joerges, ' "Good Governance" through Comitology?', in ibid., at 311.

[81] K.-H. Ladeur, *Negative Freiheitsrechte und gesellschaftliche Selbstorganisation: Die Erzeugung von Sozialkapital durch Institutionen* (2000); and Ladeur, 'The Theory of Autopoiesis as an Approach to a Better Understanding of Postmodern Law. From the Hierarchy of Norms to the Heterarchy of Changing Patterns of Legal Inter-relationships', EUI Working Papers Law no. 99/3, at 5 et seq.

[82] A. Heritier, *Policy-Making and Diversity in Europe: Escape from Deadlock* (1999).

[83] Proceeding from the idea that '[t]ransnational systems must draw their legitimacy from the deliberative quality of their decision-making process'. Joerges proposes to interpret comitology as a 'forum of deliberative politics' (311). Comitology—he says—'by virtue of its feedback links to the Member States, . . . can, in principle, take all social concerns and interests into account while, at the same time, links with science (as a social body) can be shaped so as to allow for the plurality of scientific knowledge to be brought to bear'. He suggests to understand comitology as the paradigmatic case of what he describes as a new European 'deliberative supranationalism'. Comitology, although 'probably the least transparent of all the European institutions', thus, rather than subverting the practice of democratic constitutionalism as Weiler feared, according to Joerges 'marks the transformation of the "old" European Economic Communities into a European polity' (3).

Joerges' starting point is the idea that European primary law, as a matter of paradigmatic orientation, operates neither merely as a bulwark against political interventionism, nor merely as a discipline on domestic debate. Rather, it 'compels the public presentation of one's own position in each individual case' and necessitates actors to 'use arguments which are compatible

Given this convergence, and in the absence of settled criteria for deciding when a non-standard technique of public problem-solving becomes a substitute for democracy, it is, finally, a short step to agreement that the new institutions are in some sense a democratically authorized substitute democracy. But this interplay of similarities and differences aside, and despite polemic flourishes, the debate on these matters is too frankly and invitingly exploratory to be usefully characterized through a contrast of positions that attributes to them more fixity than they pretend for themselves.

with European Law, not just with regard to the contents of national legal systems as such' (317). Indeed, European primary law, he says, is conceptually organized around the fundamental deliberative principle that restrictions of freedom of action can be considered as acceptable only if they are based on regulatory interests which are legitimate within the meaning of Community law.

Joerges' crucial step is to suggest that the telos of the European multi-level system of government (MLSG), permitting both empirical assessment and reform, is precisely the institutionalization of this fundamental principle of justification. As this principle binds the representatives not only of national interests, but also non-governmental actors, the MLSG transforms itself into an engine of 'good governance'. In particular, comitology becomes a key device of good governance. It permits the Member States to remain actively present, not merely in an advisory capacity, but 'also as political actors', in the process of what Joerges describes as the 'administration of the internal market': comitology permits to neutralize one-sided 'regional and sectorial arguments' (325), to curtail the parochial pursuit of national interest (316), to enhance responsiveness to politically sensitive questions, which continue to arise in the context of implementing activities and 'below the attention threshold of the legislature' (322) and thus opens framework regulations to constant revision. Moreover, the emergence of the new forms of cooperation between the Commission and Member State administrations goes hand in hand with regulatory techniques which instrumentalize the knowledge and the management potential of non-governmental organizations and firms, and which relocate control tasks into the production process itself.

In order to achieve the aim of harnessing deliberation, it is, as Joerges says, of 'constitutional importance' to secure the Member States' participatory rights in the comitology process. The persuasiveness of comitology deliberations is warranted, in the MLSG Joerges describes, by two elements. First, by the participatory entitlements of the Member States and the capacity of comitology to operate 'with due regard for all Member State perspectives' (317); second, by the capacity of comitology to integrate scientific expertise through a dialogue with the transnational epistemic community (317, 335) within which comitology-internal risk-assessments and decisions constantly have to expose themselves. Joerges, of course, notices that the committee system 'with its emphasis upon a unitary understanding of "science" . . . is largely closed to non-governmental actors' (318), and that the public which he speaks of is the specialized public of the policy community, and that influence remains mediated either by national administrations or by 'experts'. But he seems to believe that this insulation from the broader deliberation within non-specialized publics is a virtue, if not the very bedrock, of the comitology system: for '. . . because of their cognitive content, the correctness of risk decisions cannot be guaranteed by unmediated recourse to interests or their negotiation—or . . . by extending participation rights and veto-positions; and at European level in particular, the identification of representatives of European "interests" is inconceivable' (334). Accordingly, the key to enhancing the rationality of European decision-making processes lies not in the 'inclusion of ever more "interests" ', but in the strengthening of the internal 'deliberative . . . quality of decision-making processes' (334).

In this section, therefore, we will put further reflection on the commentaries to the side and stick to a brief review of critical facts. We begin with an example of the findings that cast doubt on the race-to-the-bottom view and its assumptions, then examine second-order results that cast doubt on efforts to save at least core assumptions of the de-regulation prediction by narrowing its scope. Even within this limited ambit we omit much detail, as the nuances of the findings change in this area as rapidly as the nuances of opinion. Accordingly, we present only enough to document what we think must be taken for granted in further argument. It is not the case that the logic of the market is trumping the logic of politics and regulation in the construction of the EU polity, nor is it the case that interests are inherently as fixed and irreconcilable—above all so refractory to reconsideration through debate—as participants of both sides of the debates discussed so far have assumed.

A conspicuous counter-example to the market-dominance view is the demanding and innovative regime established in the last decade to regulate aspects of occupational health and safety, and in particular equipment safety. The case counts as a counter-example, first, because the regulations concern the production process, not the marketable product. By the logic of the *Wirtschaftsverfassung* discussed above, the outcome should be determined by the interests in cost-avoidance of the median producer (state). Consumers, after all, are not concerned with injuries to workers occasioned by the production of the goods they purchase any more than they are concerned with insults to the environment, except insofar as these costs are reflected in the price. Since such costs are typically externalized—shifted to state in the form of environmental clean-up or worker compensation schemes, or directly to affected citizens (domestic and foreign workers)—their concern will usually be minimal. For one state, moreover, to impose its pretences for, say, a safe workplace on others is, in the market view, either a disguised attempt at protectionism or an unwarranted exercise of brute power. Under these conditions the poorest producers, who generally use the dirtiest and most dangerous equipment, and can also least afford to improve it, will have strong interests in keeping regulatory levels low, and face little legitimate opposition in their assertion of the right to do so.

But in the case of the machinery safety guidelines the putative interests did not prevail. The lowest common denominator in an area as technically complicated, as, for example, the safety devices to be incorporated into production equipment proved dauntingly difficult to define. Comitological structures helped surmount this impasse by allowing exploration of possible solutions without political tutelage. In this setting attention turned to regulatory architectures that generate rules from the best practices of the relevant actors, rather than requiring a central administrator to all current rules on a continuum ranging from lax to strict, and pick as strict a point on that line as political conditions allow.

Three related innovations, each with a complex history in specialized areas of regulatory debate, were linked to achieve an acceptable solution. First, the notion of *occupational* health and safety was broadened to allow for a more capacious understanding of *occupational*. Instead of referring chiefly to tools, machines, plant and workplace, occupational came to be interpreted as meaning the world of work, including in addition to the foregoing the organization of work, work time, social relations at the workplace, and training. Second, the notion of *health and safety* was extended from physical integrity or reduction of the risk of physical harm to well being as the physical and psychological basis pre-condition of flourishing. Third, employers were required to assess risks to the well being of employees arising from the world of work, and to respond to the risks identified in the light of the most effective responses to similar threats implemented by others.

This new EU regulatory architecture counts as a counter-example to the market-dominance view because the standards it establishes are 'higher' or more demanding than the domestic rules it supersedes in at least two senses. First, with the partial exception of Denmark and Sweden, which anticipated different aspects of the eventual European solution in national practice, the new system covers a broader range of risks arising from more varied sources than did the old. Thus Germany, long regarded as a leader in this area of regulation, had a settled practice of narrowly interpreting both occupational and safety, and this practice is open to challenge under the new system. Second, given that current rules are linked to current best practices, and these latter are raised over time as leading employers improve working conditions and advertise this to put pressure on competitors, future rules will likely be more demanding than current ones. In this the new regime instigates a race to the top whose protagonists in theory will eventually overtake the most advanced representatives of the old system regardless of their respective starting points. Whether the ground-level agents comply sufficiently with this regime, or others like it, to actually produce this effect is difficult, so far, to say. But even without a crisp answer to this and related questions, it is clear that the output of the rule-making machine and its mode of operation are both sufficiently different from what the theory leads us to expect that its advocates are obliged to respond.

A first reaction might be to observe that this exception is itself exceptional, the product of freak political circumstances—sage committee members or machine-tool builders run by former skilled workers with loyalties to the blue-collar world—and not an expression of a fundamental flaw in the market-dominance view. It is insufficient to note, correctly, that the list of exceptions is long. It includes environmental regulation (rules covering the protection of flora and fauna, for instance) and transportation (as infrastructure it is, very roughly speaking, more a process than a product from the point of argument under consideration), as well as, via the ECJ, social welfare policy (a 'solidary' institution in the crucial reserve of the old welfare state). For all of these exceptions might be countered by a generalization of the objection to the first one: the translation of interests into policies is never automatic; it depends on political action, which in turn depends on the structures of politics. If the political structures tend to obstruct the articulation of some interests while permitting or encouraging advocacy of rival ones, then the regulatory outcome will reflect the surface accidents of politics rather than the underlying geology of interests. When a second accident accidentally undoes the first, the bedrock will reshape the landscape in its own image.

This argument is naturally suspect. It might just be a counter-fallacy, 'correcting' one wrong argument with another, in a way that renders both hard to falsify. But a more convincingly empirical objection to the objection is available in the work of Eichener. Suppose for a moment that there is some explanation in political structure for the 'aberrant' outcomes of high-standard regulation. Then there should be some set of political circumstances that is either necessary or sufficient or both for such results. But Eichener could find neither, although he considered a carefully drawn list of reasonable candidates, including: qualified majority, rather than unanimous voting rules (unanimity increases the chances of hold-ups); supranational actors such as the Commission as process managers (with an interest in outcomes that validate their own activity by going beyond the lowest common denominator); spillover effects (that might entail regulation as the price of 'negative' integration); legislative eclecticism (novelty arrived at through syncretic combinations of bits of diverse national traditions is more acceptable to all than wholesale adoption of the principles of an 'advanced' country); consensus building in comitology (comitology is a necessary or sufficient means for achieving the revaluation of interests described above); and so on.[84] His conclusion, which we follow here, is accordingly that the political institutions of the EU are now such that 'high' outcomes are possible in many, if not all, regulatory areas. Indeed, he argues on the basis of historical experience that changes in the political institutions are more likely to increase the probability of such outcomes than reduce them.[85]

What we need on this account, then, is not an explanation of the exceptions that can be explained away as narrow accidents, but rather one that takes seriously the possibility that they may point the way to new forms of effective and democratic decision-making. That is the kind of explanation we begin to offer next.

---

[84] V. Eichener, *Das Entscheidungssystem der Europaeischen Union. Institutionelle Analyse und demokratietheoretische Bewertung* (2000), at 323.

[85] See ibid., 335–341, noting, for instance that comitology itself originated in an effort by the Council to domesticate the Commission, but had the opposite effect in some sense. Such 'perversion' of efforts to create a pristine representative democracy at the EU is the rule, not the exception. The why is another story.

IV. AN ALTERNATIVE APPROACH

An alternative conceptualization supposes, in contrast to the theories examined so far, the pervasiveness of ambiguity. Recall that in the demos view meaning is transparent and self-evident within the nation, but only there. Citizenship is the identification with others that makes explication unnecessary. Signs are virtually superfluous because understanding is intuitive. Taken to the extreme, as in the work of Schmitt, the intuitive identification of friend and foe becomes the wordless act from which all politics flows. The market view comes to a similar conclusion but uses signs to get there. It assumes that all meaning can be reduced to unequivocal symbols—prices—which need only to be publicized to guide co-ordination. At the extreme this co-ordination by price is seen as a more precise and continuous version of co-ordination by (national) politics, as in Böhm's remark that the market is the 'plebicite de tous les jours'.[86]

The alternative is to assume that all language is ambiguous, and that the world language describes cannot be encoded in unequivocal signs or signals, even if some formalization is an indispensable scaffolding for the construction of meaning. In this view semantics—the meanings of words—depends in part on pragmatics—the contexts of their actual use. Thus it is only in addressing particular persons or audiences for particular purposes, and noting the response, that I come to understand what I mean. One upshot of this view is that meaning is dialogic: only in exchanges with others can I fix, however provisionally, what I think. A second is that communication within any one language shades into translation, between languages: the mutual attribution of serviceably coherent conceptual frames, and the effort to compare and adjust them that occurs in translation is just an explicit form of the mutual scrutiny and adjustment of category that occurs routinely in communications between speakers of the same language. Put another way, the very differences that obstruct understanding in the demos view, and disappear completely in the market perspective, are the engine of understanding in a world of pervasive ambiguity. We will see in a moment how this reversal in the role of difference makes it possible to speak of boundaries, interests and identities and even sovereignty without invoking the demos or the nation state.

In this alternative perspective language and formal conceptual schemes both enable acts or episodes of understanding, and are transformed, piecemeal, by them. Without conceptual frames or the categories of language we would be unable to orient ourselves towards each other and the aspect of the world that commands our attention; still less would we be able to fix our differences clearly enough to allow further, mutual clarification to begin. Once

---

[86] Böhm, 'Privatrechtsgesellschaft und Marktwirtschaft', 17 *Ordo* (1966) 75.

clarification does begin, however, it can lead to re-conceptualization of the orienting categories, and so revision of the framework itself. This revision is piecemeal because the clarifications, triggered by differences arising in particular situations, are always in some sense local, concerning only part of the skein of concepts. (The language or conceptual scheme orients thought and investigation precisely because it is so much an all-encompassing matter-of-fact that we can't call it into question as a whole, even if we set our minds to it.) But the local re-categorizations can be cumulatively transformative, so that in time one formal framework of categories or signs is replaced, through use, with another. A slow revolution in the formal system of signs that relate our categories to each other is thus the indispensable instrument and the visible track of our dialogic re-characterization of the world.

To connect this way of thinking about meaning with an understanding of action is to emphasize its close affinity with the pragmatism of Peirce, James and Dewey. Shocks to (parts of) our understanding lead to doubt; doubt prompts inquiry; inquiry leads to differing, formal understandings of previously undetected conceptual ambiguities. Some variants fare better in worldly use, and those that do reshape the categories that guide initial response when doubt strikes again. When this process is deliberate, in the sense that the provisionality and partiality of starting points and results is recognized from the first, and the meaning of concepts is acknowledged to be implicated in their use, the process as a whole can be called experimentalist.

Many aspects of this alternative view are of course controversial. What exactly, for example, must interlocutors suppose about the commonality of their concerns and understandings so that what they share can serve as a vantage point for examination of their differences? Or, how exactly does clarification of closely related, local categories ramify in changing the broader system of categorization of which they are a part? But even neglecting such questions, and many more like them, the sketchiest presentation of the pervasive-ambiguity view is sufficient to suggest that the accounts of meaning presumed so far do not exhaust the theoretical possibilities. On the contrary, contemporary thought is deeply marked by the repeated failure to establish foundational or indubitably self-evident knowledge under any conditions, and hence the conviction (though not of course the demonstrable certainty) that it is impossible to do so. Given this chastened conviction, the alternative view is a more plausible account than its competitors of what it means for us to come to an understanding, even if it is incapable of saying how precisely we do so. In challenging the ideas of sovereignty and democracy associated with the personification thesis and economic constitutionalism we are thus standing on conceptual ground as firm as there is.

Beyond providing such grounding, however, the semiotic or experimentalist view is crucial to our argument as a heuristic for the interpretation of the novel institutional developments that both contribute to the undeniable success of Europe as a project in public decision and deepen the puzzle of its democratic legitimacy. Indeed, arrangements such as comitology can be thought of as precisely the institutional embodiment of the semiotic view of language and meaning. With regard to particular policy areas, comitology establishes a framework that enables discussion of contrasting views of a common object, and is in turn transformed (with respect to the outcomes that continue to be explored and elaborated) by that discussion itself. The common object sought is, as we saw, typically a regulation (for the safety of foodstuffs or machine tools or cosmetics) which respects both the integrity of the common market and the public interest in its well being, where the public(s') interest in this regard reflects differing national traditions regarding the burdens to be assumed by the state, the market and citizens. The contrasting views are the various proposals for the requisite EU regulation that arise from the distinctive national traditions. In subjecting these proposals to a common test—how well they meet the characteristic double constraint of EU regulations—comitology makes explicit, and so heightens differing national styles of regulation. But in so doing, as we saw, it also allows for a re-combination of the elements and tropes of these traditions, suggesting possibilities obscured by the implicit assumption that continuing (that is, traditional) differences amounted to a kind of proof of fundamental incommensurability. In short, difference in comitology, as in the semiotic view, is the engine of understanding. Finally, the outcome of comitology is not a fixed rule—a once and for all solution to the initial demand for regulation—but rather a new framework for continuing re-evaluation, within new boundaries, of the provisional solution.

Accompanying the emergence of comitology as a transnational form of governance is a shift from a vertical and Court-oriented towards a horizontalized and polyarchical conception of constitutionalism. The experimentalist view proposed to understand the emergence arrangements such as comitology in terms of a move of constitutional interpretation away from the Court to 'political' and non-court-centric arenas of law-making. The judiciary is not alone in claiming a rational standing; the new arenas also have their share of 'tribunality',[87] that is, they operate as self-authenticating (as opposed to derivative) sources of constitutional interpretation and can be viewed as devices of extending procedural due process requirements 'horizontally' from state into society itself. This move, in turn, prompts—as we will show—not only a new understanding of the role of the Court when assessing the constitutionality of the comitology procedure in individual cases, but also a transformation of the background of constitutional categories which provides the conceptual framework for such an assessment. Rather than assessing comitology's constitutional and democratic credentials in the traditional terms of 'delegation' which are

---

[87] On the idea of tribunality, see Shklar, 'Political Theory and the Rule of Law', in S. Hoffman (ed.), *Political Thought and Political Thinkers* (1998) 21.

reminiscent of the personificationist thesis, the experimentalist view reverses the current set of priorities by putting to the foreground notions of transparency, equality of access, fair participation and direct political accountability, i.e. notions which aim at holding society as a whole accountable for the integrity of constitutional practice. An adjudication which would insist on 'delegation' would run counter to the telos of the novel law-making arrangements of establishing a catalyst for a deliberative re-combination of heterogeneous viewpoints and would risk destroying the very fabric of deliberation.

Consider, in order to trace the idea of non-court-centredness within the EU's constitutional development itself, the jurisprudential progression from *Dassonville*[88] to *Cassis*.[89] Article 28 (ex 30) TEU not only prohibits quantitative restrictions on imports, but also 'all measures having equivalent effects'. The concept of a measure having an effect equivalent to quantitative restrictions had been given a very broad interpretation through the *Dassonville* formula ('D') to cover 'all trading rules enacted by Member States which are capable of hindering, directly or indirectly, actually or potentially, intra-Community trade'. Thus, a crucial consequence of D was that, when a Member State violates the *Dassonville* formula, the Member State was required to justify its social choices in regulating the market sphere by reference to the derogation clause of Article 30 (ex 36) TEU, which was supposed to represent the crucial areas where social policy was allowed to trump the interest in free trade. At the same time, however, the Court in *Dassonville* enshrined another important principle, namely that the derogation clause of Article 30 must be construed as narrowly as possible. As one commentator notes, this meant 'an inbuilt conservative bias, or at least presumption, in favour of free trade, creating an ethos that any obstacle to free trade is in some ways improper and has to be justified'.[90]

In *Cassis*, then, the Court moved beyond this narrowness—beyond the 'conservative bias' implicit in its *Dassonville* jurisprudence. By introducing the concept of 'mandatory requirements' the Court now allowed Member States to plead hitherto unforeseen non-economic policies which were not mentioned—and not recognized—in Article 36 TEU. Article 36 TEU, as Weiler notes, had been 'written with the sensibilities of the 1950s'—the scope of 'legitimate social reasons' being focused mostly on consumers' physical safety, but not on fairness, transparency or environmental concerns. The point of *Cassis*, accordingly, was to unfreeze the EC's constitutional development by expanding the class of legitimate social reasons to include general-clause-like

---

[88] Case 8/74, *Procureur du Roi v Dassonville* [1974] ECR 837.

[89] Case 120/78 *Revue-Zentreal AG v Bundesmonopolverwaltung für Branntwein* (*Cassis de Dijon*) [1979] ECR 649.

[90] Weiler, 'Epilogue: Towards a Common Law of International Trade', in J. H. H. Weiler (ed.), *The EU, the WTO and the NAFTA. Towards a Common Law of International Trade* (2000) 217.

'way-of-life-reasons'—and thus to broaden the scope of, to dynamize and to adapt to changing realities and public sensibilities, the process of constitutional balancing. Hence, the first effect of the progression from *Dassonville* to *Cassis* is the emergence of an (argument-theoretical) constellation in which it is possible for Member States to plead any social policy as a justification for violating economic freedoms as long as it can be shown that the importance of such policy trumps the interest in the free movement of goods and is proportionate. This constellation, in turn, transforms the EU's substantive constitutional commitments: policy reasons which were hitherto seen as *exceptions* to a narrow set of constitutional commitments premised on a presumption in favour of free trade—i.e., as 'derogation clauses'—can now be seen as *extensions* of an evolving core of substantive constitutional commitments; they are subsumed into the core and become part of a constitutional continuum, which expands as the practice of principled justification proceeds.

The second effect of the progression from *Dassonville* to *Cassis*, however, was that by drawing the Court into the very centre of substantive policy dilemmata it raised the spectre of judicial supremacy. As Member States are required to justify state measures by reference to a constitutional core of European law criteria (ex Article 30 or as a mandatory requirement à la *Cassis*), the Court's involvement in the evaluation of Member State social policies in conflict with economic freedoms and the fundamental principle of free movement is deepened. The Court is more and more pushed into the role of the ultimate guardian of the right balance between market integration on the one hand and social policy on the other. Thus, in *Cassis* the Court had no scruples to rely on its own factual risk determinations in order to invalidate a particularly far-fetched justification proffered by the German government for a measure aiming at ensuring that consumers could not be misled into buying a liqueur believing it to have a certain alcoholic content—and it is clear that this kind of self-referential judicial 'self-programming' implicit in the Court's assertion of its competence to assess the reasonableness of the Member States' health, safety, or environmental product regulations that could negatively affect free trade will pose a formidable legitimacy problem when more sensitive policy assessments pertaining to, e.g., food or environmental regulations are at stake. The spectre of judicial supremacy was, however, also raised by another doctrine the Court famously had developed in *Cassis*—the doctrine of mutual recognition. Whenever a state measure cannot be justified by reference to European law criteria—as ultimately defined by the Court—the measure is inapplicable and there is, by judicial fiat, no need for harmonization, since goods complying with the technical standards required in one Member State could now be marketed freely in all Member States provided that standards are functionally equivalent.[91] Only when the Court comes to the

---

[91] There is a vast bulk of 'neo-hayekian' literature on mutual recognition which, of course, welcomes this outcome.

conclusion that a measure in question does serve a valid public-interest purpose and can, thus, be upheld, do Articles 100 and 100a come into play—with the requirement in Article 95 (ex 100a (3)) EC that harmonization measures aiming at the completion of the internal market 'will take as a base a high level of protection, taking account in particular of any new development based on scientific facts'.

Seen from the experimentalist vantage point the telos underlying new institutional arrangements such as comitology is to move the process of constitutional justification—the process of bringing social policy reasons and economic liberties into a coherent order—away from the Court to new, politically accountable arenas of justification. Constitutional interpretation, thus, remains no longer exclusively tied to the Court, but shifts to non-court-centric arenas of law-making—arenas which obliterate the delegatory aspects of committee membership and which transform the committee members' respective outlook from one of being representatives of the Member States' interests to one of being partners in a transnational constitutional project. Euro-constitutionalism now can be seen as a process with two sides. On the one hand, there is, through the progression to *Cassis*-and-onwards, an 'upward drift'—or justificatory ascent—which expands the EU's constitutional core. On the other hand—and complementary to the core's expansion—there is a 'downward drift' in which burdens of justification are extended beyond the Member States (as the original addressees of justificatory burdens) to new, non-court-centric deliberative settings, in which the veil of the nation state is pierced and, through the practice of comitology, a new transnational point of view and form of solidarity among heterogeneous actors is forged.

This changed perspective on comitology, in turn, would prompt a transformation of fundamental constitutional concepts the Court applies to comitology. The Court, in order to be able to monitor and to hold accountable the comitology procedure in individual cases without at the same time distorting comitology's identity-forging constructivist dimension, would have to define notions of political accountability and of constitutionality no longer in terms of delegation, but in terms of equality of access, participation, transparency and deliberativeness of the reason-giving process. To frame comitology in terms of delegation (pursuant to the Court's *Meroni* jurisprudence[92]) would only uphold the fiction that the Commission remains the author of the comitology process and that committee members act 'atomistically' as representatives of the Member States. The belief—implicit in the concept of delegation—that certain well-circumscribed powers can be assigned to functionally defined actors would not only miss (and distort) the constructivist and dialogic dimension of comitology, but would exempt actors from juris-

---

[92] See *supra* n. 10.

generative responsibility—from their role as suppliers of reasons—indeed, immunize them from scrutiny. 'Delegation' would become a prescription for judicial supervision of both the form and the substance of the comitology process, without the existence or even possibility of coherent, principled or judiciable standards. It would magnify the role of the judiciary in overseeing the comitology process, and thus undermine the very telos underlying comitology—the removal of the practice of constitutional principle to non-court-centric arenas of law-making.

Consider as an illustration of the problems of bringing constitutionalism to comitology a recent case decided by the Court of First Instance. Relying on Declaration No. 17 of the Treaty of Maastricht and the Code of Conduct[93] which lay down the general principle that the public should have the greatest possible access to the documents held by the Commission and the Council, the applicant—the Rothmans group—had requested from the Commission access to a number of documents which included the minutes of the Customs Code Committee. The Commission refused to hand over the minutes of the Committee, arguing that it was not their author and that the minutes of the Committee were not the Commission's documents. The Court's dilemma in its attempt to categorize comitology in *Rothmans*[94] was that on the one hand it did not want to leave comitology outside the EC constitutional structure, but on the other side it did not want to go so far as to develop a new and bolder theory of its monitoring of comitology committees by endorsing the idea of a direct and horizontal application of the right to committees. In the end the Court did attempt some variant of the delegation doctrine by deeming the Commission to be responsible for giving access to information contained in the committees' minutes (para. 61) and by affirming that ' "comitology committees" come under the Commission itself'.[95] But the substance of the Court's reasoning was that the principle of transparency should trump the Commission's formal-legal arguments about its non-authorship of the documents and that the importance of that principle should prevail. However, in its reasoning the Court did not go so far as to put values before structure and to horizontalize the constitutional principle to the novel comitology arenas and settings; rather, through the authorship question, it upheld the fiction that the committee is presided over by the Commission. Comitology's responsibility to citizens is a mediated—but not a directly-deliberative—one; it is mediated through (or derived from) the Commission, but does not originate within comitology itself and from its interconnectedness with society as a whole.

Looked at as an experimentalist framework for generating (experimentalist) rules, comitology seems less a curious, idiosyncratic response to the

---

[93] OJ 1993 L 340/41.
[94] Case T-188/97, *Rothmans v Commission* [1999] ECR II-2463.   [95] Ibid.

problem of the regulatory integration of the EU and more a key instance of a broad re-orientation of law-making. To see comitology as both example and component of a general movement in the direction of experimentalism, it is necessary only to peer 'down' from the level of comitological decision-making into the national administrations that, among other things, must implement EU decisions, or gaze 'up' at the level of macro-policy-making—the procedures for encompassing policy areas, such as 'employment', that affect countless particular programmes and regulations. Although the actors and their scope of action are only distantly, if at all, comitological at these levels, the institutional architecture of decision-making has a strong family affinity indeed.

At the level of national administration of EU Member States, and of course with greater clarity in some than others, there is a blurring of the distinction between the making and administrative application of law, and more particularly a tendency—central to comitology—for the actors who will eventually be subject to the law to constitute a framework for its articulation and continuing revision. Developments in France and Italy are particularly salient. There administration at the local, regional and even national level, across policy areas from economic development, to environmental protection and transport, is increasingly by a process referred to as 'contracting', but better rendered by convocation. A nominally superordinate authority—the ministry of finance, say—enters 'contracts' with nominally subordinate entities—regions or municipalities interested in economic development projects funded by the ministry—by which the latter 'obligate' themselves to develop plans for using the funds, and further to 're-contract' periodically so that initial plans can be adjusted in the light of pooled experience. Thus 'contract' in this setting is a misnomer, though perhaps a reassuring one insofar as it evokes the notion of considered mutual obligation. The parties are indeed exchanging a promise. But the promise they exchange is not, as is conventionally the case, to undertake some well specified task in return for a like undertaking by the other; but rather to elaborate with other promisors, in a mutually transparent and accessible way, what each will do given their joint experience. In 'contracting' the administration thus an experimentalist frame for law-making is developed in which the means of executing or implementing a policy and the definition of its very purpose are determined together in a collaborative effort by those whose formal responsibilities tend to the latter (the national administration, acting under authority of the legislature) and those whose responsibilities are in theory limited to the former (the subordinate entities). (A similar blurring of the conception and execution of administrative tasks has been observed in Great Britain (and the other Whitehall countries) which were at pains to separate them as part of a private-firm inspired programme of administrative modernization known as the New Public Management.)

Most of the studies of the new currents in administrative organization focus on one, or at most several closely related countries. They typically pay scant attention to European developments in general, or the connection between comitological regulatory efforts at the EU level and the shift towards what we can call experimentalist framework administration nationally. But it seems reasonable to suppose (and very preliminary accounts encourage the speculation) that the EU and national changes are mutually re-enforcing. Looked at narrowly, from the point of view of the jostling for place endemic in institutions, national-level decision-makers who take part in comitological deliberation by difference are likely to encourage or at least tolerate similar methods domestically because the domestic exercise increases the range of experience they can bring to bear on the EU-wide discussion, and thus the authority with which they speak. Conversely, national-level administrators who have experience of domestic framework regulation would have an interest in participating in comitology as a way of canvassing possibilities that can be brought to bear in discussion at home. More generally, the methods, more or less particular to each policy area, for arriving at solutions serviceable as current instruments of regulation and open to correction through the experience of the regulated parties are likely to encourage, perhaps even require, learning across the two levels. Put another way, in the medium term, experimentalist administration is likely to help national governments exploit the half-hidden resources of domestic diversity to accommodate the 'irritating' introduction of elements of 'European' law through court decisions or regulation. In the long run an experimentalist national administration could become a kind of local comitology, and comitology an extension across national boundaries of local experimentalism.

A similar pattern is emerging at what might be called the supra-comitological level, as broad policy areas encompassing many distinct regulatory regimes within each Member State are constituted as distinct, politically tractable entities in the very process of becoming 'Europeanized' through EU scrutiny and criticism. An example is employment policy. Each EU Member State of course had an implicit employment policy insofar as it had policies for vocational training and continuing education, unemployment insurance, pensions arrangements, taxes on wages and salaries (to finance social insurance schemes), collective bargaining, other policies affecting job creation and the 'investment climate' generally, and much else besides. Together these policies amounted analytically and de facto to an employment policy. But few countries tried to integrate these policies systematically, adjusting each part to the emergent whole; fewer, if any, systematically compared such explicit employment policy with the employment policies, explicit or not, of other countries.

However, at the Brussels meeting of the European Council in December 1993, as unemployment in the EU neared a peak of 10 per cent, the Member States began to formalize discussion of employment policy among themselves, with the effect of requiring increasing explication of their respective internal measures. By a process elaborated at subsequent meetings at Luxembourg and Cologne the Member States were required to take detailed stock of their domestic labour markets and formulate multi-year national-employment policy plans. The first plans addressed matters suggested by a rough, initial comparison of the then current policies. These plans were then evaluated collaboratively so as to allow both criticism of the individual national strategies for data-collection, decision-making, and policy integration, and refinement of the criteria of evaluation. It is becoming routine for the national employment policies to be judged, in part, on the extent to which they and the accompanying report on actual developments document improvement in areas of weak performance; and the pooled judgements of the plans then routinely prompt further elaboration of the criteria for subsequent judgement. The infrastructure for the continuing discussion and re-definition of employment policy at the EU level and between the EU and the relevant administrations of Member States is provided by a series of secretariats and committees, some created expressly for the purpose and others re-directed from other tasks to it. Thus as in comitology, the comparison of different strategies creates a framework that both disciplines current activity and prompts continuing re-examination of the criteria by which discipline is to be applied. The actors, of course, are substantially different actors: Member States have the initiative in 'Europeanized' employment policy, as opposed to the Commission, and they have ad hoc secretariats rather than the committees that give comitology its name. Moreover, the possibilities for sanctions are different in the two cases. Disputes over comitological regulation can be carried to tribunals. Disputes over differing interpretation of comparisons of employment policy are fought out before a—highly attentive—public opinion. But if the process of formalized comparison proceeds, and becomes (as it is just starting to be) entwined with macro-economic policy and the management of the single currency, Member States and the EU could well begin to hold individual countries to account for aspects of their labour market performance. In any case, the early evidence is that, as with the spread of experimentalist administration at the national level, the probability is high that 'horizontal' comparisons of policy and performance will lead to a re-definition of the relation between super- and subordinate levels of decision-making.

In calling attention to these separate, but linked and potentially mutually re-enforcing occurrences of an experimentalist institutionalization of the pervasive-ambiguity or dialogic view of meaning, our intent is to broaden the debate about the possibilities of EU constitutionalization and democratization, not to offer a new suggestion for concluding it. We are not, to be direct about it, suggesting that, appearances to the contrary, the EU and its Member States have already adopted experimentalist decision-making. Even if we lengthened the list above—for example, by including cases where national governments (as opposed to parts of their administration) compare their understanding of the 'welfare state' with each other directly and via the EU—we simply lack the evidence to make the case. Nor are we suggesting that the adaptive advantages and tendencies for mutual re-enforcement of partial and limited innovations that we are tracing will somehow enable the novel institutions to metabolize traditional ones. We lack the faith in the functional superiority of the new forms (and in functional arguments in general) to advance such a claim.

But excluding these extravagant claims the evidence just introduced, combined with the continuing 'surprises' of successful collaborative rule-making amidst the diversity of the EU, suggests the possibility that there is in the core of the 'new' Europe a distinctive institutional architecture—one that takes for granted, indeed depends on kinds of ambiguity that, from a traditional perspective, seem inimical to any kind of 'constitutionalization' at all. Supposing that this possibility is still ruled in by the evidence—and that current debate gestures at, but cannot identify it clearly—we proceed to enquire whether, from a constitutional point of view, the new forms of collective decision-making may not fall victim to the same paradoxes—the problem of delegation, boundaries, and so on—that felled the familiar ones, and, if they do not, whether (or under which conditions) they should count as democratic.

The point of departure of this enquiry is the idea that the emergence of the distinctively new forms of collective decision-making is accompanied by a transformation of the constitution of constitutionalism itself. In a world of pervasive ambiguity constitutionalism cannot coherently be understood any more in terms reminiscent of (soft-) positivism as an application practice uncontroversially fixed by rules which are known in advance, which make the law independent of any commitment to any controversial theory of status of moral judgements and, at best, allow for a 'debatable penumbra of uncertainty', and which should, in the interest of legal certainty, be administered by the courts. Rather, the task of constitutionalism becomes to set a framework for deliberation among heterogeneous social actors, to ensure that those framework conditions can themselves be transformed in the light of insights brought to bear by hitherto excluded or marginalized voices—and thus to enable the parties to a conflict to construct the pragmatic settings themselves which are adequate to the resolution of contested policy issues. This forward-looking and constructivist character of constitutionalism is meant, when it is said that constitutional practice is not a matter of investigating a holistically closed space of meaning, reflecting a common aspiration of society, but a matter of 'design'.

The new understanding of constitutional practice sheds a new light on the long-standing debate on legal indeterminacy. The underlying question, as perceived by the protagonists of this debate, concerns 'the degree or extent of uncertainty which a legal system can tolerate if it is to make any significant advance from a decentralized regime of custom-type rules in providing generally reliable and determinate guides to conduct identifiable in advance'.[96] Against the view of constitutional practice as essentially fixed by linguistic rules shared by lawyers and judges, Dworkin, as we saw, had urged the distinction between rules and principles and had pointed to the inevitably controversial, open and discursive character of the interpretive process. The application of abstract constitutional principles to particular cases, Dworkin had argued, not only takes fresh judgment, but 'must be continually reviewed, not in an attempt to find substitutes for what the Constitution says, but out of respect for what it says'.[97] But, as we also saw, the translation of constitutional meanings to the citizens, according to Dworkin, ultimately has to rely on personification, and the reviewing process remains mediated by a supremely competent judiciary which represents the Constitution to the people. Yet, considering the kinds of controversies and political struggles in which this programme must inevitably embroil the judiciary, in the more recent debates the idea of centring constitutional practice on the judiciary (acting as a guardian of constitutional principle, removed from society) has become problematic. One strand within the contemporary debate has embraced the idea of a 'democracy-forcing judicial minimalism'[98] and thus tries to defend a chastened role for the judiciary and for constitutionalism itself as a democratic virtue. For reasons of both policy and principle, the argument goes, the development of comprehensive theories of the right and the good is a democratic task, not a judicial one. A 'moral reading of the constitution' (as proposed by Dworkin) would impose the large-scale theories of the judiciary on a public that would ultimately reject them—and would thus practically-performatively undermine the very idea of mutual recognition among free and equal citizens which originally and aspirationally may have motivated them. Judges should, precisely in order to promote democracy, resort to conceptual or justificatory descents and offer low-level rationales on which diverse people may reasonably converge in the face of reasonable interpretive pluralism. The objection to this view is that a moral reading of the constitution remains necessary—precisely for reasons of avoiding government by the judiciary.[99] Judicial abstinence and constitutional down-sizing would not produce more democracy, but the paralysis of the process essential to democracy. In a world where minimalist judicial opinions are the rule, one can never be confident that a piece of law-making is constitutional—hence the judiciary becomes the focal point with regard to every piece of law-making.

---

[96] Hart, *The Concept of Law* (2nd ed., 1997), at 128 and 251.

[97] Dworkin, 'Comment', in A. Scalia, *A Matter of Interpretation. Federal Court and the Law* (1997) 115, at 122.

[98] Sunstein, 'Agreement Without Theory', in S. Macedo (ed.), *Deliberative Politics, Essays on Democracy and Disagreement* (1999) 123.

[99] M. Tushnet, *Taking the Constitution Away from the Courts* (1999); Dworkin, *supra* n. 51.

The experimentalist view of constitutionalism moves beyond this debate by pointing to the possibility of a non-court-centric notion of due process. The experimentalist view thus breaks with the traditional understanding according to which an independent judiciary has a privileged or exclusive role in the allegedly 'judgement-driven' (as opposed to 'preference-driven', erratic and 'societal') work of finding justice-serving answers to questions of constitutional interpretation. In the experimentalist view, not only judges, but the newly emerging societal arenas, too, are guardians of constitutional principle and must be considered as *fait normatifs*. Moreover, the experimentalist view pays attention to the fact that issues of constitutional principle cannot be pursued without deciding lots of closely connected questions, not themselves matters of justice, but nevertheless of concern to citizens—matters of strategy, institutional arrangement, local self-understanding. Whoever deals with questions of constitutional principle will have to deal with these non-justice considerations, too. The general idea, suggested by this notion of constitutional principle itself, is that the success of the practice of constitutional interpretation depends on its inclusory and participatory character, i.e., on its capacity to draw even excluded and marginalized voices into the interpretive process. Accordingly, and as indicated above, the experimentalist view argues that the rationale lying behind the new institutional arrangements is the expansion of the process of constitutional interpretation beyond the judiciary to non-court-centred 'societal' arenas of decision-making; and the task of constitutionalism becomes to ensure that these settings have their share of 'tribunality'—i.e., are *participatory* and *deliberative*, in that they enable actors to decide contested policy issues in the appropriate pragmatic settings; *constructivist* in that the process itself reconstructs identities; and *experimentalist* in that the process is open to new facts and arguments and to learning.

More radically than in municipal contexts, the guiding telos of the new constitutionalism becomes to transform the actors' perspectives from polarized conflict to collaboration, from confronting each other in the role of representatives of the Member States' interests to collaborating as partners in a shared transnational constitutional project. The new constitutionalism aims at achieving this shift in perspective from atomism to dialogue by extrapolating from the practice of balancing framework rules of discussion which not only force the innovative re-combination of perspectives, but also, by requiring actors to see conflict as a process to be managed rather than as an evil to be avoided or suppressed,[100] forge a new kind of *constructivist solidarity* which pierces the veil of the nation state and becomes a powerful source of law without the state. This transformation of perspectives is, as we argued, the

---

[100] Slaughter, 'Agencies on the Loose?', in G. Bermann, M. Herdegen and P. Lindseth (eds), *Transatlantic Regulatory Cooperation. Legal Problems and Political Prospects* (2000) 521, at 545.

underlying telos of a new type of rules which provide for recursive processes of joint problem analysis and goal setting, self-commitment and self-evaluation, combined with common monitoring and central benchmarking capacities. These rules re-orient and unite the whole regulatory spectrum, from 'open coordination' all the way down to the questions of manufacturers' liability and tort law.

One might object to the experimentalist picture that it remains just that—a picture—and that it does not 'really' resolve the question whether the new arrangements can count as 'democratic' or are just examples of an impossible delegation of authorities from the nation states to transnational governance regimes. The reply is to point to the interconnection between experimentalism and pragmatism, understood as a strategy of reforming practices through principles and counterfactuals drawn from the practices themselves. From a pragmatist standpoint, delegation is neither possible nor necessary, and the task ahead lies in embracing the shift within the operative constitutional vocabulary from notions of delegation to 'constructivist' notions of participation, transparency, accountability, etc.

Because very generally speaking our constitutional horizontalism position shifts the burden of public decision-making from the formal institutions of representative democracy back to civil society, it is easily confounded with two schools of thought which dissolve the state into society, but under different assumptions, and with correspondingly different conclusions, than those advanced here. The first takes was inspired by Durkheim, and found its fullest modern expression in the social law theory of Georges Gurvitch.[101] The second, system-theoretic view is more recent. It derives from work on complexity in sociology (in part also traceable to Durkheim), as well as in biology and chemistry, and finds its authoritative exponent in Gunther Teubner.[102] To clarify our own views we briefly distinguish them from these affine schools of thought.

What these views share with our own is the assumption of strong constraints on the co-ordinating capacities of central agents given the cognitive limits of the latter in relation to the tasks they face. Scepticism about the effectiveness of a unitary, centralized sovereign with pretensions of panoramic comprehension, however democratically it is constituted, follows directly. From this scepticism follows in turn the recourse to 'the social' as, very broadly speaking, the alternative to the sovereign, centralized state.

The differences between these schools, and between their views and ours, concern further assumptions about the character and communicability of the knowledge of the local agents themselves. The Durkheimian, social-law

[101] Gurvitch, *supra* n. 4 above.
[102] Teubner, 'Contracting Worlds: The Many Autonomies of Private Law', 9 *Social and Legal Studies* (2000) 399.

school takes local knowledge to be tacit—the capacity to do, without the ability to explain what is done—and occupation-specific in the sense of arising through mastery of a profession or craft. Occupations are taken to be inherently complementary: 'Toutes les industries sont soeurs' is the famous dictum of Proudhon that Gurvitch adopts as his own. Local knowledge of different occupations is therefore complementary in principle but incommunicable, at least directly, because tacit. Co-ordination among occupational groups is accomplished by the collaboration of expert representatives of each (whose temporary differences of interest are in the end tamed by their mutual dependence). These representatives are schooled in particular crafts and professions—and therefore possessed of its tacit understanding—but also in formal languages that permit a measure of articulate exchange with one's peers in other groups. As a principle of government this view yields (neo-)corporatism, in which sovereignty rests in a federation of occupational groups and is exercised by their representatives acting directly as a chamber of occupations or indirectly as the indispensable interlocutors of a parliament too removed from practical knowledge to act without them. A vast literature recounts how, particularly in Western Europe and the Nordic countries, neo-corporatism came to define the practice of representative democracy from the inter-war years through the mid-1980s. An equally vast literature documents how, having entrenched themselves in the de facto constitution, the occupational groups came to reject as threatening (not least to their own institutional prerogatives) adjustment to the vast changes transforming the world of their immediate constituents and society as a whole. In the end the 'organicist' constitution of groups, intended to make mute know-how just audible enough to permit collective action, winds up silencing the public voice and paralysing public action. Beneath much of the social democratic nostalgia for the nation and the welfare state lies nostalgia for the world of occupations stable enough to permit corporatism to work.

For the systems-theory school local knowledge (meaning, more exactly, knowledge sufficiently more particular than the panoramic perspective to be of use) is always formal, and its formalisms are always tied to one, and only one, of a small number of fundamental systems which together constitute complex modern societies. The economy, law and politics always figure on the list of these systems. The very formalization that allows for inter-local communication within each system, however, forecloses communication among them. The formalisms of law being deemed incommensurate with the formalisms of the economy, for instance, mutual comprehension is impossible. Yet the co-ordination across systems that social integrity requires is in fact possible, on this view, through a process of reciprocal 'irritation'. Thus changes in the economy, although not directly perceived as such by lawyers, irritate or perturb legal categories, calling forth a response in law that in turn irritates the economy and other systems, provoking within each a response in (its own) kind. Or in Teubner's more delicate language, where 'discourse' replaces 'system': although, '[i]n a precise sense, interdiscursive translation is impossible', there is nonetheless, because of the perturbing effects of 'conflictual polycontexturality' on each discourse, a 'fragile symmetry of chances of translation' between them.[103]

As a principle of government systems theory yields technocracy, more in the sense of government by techne or technique itself than of government by a class of experts. For in systems theory the environment—the world in which society finds itself—and the reciprocally irritating systems that define social life co-evolve, with little place for the agency of individuals and, by definition, none for a co-ordinating centre of any kind. It holds out the vague promise that society can somehow control itself in a complex age without becoming hostage, as in the social-law school, to entrenched and self-interested groups or even deciding once and for all which groups are 'weak' and worthy of protection, and which can fend for themselves. This is the thrust of Teubner's suggestion that private law can protect 'weaker'—non-economic—discourses from colonialization by the 'stronger' rationalities of economic or technocratic discourse by strengthening their powers of systemic perturbation or 'discourse rights'. But since systems theory does not afford a place for us to constitute ourselves as a 'we' that can choose to favour this, or any other systemic outcome, the hope is just that. Put another way, the price systems theory exacts for the prospect of escape from corporatist self-blockage and market domination is submission to the tyranny of self-determining or autopoetic systematicity itself. In the end both social law and systems theory are alike in sacrificing sovereignty conceived most generally as the capacity for public decision-making on the altar of complexity.

In our view, in contrast, local knowledge is neither tacit nor fully and self-referentially systematic. Co-ordination among local collaborators is necessary because of the diversity of their views and possible because, as we have argued, the exploration of the ambiguities internal to each shades into exchange with the others. But as local co-ordination yields new ambiguities of its own, there is both need and possibility for inter-local exchange through a new centre that frames discussion and re-frames it as results permit.

As a principle of government this view yields what we called at the outset directly deliberative polyarchy. It is directly deliberative because local agents—acting in geographic localities or as the ground-level actors in specific policy regimes regarding anything from education to the environment—can participate directly in problem-solving, representing as it were themselves, rather than delegating responsibility for their choices to an actor who com-

---

[103] Teubner, *supra* n. 102. For a discussion of Teubner's views, see Gerstenberg, 'Justification (and Justifiability) of Private Law in a Polycontextural World', in *Social and Legal Studies* (2000) 419.

mands a language beyond them. It is polyarchic because, even as they gain freedom of initiative, locales (generally: ground-level units of policy regimes from schools to pollution-producing firms) remain accountable to a public informed by the doings of their peers. A horizontal constitution is one that avowedly makes its interpretative choices, large and small, on the basis of such polyarchic exchange, rather than on the judgement of judges trying, for instance, to preserve the moral integrity of the citizens personified.

The thrust of the new constitutionalism is no longer exclusively to protect a set of well-circumscribed (economic) rights from the vicissitudes of pluralist politics, placing them beyond the reach of bargaining by establishing them as legal principles to be applied by the courts. Rather, the telos underlying new constitutionalism (and its conceptual vocabulary) becomes to provide, and to operate as, an *enabling constraint* with regard to transnational fora of principle-guided 'deliberative' problem-solving and democratic participation.

Index

The Collected Courses of the Academy of European Law
Edited by Professor Philip Alston and Professor Gráinne de Búrca

This series brings together the Collected Courses of the
Academy of European Law in Florence. The Academy's mission is to
produce scholarly analyses which are at the cutting edge of the two
fields in which it works: European Union law and human rights law.
A 'general course' is given each year in each field, by a
distinguished scholar and/or practitioner, who either examines the
field as a whole through a particular thematic, conceptual or
philosophical lens, or who looks at a particular theme in the context
of the overall body of law in the field. The Academy also publishes
each year a volume of collected essays with a specific theme in each
of the two fields.